Regional Histories of Austria

Günter Bischof/Marc Landry, eds.,
Ingrid Böhler, guest editor

CONTEMPORARY AUSTRIAN STUDIES | VOLUME 33

UNIVERSITY OF NEW ORLEANS PRESS   *innsbruck* university press

University of New Orleans Press
2000 Lakeshore Drive, Earl K. Long Library, Room 221
New Orleans, LA, 70148, USA
www.unopress.org

Printed in the United States of America on acid-free paper

Published in the United States by
University of New Orleans Press
ISBN: 978-1-60801-277-0

UNIVERSITY OF NEW ORLEANS PRESS

Published and distributed in Europe
by *innsbruck* university press
ISBN: 978-3-99106-167-0

iup

Library of Congress Control Number: 2025932974

Publication of this volume has been made possible through a generous grant by the Austrian Federal Ministry of Education, Science and Research through Austria's Agency for Education and Internationalization (OeAD). The Austrian Marshall Plan Anniversary Foundation in Vienna has been very generous in supporting Center Austria: The Austrian Marshall Plan Center for European Studies at the University of New Orleans and its publications series. The College of Liberal Arts at the University of New Orleans, as well as the Vice Rectorate for Research and the International Relations Office of the University of Innsbruck provided additional financial support.

THE UNIVERSITY *of* NEW ORLEANS
CENTER AUSTRIA

universität innsbruck

The Dietrich W. Botstiber FOUNDATION

Federal Ministry
Republic of Austria
Education, Science
and Research

Marshallplan-Jubiläumsstiftung
Austrian Marshall Plan Foundation

Contemporary Austrian Studies

Sponsored by the University of New Orleans and University of Innsbruck

Table of Contents

FORUM

The World War II Bombing War Over Austria and Archeology: The Case of Matrei am Brenner

HISTORIOGRAPHY ROUNDTABLE ON JOHN BOYER'S *AUSTRIA 1867-1955*

REVIEW ESSAY

BOOK REVIEWS

Regional Histories of Austria

Introduction

Günter Bischof

Martin Knoll is right to remind us that regional history is situated between "*Landesgeschichte, Landeskunde*, and *Regionalgeschichte*" and has to critically reflect the role it played as an "anti-modernist and fascist *völkische Wissenschaft*" during the interwar years. He also reminds us that regional history was first practiced in the nineteenth century by learned societies in the Austrian *Länder* and not in the universities. He quotes the University of Salzburg historian Ernst Hanisch as to the difference between *Regionalgeschichte* and *Landesgeschichte*: "But one decisive difference remains: *Landesgeschichte* is bound to the political boundaries of the area; *Regionalgeschichte* creates its own boundaries through its questions." What also needs to be kept in mind is that, in Austria, regional archives and museums play a decisive role in promoting regional history also by publishing regional book series and journals.

Nowadays the Universities of Vienna and Salzburg have chairs in regional history. Vienna and Innsbruck harbor research centers that cooperate transregionally with Lower Austria in the case of Vienna and the South Tyrol and Trentino region in the case of Innsbruck. Martin Knoll stresses the "paradigm shift from the nationalistically influenced older regional history to the new pluralistic and transnational regional history research." The University of Innsbruck, moreover, has been a trailblazer in integrating regional history and contemporary history. The historiography of regional and economic, social, and environmental history is also closely linked. Moreover, as the case of Lower Austria shows, regional history has been closely linked with rural history. More recently, regional history has been productively linked with global history.

H. Glenn Penny's paper is re-published from the *Bulletin of the German Historical Institute* in Washington, DC. He is suggesting to "globalize *Landesgeschichte*." From his research on German "coffee capitalists" in Guatemala, he arrives at the conclusion that many of them came from Bavaria and Baden-Württemberg and succeeded in integrating quickly in Guatemalan society due to their interest in local culture and learning the local languages. This brings him to the "south German borderlands" from "Salzburg through Innsbruck and Bregenz to Freiburg and Basel." Here is a regional history construct whose territorial extent he defines himself along the lines of Hanisch's definition mentioned above. He is interested in the labor migrations and mobility of the people living in that stretch of southern Germany. To understand this history, he also reaches back to the valuable "*Heimat* histories" written by *Volkskundler* and scholars of *empirische Kulturwissenschaft*.

After these more general considerations of writing regional histories, we have a number of studies dealing with western Austria's states of Tyrol and Vorarlberg, situated in these "south German borderlands." This reflects the agenda of the University of New Orleans' long-standing partner university in Innsbruck. It also reflects my own interests as a Vorarlberger. Ingrid Böhler, a Vorarlbergerin who heads the Institute of Contemporary History of the University of Innsbruck, opens these case studies with her considerations of early industrializing Vorarlberg. Vorarlberg used to be an agrarian region with out-migration; in the nineteenth century, it turned into an industrializing region that needed an in-migrating workforce. Early industrialization came out of nearby eastern Switzerland's textile industry, taking a foothold across the border in Vorarlberg. Böhler thusly gives us a nice case study on how closely economic history is linked to regional history, as Knoll argues in his lead essay.

Martin Kofler's essay on the stereo photographer Wilhelm Dronowicz is a case study of regional visual history. Dronowicz documented the eastern and southern frontlines in the First World War, where he did his service. In the process he left the *Tiroler Photoarchiv* (TAP) with a lot of valuable pictures from Ukraine, Poland, and South Tyrol during World War I. This kind of visual history has become a valuable source in documenting vital events.

Hester Margreiter's essay compares the cities of New Orleans and Innsbruck and their vital tourism industries. Margreiter and Kofler were both fellows at UNO's "Center Austria" and are thus beneficiaries of the UNO–Innsbruck partnership. Margreiter looks at both cities as "gateways" and is excited how the "water region" and the "mountain region" are advertised, arguing how "touristic advertising concepts are one factor in the cultural construction of regions." She is interested in both advertising as a "cultural construct" and in the "tourist gaze." Her article is meant to show how the analysis of historical tourism advertisements can contribute to regional history research.

Markus Barnay, a Vorarlberger, and Beat Gugger, a Swiss, present the fascinating case study of the making of the new Vorarlberg Museum in Bregenz. They argue that in a "highly differentiated and fractionalized society," no master narrative is possible in a "dialog with society," the new museum had to position itself in the social environment. A "core exhibition" was designed in workshops and numerous discussions with experts. The curators "had to try to reconcile a collection that had grown over 150 years of museum history with the demands of a modern presentation of regional history." The objects collected did not tell the story they wanted to tell. They had to rely on loans and donations from some eighty archives and private collections. This allowed for changeability of objects displayed. In the end, the exhibitions told no master narrative but rather tried to answer four key questions. The end result became an exhibition named "vorarlberg: a making-of." The new Vorarlberg Museum became a model for presenting regional history even beyond the region. This again make Knoll's point how regional museums played an important role in constructing state/regional history.

The next two essays on migration history were written by scholars affiliated with the Institute of Contemporary History of the University of Innsbruck. Eva Pfanzelter, herself from the South Tyrol, tackles the complex issue of migrations from and to the South Tyrol region in the twentieth century. She discusses the 1939 *Option*, agreed to by the fascist dictators Hitler and Mussolini, that gave the South Tyroleans the option to move to Germany. But soon Italy dropped out of the war in 1943, and after 1945, one third of these 25,000 to 40,000 "optants" chose to return to the South Tyrol (re-optants). In the 1960s and 1970s, thousands of *Südtiroler* emigrated for economic reasons; most went to Germany, Austria, and Switzerland. More recently, after the end of the Cold War, South Tyrol has been attracting immigrants from various parts of the European Union and the Mahgreb.

Marcel Amoser, a young researcher from the North Tyrol, presents us with a fascinating comparative case study of the North and East Tyrol vs. the Italian South Tyrol. His approach makes migration and diversity visible as constitutive elements of coexistence in Tyrol and South Tyrol. He looks at the work of the Catholic Church social organization *Caritas* and the role it played in helping to settle and eventually integrating immigrants. In the North and East Tyrol, this work began in the 1960s with arrival of "guest workers" from Catholic Croatia. In the South Tyrol, the *Caritas* organization began to take care of immigrants from Eastern Europe and the Maghreb region of North Africa in the late 1980s/early 1990s. While the *Arbeiterseelsorge* in the North and East Tyrol was a form of Christian charity, in the South Tyrol it took on the form of a "profane service orientation," helping immigrants with their social problems toward integration.

The final essay by Duncan Bare and Siegfried Beer, both intelligence experts from the University of Graz, deals with American intelligence services in Austria (Office of Strategic Service, OSS; Strategic Services Unit, SSU). They provide a careful survey of these intelligence units' work (the

OSS from the end of the war until October 1945; the SSU from October 1945 to October 1946) in postwar Austria 1945/46 in the "provinces," the *Länder*. They define "provincial" as "everything outside of Vienna," but note from the perspective of a US intelligence officer "all of Austria would seem 'provincial' outside of Vienna and (possibly) Salzburg." From Washington's perspective, the importance of Austria declined sharply in the late fall and winter of 1945; eastern Austria was used for observing Communist Eastern Europe. They argue that intelligence, particularly in the modern era, is often understood in geopolitical terms and/or as it impacts (inter)national security; however, it does have regional and local contexts.

The FORUM on "The Bombing War in the Tyrol: The Case of Matrei am Brenner" deals with Allied bombing of an Austrian province during the Second World War, specifically the town of Matrei am Brenner. The essay by Ryan Gray and Harald Stadler covers World War II archeology of bomb sites more specifically; Elisabeth Waldhart looks at castles that were bombed during the war in the Tyrol; and Emily Hanish covers the bombing of Matrei, when during a raid on March 22, fifty-six people were killed in the village.

The HISTORIOGRAPHY ROUNDTABLE deals with the monumental recent history of Austria by John Boyer, *Austria 1867-1955* in the "Oxford Modern History of Europe" series. Gary Cohen, Pieter Judson, Maureen Healy, and Peter Becker each write a review of this masterpiece, and John Boyer responds to the reviews. A number of book reviews conclude the volume.

We would like to thank a number of people for their help in making the completion of this volume possible. Working with Ingrid Böhler, an old friend, as the guest co-editor of this volume has been smooth and easy since the very first days of putting this volume together. We are sincerely thankful to all the contributing authors for submitting their essays in a timely fashion and responding favorably to all editing suggestions from our production team. Amin E. Aghjeh, the 2023-24 Austrian Ministry of Education, Science, and Research Doctoral Research Fellow at UNO and a PhD student in the Department of Eastern European History at the University of Vienna, has done a fine job in tracking every manuscript through both the copyediting and proofreading processes and toward final publication. He also has been relentless in correcting and aligning footnotes with our style sheet and humoring authors toward completion of their manuscripts.

Many archives and archivists have been helpful in helping us illustrate this volume. Lukas Morscher from the Innsbruck City Archives was kind enough to allow us to use an image from his collection in Hester Margreiter's essay to serve as the photo for our cover. The Historic New

Orleans Collection gave Margreiter permission to use one of their photos. Martin Kofler used images from the collection of Wilhelm Dronowicz of the Tyrolean Photo Archives for his essay. We are grateful to H. Glenn Penny and the German Historical Institute in Washington, DC, for allowing us to reprint his essay on "Globalizing Regional History" from the *Bulletin of the German Historical Institute* (Spring 2023 issue). Richard Wetzell, the editor of the *Bulletin* and the GHI, was also kind enough to provide the photos and the rights to them to illustrate Penny's essay.

We would also like to thank our anonymous outside peer reviewer for his thorough and timely assessments.

Katie Pfalzgraff at UNO Press put her enthusiasm into the final round of copyediting the individual manuscripts; Alex Dimeff skillfully typeset the final text of the volume and designed the cover. G.K. Darby and Abram Himelstein, the leadership team at UNO Press, have been hugely supportive to spirit this volume through to final publication. At Center Austria: The Austrian Marshall Plan Center for European Studies, Marc Landry, the Director, was helpful with sage advice. Gertraud Griessner conducted the Center's daily business with superb efficiency to allow the co-editor to work on managing the completion of this volume. Without the dedicated teams at Center Austria and the UNO Press, there would be no CAS series. At the innsbruck university press, Birgit Holzner and her team were helpful with the final round of proofreading and then producing the volume for the European market. Cooperating with her has become a big bonus in the production of these volumes.

As always, we are happy in acknowledging our sponsors and supporters for making the publication of the *Contemporary Austrian Studies* series possible at all, not a small matter in the age of diminishing budgets for higher education in general and the social sciences and humanities in particular. At the universities of Innsbruck and New Orleans, our thanks go to Vice *Rektor* for Research Gregor Weihs for a grant toward the printing of this volume and Matthias Schennach, Barbara Tasser, Gerhard Rampl, and Leonie Kaupert in the New Orleans Office. At UNO, Provost Darryl P. Kruger, Samuel Gladden, the Dean of the College of Liberal Arts and Education, and Katherine Dungy, the chair of the History Department, have given us green lights and much support whenever needed. We are also grateful to UNO President Kathy E. Johnson and Innsbruck *Rektor* Veronika Sexl for their support of the entire UNO-University of Innsbruck partnership agenda, including its publication series. In the Federal Ministry of Education, Science, and Research and its student exchange office *Österreichischer Auslandsdienst* (ÖAD), we are grateful to Barbara

Weitgruber, Christoph Ramoser, Felix Wilcek, Regina Radax, and Sigrid Koller. Markus Schweiger, the executive secretary, Ambassador Wolfgang Petritsch, the chairman of the board, as well as the board members of the Austrian Marshall Plan Foundation have been Center Austria's strongest supporters for two decades now. It is a great pleasure and privilege to work with them all and acknowledge their unwavering support of Center Austria: The Austrian Marshall Plan Center of European Studies at UNO and its activities and publications.

Larose/New Orleans/Innsbruck, April 2024

The Status of Regional History in Austria[1]

Martin Knoll

In June 2023, the Johannes Kepler University Linz and the State Archive of Upper Austria hosted a workshop entitled "*Landesgeschichte Lebt*."[2] Apart from its alliterative quality, the title is remarkable in two respects. First, it could be translated either optimistically as "Regional History: Quite Lively" or pessimistically as "Regional History—Still Alive." The second aspect concerns a semantic peculiarity in the designation of regional historiography in German-speaking countries. There is a difference between two terms used to designate regional history: "*Landesgeschichte*" and "*Regionalgeschichte*." Thus, "*Landesgeschichte Lebt*" can also be read as a positioning within a historiographical debate about different approaches. This plurality of approaches and the respective debate does in fact exist, while according to the latest diagnosis by regional historians Nina Gallion, Martin Göllnitz, and Frederike Maria Schnack the "gun smoke of the trench warfare" of such debates has now dissipated: "In current academic research, even genuine *Landeshistoriker*innen* are increasingly using a regional historical method by defining their object of investigation according to the research question and advocating comparisons—or to put it in Joachim Schneider's words: they want to 'emphasize less the individual and more the exemplary nature of a research area.'"[3]

Having this in mind, it seems impossible to comment on the regional history scene in Austria without briefly addressing this sub-disciplinary difference. Nevertheless, differences should not be given a too great emphasis, as in the scientific everyday life a broad, integrative concept of regional history gains more and more weight, which pragmatically subsumes both concepts and which has helped to develop a flourishing and dynamic research landscape.

A. Regional History between *Landesgeschichte*, *Landeskunde*, and *Regionalgeschichte*

The German historian Wolfgang Schieder once polemically pointed out that regional history in Germany, as in Austria, was a political child of the interwar period, an attempt to construct cultural spaces that were intended to overcome the new, unpopular demarcations of the Paris suburban treaties.[4] While Schieder was right to point at the necessity for regional history communities in Austria and Germany to critically reflect on the political dimension of their discipline—a reflection that necessarily sheds light on the role it played in the context of anti-modernist and fascist *völkische Wissenschaft* of interwar years, during the National Socialist regime, as well as on continuities and legacies after 1945[5]—he is not precise in his chronology. *Landesgeschichte* and the broader and interdisciplinarily shaped *Landeskunde* are not projects of the twentieth century but of the nineteenth century. And for those who want to discover even much older roots of this historiography, I recommend a still worthwhile article published by Ernst Hinrichs in 1985.[6] In his reflection on an open and inclusive approach to regional history, Hinrichs convincingly traced back the origins of regionally focused historiography to late medieval times, clustering the impressive diversity of approaches that have appeared and developed since then in three layers: a state-political and sovereign oriented historiography, a geographical and regional historiography, and a social-scientific-anthropological historiography. *Landesgeschichte* and the interdisciplinary *Landeskunde* have been visible also in the names and agendas of learned associations. To name two Austrian examples, the founding of the *Historischer Verein für Steiermark* (Historical Society for Styria) dates back to 1849,[7] while the *Gesellschaft für Salzburger Landeskunde* (Society for Salzburg Regional Studies) was launched in 1860.[8] Using two examples from the world of associations here is not for incidence, as the non-university sphere has played a central role in the development of regional history and still does so. This distinguishes it from other historical sub-disciplines. A specific historical awareness of the country was the inspiration for the founding of associations. In the case of the Styrian association, the name reflects a more exclusively historically focused interest, while in the case of the Salzburg association it reflects the more interdisciplinary concept of *Landeskunde* (regional studies), which is sketched in the purpose of the association's statutes since 1860: "the promotion of knowledge of the province of Salzburg and its inhabitants with regard to the present and past."[9] Also the introductory chapters of the initial issues of the two associations' journals underline the different approaches. Abbot Ludwig, president of the Styrian association, in the printed text of his opening speech of the general assembly held on June 21, 1849, in critical distance to the revolutionary events having taken place in Europe 1848/49, argued politically, attributing to regional history the role of helping to reconstruct a reliable political order.[10] However, eleven years later in the Salzburg case, Valentin Zillner outlines a broad spectrum of cultural and scientific fields of knowledge, which he recommends to his society for exploration under the auspices of regional studies. This latter claim has been and continues to be put into practice, and so when you browse through the society's annual volumes, you will find not only historical articles but also articles on art history, cultural geography, geology, mineralogy, and botany.

In the Austrian context, this highly interdisciplinary format of regional studies could, for example, be linked to the descriptive statistics of Ignaz de Luca (1746–1799) or, in the regional Salzburg context, to the regional description of Lorenz Hübner (1751–1807) or the works of Karl Ehrenbert Freiherr von Moll (1760–1838) with a more natural history focus. The interdisciplinarity and, above all, close relationship between geography and historiography was and is a formative element in the development of regional historiography. *Land* and *Region* still are two different concepts, used by the proponents of the different approaches. The essentialist category of *Land* can be attributed either in a geographical sense to historical cultural landscape or a political territory (historical or present), as applies for the territories of the Holy Roman Empire before 1803 or the provinces (*Bundesländer*) of present Austria. Historian Heinz Dopsch convincingly pointed out that the category of the *Land* provides a plausible point of reference, especially where today's countries can look back on a long territorial tradition, as applies for most of the Austrian provinces.[11] However, to make a long story short and hereby also set aside the role of regional history in Marxist historiography in Eastern Europe during the Cold War period, there was a younger generation, inspired by social sciences, claiming for *Region* as a non-essentialist, more flexible category. In his retrospective consideration of the differences and similarities between *Regionalgeschichte* and *Landesgeschichte*, the Salzburg historian Ernst Hanisch once pointed out—over and above pragmatic rapprochement and all the new developmental pathways opened up by micro and macro perspectives: "But one decisive difference remains: *Landesgeschichte* is bound to the political boundaries of the area; *Regionalgeschichte* creates its own boundaries through its questions."[12] It is this core difference that delineates the decisive research method in regional history, as also the above cited observation by Nina Gallion et al. shows: the historian, in applying a regional perspective, constructs their study object based on their interests and questions, be it a mining region or an industrial district as a study object of economic history, a tourist destination in the history of tourism or a political territory when guided by the interest in political history. A region in this sense can be understood as, on the one hand, an epistemological and historical-social construct with flexible boundaries that need to be precisely defined and argued in the respective context, but on the other hand it owes its existence to concrete spatial-material factors, i.e. a real substrate with tangible effects. A region is part of a superordinate geographical, political, socio-economic or ecosystemic whole and is interwoven with its outside in many ways.

The spatial extent can extend beyond national borders (macro-regions) and affect spaces below the national level such as federal states or much smaller units such as towns or villages (micro-regions). Regions and regional identities are actively and passively constructed, shaped, staged, cultivated and lived by individual (e.g., people from politics, journalism, science, art or advertising) and collective (mass media, associations, institutions, parties, companies, etc.) actors–this happens in stories, songs, pictures, etc. and is anchored in the collective memory through museums, exhibitions and the like. By whom, why and in what way regions are shaped depends on the context and is sometimes a question of power.[13]

In order to define the working methods and agenda of an up-to-date regional history, the historian Winfried Speitkamp has suggested that four configurations of region should be examined: firstly political, secondly economic-social, thirdly ecological, and fourthly cultural configurations.[14] He demands of regional history that it should work in an interdisciplinary, in the best sense a transdisciplinary way; that it should work transnationally beyond mere comparison as a method; that it should not primarily ask about statics and structures but about processes and dynamics; and finally that it should examine negotiation processes, practices, and actions that create spaces.[15] According to my observations, these standards formulated by Speitkamp for a theoretically reflected and methodologically updated regional historical research meet with a broad consensus in the community, regardless of whether the respective researchers locate themselves more in *Landesgeschichte* or in *Regionalgeschichte*. This observation also applies to the Austrian research landscape, which is examined and commented on in the following section.

B. Regional History in Austria: An Exploration

Browsing the scene in Austria could be based on an institutional perspective identifying institutions active in the field, or it could refer to research topics and trends indicating the recent state of the art. In the following passage, I will follow a mixed strategy without claiming to be exhaustive.

As indicated earlier, considerable work in regional history research is done outside the walls of historical university institutes. Thus, merely counting the number of professorships at Austrian universities dedicated to regional history would provide a rather incomplete and one-sided image.[16] In all Austrian provinces, the provincial archives play a decisive role as promoters of regional history, not only through their archival collections, but also by hosting specialist events and publishing regional history book series and journals.[17] A similar role is played by many municipal archives and ecclesiastical archives. They often have established tight cooperations with the already mentioned regional history societies. Due to the close thematic and institutional links between urban history and regional history, the Austrian Working Group for Urban History Research also plays an important role in regional history research.[18] The working group has been the publisher of the *Austrian City Atlas* since 1982. Furthermore, museums are also important partners in regional history. The regionally focused museums in particular are on the one hand mediators of regional historical content and, on the other hand, they offer students and researchers opportunities for cooperation.[19]

Regional History on the Move: Institutions, Innovations, Approaches

One institution deserves special mention in my list, even though it is not based in Austria: the Competence Center for Regional History at Bozen-Bolzano (Italy). At the moment being transferred from the Free University of Bozen-Bolzano to the provincial museums of South Tyrol, the Center is well connected to the Austrian community through many cooperation partners. Together with the provincial Archive of Bozen and the working group "*Geschichte und Region / Storia e regione*," the Center is co-publisher of the journal *Geschichte und Region / Storia e regione*, which has been a trendsetter in the regional history debate for years.[20]

In recent years, the regional history research scene in Austria has been characterized by a phase of remarkable innovation and interdisciplinary openness. In 2020, the Faculty Center for Transdisciplinary Historical and Cultural Studies began its work at the Faculty of Historical and Cultural Studies at the University of Vienna to complement the work of the existing fifteen disciplinary institutes.[21] A professorship for historical transregional studies, held by Dietlind Hüchtker, is based at this center. Historical transregional studies in this context are defined as being "dedicated to historical questions based on a relational concept of space. Spaces are conceived in terms of their shifting boundaries, overlapping, and their mobile constitution. Historical transregionality considers three aspects in particular: first, the conception of classic spaces such as urban and rural as relational and historical, second, mobility and interdependence, thus the construction of spaces via transgression and, third, situated realms which are commonly perceived as supra-spatial such as knowledge and science."[22]

The Vienna department co-operates with—among others—the "Research Network for Interdisciplinary Regional Studies," in which six research institutions based in Lower Austria bundle their efforts to develop interdisciplinary approaches based in the humanities, social sciences, and cultural studies for regional studies. The Research Group for "Regionalities" in this network is working on an up-to-date conceptual understanding of regionality. The research group has published a framework paper, which states that "the main interest of the Research Group for Regionalities lies in the critical examination of the (historically grown) ambiguity of the conceptual complex 'region' / 'regionality' / 'regional,' its utilization as a category of analysis for the scientific disciplines represented in the research group as well as for transdisciplinary studies. Subsequently, the research interest lies in questions about the dynamics of current and historical regions."[23] Hereby, the focus of the Research Group for Regionalities is not to work out and define what a region is, but rather to 'describe regions "densely" on the basis of the actors' logics of action that extend to all [their] levels,' taking into account the diversity of the affiliations and interaction contexts involved—both internally and externally. The aim is to avoid essentialist definitions and definitions that are predetermined by research. It is in the interest of the research group to show the dynamic interdependencies of actors, dispositives, and practices and to make transformation processes of regions comprehensible. In this way, common characteristics of regions that distinguish them from other spatial-social entities, such as states or nations, but also villages and municipalities, can be developed and serve as a basis for further comparative studies—also of a transdisciplinary nature.[24]

This atmosphere of conceptual openness and theoretical dynamism is a breeding ground for the contemporary development of regional history in Austria. As the recently founded Research Center for Regional History at the University of Innsbruck shows, this development also provides solutions that make the old dichotomy of *Landesgeschichte* vs. *Regionalgeschichte* obsolete. In the Innsbruck case, the focus on a specific regional context (Tyrol, South Tyrol, Trentino, Cortina d'Ampezzo, Buchenstein) goes hand in hand with the explicit claim to work transregionally and to overcome the national-historical paradigm.[25]

"For the research center it is important in an overriding sense to illuminate the standpoints of regional history research in the twenty-first century. Not least, the challenges of global history and the rejection of national historiography make it necessary to determine where we stand. The establishment of the research center enables a better illumination of a paradigm shift from the nationalistically influenced older regional history to the new pluralistic and transnational regional history research."[26]

Linking Regional History and Contemporary History

The fact that the new Innsbruck Center can build on well established relationships between regional history and contemporary history is less surprising than one might think, given the affinity between older regional history approaches and pre-modern eras. Necessity and scope of regional history as a "contemporary history of manageable spaces"[27] have been conceptualized as early as in the 1990s[28] and updated recently. At Innsbruck University, the Department of Contemporary History, broadly facilitating research activities examining contemporary historical topics such as migration history, dictatorship, world wars, the culture and politics of remembrance, musealization, and media history within the prism of regional history,[29] proves to be an important player at the intersection between regional history and contemporary history. Also in other parts of Austria, research along this intersection has proven to be very productive, as for example a large scale project dedicated to the history of National Socialism in the city of Salzburg, just recently completed by the launch of the eighth volume of a comprehensive handbook, shows.[30] The research project,[31] conducted by the city magistrate of Salzburg in co-operation with two universities, several archives, and further institutions and researchers, offers a comprehensive reappraisal of the prehistory; the political, administrative, economic, and social structures; the cultural staging; and the oppression and persecution under the Nazi regime but also studies the history of the impact and reception after 1945 and is therefore of direct relevance for discussions and controversies in the local and regional culture of remembrance today. Regional history in projects like the one showcased here is more than "contemporary history of manageable spaces"; it is historiography close to and in dialog with society. It is public history.

Integrating Economic, Social, and Environmental History

Economic history has a high affinity with regional history not at least because various economic and economic-historical concepts offer their own economic definitions of regionality, such as economic clustering or processes of transregional division of labor.[32] As regional history analyzes processes of transformation, changes in regional economies and their social, cultural, and ecological consequences—be they grounded in (de-)industrialization,[33] tourism,[34] or else—necessarily have a prominent position as objects of investigation. The fact that the integration of social ecology into the perspective of economic and social historians becomes more and more common sense at Austrian universities (Innsbruck, Linz, and Salzburg host departments or professorships of Economic, Social, and Environmental History), deepens the common ground. On a conceptual level, Verena Winiwarter already defined the close relationship between regional history and environmental history earlier.[35] Building on this common ground, more recent contributions conceive the framework of a comprehensive perspective on the economic, social, and environmental history of the province of Tyrol[36] or attempt to derive a new social awareness of space and region from the crisis experiences of the 1970s.[37] Projects that contextualize regional structural change in Styria to an interregionally and internationally comparative perspective,[38] or that relate regional economies to global crises,[39] stand for the historiographical productivity of the overlapping zone of regional, economic, social, and environmental history.

Linking Regional History and Rural History

In November 2023, the Institute of Rural History, located in St. Pölten, Lower Austria, celebrated its fortieth anniversary.[40] Looking through the institute's publications and the *Rural History Yearbook* most notably, it becomes clear that the approach of examining rural areas in their social dynamics; in their modernization, mechanization, and (sub-)urbanization; in their supra-regional to global interdependence; in their complementary functioning to and with urban areas; and, last but not least, as an identification-creating topos, represents nothing less than a pillar of contemporary regional historiography. The Institute's self-image of offering "regional perspectives, globally linked,"[41] gives it an important significance for regional history—in Austria and beyond.

Regional Perspectives, Globally Linked

"However, pitting global history against regional history neither helps nor works. Globalization and regionalization are interrelated, just like the global, the regional and the local, and globalism, regionality and locality grow out of this."[42]

Hardly anyone in regional history research would disagree with Michael Gehler's diagnosis. An isolationist or static concept of region is obsolete. Whether through colonial expansion or military conflicts; whether trade, division of labor, or migration; whether cultural contact or science; whether vulnerability or resilience to global ecological processes—no region in the world is not intertwined with other regions in many ways.

From the perspective of the history of the historical discipline, the point made by Francesca Brunet, Marcus Gräser, and Ernst Langthaler that both regional history and global history in the twentieth century challenged the methodological nationalism of traditional national history deserves attention.[43] However, this complicity did not necessarily lead both disciplines to the development of common approaches. The Spatial Turn, with its relational space concept as an alternative to previous space-absolute container spaces, acted as an important incubator here. Angelika Epple's concept of a "global microhistory"[44] or Ernst Langthaler's call for a "transterritorial microhistory"[45] have shown theoretically reflected ways to secure the analytical place of the regional small space within this complex framework. "Globalizing *Landesgeschichte*," as H. Glenn Penny so excitingly illuminates it from a perspective of mobility and migration history, (this volume), is underway.

C. Concluding Remarks

Regional history in Austria builds on a solid foundation not least because of the long-standing work of non-university institutions in the field, such as archives, museums, and societies, being strong partners of the university departments. At the same time, the development of the discipline over the past twenty years has been marked by a considerable thematic, epochal, and methodological opening. Regional history explores intersections with global history, and it is actively engaged in contemporary history. It will have to continue the pleasingly dense debate on theory and methods that has characterized the past years. It will also have to question its potentials and social tasks even more. Without claiming to be comprehensive, I would like to single out three fields: sustainability, urban-rural relations, and digitization.

As indicated earlier, regional history and environmental history have long been closely intertwined, and the number of publications in this overlapping area is increasing. Environmental history demonstrated the potential of regional case studies. On the other hand, regional historians have discovered their enthusiasm for experimenting with themes and approaches to environmental history. This area of research needs to be expanded in the face of ever more pressing societal sustainability issues, which always have a very tangible regional and even local component. The hope is that research into regional evidence of historical societies, sustainable economic strategies, and unsustainable economic practices will broaden our evidence base for dealing with the problems we face today. It is not a question of naively believing that history can teach us lessons, but it is certainly a question of identifying patterns and broadening our knowledge of possible options and successful and unsuccessful policies.

Urban history and rural history are both closely related to the history of the region. Unfortunately, despite undeniable advances in research, they are still not integrated to the extent that would be desirable. The relationship between urban and rural areas is one of the great unresolved problems on the planet: migration movements; urban growth; suburbanization; infrastructure development and infrastructure deficits; the repeatedly claimed, but ultimately not reliably evidenced, convergence of urban and rural areas under the auspices of the global village. If proof of a real separation and increasing division between urban and rural areas were needed, it would be the increasingly divergent election results in democratic states. In order to be able to better understand the complexity of the problem, we need regional historical competence and a long-term perspective that has been elaborated in a comparative manner.

Digitization has affected and profoundly transformed societies around the world. This is particularly true of the academic world, not less of the social and cultural sciences. With buzzwords such as "digital humanities" come the promise of completely new analytical possibilities and, for example, in historical studies, easy access to ever-expanding universes of literature and digitized sources. In many places, actors in regional history are involved in digitization projects and are thus very close to them. This is great, but what is leading is the discussion of the methodological and epistemological implications for regional history. In global history, for example, it has long been debated whether digitally facilitated access to geographically increasingly distant source corpora has led to an overemphasis on global connections and a leveling of what divides.[46] Similar discussions can be conducted on different spatial scales. We can break it down to our everyday work: for example, we all value "Austrian Newspapers Online,"[47] the online database for historical newspapers and periodicals set up by the Austrian National Library, as an immense source pool and are happy to assign topics for seminar and qualification papers that are easy to work on. But doesn't that mean, on the other hand, that we discriminate against subjects that still require a strenuous visit to the analogue world of the archive or library? That's one of the many questions that digitalization poses, and we haven't even started talking about AI yet.

Regional history in Austria is on a solid footing. But for its further development in turbulent times, it needs both the joy of experimentation and the foresight.

Endnotes

1. Parts of this text were presented as part of the lecture "Gedanken zur Geschichte kleiner Räume in bewegten Zeiten" at the ceremony to mark the fortieth anniversary of the *Tiroler Geschichtsverein* on Nov. 7, 2022, in Innsbruck.

2. Symposium, LandesgeschichteLEBT 2023, June 14, 2023, Johannes Kepler Universität Linz, *jku.at*, accessed Feb. 24, 2024, https://www.jku.at/news-events/events/detail/news/landesgeschichtelebt-2023/.

3. Nina Gallion, Martin Göllnitz, Frederieke Maria Schnack, "Potentiale des historischen Raumbezugs. Einleitende Bemerkungen zu Historiographie und Systematik der Regionalgeschichte," in *Regionalgeschichte. Poetentiale des historischen Raumbezugs*, ed. Nina Gallion, Martin Göllnitz, Frederieke Maria Schnack (Göttingen: Vandenhoeck & Ruprecht, 2021), 9-26, 14. Please note: all German-language quotations in this text were translated into English by the author with the support of DeepL.

4. Wolfgang Schieder, "Regionalgeschichte als Problem. Ein Kommentar," in *Landes-, Regional- und Mikrogeschichte. Perspektiven für die Pfalz und ihre Nachbargebiete*, ed. Frank Konersmann, Joachim Paul Heinz (Speyer: Verlag Regionalkultur, 2014), 149–157, 151–152.

5. Werner Freitag, "Die disziplinäre Matrix der Landesgeschichte. Ein Rückblick," in *Methoden und Wege der Landesgeschichte*, ed. Sigrid Hirbodian, Christian Jörg, Sabine Klapp (Ostfildern: Thorbeke, 2015), 5–27.

6. Ernst Hinrichs, "Zum gegenwärtigen Standort der Landesgeschichte," *Niedersächsisches Jahrbuch für Landesgeschichte. Neue Folge der Zeitschrift des Historischen Vereins für Niedersachsen* 57 (1985): 1–18.

7. "Vorbemerkung," *Mittheiungen des historischen Vereins für Steiermark* 1 (1850): II.

8. Franz Valentin Zillner, "Ein kurzes Vorwort zur Gründung der Gesellschaft für Salzburger Landeskunde," *Mittheilungen der Gesellschaft für Salzburger Landeskunde* 1 (1860): 2–13.

9. Statuten der Gesellschaft für Salzburger Landeskunde, § 2, *landeskunde.at*, accessed Feb. 24, 2024, http://www.landeskunde.at/index.php?option=com_content&task=view&id=12&Itemid=33.

10. Ludwig, Abt zu Rein, "Eröffnungsrede des Vereinsdirectors, des hochwürdigen Herrn Ludwig, Abtes zur Rein, bei der allgemeinen Versammlung am 21. Juni 1849," *Mittheilungen des historischen Vereins für Steiermark* 1 (1850): 3–6.

11. Heinz Dopsch, "Vergleichende Landesgeschichte in Österreich: Realität, Vision oder Utopie?," *Zeitschrift des Historischen Vereines für Steiermark, Festschrift 150 Jahre Historischer Verein* 91/92 (2000/01): 53–92.

12. Ernst Hanisch, "Kleine Meditation über Globales und Regionales. Die Landesgeschichte zwischen Mikro- und Makrogeschichte," *Zeitschrift des Historischen Vereines für Steiermark, Festschrift 150 Jahre Historischer Verein* 91/92 (2000/01): 41–50 (here 47).

13. Martin Knoll, Katharina Scharf, *Europäische Regionalgeschichte. Eine*

Einführung (Vienna: Böhlau, 2021), 36.

14. Winfried Speitkamp, "Raum und Erinnerungsorte. Das Dilemma der Landesgeschichte," in *Methoden und Wege der Landesgeschichte*, ed. Sigrid Hirbodian, Christian Jörg, Sabine Klapp (Ostfildern: Thorbeke, 2015), 81–93 (here 84).

15. Ibid., 85.

16. Knoll/Scharf, *Europäische Regionalgeschichte*, 168-170, provides a list of relevant professorships and research labs at universities in German-speaking countries.

17. The recently published impressive two volumes on the history of nineteenth century Lower Austria may serve as an example for this productive role: Oliver Kühschelm, Elisabeth Loinig, Stefan Eminger u. Willibald Rosner (Eds.): *Niederösterreich im 19. Jahrhundert, Vol. 1: Herrschaft und Wirtschaft. Eine Regionalgeschichte sozialer Macht*, (St. Pölten: NÖ Institut für Landeskunde, 2021), Vol. 2: *Gesellschaft und Gemeinschaft. Eine Regionalgeschichte der Moderne*, (St. Pölten: NÖ Institut für Landeskunde, 2021).

18. Austrian working group for research on urban history, *stadtgeschichtsforschung.at*, accessed Feb. 24, 204, http://www.stadtgeschichtsforschung.at/.

19. Martin Knoll, Robert Moretti, "Geschichte vor Ort - aber wie? Einführendes," in *Geschichte vor Ort - Salzburger Museen und Sammlungen*, ed. Dagmar Bittricher, Andrea Dillinger, Martin Knoll (Salzburg: Edition Tandem, 2022), 9–20.

20. Storia e Regione, accessed Feb. 24, 2024, https://storiaeregione.eu/en/home.

21. The Faculty Center for Transdisciplinary Historical and Cultural Studies, *univie.ac.at*, accessed March 10, 2024, https://fakzen-thks.univie.ac.at/en/.

22. Historical Transregional Studies, *univie.ac.at*, accessed March 10, 2024, https://fakzen-thks.univie.ac.at/en/about-us/historical-transregional-studies/.

23. Sabine Miesgang, *Research Group for Regionalities (FIRST), Conceptual Framework, Status quo 16th January 2024*, 2, accessed Feb. 24, 2024, http://first-research.ac.at/wp-content/uploads/2024/01/Rahmenkonzept_Regionalitaeten_engl.pdf.

24. Ibid., 8–9.

25. Mission statement Research Center for Tyrolean Regional History, *uibk.ac.at*, accessed March 11, 2024, https://www.uibk.ac.at/fsp-kultur/themen/fz-regionalgeschichte-europaregion.html.en.

26. Ibid.

27. Michael Gehler, "Begriffe und Entwicklungen zur Hintergrunderfassung von Landes- und Regionalgeschichte in Europa," in *Regionen der Geschichte / Ragioni della storia. Festschrift für / Scritti in onore di Helmut Alexander* (Geschichte und Region, Storia e regione Special Issue) ed. Andrea Bonoldi, Hans Heiss, Stefan Lechner (Innsbruck: StudienVerlag, 2022), 99-132 (here 99).

28. Michael Gehler, "'Regionale' Zeitgeschichte als ‚Geschichte überschaubarer Räume'. Von Grenzen, Möglichkeiten, Aufgaben und Fragen einer Forschungsrichtung," *Geschichte und Region, Storia e regione* 1 (1992): 85–120.

29. "Regional history," *uibk.ac.at*, accessed March 15, 2024, https://www.uibk.ac.at/zeitgeschichte/regionalgeschichte/.

30. Thomas Weidenholzer, Peter F. Kramml, Sabine Veits-Falk, "Erinnerungskultur braucht Fakten: Die Stadt Salzburg im Nationalsozialismus. Ein Projekt des Stadtarchivs und der Universität Salzburg," in *Außerordentliches. Festschrift für Albert Lichtblau*, ed. Regina Thumser-Wöhs et al. (Vienna: Böhlau, 2019), 402–415.

31. "The City of Salzburg during the Nazi Era," *stadt-salzburg.at*, accessed March 15, 2024, https://www.stadt-salzburg.at/ns-projekt/.

32. Knoll/Scharf, *Europäische Regionalgeschichte*, 64–65.

33. Walter M. Iber, Thomas Krautzer, "Wirtschaft und Region – Transformationsprozesse im internationalen Vergleich. Einleitung, Synthese, Ausblick," in *Wirtschaft und Region. Transformationsprozesse im internationalen Vergleich*, ed. Walter M. Iber, Thomas Krautzer (Vienna: Lit Verlag, 2021), 7–26.

34. Cédric Humair, Martin Knoll, Laurent Tissot, "How to Deal with Regional Tourism? Historical (and interdisciplinary) Reflections," *Zeitschrift für Tourismuswissenschaft* 9 (2017) no. 1, 5–31.

35. Verena Winiwarter,"Regionalgeschichte als ‚histoire totale'," in *Nachhaltige Geschichte. Festschrift für Christian Pfister*, ed. André Kirchhofer et al. (Zürich: Chronos, 2009), 271–283.

36. Wolfgang Meixner, "Prolegomena zu einer Wirtschafts-, Sozial- und Umweltgeschichte des Bundeslandes Tirol im 20. Jahrhundert," in *Regionen der Geschichte / Ragioni della storia. Festschrift für / Scritti in onore di Helmut Alexander* (Geschichte und Region, Storia e regione Special Issue) ed. Andrea Bonoldi, Hans Heiss, Stefan Lechner (Innsbruck: StudienVerlag, 2022), 133–157.

37. Hans Heiss, "Regionen ‚nach dem Boom'. Krisenerfahrungen der 1970er Jahre – Basis neuen Bewusstseins für Raum und Regionen. Ein Essay," in *Regionale Wirtschafts- und Sozialgeschichte im Zeitalter globaler Krisen*, ed. Wirtschaftsarchiv Vorarlberg, Wolfgang Meixner, Gerhard Siegl (Vienna: Böhlau, 2024), 13–39.

38. Walter M. Iber, Thomas Krautzer ed., *Wirtschaft und Region. Transformationsprozesse im internationalen Vergleich* (Vienna: Lit Verlag, 2021).

39. Wirtschaftsarchiv Vorarlberg, Wolfgang Meixner, Gerhard Siegl ed., *Regionale Wirtschafts- und Sozialgeschichte im Zeitalter globaler Krisen*, (Vienna: Böhlau, 2024).

40. Events at the Institute of Rural History, *ruralhistory.at*, accessed March 15, 2024, https://www.ruralhistory.at/en/events.

41. The Institute of Rural History, *ruralhistory.at*, accessed March 15, 2024, https://www.ruralhistory.at/en.

42. Gehler, *Begriffe und Entwicklungen*, 117.

43. Francesca Brunet, Marcus Gräser, Ernst Langthaler, "Editorial," *Geschichte und Region / Storia e regione* 30 (2021), no. 1, 5–17.

44. Engelika Epple, "Globale Mikrogeschichte. Auf dem Weg zu einer Geschichte der Relationen," *Rural History Yearbook* 9 (2012), 37–47.

45. Ernst Langthaler, "Vom Behälter zum Netzwerk? Raum in mikrohistorischer Perspektive," *Rural History Yearbook* 9 (2012), 57–68, 61–62; Ernst Langthaler, "Orte in Beziehung. Mikrogeschichte nach dem Spatial Turn," *Geschichte und Region / Storia e regione* 21 (2012), no. 1–2, 27–42.

46. Lara Putnam, "The Transnational and the Text-Searchable: Digitized Sources and the Shadows They Cast," *The American Historical Review*, Vol. 121 (2016) no. 2, 377–402.

47. "AustriaN Newspaper Online," *anno.onb.ac.at*, accessed March 15, 2024, https://anno.onb.ac.at/.

Globalizing *Landesgeschichte*: Reflections on Narrating Germans' Histories in the Modern Era[1]

H. Glenn Penny

I came to the notion of globalizing *Landesgeschichte* rather inadvertently. I have often said that my primary research strategy is to stumble into problems that irritate or perplex me and then try to figure them out. In that sense, my incompetence with things like the history of Bayern, Baden-Württemberg, Switzerland, the Tyrol, and Vorarlberg—all political entities scattered across what I have come to call the southern German borderlands—became a virtue of sorts. Essentially, I happened upon people from these places during my work on German migrants in Latin America; they made me want to know more about the region; and once I started digging into it, I started rethinking German history in productive ways.

Part of this rethinking was already in motion as I was writing my most recent book, *German History Unbound*.[2] It grew out of a culmination of problems I had been wrestling with over the last couple of decades, the biggest of which was trying to figure out how to narrate a polycentric German history that places communities of self-proclaimed Germans and their interconnections at its center, rather than the history of the German nation-state, or any states for that matter.

As I did that, I spent a lot of time thinking about Germans all over the world, and I spent a good deal of energy pursuing them throughout Latin America. In part, that was because those migrants had seen much less scholarly attention than their counterparts in Eastern Europe, Russia, and North America. Yet they also appeared to be just as important, if not more important, to what I was starting to think of as a globalized German history, one punctuated less by the radical ruptures of major geo-political events, or the lives and fates of the regimes dominating the German nation-state, than the many consistent networks and relations that have persisted through them.

To be honest, I also simply wanted to understand why there were so many German communities in Latin America, particularly across the southern cone, and I wondered what their histories might tell me about the last couple of centuries of European and German history, which I had not learned from the secondary literature.

It turns out that the many German communities that took shape across

Latin America after the 1880s had quite a lot to teach me, particularly when I thought about things like the soft forms of power that grew along with the emergence of global Germanophone networks of transportation, travel, and trade in the modern era. I also learned a great deal about Germans' interactions with non-Europeans, a topic that has interested me since I entered this profession.

I could continue at length about the arguments in that book, but I would prefer to use this opportunity to open up discussions about three things I have been thinking about since completing it: 1) the often-overlooked historiographical importance of the southern German borderlands, 2) how globalizing the *Landesgeschichte* of these regions might draw that into relief, and 3) how the work of generations of *Volkskundler* (or practitioners of *Empirische Kulturwissenschaft*) who have focused on these regions might help us do all of that.

To get to those points, I need to take you through a bit of my own intellectual journey, which has been filled with poignant false steps and miscalculations that have proven to be surprisingly fruitful; the place I would like to begin is Guatemala.

When I think of being German in Guatemala, I think of highly inclusive transcultural communities that were locally grounded but globally oriented. These German communities were well-established in Guatemala by the turn of the twentieth century; although there were never more than a few thousand German-speakers in Guatemala at any moment between the 1880s and the 1940s, those communities were and remain the largest concentration of German-speakers in Central America, and throughout those decades they generated a large percentage of Guatemala's GDP. Moreover, while most of them were well-integrated into Guatemalan society, they clearly lived transcultural and transatlantic lives. Many of the leading trading families, in fact, worked simultaneously in Bremen and/or Hamburg while living in the capital of Guatemala City and/or (in the case of the coffee capitalists) on one of their many plantations. Moreover, most of them made sure that their children were Guatemalan as well as German citizens.[3]

Figure 1: "Inside Plantation Life on El Peru," n.d.
courtesy of Regina Wagner

Figure 2: "Inside the Nottebohm Bank, Guatemala City,"
courtesy of Regina Wagner

On the one hand, that gave these Germans many advantages—most importantly, they could draw on the many forms of cultural, economic, and social capital tied to being German in Guatemala. For example, and this is quite important, until the 1930s, most of the coffee they produced was traded almost exclusively on the Hamburg coffee exchange. But their insider/outsider status also made these German-Guatemalans incredibly vulnerable because even though they were the people who most linked other Guatemalans into international trade networks that connected Central America to Central European industry and markets, the shifting

Guatemalan regimes always had the monopoly on violence within their borders.[4] That, in fact, is one of the things that made German connections so appealing to Latin American regimes: they offered a less threatening alternative to the British, the French, and later the United States—all of whom sought economic and political hegemony in the region. So, Imperial Germany's political and military weakness at the turn of the century, in fact, was part of these Germans' secret to successes.[5]

Moreover, while Imperial Germany did set up a favored nation trading agreement with Guatemala in the 1880s, that was only after Germans living there had done the hard work of building relations. Characteristically, and this is critical to bear in mind, in Latin America, the German nation-state followed the actions of German speakers living abroad. It did not take the lead in building those relationships. Nor could it control them. It also could not defend them, and thus in both world wars, as the Guatemalan state broke relationships with the German nation-state, Germans in Guatemala suffered property seizures, and in the Second World War there were widespread confiscations as well as internments. In both cases, the Guatemalan state's political elites enriched themselves on German properties during the crises. In neither case could the German nation-state help, and in both cases the rebuilding had to take place by those networks of Germans in Central America—because neither the Weimar Republic nor the young West Germany proved of much value.[6]

None of this sounds much like the kinds of informal imperialism or neocolonial situations that dominate the postcolonial literature on Latin American relations with foreign actors or even most of the literature on Germans in the world—which tends to privilege analyses of colonial connections, particularly forms of exploitation. Except that one might argue that the Germans who came to dominate a great deal of coffee production and other businesses in Guatemala from the 1880s into the 1930s benefitted from the Guatemalan state's efforts at internal colonialism—because the labor on German plantations, like all the plantations in Guatemala, was largely Mayan labor that was forced into debt peonage by Guatemalan state statutes. German capitalists, like everyone else in Guatemala, participated in that system.[7]

And this is where the story gets most interesting and where my own incompetence turned into a kind of virtue that took me to Baden-Württemberg and Bavaria. What we find among the coffee capitalists in Guatemala, and this is something that British, French, and US observers consistently noted and lamented from the 1880s through the 1930s, is that Germans in Guatemala, as in much of Latin America, were quite good at integrating into local cultures, learning local languages, and finding ways to do business that benefited their partners as well as themselves. In the case of many German plantation owners (but by no means all), they quickly found ways to integrate into local kinship networks, learn local languages, including Mayan as well as Spanish, and make themselves the lesser evil among the property owners. There is no question that that paid large dividends, but there is also little question that it was never all about the money. In general, Germans in Guatemala showed a great deal more interest in those cultures and peoples than did their British or US counterparts—not to mention the Ladinos, (native born-Spanish speaking elites), who had absolutely no interest in speaking Mayan languages or learning about the cultures of their underclasses.[8]

I was pretty intrigued when I learned about this characteristic, and I spent a lot of time trying to figure it out. Everyone working on coffee capitalism in Central America knew that the Germans in Guatemala were simply better capitalists than their American, European, or Ladino counterparts. And everyone essentially agreed that this was largely due to the fact that many of them were quick to learn the languages and integrate into the cultures of the plantation workers. But no one could tell me why. Most of the scholars who put their postcolonial theories first, or who reached back to old models of dependency theory, thought that this was simply base opportunism, a kind of cynical business model that allowed Germans to better control their labor forces and even lure laborers away from other owners' plantations.[9] And that was indeed one function of their efforts, but it did not take me long to realize that it was not their only intention.

Figure 3a: Erwin Paul Dieseldorff

Figure 3b: One of Dieseldorff's many books

The thing is, people such as Erwin Paul Dieseldorff, who was one of the leading coffee capitalists of the age, was never trained at a university but came from a Hamburg trading family. He not only learned Mayan languages (there are at least thirty-two) and integrated himself into kinship networks while he built a vertically-integrated coffee empire, he also dove deep into the history of the region—the natural history, the ethnology, the archeology, becoming a central interlocutor with a whole series of American and European scholars interested in Central American and particularly Mayan cultures and history. In fact, Dieseldorff became a reigning expert by the interwar period, publishing essays on artifacts, languages, and natural history in scholarly journals, participating in international scholarly meetings, and creating sizable archeological collections that he donated to museums in Europe and Guatemala.[10] There was no profit in that.

But Dieseldorff also understood the utility, or the cultural, social, and political capital, of his knowledge gathering, and while I was reading the private papers of David Sapper, the cousin of Richard Sapper, another equally important coffee capitalist in Guatemala, I was fascinated to learn that David Sapper, who traveled alone from Germany to New York and then from New Orleans to Guatemala when he was only fifteen years old, learned to speak Q'eqchi' from Dieseldorff after they met by accident on the ship that took Sapper across the Caribbean. It was a chance encounter, but once Dieseldorff learned who David Sapper was, and on which plantation he would be working, he made a point of teaching him the Mayan language he would need on that plantation so that the young Sapper would be ahead of the game when he arrived.[11]

I found that amazing, particularly because it was relatively easy for the fifteen-year-old David Sapper to learn the language. But then he could already speak German, English, French, Italian, as well as the dialect common around the southern Italian city of Bari, on the Adriatic Sea, where he had attended a German school supported by its German colony while his father worked there as a merchant. As a result, David Sapper learned his first Mayan language before he even learned Spanish, because, as Dieseldoff taught him, it would be much more important for his work, just as the local Italian dialect around Bari had been more important for his father's work than written Italian based on Tuscan, the standard literary dialect in Italy.

This linguistic talent, it seemed to me, was typical of trade families from Hansa states. In fact, it also seemed to me that it was the history of Hansa city states, much more than the German nation-state, that best explained a great deal of these Germans' successes in Guatemala, as people like the Dieseldorffs and the Sappers continued to live and work in places where others held the monopoly on political power and violence while they simultaneously tied themselves into local cultural and linguistic networks and worked within transnational and transcultural Germanophone networks of travel, transportation, and trade. After all, Hansa trading families had been doing that for centuries.

In fact, I was rather pleased with myself when I made this argument in a 2017 essay for *Geschichte & Gesellschaft* about migrants and knowledge production.[12] It was not until a few years later, however, that it dawned on me that there was a problem in my thinking: David Sapper's family was not from Bremen or Hamburg or one of the northern trade cities. They were from Stuttgart. In fact, a good number of people who worked on their plantations were from this region as well, which is why one could still encounter the mixed-race children of those people speaking Schwäbisch on those plantations right through the Second World War and into the postwar period.[13]

Moreover, there also was no shortage of people from the region living in Latin America. Franz Joseph Lentz, who had worked as a teacher at the German school in Guatemala City before publishing his massive *Aus dem Hochlandder Maya* (1930), made this abundantly clear in a 1965 letter to the Hamburg ethnologist Franz Termer. During his decades of working as a teacher near the Bodensee, he explained, he had continued to give slideshows and public talks about Guatemala across the region. They "aroused a great deal of interest here in Schwaben," he noted, "because almost every family here has relatives in Latin America."[14]

Is that not striking? Mayan workers speaking Schwäbisch in the hills of

Guatemala? Families across Schwaben with relatives in Latin America? It is not as if I was not aware of the global trade networks that cut across southern Germany or the great amount of out-migration from Baden and Württemberg to places as diverse as the Caucuses, Minnesota, Argentina, Venezuela, or Chile. In fact, one of the interesting things I discovered while working through the files of the *Deutsches Auslands Institut* (DAI) in the Bundesarchiv in Berlin is that while the DAI compiled lists of leading Germans, their businesses, and opportunities for German migrants all over the world, and particularly in Latin America during the interwar period, they also had a second list for Schwaben. Really, the DAI was not only one of the most important organizations for emigrants in Weimar Germany, and one of many meant to promote the safe migration of Germans abroad and their continued connections to their homeland, it also actively promoted global Schwaben networks and connections to that homeland as well.[15] That should not surprise us; after all, the DAI was in Stuttgart.

So, once I realized my mistake, once I understood that I had allowed the almost hegemonic tale of Hamburg's dominance over Germanophone global trade in the modern era to color my analysis of Germans in Guatemala, as well as other parts of Latin America, I started to pay even more attention to the eclectic mixes of Germans in Latin American locations and think about what allowed them to succeed in such a wide variety of places. I also started to wonder more concretely about the integrative character of these German communities abroad—both the ways in which they often brought together wide varieties of German speakers into so-called German communities, associations, businesses, churches, schools, and other organizations, which included Germans from all over Central Europe as well as Russia and North America, and how and why they often did so well economically and professionally within their various host communities.

Here again I wondered about fluidity, mobility, and transcultural and multilingual communities, and after a while, I realized that all those things would have been familiar to people from the southern German borderlands during the nineteenth and twentieth centuries—perhaps even more so than among Germans from the north, in places like Prussia. That was true even if the southern borderlands and those characteristics get very little attention in the broader narratives of German history.

So, now I am coming to the point: as my time researching and teaching in Tübingen over the last few years has taught me, people from Württemberg have long been steeped in a great deal of polycentrism, cultural diversity, and multiplicities of dialects and landscapes. Moreover, the people from this region, like much of what I keep calling the southern German borderlands for lack of a better term, have been quite familiar with labor migrations and other forms of mobility for a very long time—centuries really. In that sense, what I was analyzing in Latin America would have been familiar to people from the region running roughly from Salzburg through Innsbruck and Bregenz to Freiburg and Basel. It was only, like so many other things by the end of the nineteenth century, a question of upscaling—greater distances, larger numbers of people, and more mixing. But in that sense, it was not unlike the shift by southern German trading houses around Augsburg from Mediterranean to global trade in the preceding century—which also was pretty seamless.[16]

In a lot of ways, I credit COVID-19 for helping me figure this out. In 2020, I received a Guggenheim fellowship to complete a project I had been calling "Being German in Guatemala." That was going to require about another six months of archival research in Guatemala City, which I expected to complete that year. Unfortunately, I still have not been able to return. In addition, my effort to shift my focus to completing work I had begun in Chile in 2019 was stymied by the same problem because although Chile managed to do very well during the first wave of COVID-19, many of the members of the Chilean middle classes had the regrettable idea to travel to Brazil for vacation in the summer of 2020, shutting down that country to me soon afterwards.

As luck would have it, however, I was able to turn my lemons into lemonade (so to speak) by traveling to southern Germany instead. Initially, my thought was that if I wanted to better understand German speakers in places like Argentina and Chile, where such eclectic mixes of Germans and Swiss founded colonies and communities and thrived, I might do well to learn more about the communities that produced them in Europe.

That proved to be true. At the same time, however, I learned a great deal about the region that made me want to study it more closely for its own sake, which is what I am doing now: thinking about the global implications of the *Landesgeschichte* and allowing that to help me rethink our narratives of German history and Germans in Latin America and other parts of the world.

To begin with, and this seems so obvious to me now, but after I had spent a little time in Tübingen teaching at the Ludwig Uhland *Institut für Empirische Kulturwissenschaft* (EKW), I started to wonder why the southern German border had received so little attention in the more general narratives of German history. After all, historians have filled rooms with books about the eastern German border: where it was, where it should have been, how it moved, how its role in people's lives shifted and changed across our clearly periodized political histories. The eastern border seems, at least from the view of states and the historians who study and promote them, to be a perennial problem, one demanding solutions, which led to a great deal of violence. I certainly would not want to dispute its importance.

I wonder, however, if the eastern border is any more important than the southern German border, which, if we are seeing like a state, does not appear to be much of a problem at all. It is true, of course, that Bavarian armies invaded the Tyrol during the French Revolutionary Wars—we know that; there is a huge panorama exhibit in Innsbruck dedicated to that outrage. Vorarlberg's citizens also tried to leave Austria and become a part of Switzerland after the First World War—we know that too; and during the National Socialist period, Nazi officials redrew their administrative boundaries across that border.[17] But it always seemed, more or less, to snap back into place with little bloodshed or much consternation on the part of the states involved.

So, I wonder: are we missing some critical lessons by ignoring that process or the fact that it was actually a relatively peaceful one as well? Are peaceful historical processes not instructive? I think they should be. And what about the people who lived in this borderland region? What can they teach us? In what ways, for example, did their mental maps compare to the political maps we use in our textbooks?[18] I am afraid that German history, particularly as it is narrated in English-language texts, has very little to say about this, and the political maps we use are often exercises in all kinds of reification. In addition, in many of our history books the lack of violence seems almost synonymous with a lack of importance. But again, I would like to suggest that the opposite is true. In some ways, I believe this neglected region can tell us more about the contours of a globalized German history than those regions that were animated for so long by a series of titillating and often violent ruptures.

To see that importance, I am afraid we must see less like a state and perhaps more like a region.

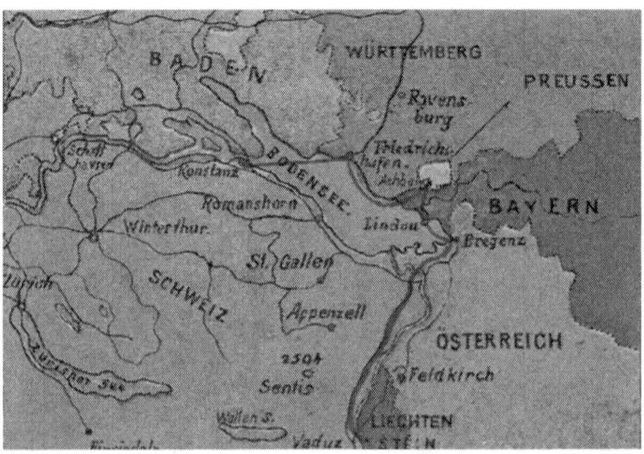

Figure 4: Map of the Bodensee region, c. 1899

The Bodensee, for example, is the kind of region I have in mind, not a regional state. Yet it is clearly a place of belonging, one bordered by political borders that played limited roles in many people's mental maps, while the Bodensee itself has long been a point of orientation, a center, or perhaps a set of many centers, for people living all around it and oftentimes rather far from its shores.[19] Or the Alps, which cut across many political borders as well but are filled with people, mountain people, who share many affinities; some of these people are not just Swiss-German, but also *Bergler*, an idea that crosses many political borders, linguistic borders, and mountain ranges, but does not include those who live in the valleys in-between.[20] The Alps are also filled with mountain resorts, ski areas, and spas, places that a number of scholars have shown were decidedly cosmopolitan even if their locations were incredibly provincial, even purposefully so.[21] That means that the provincial, some even said primitive, regions of the Alps were long animated by networks of cosmopolitan, transnational, and quintessentially modern interconnections while many nearby cities were not. Which tells us what?

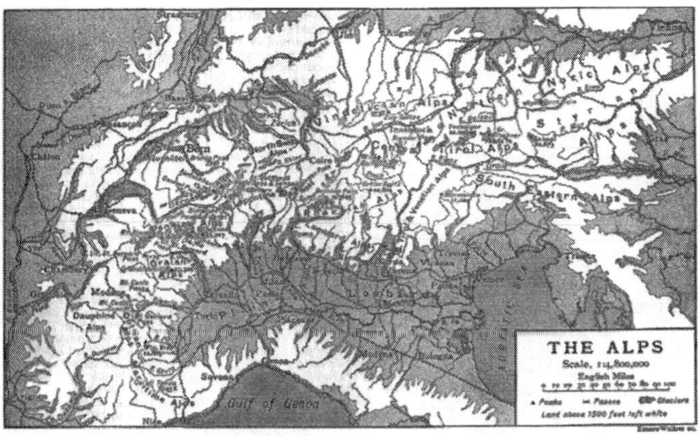

Figure 5: Map of the Alps, Encyclopedia Brittanica, 1911

I think it is also worth noting that the wild animals that move through these mountains do not seem to notice the political borders—it is one of the controversies at the center of the reintroduction of wolves into the region. There has seen some fantastic scholarly work recently.[22] Moreover, many of the people who tended domesticated herds and flocks nearby moved regularly across those borders for generations and over centuries in instructive ways. That is just how life worked; that is what was necessary to regulate the lives of cows and the production of hay—and none of the big, geopolitical shifts that punctuate our typical national narratives of Central

Europe managed to upset much of that.[23] So, what does that tell us about our reliance on those narratives as we both structure our analyses at home and abroad and live our lives in modern Europe?

Of course, we could choose to be splitters rather than lumpers and still make the same point. After all, why is Vorarlberg, and Bregenz in particular, so affluent today? In many ways, it has a great deal to do with a history of labor mobility, which not only included many peddlers and the now famous *Schwabenkinder*, who streamed north across the border during the last decades of the nineteenth century to seek employment during times of need, but also the highly-skilled weavers who were able to travel all over Europe and the Americas by the end of that century working for the highest bidders.[24] They could do that because of their skills, developed largely in textile industries founded by Swiss industrialists who saw advantages in setting up business just down the shore, so to speak. Because down the shore was also across the border, which gave them untaxed access to the Austrian-Hungarian Empire as well as its cheap labor, and those interconnections persisted for, well . . . more than a century—before, during, and after the fall of that empire.[25] I could continue down the list of things that crossed the borders and tied more places and people together, like the ubiquitous tourism that grew with mountaineering as a leisure activity and tied the region to a great many major cities, including most major cities in northern Germany.[26] The ski industry, as Andrew Denning taught us, only expanded that during the postwar era.[27]

Figure 6: Image of Lucie Varga

We could also talk about the Annales historian Lucie Varga's fantastic 1936 ethnography of a valley in Vorarlberg, which demonstrated that while Vienna remained the capital of Austria at that time, its auspicious place on political maps did not have its counterpart in her subjects' mental maps. Vienna was no center for them, and when they thought of cities it was first Bregenz, Innsbruck, Munich, or Zürich, where many of her subjects had been, long before it would have been interwar "*Rote* Wien," which few bothered to think about much less to visit.[28]

There was, in fact, a great deal of transnational life happening in this region and a great many transcultural places there as well. To see those, however, it helps to look on these borders through the eyes of ethnologists rather than historians of Germany. *Volkskundler*, in particular, have been casting their focus on the border regions for generations, paying a great deal of attention to a multitude of borders, not just national ones, and to a whole range of languages many of us would call dialects. So too have the people engaged in what is sometimes dismissed as *Landeskunde*, who have long been aware of the diversity in their regions.

I think it is part of the cunning teleology of thc nation-state that causes those of us who claim to be historians of Germany to frequently dismiss *Landeskunde* in the first place—as something with only local importance, perhaps useful to cite but seldom to engage. As for the *Volkskundler*, well, recast as European ethnology or EKW, many historians interested in *Alltagsgeschichte* began working with them in the 1990s—particularly in urban settings, sometimes within the context of *Werkstattsgeschichte*—but dialects, villages, and rural communities not so much.

For my own work, however, getting over such disciplinary divisions is part of the practice of rethinking German history, and I find the scholarship produced by people devoted to EKW particularly compelling. To some degree, that is clearly because the field formerly known as *Volkskunde* was forced generations ago to come to terms with the nation-state's influence on it—as scholars such as Hermann Bausinger focused on the lives of people rather that the lives and fates of states. Or as he once wrote, while riffing on Berthold Brecht—focusing on *Bevölkerung* rather than *Volk* or *Völker*. It is an important distinction that, particularly when combined with his ongoing response to the putatively rooted character of Heimat histories, people have legs, not roots.[29] Those are two powerful insights that remind us of the importance mobility has long played in the region.

As a result, already in the 1950s and 1960s much of Bausinger's work around Tübingen focused on questions of migration, transference, and large and small networks crisscrossing the region. He was writing, in fact, about the influx of foreigners, *Vertriebene*, long before it was fashionable; he was teaching us about the great variety of dialects in the region, some imported by those new arrivals; and he was tying all of that into notions of belonging a half century before I took part in a conference devoted to just that topic in Tübingen in 2021.[30]

It is stunning, in fact, to read his 1971 *Volkskunde: von der Altertumsforschung zur Kulturanalyse*, which underscores two incredibly important forms of post-war mobility that mattered a great deal: flows of refugees across the new Bundesrepublik and tourism beyond localities and across all borders. Both of those helped to usher in fundamentally new forms of spatial orientation, which gave many traditional cultural markers new meanings and functions—which he traced and analyzed.[31]

One of the most important things he wrote about is the constructed character of culture, particularly historical traditions, and their transference through these new forms of mobility. I honestly almost fell out of my chair last summer when I read this. It is amazing to realize that he wrote about that more than a decade before Eric Hobsbawm and Terrance Ranger transformed cultural history pretty much globally while introducing their arguments about the "invention of traditions."[32] Clearly, they were not aware of the fact that Bausinger and his colleagues in Tübingen had already been thinking and writing about just that for decades. But I do not feel comfortable criticizing them because, until quite recently, neither was I.

Please do not misunderstand me. I am not interested in hagiography, and I am not looking to convince anyone to join me as the new Bausinger disciples. That is not the point. I think it is also important to understand that Bausinger too was channeling things that predated him. He seemed to understand that. For close to a century, in fact, and even after the hyper-nationalization of the field by the end of the nineteenth century, *Volkskundler*, he wrote in 1971, had been exploring overlapping notions of belonging, thinking about the many borders that persist in our heads: where, for example, is *Oberösterreich*? And how many people in Baden-Württemberg know when they enter former Hohenzollern lands today? Some people do, and for them it matters—for others it does not.[33] Which means what? We all move through our own worlds and mental maps often unaware of the phantom landscapes animating the lives of others around us? There is some great work on this by Kathleen Conzen, who wrote a lot on German communities in the American Midwest.[34] Its application, however, is not limited to that location.

Let me return, for a moment, to those older practitioners, who included people such as Wilhelm Heinrich Riehl, who sought unity in diversity, and who also were pursuing questions about performing identity, a topic that was long a great interest of mine. Moreover, as Bausinger later realized, they did that precisely at the moment when radical modernization had gripped these landscapes during the middle of the nineteenth century, causing a dramatic uptick in the scale of mobility and industry. So, while historians during that era ignored everyday life, *Volkskundler* began studying it, collecting material culture from people's homes and hometowns and exploring the fluidities on the southern German borderlands.[35]

The important point is not to celebrate them, but to recognize that those records are extant. Of course, such records are never unbiased, unfiltered, or complete; but then neither are the ethnologies of non-European cultures that a variety of scholars, including many working with indigenous interlocutors, many of whom are scholars as well, are successfully harnessing to reconstitute histories and revitalize languages and cultures in a great variety of non-European locations today.[36]

I would like to suggest that we can use the records of European ethnologists who moved throughout the southern German borderlands in equally successful ways, and we can place them into productive comparative analyses. After all, in many cases they used the same collectors. I would be remiss if I did not point out that, after Adrian Jacobsen traveled to the coast of British Columbia in the 1880s to collect what remains one of the most complete assemblies of material culture from that part of the world for Adolf Bastian's *Museum für Völkerkunde* in Berlin, Rudolf Virchow hired him to travel to Bavaria and the Tyrol to generate one of his earliest *Volkskunde* collections—which he did for precisely the same reasons: to capture the vestiges/records of cultures on the cusp of radical transition, using exactly the same methods and encountering, in many cases, some of the very same challenges he had faced in British Columbia and Alaska.[37]

Those records, and the work compiled by later ethnologists, sometimes called *Volkskundler*, can, for example, teach us a great many things. Just reading Bausinger's accounts of singing cultures in Alpine villages, for instance, reminded me a lot of the compartmentalized character of Hopi religion. Not everyone on the three Hopi mesas knows it all. But until this moment, neither I nor anyone else had thought much about comparing those two locations. Maybe we should; if not with the Hopi, than other non-Europeans.[38]

I apologize for returning again to my revelations about Bausinger, but it is pretty stunning to read his work from the 1970s, which underscores the reifications inherent in mapping; the fundamental problems with any system of typologies; and explanations that *Volkskundlers*' efforts to sort things like varieties of German houses only led to the disheartening conclusion that those types of houses were never only created and used by German-speakers, nor were they generally exclusive to one clearly inscribed region. Even terms like Schwaben, he warned us, elide differences, and they obscure things like class, whereas the reanimation of Volk art he witnessed and wrote about in subalpine regions during the postwar era is stunning for several reasons.[39]

Here again, his observations resonate in instructive ways with those of ethnologists focused on similar problems in other parts of the world. Alpine artisans working in the age of high tourism, he realized, increasingly produced objects, like furniture, for urban tastes rather than due to any devotion to tradition or an undying artisanal culture.[40] Well, that response to market mechanisms was commonplace on the Hopi mesas as well.[41] That's well documented, and in fact, that dialogic is something that Sally Price wrote about in her 1989 blockbuster *Primitive Art in Civilized Places*—but again, only decades after Bausinger's studies had analyzed similar processes in Europe.[42]

Even the ties Bausinger wrote about between the postwar Heimat renaissance of the 1980s and the histories of German-speaking refugees and guest workers in Baden-Württemberg speaks volumes about the global cultural mobilities through and from this region and the many modes of performing Germanness that scholars are only now discovering as they compare the current semiotics of beer, festivals, and trachten in places like Brazil and Bayern or ponder the longer histories of in-migration and integration into German-speaking Europe, while arguing about the implications of the so-called welcoming culture of the Federal Republic today.[43]

So again, it seems to me that a return to reading the writings of those scholars who, before and after Lucie Varga's stunning work on Vorarlberg, were and have been digging into everyday life in the southern German borderlands, means the chance to engage a complex *Alltagsgeschichte* that most historians of Germany have long overlooked. And again, it is often the quiet instances in this history that are the most compelling: be they the rather peaceful history of the region in the modern era; the seldom told success stories of well-integrated guestworkers before and during that period, but especially in the second half of the twentieth century; the equally overlooked fact that postwar Germany was incredibly diverse and able to integrate a large percentage of outsiders; or the fact that the polycentrism I like to place at the center of German history always has had its counterpart in such a striking number of distinct cultures, dialects, and landscapes in even small areas of the southern German borderlands.[44] If you do not believe me, take the trip between Isny im Allgäu and the interior of the Schwarzwald, which Bausinger sketched out in great detail some decades ago, and which I did on a bike. If you do, get ready for a treat; you will encounter incredibly varied and polycentric regions and spaces all along the way.[45]

Moreover, it is not just Bausinger, and none of this is limited to Tübingen or Baden-Württemberg. I've been stunned by some of the work by Konrad Kuhn, who teaches *Volkskunde* in Innsbruck, on the origins of Swiss masks, or Walter Lehmgruber from Basel on dialects and code switching in Switzerland and the many histories of mobility and migration that were overlooked by scholars and politicians for far too long—all the Swiss living outside of Switzerland, and all the non-Swiss living inside it, creating it, building and maintaining it.[46] Here too, the longer history of those successful labor migrations (white as well as blue collar) and multiple modes of belonging are often lost in political debates, but many scholars today on all sides of the national borders are now drawing them out, and to my mind, that mobility needs to be given more attention in our more general narratives of German histories in Europe and abroad.[47]

I will just end by underscoring that one of the most compelling arguments coming out of Switzerland, for example, has been about colonialism without colonies—which is also simply about Swiss people and things in the world.[48] These arguments have been animating the Swiss academy for over a decade, but they also have a lot to teach us about how to think of colonial connections in the German-speaking world north of Switzerland. Official colonialism, and particularly violence, gets all the scholarly and political attention. The Swiss story reminds us, however, that one need not have participated in official colonialism or even visited a colony to have moved in and been part of the imperial world.

In that sense, our obsession with official colonies often reifies the many ways in which people from German-speaking Europe engaged with the non-European world either during or after that era. It makes us overlook many of the ways in which German speakers came together and worked together while abroad. Some reflection on that can remind us of the fact that there were many more Germans in Argentina than all the official German colonies combined and that places like Guatemala far outshined the economic importance of Imperial Germany's official colonies. It also reminds us that those people from German-speaking Europe who went abroad frequently remained connected to it across the radical ruptures of the twentieth century. Perhaps even more importantly, as Franz Joseph Lentz, the schoolteacher from ostensibly provincial Sigmaringen explained in the 1960s to the Hamburg Museum director Franz Termer, they also helped to connect individuals, families, and groups in incredibly varied and polycentric locations within the southern German borderlands to people and places throughout Latin America and, we can imagine, many other parts of the world.

Endnotes

1. Reprinted with permission of the Bulletin of the German Historical Institute in Washington D.C. 71 (Spring 2023): 41-64.

2. H. Glenn Penny, *German History Unbound: 1750s to the Present* (Cambridge, UK and New York, NY: Cambridge University Press, 2022).

3. The standard text is Regina Wagner, *Los Alemanes en Guatemala, 1828-1944* (Guatemala City: IDEA, 1991).

4. Christiane Berth, *Biographien und Netzwerke im Kaffeehandel zwischen Deutschland und Zentralamerika, 1920-1959* (Hamburg: Hamburg University Press, 2010).

5. Penny, *Unbinding German History*, 172-76.

6. Ibid., chapters 5-7.

7. See inter alia: J. C. Cambranes, *Coffee and Peasants: The Origins of the Modern Plantation Economy in Guatemala, 1853-1897* (South Woodstock: CRIMA, 1985); Julie Gibbings, "The Shadow of Slavery: Historical Time, Labor, and Citizenship in Nineteenth-Century Alta Verapaz, Guatemala," *Hispanic American Historical Review* 96, no. 1 (2016): 73-107; Matilde González-Izás, *Modernización capitalista, racismo y violencia: Guatemala (1750-1930),* (México City: El Colegio de México, 2014).

8. Thomas Schoonover, *Germany in Central America: Competitive Imperialism, 1821–1929* (Tuscaloosa: University of Alabama Press, 1998). On integration, see: H. Glenn Penny, *In Humboldt's Shadow: A Tragic History of German Ethnology* (Princeton: Princeton University Press, 2020), chapter 4.

9. See, for instance, Cambranes, *Coffee and Peasants;* and González-Izás, *Modernización capitalista, racismo y violencia.*

10. For a complete Dieseldorff bibliography and much more on his life and work, see: Guillermo Náñez-Falcón, *Erwin Paul Dieseldorff, German Entrepreneur in the Alta Verapaz of Guatemala, 1889-1937* (Ph.D. Dissertation, Tulane University, New Orleans, 1970).

11. David Sapper, *Erinnerungen von David Ernst Sapper, Guatemala. Seine Schwester Marida gewidmet.* Typescript in the possession of Regina Wagner. I remain grateful to her for providing me with this text.

12. "From Migrant Knowledge to Fugitive Knowledge? German Migrants and Knowledge Production in Guatemala, 1880s-1945," *Geschichte & Gesellschaft* 43, no. 3 (2017): 381-412.

13. See, for example, the detailed letter from David Sapper in Guatemala to Karl Sapper in Germany, February 13, 1936, in Karl Sapper Nachlass, Karton 4, Signatur 2.2., MARRK Museum Hamburg.

14. Lentz to Franz Termer, November 18, 1965, Franz Termer Nachlass, Folder 22.2, MARRK Museum Hamburg.

15. Penny, *In Humboldt's Shadow*, 110.

16. Christine R. Johnson, *The German Discovery of the World: Renaissance Encounters with the Strange and the Marvelous* (Charlottesville: University of Virginia Press, 2008).

17. Tirol Panorama with the Museum of the Imperial Infantry, accessed December 31, 2023, https://www.Tiroler-landesmuseen.at/en/Tyrolean-state-museums/; Ulrich Nachbaur, *Vorarlberger Territorialfragen, 1945-1948: Ein Beitrag zur Geschichte der Landesgrenzen seit 1805* (Konstanz: UVK Verlag, 2007).

18. Barak Kalir, "Moving Subjects, Stagnant Paradigms: Can the 'Mobilities Paradigm' Transcend Methodological Nationalism?" *Journal of Ethnic and Migration Studies* 39, no. 2 (2013): 311-327.

19. Since 1869, the Bodensee also has had a scholarly association devoted to it, which has consistently underscored its transnational membership while producing a journal devoted to all aspects of the region's history: *Schriften des Vereins für Geschichte des Bodensee's und seiner Umgebung* (Lindau: 1869-2022). On regional networks, see: Roland Scherer, "Eine Grenzregion als Wachstumsregion: was man von den Governance- Strukturen der Bodenseeregion lernen kann," in *Grenzen. Theoretische, konzeptionelle und praxisbezogene Fragestellungen zu Grenzen und deren Überschreitungen*, ed. Martin Heintel, Robert Musil, and Norbert Weixlbaumer (Wiesbaden: Springer VS, 2017), 237-53. For belonging, see: Bernhard Tschofen, *GrenzRaumSee. Eine Ethnographische Reise durch die Bodenseeregion* (Tübingen: Tübinger Vereinigung für Volkskunde, 2008); and Bernard Tschofen, "Der See: Deutungsgeschichten eines grenzüberschreitenden Gedächtnisortes," in *Baden-Württembergische Erinnerungsorte*, ed. Reinhold Weber, Peter Steinbach, and Hans-Georg Wehling (Stuttgart: Kohlhammer Verlag, 2012), 312-23.

20. Corinna Peniston-Bird, Thomas Rohkrämer, and Felix Robin Schulz, "Glorified, Contested and Mobilized: The Alps in the Deutscher und Österreichischer Alpenverein from the 1860s to 1933," *Austrian Studies* 18 (2010): 141-158; most importantly: Bernhard Tschofen, *Berg, Kultur, Moderne: Volkskundliches aus den Alpen Sonderzahl* (Vienna: Sonderzahl Verlagsgesellschaft, 1999).

21. Alison Frank Johnson, "The Air Cure Town: Commodifying Mountain Air in Alpine Central Europe," *Central European History* 44, no. 2 (2012): 185-207; Adam T. Rosenbaum, *Bavarian Tourism and the Modern World, 1800-1950* (New York, NY: Cambridge University Press, 2016); and Ilaria Scaglia, *The Emotions of Internationalism: Feeling International Cooperation in the Alps in the Interwar Period* (Oxford: Oxford University Press, 2020).

22. See, for example, Michaela Fenske and Bernhard Tschofen, *Managing the Return of the Wild: Human Encounters with Wolves in Europe* (London, UK: Routledge, 2020).

23. Nicole Stradelmann, Martina Sochin D'Elia, Peter Melichar eds., *Hüben & Drüben: Grenzüberschreitende Wirtschaft im mittleren Alpenraum* (Innsbruck: Universitätsverlag Wagner, 2020).

24. Michael Kasper und Christof Thöny, "Schwabenkinder und andere Formen

der alpinen Arbeitsmigration – eine Spurensuche zwischen gestern und heute," *Zeitschrift für Agrargeschichte und Agrarsoziologie* 68, no. 2 (2020): 81-96; Stefan Zimmermann and Christine Brugger, *Die Schwabenkinder: Arbeit in der Fremde vom 17. Bis 20. Jahrhundert* (Ulm: Süddeutsche Verlagsgesellschaft im Jan Thorbecke Verlag, 2012); and Loretta Seglias, *Die Schwabengänger aus Graubünden: Saisonale Kinderemigration nach Oberschwaben* (Chur: Verlag Desertina, 2004).

25. Meinrad Pichler, *Auswanderer: Von Vorarlberg in die USA 1800-1938* (Bregenz: Vorarlberger Autoren Ges., 1993).

26. Kurt Luger and Franz Rest eds., *Der Alpentourismus: Entwicklungspotenziale im Spannungsfeld von Kultur, Ökonomie und Ökologie* (Innsbruck: Studienverlag, 2002).

27. Andrew Denning, *Skiing into Modernity: A Cultural and Environmental History* (Berkeley: Berkeley University Press, 2015).

28. Lucie Varga, "Ein Tal in Vorarlberg—zwischen Vorgestern und Heute," in *Lucie Varga Zeitenwende: mentalitätshistorische Studien, 1936-1939*, ed. Peter Schöttler (Frankfurt am Main: Suhrkamp, 1991), 146-169.

29. Hermann Bausinger, *Volkskunde: von der Altertumsforschung zur Kulturanalyse* (Berlin: Habel, 1971); Muhterem Aras and Hermann Bausinger, *Heimat. Kann die weg?* (Tübingen: Klöpfer, Narr, 2019).

30. Hermann Bausinger, Markus Braun, and Herbert Schwedt, *Neue Siedlungen: Volkskundlich-soziologische Untersuchungen des Ludwig-Uhland-Instituts Tübingen* (Stuttgart: Kohlhammer, 1959); Bausinger, *Dialekte, Sprachbarrieren, Sondersprachen* (Frankfurt: Fischer Taschenbuch, 1972).

31. Hermann Bausinger, Wolfgang Kaschuba, Gudrun M. König, Dieter Langewiesche, and Bernhard Tschofen, *Ein Aufklärer des Alltags. Der Kulturwissenschaftler Hermann Bausinger im Gespräch mit Wolfgang Kaschuba, Gudrun M. König, Dieter Langewiesche und Bernhard Tschofen* (Vienna: Böhlau, 2006), 22-29.

32. Eric J. Hobsbawm and Terrance O. Ranger eds., *The Invention of Tradition* (Cambridge, UK: Cambridge University Press, 1983).

33. This continued during his career; see, for example, "Grenze a. D.: Zum Nachleben von Baden und Württemberg," in Weber et. al., *Baden-Württembergische Erinnerungsorte*, 52–63.

34. Kathleen Conzen, "Phantom Landscapes of Colonization: Germans in the Making of a Pluralist America," in *The German-American Encounter: Conflict and Cooperation between Two Cultures, 1800–2000*, ed. Frank Trommler and Elliott Shore (New York, NY: Berghahn Books, 2001), 7–21.

35. Bausinger, *Volkskunde,* 53; Aras and Bausinger, *Heimat,* 94.

36. See, for example, Philipp Schorch, *Refocusing Ethnographic Museums through Oceanic Lenses* (Hololulu: University of Hawaii Press, 2020). More generally, see: Indigeneities in the 21st century, available at: https://www.indigen.eu/about.

37. "Ausstellung in Chicago 1888-1893," in Jacobsen Nachlass, MARRK, Hamburg. For a Pacific Northwest Coast perspective on Jacobsen's collecting in Alaska and Canada, see: Ann Feinup-Riordan, *Yup'ik Elders at the Ethnologisches Museum Berlin, Fieldwork turned on its Head* (Seattle: University of Washington Press, 2005), especially, xii-xiii and 33-35.

38. The Hopi Foundation, available at: https://www.hopifoundation.org/about-hopi

39. Bausinger, *Volkskunde,* 113-21, 160-66; Bausinger, *Dialekte, Sprachbarrieren, Sondersprachen;* Bausinger, *Die bessere Hälfte: Von Badenern und Württembergern* (Stuttgart: Deutsche Verlags-Anstalt, 2002).

40. Bausinger, *Volkskunde,* 160.

41. Franzke, Andreas, Wolfgang Haberland, Hans-Ulrich Sanner, and Brigitte Templin, eds., *Katsinam: Figuren der Pueblo-Indianer Nordamerikas aus der Studiensammlung Horst Antes* (Lübeck: Kulturstiftung Hansestadt, 2000).

42. Sally Price, *Primitive Art in Civilized Places* (Chicago: Chicago University Press, 1989).

43. Aras and Bausinger, *Heimat,* 73.

44. Reinhard Johler, *Die Formierung eines Brauches: Der Funken- und Holepfannsonntag. Studien aus Vorarlberg, Liechtenstein, Tirol, Südtirol und dem Trentino* (Vienna: Universität Wien Institut für Europäische Ethnologie, 2000).

45. Werner Richner and Hermann Bausinger, *Baden-Württemberg: Landschaft und Kultur im Südwesten* (Karlsruhe: Braun, 1994), 6.

46. See, for example, Konrad J. Kuhn, "Markt-Masken. Dinge zwischen materieller Produktion und ökonomischen Marktbedinungen," in *Materialisierung von Kultur. Diskurse - Dinge – Praktiken*, ed. Karl Braun, Claus-Marco Dietrich, and Angela Treiber (Würzburg: Königshausen & Neumann, 2015), 155-164; Kuhn, "Relics from the "Lost Valley" – Discourses on the Magic of Masks," in *The Ritual Year 10. Magic in Rituals and Rituals in Magic*, ed. Tatiana Minniyakhmetova and Kamila Velkoborskà (Innsbruck, Tartu: ELM Scholarly Press, 2015), 203-212; and Walter Leimbruger, "Assimilation, Integration, Kohäsion, Partizipation," in *Konfliktfeld Fluchtmigration: Historische und ethnographische Perspektiven*, ed. Reinhard Johler and Jan Lange (Bielefeld: transcript Verlag, 2019), 65-80; and Leimgruber, "Aktuelle Entwicklungstendenzen des Profils der Auswanderinnen und Auswanderer aus der Schweiz," *Politorbis* 62, no. 2 (2016): 33-40.

47. André Holenstein, *Mitten in Europa: Verflechtung und Abgrenzung in der Schweizer Geschichte* (Baden: Hier und Jetzt, 2014); Barbara Lüthi and Damir Skenderovic eds., *Switzerland and Migration: Historical and Current Perspectives on a Changing Landscape* (Cham: Palgrave Macmillan, 2019); Peter Melichar, Andreas Rudiger, Gerhard Wanner eds., Wanderungen. Migration in Vorarlberg, Liechtenstein und in der Ostschweiz zwischen 1700 und 2000 (Vienna: Böhlau, 2016).

48. See, inter alia, Patricia Purtschert and Harald Fischer-Tiné eds., *Colonial Switzerland: Rethinking Colonialism from the Margins* (Basingstoke, UK and New

York, NY: Palgrave Macmillan, 2015); Andreas Zangger, *Koloniale Schweiz: Ein Stück Globalgeschichte zwischen Europa und Südostasien (1860-1930)* (Bielefeld: transcript Verlag, 2011).

Vorarlberg: From a Poor Country of Emigration to a Rich Country of Immigration Thanks to Industrialization - Regional History Viewed in Context

Ingrid Böhler

At the turn of the twentieth century, only a third of Vorarlberg's population made a living from agriculture. An agricultural region once poor and characterized by emigration had turned into an expanding industrial region characterized by immigration. Regardless of much more complex patterns and dynamics of both regional economic life and the influx of immigrants, as well as phases of crisis and setback, to this day, industrial production continues to play a defining role in Vorarlberg, one of the leading federal states in Austria in terms of per capita income. Based on this success story, which is central to the country's identity, this text attempts two things. For one, it aims to trace the connections between the phenomena of industrialization and migration—oft-described in historiographical literature on Vorarlberg—the latter of which remains a highly explosive socio-political topic to this day. Based on the socio-economic structural change outlined, the central concern of the text, however, is to highlight that the key to a regional historical perspective—one that avoids back-slapping when presenting specific, positively connoted regional "peculiarities" of the region while at the same time enabling deeper historical insights—lies in contextualization. In this regard, it seems essential to look back from the present day into history and to classify and embed local events in larger spatial reference systems.

* * * * * *

Vorarlberg is the westernmost and, in terms of both size and population, the second smallest of the nine Austrian federal states. At the end of 2020, Vorarlberg had a population of 430,000, twice as many as at the beginning of The Second Republic. Twenty percent of those did not have Austrian citizenship, the second highest figure after Vienna.[1]

Vorarlberg's economy has been attracting workers from outside the region since the last third of the nineteenth century. The first massive wave of immigration commenced in 1870 from the impoverished Austrian Trentino and, to a lesser extent, from the Kingdom of Italy. The migrants were Italian-speaking, mostly female factory workers who were needed in the cotton industry or construction workers who immigrated to build railway lines and other infrastructure. In 1910, almost 8,000 people from the Trentino region and approximately 1,000 Italians lived in Vorarlberg.[2] During the Second World War, so-called South Tyrolean settlements were established at cotton industry sites. This created living space for around 10,000 members of the German-speaking minority who were subjected to reprisals in fascist Italy and had decided to emigrate to the German Reich as a result of the South Tyrol Option Agreement negotiated by Hitler and Mussolini in 1939. Their motivation to migrate was thus not driven by the search for work. But the large Vorarlberg textile companies, with their need for unskilled, cheap labor, knew how to instrumentalize the cynical "solution" to the situation in South Tyrol for their own purposes.[3] During the long period of growth that started with what came to be known as the years of the "economic miracle" following the Second World War, the job seekers initially recruited came from the structurally weak rural regions of Carinthia and Styria. They were followed by migrant workers known as "*Gastarbeiter*" from Yugoslavia and Turkey. In 1969, 10,372 Yugoslavs and 4,248 Turks lived in Vorarlberg; in 1982, the Turks (13,897 people) had become the largest group of immigrants, followed by the Yugoslavs (13,765 people), who now came in second place.[4] In 1995, Austria joined the EU. It is one of the fundamental rights of EU citizens to be free to work anywhere in the EU without the need for individual authorization. This has resulted in other EU nationals making up the largest group of immigrants to Vorarlberg, with those from neighboring Germany comprising the majority.[5]

In view of this development, a high quota of foreigners is nothing new in Vorarlberg. It is an expression of economic prosperity and is closely linked to Vorarlberg's emergence as an industrial region. Vorarlberg sees and "markets" itself as such to this day. This characteristic, which is presented in an unconditionally positive manner, can also be supported with facts. In 2020, at 35.3 percent Vorarlberg had the highest proportion of employed people in the industrial and commercial sector of all federal states in Austria.[6] The textile industry, which had been dominant for a long period and whose decline was finally sealed in the 1990s, was replaced by new businesses, particularly in the mechanical, metal, and electrical industries. At the same time, the integration of computer technologies permanently changed the industrial world. The former textile region now advertises its benefits as an industrial location, labeling itself as "*Technikland*" ("engineering region").[7] The majority of Vorarlberg residents now earn their living in the tertiary sector. The service society, which emerged in the 1970s, can also be seen as a facet of the industrial economic system. Ultimately, its "completion" lies in mass consumption.

Industrialization spread across European societies starting from England. Those historians who are considering the bigger picture like to compare the scope of the industrial revolution with the neolithic revolution, which turned nomadic hunters and gatherers into settled farmers. At the beginning of the age of industrialization, agricultural societies were still the norm. Agriculture at subsistence level or just above it, "with urban sprinklings that offered space for crafts and trade,"[8] were characteristic of pre-modern economies in all regions of the world. Newer global historical research that goes beyond the Eurocentric perspective highlights their fundamental similarity, just as it argues that, until 1800, the general population's living standards in Europe and Asia were still very similar. But then came the unique European path: the start of a sustainable growth that withstood both economic fluctuations and wars, with its driving force being the industry, i.e., the specialized, machine-based mass production of goods aimed at supra-regional markets, which not least gave rise to new social classes: entrepreneurs and the workforce. In this way, Western Europe and its "offspring"—North America, Australia, and New Zealand—left almost all other nations and regions of the world behind in terms of goods produced, income per capita, and technical knowledge for more than two centuries. It is undisputed that a multitude of natural, political, and cultural forces were at play and that they intertwined and reinforced each other. Precisely for this reason, we have to think of the industrial revolution as neither intentional nor foreseeable but as a contingent phenomenon; in other words, a phenomenon associated with random elements.[9]

Even if only considering today's federal territory instead of the territory of the Habsburg Monarchy or Cisleithania, Austria was not one of the pioneering nations of the industrial revolution. Nevertheless it was and remained part of a Western European "force field" that had taken shape over a long period of time and enabled the quantum leap on English soil. The establishment of the Pottendorf cotton mill south of Vienna in 1801 is of importance due to its symbolic power. It is considered the first factory in Austria.[10] However, it took until the pre-March era for industrialization to really gain momentum. As elsewhere, textile production took on the role of leading sector as—starting with the spinning mill—it was the first to be mechanized. Due to the concentrated purchasing power of the royal capital, its center was in Vienna and the Vienna Basin. A second, smaller center emerged in the very west of the empire for completely different reasons, namely an "overspill of the Swiss textile industry," as economic historian Felix Butschek puts it.[11]

Merchants from St. Gallen had been conducting long-distance trade in textiles since the Middle Ages. In the seventeenth/eighteenth centuries, these trading houses from eastern Switzerland proceeded to organize the manual spinning and weaving of flax in a workshop system, i.e., working from home, on either side of the Rhine. Parallel to the increased processing of cotton, embroidery was added from the second half of the eighteenth century.[12] Emulating their Swiss role models, more and more locals now joined the workshop movement in Vorarlberg. It was in the hands of these domestic merchants to make the switch to mechanical production once it became essential for maintaining competitiveness. The first mechanical spinning mill in Switzerland had gone into operation in St. Gallen in 1801, the same year as in Pottendorf; around 1812/13, Lorenz Rhomberg and Michael Lenz founded the first mechanical spinning mill in Vorarlberg, located in Dornbirn-Juchen. It was the third one in what is Austria today. Hubert Weitensfelder's important research also substantiates the direct influence of the Swiss neighbors in this implementation of technical progress.[13]

Originally, latching onto the flourishing textile industry in eastern Switzerland had served as an outlet to counter the overpopulation that Vorarlberg suffered from in the early modern age. Around 1750, there were twice as many inhabitants (around 60,000) in the region than at the beginning of the modern age, far more than could be supported by agricultural income. However, the opportunities for business and profit were few and far between in Vorarlberg, not least because there was neither a large city nor profitable raw material supply. Therefore, funds to finance grain imports had to come from outside. Another feasible strategy was seasonal emigration, which around 1850 was still estimated at just under 6,000 people. The most noted groups among these temporary "economic refugees" are the master builders and craftsmen hailing from the Bregenz Forest, who created hundreds of baroque buildings throughout southern Germany, Switzerland, and Alsace; the cabbage shredders from the Montafon area; and the Swabian children, who worked as herders, domestic help, etc. on farms between Lake Constance and Ulm each year from early summer until fall. The export of livestock and hard cheese also brought in money. However, the inflow of money from textile production far exceeded the income from livestock farming. What was much more important, though, was the fact that the production of textiles had already set the course for the future in pre-industrial times. The disparity between the number of people to be fed and the natural resources increasing from previous centuries resulted in both seasonal and sometimes permanent migration but also the emergence of an expanding industry.[14]

Vorarlberg's economic path of development owed its decisive impetus to its proximity to Switzerland. In the long term, it brought with it remarkable improvements in the living conditions of the population. Nevertheless, there was a recurring occurrence of adjustment crises—including social upheavals. Problems in the sales and raw materials markets of the textile industry between 1850 and 1870 and again between 1890 and 1914, for example, caused waves of emigration to the United States, with several thousand leaving the country during each of those periods.[15]

The flipside of industrialization was de-agrarization, a fact not to be neglected. The factories were concentrated in the Rhine Valley and Walgau. In Vorarlberg's side valleys, the industrialized high-yield agriculture that became increasingly common in the second half of the twentieth century and required a lot of machines yet few people was not an option. Here, tourism, whose beginnings date back to the interwar period, was the industry that most notably paved the way to modernity. From the 1950s onwards, it created new jobs and improved living standards at an increasing rate.[16] Now, even in mountainous regions, the rather static way of living and doing business associated with peasants gave way to the central dynamics of an industrial society—progress, growth, and acceleration.

* * * * * *

The COVID-19 pandemic with its massive impact on the exchange of goods, long-growing income disparities, and climate and refugee crises points to the destructive sides of the capitalist economic model. This is also palpable in Vorarlberg. The future seems threatened despite, or perhaps because of, the progress promised by capitalism. Are we facing another turning point in history? That much is certain: the break in development that paved the way to the present day took place in the late eighteenth century. Its scope can be seen as an indicator of how much not only Vorarlberg's future, but also its successful past, is, or was, an embedded part of a European or global economic transformation process.

Endnotes

1. Amt der Vorarlberger Landesregierung/Landesstelle für Statistik, "Die Bevölkerung Vorarlbergs und die Staatsbürgerschaftsverleihungen im Jahr 2020," *vorarlberg.at* 56 (2021), accessed Jan. 6, 2024, https://www.vorarlberg.at/statistik.

2. Franz Mathis, "Vorarlberg als Zuwanderungsland: Ursachen und Voraussetzungen," in *Auswanderung aus dem Trentino – Einwanderung nach Vorarlberg. Die Geschichte einer Migrationsbewegung mit besonderer Berücksichtigung der Zeit von 1870/80 bis 1919*, ed. Karl Heinz Burmeister and Robert Rollinger (Sigmaringen: Thorbecke, 1995), 101–126 (here 108–109, 117); Meinrad Pichler, *Das Land Vorarlberg 1861 bis 2015* (Innsbruck: Universitätsverlag Wagner, 2015), 71.

3. Ibid., 238.

4. Erika Thurner, *Der "Goldene Westen"? Arbeitszuwanderung nach Vorarlberg seit 1945* (Bregenz: Vorarlberger Autoren Gesellschaft, 1997), 114.

5. okay. zusammen leben/Projektstelle für Zuwanderung und Integration, "Die Entwicklung Vorarlbergs vom Gastarbeiter- zum Einwanderungsland," *okay-line.at* (2005), accessed Jan. 6, 2024, https://www.okay-line.at/file/656/2vorarlbergalseinwanderungsland.pdf.

6. Wirtschaftskammer Vorarlberg, "Bundesländer im Vergleich/Basisdaten für Österreichs," *wko.at* (2021), accessed Jan. 6, 2024, https://wko.at/statistik/bundesland/basisdaten.pdf?_ga=2.62037039.2039205498.1618250149-374231131.1617532071.

7. Wirtschaftskammer Vorarlberg/Sparte Industrie, "Zukunft leicht gemacht im Technikland Vorarlberg. Karrierechancen für Technikerinnen und Techniker," *technikland.at*, accessed Jan. 6, 2024, https://www.technikland.at/

8. Felix Butschek, *Industrialisierung. Ursachen, Verlauf, Konsequenzen* (Vienna: Böhlau, 2006), 17.

9. Peter Kramper, "Warum Europa? Konturen einer globalgeschichtlichen Forschungskontroverse," *Neue Politische Literatur*, no. 1 (2009): 9–46 (here 44).

10. Felix Butschek, Österreichische Wirtschaftsgeschichte. Von der Antike bis zur Gegenwart, second edition (Vienna: Böhlau, 2012), 90–97.

11. Ibid., 111.

12. Stefan Sonderegger and Marcel Mayer, "St. Gallen (Gemeinde)," *Historisches Lexikon der Schweiz (HLS)* (2012), accessed Jan. 6, 2024, https://hls-dhs-dss.ch/de/articles/001321/2012-01-06/.

13. Hubert Weitensfelder, *Industrie-Provinz. Vorarlberg in der Frühindustrialisierung, 1740–1870* (Frankfurt am Main: Campus, 2001), 94–96.

14. Mathis, "Vorarlberg als Zuwanderungsland," 103–105; Arno Fitz, "Textile Heimarbeit," in *Vorarlberger Wirtschaftschronik*, ed. Gesellschaft für Wirtschaftsdokumentationen (Vienna: GFW-Verlag, 1993), I/21–I/40 (here I/22–I/26); Weitensfelder, *Industrie-Provinz*, 11, 13–18.

15. Pichler, *Das Land Vorarlberg*, 62–65.

16. Franz Mathis, "Neun Wege – ein Ziel. Zur Wirtschaftsgeschichte der österreichischen Länder im 19. und 20. Jahrhundert," *Geschichte und Region/Storia e regione*, no. 1 (2001): 13–41 (here 29–30).

Casting a New Spotlight on the Russian and Italian Front: Wilhelm Dronowicz and His Austrian Stereo Photographs during the First World War

Martin Kofler

Introduction

What is the contribution of a regional photo archive to modern regional history? How can newly found visual objects shed new light on specific theaters of the First World War? The more you collect photographs in a rather manageable geographical area, combine different accumulations of the same topic, and put it all together with sources and well-researched literature, the more you get out of these more and more important visual pieces of singular memory regarding general patterns of day-to-day life or developments. A few photographs alone are too little to come up with fruitful and successfully nuanced results, but there are photo albums or piles of pictures—hopefully with at least some information about persons, date, place—that give us more than just additional insight. This article presents such a private collection with high potential as well as the detective research about its creator.

The Tyrolean Photo Archive and World War I Visual History

The Tyrolean Archive of photographic documentation and art, in short TAP, was founded in 2011 as a trans-national institution with funding mostly stemming from the European Union as well as the State of Tyrol/Austria and the State of South Tyrol/Italy.[1] It collects, digitizes, and presents old photos from the historic entity of Tyrol (Tyrol, South Tyrol, and Trentino). It has two offices in Lienz and Bruneck/Brunico. Besides its almost 700,000 pictures handed over as donations, loans, and rights use during the past thirteen plus years, it has always been its mission from the start to show the findings on the archive's website[2] as well as especially in exhibitions,[3] books,[4] and articles.[5]

Within the large field of activities commemorating one hundred years since the outbreak of the First World War,[6] TAP prepared a big exhibition in 2014, called "Grenzgang: The Puster Valley and the War 1914-1918," set up in free space in the four border communities of Sillian and Kartitsch in East Tyrol/Austria and Sexten and Bruneck in South Tyrol/Italy. Already back then we showed new photographic findings (including a bit of Dronowicz[7]), which were still groundbreaking and not (!) representing the general manipulating view of the Habsburgian propaganda machinery.[8] On the contrary, they give a merciless insight into day-to-day life in the Dolomites in the First World War and the retreat in early November 1918. Of course, these private pictures never made it into official newspapers, nor were they the front covers of postcards. They are much more than basic illustrations besides written statements: they represent very important and highly emotional historic sources on their own that counter long-lasting WWI mountain warrior myths as well as give evidence to events that are not documented in written form at all. And only a few weeks after the Russian invasion of Ukraine starting February 24, 2022, TAP published a new virtual exhibition with the title "Tyrol and the Eastern Front in the First World War" as a historical contribution to this present war of Moscow against Kyiv—with quite a few Dronowicz photographs of Galicia/Volhynia (today Western Ukraine).[9]

The First World War was the first war of pictures—of propaganda pictures and also the first war mostly remembered via photographs.[10] You have to look at Anton Holzer's influential and critical picture books and articles[11] and Oswald Überegger's work on the construction of national-conservative politics of remembrance of the 1920s and 1930s.[12] For the Eastern Front, Wolfram Dornik has especially put out groundbreaking work.[13]

The general context to be taken into account is the following: a photographer chooses the focus, the right time, the right place, and also manipulates to a certain degree. He sets a description and hands over the picture to the official departments. Each photograph offers one glimpse of past reality, but has to be set into a wider perspective of questions and tempting ways of interpretation. Parallel to press photographers, as well as photographers hired by the War Press Office, you had officers or regular soldiers shooting pictures starting about 1915/16—with cheap celluloid roll film cameras rather than with expensive, unwieldy glass negative cameras. The Austrian War Press Office was increasingly interested in these private pictures because the need for visual documentation could not be satisfied by army or press photographers. Amateur photographers were even supplied with photo materials or received prizes and laudatory decrees for their efforts.[14] But as far as we know now, there is no evidence for an official use of any of Wilhelm Dronowicz's pictures.

Short Biography of Wilhelm Dronowicz (1892–1966) and History of the Collection

Biography

Figure 1: Wilhelm Dronowicz, about 1915 (ID card "Willi Dronowicz," "Akademische Sektion WIEN des Deutschen und Oesterreichischen Alpenvereins") (Photographer: Unknown; Collection TAP)

Wilhelm Dronowicz was born in 1892 in Trient/Trento, back then the most southern part of Tyrol in Austria-Hungary. His father Wilhelm Senior—born in Habsburgian Czernowitz/Bukovina (today Chernivtsi/Ukraine) in 1857, attended the k.u.k. Military Academy in Wiener Neustadt, and joined the Austrian Army in 1880—was stationed in Trient/Trento (*Genie-Direction*) and Innsbruck (*Militärbauabteilung*) and moved with his family (wife Franziska, born in Iglau/Moravia Mähren in 1856; daughter Luisa, born in 1889)[15] to Vienna later on. So, the son Wilhelm was mainly raised in the Habsburg capital where his father had his career in the financial section of the War Department (*Militärrechnungsrat* since 1907). Wilhelm Junior studied engineering in Vienna and went to war in 1914 at age twenty-two. After the First World War, Dronowicz left the army as *Oberleutnant i. d. R.*; he was an assistant at the *Technische Hochschule Wien* and later became a teacher in the *Bundeslehranstalten* in Mödling and Wiener Neustadt/Lower Austria.[16] In the 1930s, Dronowicz worked in Klagenfurt/Carinthia as a teacher in the local *Bundesgymnasium*;[17] his guidance of a Klagenfurt Alpenverein's boys group in the summer of 1935 is also documented.[18] At least since 1944, he lived in Vorarlberg, first in Feldkirch, then in Bludenz, with his wife and two daughters. Dronowicz communicated with the educator and writer Erik Ludwig Tesar in Tyrol, published critical commentaries on Austrian education in the "*Vorarlberger Nachrichten*" and held lectures on psychology in the Feldkirch gymnasium.[19] In fall 1956, the court of Innsbruck sentenced the sixty-four-year-old Dronowicz to three years in prison because he had abused children during leisure activities as well as tutoring hours.[20] He died in Lienz/East Tyrol in 1966[21] where the newly established Tyrolean Photo Archive TAP has had its headquarters since 2011.

History of the Collection

In late 2012, Werner Leibetseder handed over to me as a gift for TAP a big box full of photographs, maps, and documents stemming from an apartment liquidation in Lienz. He also stated that Martin Dobernik had bought many WWI glass negative plates from him out of the same collection, which stemmed from a photographer named Wilhelm Dronowicz. I got in touch with Dobernik, and we were able to scan the whole range of about 1,500 pictures based on a loan contract.

So, as already stressed, for the TAP exhibition "Grenzgang" in 2014, I used the very first pieces out of the Dronowicz collection and in 2022 I checked about 300 photographs intensively for the selection of the TAP web exhibition on "Tyrol and the Eastern Front in the First World War," as a reference to the Russian attack on Ukraine in early 2022.

What Are Stereo Photographs?

To understand the specialty of the Dronowicz collection, you have to explain the photographic technique of stereoscopy.[22] This is the scientific term meaning to shoot pictures in a way that creates a three dimensional effect in the end. It came into existence right away with the invention of photography in 1839 and became extremely popular around 1900. In the First World War, reconnaissance planes used this technology to shoot pictures of whole front areas. Back then you had to have a stereo camera with two objectives in eye-distance as well as stereo glass negative plates. You pushed the button and exposed the plate to light. When you made a paper print afterwards, you put it into a stereoscope, or back then you visited a "*Kaiserpanorama*"—one of up to 250. Today, this technique is widely used for 3D movies; in computer game consoles like Nintendo 3DS; or in Virtual Reality (VR), for instance with your smartphone and extra-made VR videos.

Of course, you need the information, the content of the pictures. Regarding Wilhelm Dronowicz's 1,000 stereo photographs (out of collection's 1,500), it is like this: he made paper prints of his glass plate negatives, cut them out and glued them on field postcards he had received at the front. Have a look at an example.

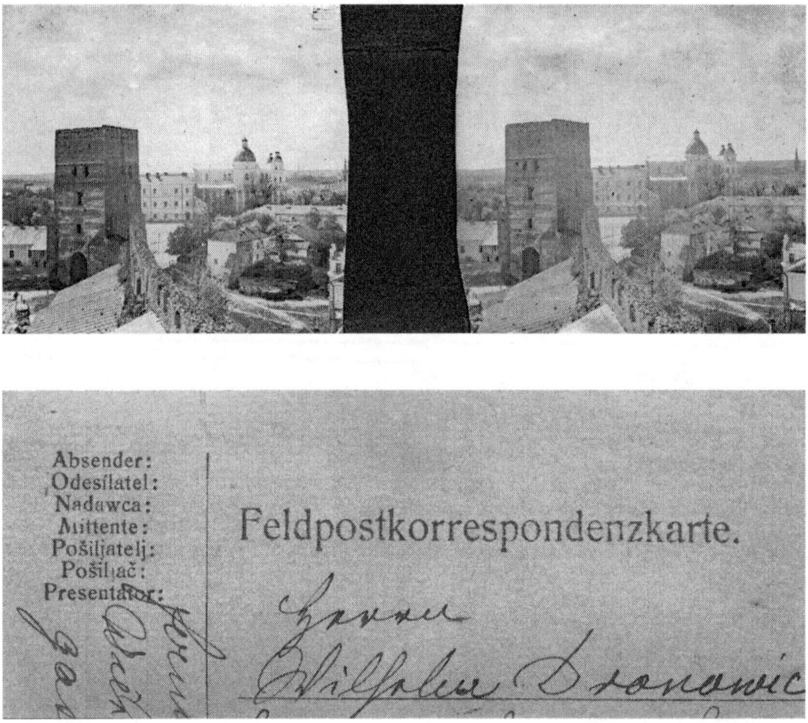

Figure 2: Stereo photography (front and back side of postcard section): Luck, today Luzk/ Western Ukraine, center of Volhynia, back then headquarters of the k.u.k. 4th Army's Oberkommando by Erzherzog Joseph Ferdinand, about September 1915 (Photographer: Wilhelm Dronowicz; Sammlung Martin Dobernik—TAP)

Russian Front

With the Austrian declaration of war against Serbia on July 28, 1914, and the following declarations, the first Habsburgian front proved to be against Russia in Galicia/Volhynia, today Southern Poland and Western Ukraine. Already in August 1914, the four k.u.k. Tyrolean regiments of the *Kaiserjäger*, three regiments of the *Landesschützen*, and the Tyrolean *Landsturm* took a two-week train ride from Tyrol to Galicia: about 45,000 men, mainly eighteen to twenty years old, but also quite many family fathers around thirty-five or forty. In a very short time, more than 10,000 were killed in battle! In total the Austrian Army had about 800,000 soldiers there; in the first weeks August/September 1914, about 300,000 were dead and wounded; 100,000 became prisoners of war of the Russians. It was a total disaster.[23]

Wilhelm Dronowicz entered the war on October 26, 1914, when he became part of the k.k. *Sappeur-Baon* 3.[24] The Sappeurs were an independent branch inside the k.u.k. troops fighting in the first row building emergency bridges, removing obstacles, and setting up fortifications.[25] Dronowicz went to the Eastern Front against Tsarist Russia in March 1915 as a member of the k.k. *Landsturm-Sappeurabt.* Nr. 2/3, Feldpost 56, of the k.u.k. *4. Armee* (about 150,000 soldiers at the beginning of the war). In 1915/16, he was in charge of building fortifications and bridges at the rivers Tanew, San, Styr, as well as Stochod in Galicia/Volhynia. In late 1916, for three months this work could only be done during the night due to heavy Russian artillery attacks (Rudka Myrinska/Stobychwa).[26] In early 1917, mortar stands ("*Minenwerferstände*") had to be built in Toboly, especially together with Bavarian troops from the allied German *Kaiserreich*.[27]

From 1915 to 1917 Dronowicz had to follow the general war's development, so to speak: marching forward in the Battle of Gorlice-Tarnów in May 1915, pushing back the Russians, freeing Przemysl and Lemberg/Lwiw, conquering Luck/Luzk (becoming High Command of the k.u.k. *4. Armee*),[28] freezing on the front with day-to-day life, longer occupation periods and quieter periods of time, fighting the Russian Brussilow offensive starting June 1916, etc.[29]

Figure 3: Stereo photography of local Ruthinians (Ukrainians), Kobche, north of Luck (today Luzk in Western Ukraine), summer 1915 (Photographer: Wilhelm Dronowicz; Sammlung Martin Dobernik – TAP)

Figure 4: Stereo photography of the battle at Maly Porsk, north of Luck/Luzk, August/ September 1915 (Photographer: Wilhelm Dronowicz; Sammlung Martin Dobernik – TAP)

Figure 5: Digging of trenches by the local population under supervision of Austrian soldiers, Sokul Navos/Volhynia, today Sokil Naviz, Western Ukraine, about July 1916 (Photographer: Wilhelm Dronowicz; Sammlung Martin Dobernik – TAP)

Figure 6: Stereo photography of a refugee camp nearby Mielnica, today Melnyzja in Western Ukraine, August 1916 (Photographer: Wilhelm Dronowicz; Sammlung Martin Dobernik – TAP)

Italian Front

Since September 1917, Wilhelm Dronowicz had to do his military duty at the Isonzo front against Italy—still in the *Sappeur-Abteilung*. With the German *Kaiserreich's* supported gaining of ground in the Twelfth Battle of Isonzo (Karfreit) in fall 1917, Dronowicz also moved forward, through Udine, Vittoria, Feltre as far as Monte Grappa—on the way, so to speak, he was in charge of the restoration of the Delizia bridge across the Tagliamento river; later on he had to check where to cross the Piave river, though Anglo-French divisions had already arrived to help the Italians.[30] Back then the private photographer Dronowicz was still unwounded, as were the official war photographers—they did not make spectacular shots right at the very front. Not one of them lost his life from 1914 to 1918. Pictures showing various battles were often made afterwards or even reconstructed in the far "hinterland." The effect made it all; there was no need for true authenticity.[31]

Figure 7: Stereo photography of the mentioned Delizia Bridge across the Tagliamento at Codroipo. Wilhelm Dronowicz was responsible for its restoration, early November 1917. In the online archive of the Austrian National Library's Bildarchiv Austria, you can find a picture of the official k.k. War Press Office (Kriegspressequartier) from November 11, 1917, where this bridge has already been fixed successfully. (Photographer: Wilhelm Dronowicz; Sammlung Martin Dobernik – TAP)

Figure 8: Stereo photography of Ponte di Piave, November 1917 (Photographer: Wilhelm Dronowicz; Sammlung Martin Dobernik – TAP)

Figure 9: Having time for something else: shooting a portrait drawing session near Masi/Cavalese, about spring 1918. (Photographer: Wilhelm Dronowicz; Sammlung Martin Dobernik – TAP)

End of the War 1918

With the Italians' new and final offensive in fall 1918 and the implosion of Austria-Hungary, Wilhelm Dronowicz accompanied the retreating armies northwards: from the Fassa Valley via the Pordoi Pass (2,239 m) to the Gader Valley and along the Puster Valley to Lienz in early November 1918. By foot, with wagons, or by train the soldiers moved further east to their home counties. Dronowicz was officially dismissed from the army as *Oberleutnant i. R.* from the *Sappeur Ersatz-Baon.* in Hainburg/Danube on November 26, 1918.[32]

Figure 10: Starting the retreat: Stereo photography of Meida near Vigo di Fassa, late October 1918 (Photographer: Wilhelm Dronowicz; Sammlung Martin Dobernik – TAP)

Figure 11 : Lost Austrian troops in chaos at Johannes Square Lienz, end of the war early November 1918 (Photographer: Wilhelm Dronowicz; Sammlung Martin Dobernik – TAP)

After the First World War, Wilhelm Dronowicz did not stop making stereo photographs. On the contrary, in the TAP collection you can find a few hundred of stereo glass plate negatives covering his mountain climbing trips in the Eastern Alps as well as journeys to the mediterranean islands of Corsica and Capri. You can even find mountain photographs of "Wilhelm Dronowicz, Wiener Neustadt" in Julius Kugy's book *Die Julischen Alpen im Bilde* from 1934.[33]

Summing Up

TAP has been lucky to be handed over the private Dronowicz photographs that have to be taken into the bigger perspective by extensive as well as detailed research. The forthright way must be to provide such a collection to the public—well-organized and with as much information as possible—for two reasons: on the one hand, scientists as well as historically interested people in general shall know about these pictures for further use and insight into the First World War; on the other hand, persons should realize the cultural value ("*Kulturschatz*") of their private visual sources and share it, for example, via a regional or local archive they trust. This snowball effect is at the core of a successful archive that supports modern regional history as well as contributes to historiography by (virtual) exhibitions, books, and articles.

The works of the formerly unknown Austrian photographer Wilhelm Dronowicz are quite unique in the sense that—contrary to the standard books with photographs from the official k.k. War Presse Office (*Kriegspressequartier*) by Holzer or from the *Kriegsarchiv* by Maderthaner/Hochedlinger[34]—you have more than 1,000 stereo photographs from an amateur that are able to cover several war theaters as well as almost the whole four years of the war: from the Eastern front (Galicia/Volhynia, today Poland and Ukraine) via the South West front against Italy up to the documentation of the end of the war in the fall of 1918 in the South and East Tyrolean Puster Valley.

The photographs of Wilhelm Dronowicz also refer to the specialty of materiality: you have glass negatives as well as photo prints—but the latter are glued on small-cut war postcards and include valuable written localization. So, the back of the prints are equally interesting and important not only because of the names of villages, towns, and front sections, but also because of some given dates.

The collection is very special, not to say outstanding, because it gives new insight in WWI history from a private "*Knipser*" perspective. Dronowicz was in a Sappeur company mainly building bridges, barracks, etc. that he shot with his camera. But he also portrayed the local population, Jewish cemeteries, and the Habsburg army's daily life in great detail, e.g. the "Josefa Farm" in Bythen/Stobychwa (Volhynia, today Western Ukraine). When looking at photographs of the Eastern Front, today's Viennese *Kriegsarchiv* has about 20,000 originals mainly focusing on Galicia (about 17,000, with about 3,000 portraying Volhynia) with the fortress of Przemysl in the center, in general mostly from 1914/15.[35] On the contrary, there are about 300 Dronowicz pictures from 1915–1917 on different areas of the front and

Hinterland in Galicia and more of Volhynia.

But no atrocities and dead soldiers can be seen on the Dronowicz photographs.[36] This refers to Markus Wurzer's analysis[37] of a photo collection of the South Western front against Italy: you do not see any cruelties in the photographs and hardly any victims; maybe they were destroyed or never made. Nevertheless, private collections and their special views strongly contribute to a broader understanding of WWI visual history—as Jay Winter has already emphasized.[38]

Endnotes

1. For the early days of TAP, see Martin Kofler, "Fotografien als historische Quelle," *Tiroler Fotografie 1854-2011*, ed. Michael Forcher and Meinrad Pizzinini (Innsbruck-Vienna: Haymonverlag, 2012), 216-231.

2. Tirol Archiv Photographie (TAP), *Tiroler-photoarchiv.eu*, accessed Jan. 21, 2024, https://www.Tiroler-photoarchiv.eu; more than 7,000 TAP photographs can also be downloaded for free under the open license Creative Commons BY at: Lichtbild Kulturschatz Historische Photograhpie, *lichtbild-argentovivo.eu*, accessed Jan. 21, 2024, https://www.lichtbild-argentovivo.eu.

3. Especially, "Frische Luft für alte Ansichten" (Lienz, 2012–2014); "Zeittreppen – Eine Bildgeschichte der Stadt Bruneck. Von Grebmer bis Hibler (1861–1932)" (Bruneck, 2012); "Sonderschau Georg Egger" (Lienz, 2012); "Volldampf. Die Pustertalbahn 1869–1918" (Lienz/Toblach/Bruneck, 2013); "Erschließung. Die Nationalparkregion Hohe Tauern Tirol im historischen Lichtbild 1880 bis 1960" (Matrei in East Tyrol, 2013/14); "Schlaglicht. Lienz und der Talboden" (Photo-Film, Lienz, 2013/14); "Grenzgang. Das Pustertal und der Krieg 1914–1918" (Sillian/Kartitsch/Sexten/Bruneck, 2014); "Kalipè. A Photographic Journey through the Life of Mountaineer Reinhold Messner" (Bruneck, 2015); "Durchbruch. Der Bau der Felbertauernstraße 1965/2015" (Lienz, 2015); "Heimat/Front. Lienz und der Krieg 1914–1918" (Photo-Film, Lienz, 2015/16); during the Interreg project "Lichtbild/Argento vivo" with partners in Bruneck/ Brunico, Bozen/Bolzano, and Innsbruck: "Platz da! Historische Photographien zentraler Orte" (2018) and "Frauenbilder. Historische Photographien. Tirol – Südtirol/Alto Adige – Trentino" (2019); constant exhibition LUMEN. Museum of Mountain Photography, Kronplatz Bruneck/Plan de Corones Brunico as well as special exhibitions there: "Ulrich Ackermann. Sagenhafte Dolomiten" (2019/20), "Jenseits des Manaslu. Friedl Mutschlechner – Bergsteiger und Fotograf" (2021), and "Zeichen am Berg" (2023/24); "Heimatfotografie und Osttirol. Politisierte Bilder von Koppitz bis Baptist; 1930–1950" (Lienz, 2023); "Osttirol – Der Weg in die Moderne, 1870/71–1970" (Heinfels, 2023); online exhibitions: "Tirol/Südtirol 1945/46: Zwischen Hoffnung und Ernüchterung" (2020/21), "Anfänge des Faschismus in Südtirol 1923–1933" (2022), and "Karl-Theo Stammer – Bäuerliches Leben" (2023).

4. For instance, see Martin Kofler, ed., *Volldampf: Die Pustertalbahn 1869–1918* (TAP-Forschungen, vol. 1) (Innsbruck-Vienna: Haymonverlag, 2013); Martin Kofler, ed., *Grenzgang: Das Pustertal und der Krieg 1914–1918* (TAP-Forschungen, vol. 2) (Innsbruck-Vienna: Haymonverlag, 2014); Martin Kofler, *Lebensader: Die Felbertauernstraße damals und heute* (TAP-Forschungen, vol. 3) (Innsbruck-Vienna: Haymonverlag 2017; Martin Kofler, *Südbahn-Heizhaus. Vom Bahnbau in Lienz 1869/71 bis zur Gegenwart* (bahnmedien, vol. 20) (Tadten: bahnmedien.at, 2021).

5. Recently, for instance, Martin Kofler and Notburga Siller, "Frauenbilder / Signora fotograf*(i)*a. Visual History in Tirol – Südtirol – Trentino: eine Fotoausstellung im Rahmen des Interreg-Projekts 'Lichtbild'," *Fotogeschichte* no. 155 (2020): 53-58; Martin Kofler, "Mountain Pictures: A Special Look into the Collections of the

Tyrolean Photo Archive (TAP)," in *Visual Histories of Austria* ed. Günter Bischof, Martin Kofler, and Hans Petschar (Contemporary Austrian Studies, vol. 30) (New Orleans: University of New Orleans Press, 2021), 259-267; Martin Kofler, "Heimatfotografie und Osttirol. Politisierte Bilder von Koppitz bis Baptist, 1930–1950," *Tiroler Heimatblätter* 99, no. 1 (2024): 2-12; a short version of this article in German has been published: see Martin Kofler, "Kriegsfronten im Lichtbild. Wilhelm Dronowicz und seine Stereofotografien im Ersten Weltkrieg," *OstTiroler Heimatblätter* 90, no. 11 (2022).

6. Looking at books that came out in 2013/14/15 just to name a few of the leading publications on the international, Austrian, and Tyrolean level: Christopher Clark, *The Sleepwalkers: How Europe went to War in 1914* (London: Penguin Books, 2013) (first edition, 2012); Manfried Rauchensteiner, *Der Erste Weltkrieg und das Ende der Habsburgermonarchie 1914–1918* (Vienna: Böhlau Verlag, 2013); Peter Fritz and Christian Rapp, eds., *Jubel & Elend. Leben mit dem Großen Krieg 1914–1918, Ausstellungskatalog Schallaburg* (Schallaburg: Schallaburg Kulturbetriebsges.m.b.H., 2014); Hermann J. W. Kuprian and Oswald Überegger, eds., *Katastrophenjahre: Der Erste Weltkrieg und Tirol* (Innsbruck: Universitätsverlag Wagner, 2014); Michael Forcher, *Tirol und der Erste Weltkrieg: Ereignisse, Hintergründe, Schicksale* (Innsbruck: Haymonverlag, 2014).

7. Two Dronowicz photographs regarding East Tyrol at the end of the First World War made it into the 2014 exhibition's essay collection, see, Kofler, *Grenzgang*, 46, 68; see also Martin Kofler, "Besiegte und Sieger. Fotogeschichte des Pustertales zu Kriegsende," *Tiroler Heimatblätter*, Heft 4 (2018), 56-65.

8. For photographs and Austria-Hungary in WWI, see above all: Anton Holzer, *Die andere Front: Fotografie und Propaganda im Ersten Weltkrieg*, second edition (Darmstadt: Primus Verlag, 2007); Anton Holzer, *Fotografie in Österreich: Geschichte – Entwicklungen – Protagonisten 1890–1955* (Vienna: Metroverlag, 2013), 47-58; Wolfgang Maderthaner and Michael Hochedlinger, *Untergang einer Welt: Der große Krieg 1914–1918 in Photographien und Texten* (Vienna: Christian Brandstätter Verlag, 2013).

9. *Kronenzeitung* (Tirol), March 25, 2022; *Dolomiten*, March 26/27, 2022; *Tiroler Tageszeitung*, May 1, 2022.

10. See, Holzer, *Die andere Front*, 14.

11. See for example, Anton Holzer, "Krieg in Bildern. Fotografie und Propaganda im Ersten Weltkrieg," in *Jubel & Elend*, ed. Fritz and Rapp, 254-259; Anton Holzer, *Rasende Reporter: Eine Kulturgeschichte des Fotojournalismus* (Darmstadt: Primus Verlag, 2014), 105-115; Anton Holzer, "Den Krieg sehen. Zur Bildgeschichtsschreibung des Ersten Weltkriegs," in *Mit der Kamera bewaffnet. Krieg und Fotografie*, ed. Fritz and Rapp (Marburg: Jonas Verlag, 2003), 57-70, here 58, 60.

12. Oswald Überegger, "Tabuisierung – Instrumentalisierung – verspätete Historisierung. Die Tiroler Historiographie und der Erste Weltkrieg," *Geschichte und Region* 11, no. 1(2002): 127-145; Oswald Überegger, *Erinnerungskriege: Der Erste Weltkrieg, Österreich und die Tiroler Erinnerung in der Zwischenkriegszeit* (Tirol im Ersten Weltkrieg. Politik – Wirtschaft – Gesellschaft, Bd. 9) (Innsbruck: Universitätsverlag Wagner, 2011).

13. Bernhard Bachinger and Wolfram Dornik, eds., *Jenseits des Schützengrabens: Der Erste Weltkrieg im Osten: Erfahrung – Wahrnehmung – Kontext* (Veröffentlichungen des Ludwig Boltzmann-Instituts für Kriegsfolgenforschung, extra vol. 14) (Innsbruck: Studienverlag, 2013); Wolfram Dornik, "Der 'überlagerte' Krieg. Österreichisch-ungarische Soldaten im 'Osten' 1914–1918," in *Jubel & Elend*, ed. Fritz and Rapp, 224-229.

14. Holzer, *Die andere Front*, 20-23, 32-37.

15. Haus-, Hof- und Staatsarchiv/Vienna, Ordenskanzlei, Zl. 3104 ex 1917 [Wilhelm Dronowicz, Militär-Oberrechnungsrat 1. Klasse, Leiter der Gruppe 7 (Transportwesen), Dienstzeit 36 Jahre und 9 Monate: Verleihung Franz Joseph-Orden (Ritterkreuz) auf Antrag Kriegsministerium.]; Kriegsarchiv/Vienna; Qualifikationslisten, Hauptreihe (A-Z), Karton 502 "Wilhelm Dronowicz"; "Grundbuchblatt Wien 1892 Karton 1356 Wilhelm Dronowicz," *familysearch.org*, accessed Jan. 04, 2024, https://www.familysearch.org/ark:/61903/3:1:3Q9M-CSJ7-99Q2?i=107&cat=2259751.

16. Archiv der Republik/Vienna, Bundesministerium für Unterricht, Personalakten 1945-1984, Sign. 3/027 "Dronowicz Wilhelm."

17. "Klagenfurt Gymnasium chronicle 1934/35," *uni-klu.ac.at*, accessed Jan. 04, 2024, https://wwwu.uni-klu.ac.at/elechner/schulmuseum/schulchroniken/gklagenfurt1934.PDF; "Klagenfurt Gymnasium chronicle 1936/37," *uni-klu.ac.at*, accessed Jan. 04, 2024, https://wwwu.uni-klu.ac.at/elechner/schulmuseum/schulchroniken/gklagenfurt1936.PDF; "Klagenfurt inhabitants register of 1938," *findbuch.at*, accessed Jan. 04, 2024, https://www.findbuch.at/files/content/adressbuecher/1938_bsoe_ktn_ab/3__I._Teil_Einwohner_und_Betriebe_Klagenfurt_A_-_F.pdf.

18. *Freie Stimmen. Deutsche Kärntner Landeszeitung*, May 16, 1935; *Kärntner Tagblatt*, May 17, 1935.

19. Letters Wilhelm Dronowicz to Erik Ludwig Tesar, May 15, 1944, January 7, 1950. Forschungsinstitut Brenner-Archiv, Nachlass Erik Ludwig Tesar, Sig. 36-121-44; driver's license "Professor" Wilhelm Dronowicz, living in Bludenz/Südtiroler Siedlung, issued on December 1, 1947. Collection TAP; Wilhelm Dronowicz, "Akademisches Proletariat," *Vorarlberger Nachrichten*, December 14, 1948; Wilhelm Dronowicz, "Vom Sinn des Studiums," *Vorarlberger Nachrichten*, January 24, 1949; *Feldkircher Anzeiger*, January 22 1949, September 24, 1949.

20. *Volkszeitung* (Innsbruck), October 17, 1956.

21. Information Meldekarte Wilhelm Dronowicz: Mail Regina Perfler/Stadt Lienz to the author, June 13, 2022. There is no information given since when he lived in Lienz or that he was married and had two children.

22. For an introduction, see, "Stereoscopy," *wikipedia.org*, accessed Jan. 4, 2024,

https://en.wikipedia.org/wiki/Stereoscopy; Tom Ang, *Fotografie: Die visuelle Geschichte* (London, 2022), 58-59.

23. Forcher, *Tirol und der Erste Weltkrieg*, 73-74.

24. Archiv der Republik/Vienna, Bundesministerium für Unterricht, Personalakten 1945-1984, Sign. 3/027 "Dronowicz Wilhelm" (Standesausweis).

25. See, "K.u.k._Sappeure," *wikipedia.org*, accessed Jan. 4, 2024, https://de.wikipedia.org/wiki/K.u.k._Sappeure.

26. Kriegsarchiv/Vienna, Belohnungsakten des Weltkrieges 1914-1918, Nr. 80469/1915, Nr. 670290/1916, Nr. 141690/1917 (Wilhelm Dronowicz); for the 4th Army on the Eastern front, see, Erwin A. Schmidl, "Der Kriegsschauplatz Galizien," in *Hinter den Fronten Galiziens: Feldkaplan Karl Gögele und sein Verwundetenspital: Aufzeichnungen 1914–1915*, ed. Monika Mader (Bozen: Edition Raetia, 2016), 36-45, here 42-43.

27. Kriegsarchiv/Vienna, Belohnungsakten des Weltkrieges 1914-1918, Nr. 209615/1917 (Wilhelm Dronowicz).

28. Regarding Luzk, see, Erwin A. Schmidl, "Das Kriegsgeschehen 1915-1918," in *Raues Leben, großes Sterben: Feldkaplan Karl Gögele und sein Deutschordensspital: Kriegstagebücher 1915–1918*, ed. Monika Mader (Bozen: Edition Raetia, 2018), 9-22, here 11, 15.

29. In general, see Dornik, "Der 'überlagerte' Krieg," in *Jubel & Elend*, ed. Fritz and Rapp, 224-229.

30. Kriegsarchiv/Vienna, Belohnungsakten des Weltkrieges 1914-1918, Nr. 209615/1917 (Wilhelm Dronowicz); on the Twelfth Battle of the Isonzo until the standstill at the Piave river: Mark Thompson, *The White War: Life and Death on the Italian Front 1915–1919* (London: Faber and Faber, 2008), 294-327.

31. Holzer, *Fotografie in Österreich*, 48-49.

32. Archiv der Republik/Vienna, Bundesministerium für Unterricht, Personalakten 1945-1984 (BMU/PA), Sign. 3/027 "Dronowicz Wilhelm" (Standesausweis).

33. Julius Kugy, *Die Julischen Alpen im Bilde* (Graz: Leykam, 1934), Dronowicz photographs on pages 73 (Siroca Pec), 83 (Skrlatica), 95 (Razor), 140 (Wischberg), 161 (Kaningruppe), 168 (Montatsch), 176 (Jof del Montasio).

34. See Holzer, *Die andere Front*, and Maderthaner and Hochedlinger, *Untergang*.

35. Hannes Leidinger, "Visualisierung des Krieges. Die Ostfront in österreichisch-ungarischen Fotografien und Filmproduktionen,"in *Jenseits des Schützengrabens*, ed. Bachinger and Dornik, 451-465, here 461, 463-464.

36. Focusing on Austro-Hungarian massacres and executions against Serbs and in Galicia from August 1914 to mid-1915—so basically before Dronowicz's duty on the Eastern Front: Hannes Leidinger et al., *Habsburgs schmutziger Krieg: Ermittlungen zur österreichisch-ungarischen Kriegsführung 1914–1918* (Salzburg: Residenz Verlag, 2014), 75-91.

37. Markus Wurzer, "In/Visibility of Violence: The First World War in Austrian Private Photo Albums," in *Visual Histories of Austria*, ed. Bischof, Kofler, and Petschar, 109-131.

38. Jay Winter, *War beyond Words: Languages of Remembrance from the Great War to the Present* (Cambridge: Cambridge University Press, 2017), especially 37-41, 61-68.

Transnational Perspectives in Regional History: Belle Époque Tourism Advertisements from New Orleans (Louisiana) and Innsbruck (Tyrol)

Hester Margreiter

New Orleans (Louisiana) and Innsbruck (Tyrol) are interesting case studies for early tourism at the end of the nineteenth and the beginning of the twentieth century.[1] Belle Époque tourism as a relatively homogenous practice allows a comparison of destinations that are quite different regarding their political, historical, and ecological context: infrastructures, from hotels to landmarks, and (tourism-induced) urban perceptions were shaped back then for and by the elite, the main tourism clientele in this era. The transformative power of tourism affected both urban development and regional identities. Besides transportation, accommodation, and entertainment infrastructures, historical advertising strategies also played a central role.

This article is meant to show how the analysis of historic tourism advertisements can contribute to regional history research. Based on theoretical foundations from the field of social and cultural studies, under special consideration of concepts by Kathrin Bonacker and John Urry, the presentation of urban structures, distinctive features, and local identities in travel guides, tourist brochures, and other advertising materials can be understood as a cultural concentrate and can thereby be examined regarding narratives of self-image, marketing, external perceptions, and historical facts. A modern understanding of regional history defines regions as cultural, political, and economic constructs, which should be analyzed as multifactor dynamic processes.[2] Tourism tends to shape regions and ideas about these regions. This contribution will showcase two important examples, which are very iconic and crucial advertisement concepts, both in the context of advertising itself but also in regard to the definition and identity-building of the respective city. The motifs, the perspectives, and especially the ideas behind these advertisements achieved an impressive longevity during the twentieth century and helped to build each distinctive regional construct.

The Golden Age of the Grand Hotels

Industrialization and urbanization processes in the late nineteenth century led to a shift in mobilities and pushed early tourism. The increasing technological possibilities enabled—and were enabled by—tourism-related infrastructures. Beginning in the middle of the nineteenth century, the extension of railway networks allowed new transport routes and volumes and stimulated tourism. In turn, tourism was a further incentive to build even more railway routes. The rise of the Grand Hotels in the Belle Époque due to leisure travel and business tourism by the upper classes shaped the images of cities. Accommodations became far more than convenient shelters; they were opulent rooms of indulgence. The luxurious architecture equipped with the latest technical innovations was part of the cultural and recreational experience.[3]

The targeted clientele and the conception of destinations designated to tourism within the Belle Époque are highly comparable: in this historical period, which is also known as the Golden Age of the Grand Hotels, new technologies allowed hitherto unknown comfort and luxuries regarding accommodations and transportation infrastructures, which did not only serve as means to an end but were also considered an attraction itself. Besides infrastructures, leisure activities and entertainment events for the travelling upper classes in this era are also internationally comparable. In Europe and overseas, Grand Hotels emerged not at the exact same time, but building structures, luxury, and technology levels, as well as the function of Grand Hotels as providers for technological and cultural innovations allow comparisons.[4]

A historic comparison of New Orleans (Louisiana) and Innsbruck (Tyrol) considers the similarities of structural shifts in perception and infrastructures combined with the awareness of dealing with two quite different cities concerning culture, politics, and environment. Nonetheless, their parallel structural redevelopment to early tourism destinations enables a trans-regional approach to discuss the transformative power of tourism and its infrastructures. In the late nineteenth and early twentieth centuries, New Orleans and Innsbruck were important destinations and already had a thriving theatre and concert culture, though in rather different cultural variations.[5] Besides the improvement of transportation, tourism was stimulated mostly by published travel reports.[6]

Both places have a long history as hubs on important trade routes. Consequently, the infrastructures needed for tourism could be built upon existing structures. A strong focus on advertising material, travel brochures, and guidebooks allows a retracing of tourism trends and the representation of these urban regions. In the Golden Age of Grand Hotels, tourism marketing designs were shaped by international trends. The crucial advertisements showcased in this article were both created in the Art Nouveau style: in Austria this style is known as *Jugendstil* or *Secessionsstil*; in the United States of America, it is also referred to as Modern Style. This style was invented in the last decades of the nineteenth century, became an international art movement, and was quite popular in the late Belle Époque era.[7]

Urbanity, Trade, and Tourism in the Mississippi River Delta

New Orleans has been an important port city since its very beginnings. Even before the French founded this city in the early eighteenth century, the area served as a gateway in the water transport routes of the American First Nations, including large settlements and landscape adaptions. Situated between the Mississippi in the south, Lake Pontchartrain in the north, and pervaded by natural bayous (the river's backwater arms) as well as artificial canals, the site allows for the movement of goods between the surrounding bodies of water. The Mississippi system's watercourses enable a vast transportation network within the northern American continent, and New Orleans is connected to the Gulf of Mexico through both the river and Lake Pontchartrain. The colonists utilized the site as a trading center and a cargo hub between oceangoing ships and river boats. So, commercial interests led to the foundation of a city, erected on top of natural levees, surrounded by swamps, in a river's flood plain, prone to natural disasters.[8] New Orleans was an important commercial hub for the plantation economy and offered an expansive network of slave trading sites up until the American Civil War.[9]

After the Louisiana Purchase in 1803 and Louisiana becoming the eighteenth state in 1812, more English-speaking Americans moved into the city. As a port city, New Orleans soon had begun to capitalize on its numerous visitors. It had developed a reputation of looser morals than the northern industrial cities and came to be a hotspot of entertainment. As part of the United States, it became more interesting as a leisure destination for tourists from the North. Tourism focused on the historic inner city, the French Quarter, and its colonial sights as well as entertainment for visiting businessmen.[10] In the nineteenth century, many hotels in this city were operated like boarding houses. The first Grand Hotels of New Orleans were built in the 1830s and located within the French Quarter. More splendid and even bigger Grand Hotels of New Orleans, serving as luxury accommodations for businessmen as well as families, were erected between the 1890s and 1920, mostly around Canal Street.[11]

Tourism investments around 1900 were often rather a reaction to tourism development than a proactive strategy. The restoration of the historic city center, the French Quarter, was led by elite preservationists who intended to stop decay and to reclaim what was understood as architectural and social heritage. The prevention of the modernization of the Quarter met the expectations of an increasing number of tourists.[12] The improvement of town squares in the historic center and the foundation of public parks (beginning in the late nineteenth century) were not primarily intended as tourism infrastructures; nevertheless, these endeavors helped to boost tourism.[13] The Mardi Gras carnival was advertised nationwide since the 1870s. Until the 1920s, tourism in New Orleans relied on conventions, fairs, and the Mardi Gras season.[14] Besides enjoyment structures for both genders, New Orleans offered plentiful carnal entertainment for male visitors. The city's image of immorality was pushed back with the closing of Storyville, the legal red-light district, in November 1917, and prohibition since the summer of 1919, which led to a decline of entertainment infrastructures in the city, including ballrooms, restaurants, and music halls. Now, taxi drivers or hotel personnel served as middlemen for illicit prostitutes; cafés and most of the city's hotels got clandestinely involved in the city's sex trade. And those who still wanted to consume alcohol found their way to illegal speakeasies, helped by people working in the tourism industry.[15]

Urbanity, Transit, and Tourism within the Austrian Alps

Innsbruck is the dominant city in the Tyrolean valley of the river Inn in the Austrian Alps. To the north, it is enclosed by a high and steep mountain range; in the south, the city faces mostly smaller mountains. Tyrol was ruled by the Austrian House of Habsburg since the fourteenth century. With the unification of the Habsburg realms in the early nineteenth century, it was designated a crown land of the Austrian Empire and continued this role as a Cisleithanian crown land of Austria-Hungary in the late nineteenth century until the end of the Empire after the First World War. By the time of the Belle Époque it had been, besides a brief interruption during the Napoleonic Wars, part of the Habsburg monarchy for centuries.

Up until the late modern period, Innsbruck was referred to as a city on a river and portrayed with its southern mountains. Since around 1820, the image of Innsbruck is tied to its northern mountain range.[16] Since medieval times, Innsbruck has been a relevant place on the important road from Verona to Augsburg. In the nineteenth century, particularly in the second half, tourism has been a relevant business; besides trade and transport, it was the most prosperous sector. People visited cultural monuments, historic structures, and the Alpine landscape.[17]

Tourism accommodations were modernized (to compete with other destinations, especially the Swiss tourism industry) and the improvement of transport systems allowed a more comfortable and faster journey to Innsbruck, which was advertised as a traditional and native area.[18] Accommodations for tourists rapidly changed at the turn of the century. Until the end of the nineteenth century, most guesthouses were oriented on transients. Meanwhile, the growing tourism sector led to the construction of modern hotels beginning in the late 1860s. Several Grand Hotels were built at the main station, including modern amenities like hot water, indoor plumbing, bathrooms in each room, telephones, electric lights, and heating.[19] Innsbruck and Tyrol benefited from events like a car race from Paris to Vienna in 1902, which helped to advertise Innsbruck and Tyrol as destinations.[20] The number of tourist accommodations in Tyrol doubled between 1890 and 1909.[21] Up until the First World War, tourism was the biggest income source for the inhabitants of the city. It was not until the mid-1920s that the level of pre-war tourism in Innsbruck was reached again.[22]

Advertising as a Cultural Concentrate

This contribution deals a lot with infrastructures in the context of advertising concepts that influenced cultural identities. Advertisements are an important factor in the tourism industry and from a structural perspective they can be understood as (marketing) infrastructures. According to Dirk van Laak, "[infrastructure systems] represent institutions, i.e. elements of long duration, but also materialized particles of memory. Conceived as 'traditions' of earlier generations, they can be read today as 'remnants' of earlier spatial and social designs."[23] To put it even more succinctly: "Infrastructures reflect commonplace social and cultural processes."[24]

The consideration of Kathrin Bonacker's thesis, that advertising can be perceived as a cultural concentrate and used to draw conclusions about historical ideas of everyday life, ideals, and desires, (as well as cultural fashions and emotional perspectives), serves as a basis for an investigation into the history of mentality: "Advertising is thus understood in a double sense as a cultural concentrate, in whose images can be found, on the one hand, what materially appears or is at least dreamed of as a contemporary cultural asset, but in which, on the other hand, cultural moods are also expressed indirectly, i.e. in which the history of mentality is reflected."[25] Bonacker uses this concept to analyze advertising in general and tourist travelers and hotel staff in particular. In my view, it can also be used to examine real and imagined images of tourist cityscapes.

John Urry's concept of the tourist gaze focuses on the complexity and interactions of the possibilities of visual enjoyment in terms of tourist consumption:

First, many of these (tourist) gazes are self-consciously organized by professionals. These include the writers of travel books and guides, travel agents, hotel owners and designers, photographers, . . . and so on. Second, different [tourist] gazes are authorized by different discourses. . . . Third, there is a distinction to note between the romantic and the collective tourist gaze. In the former, the emphasis is on solitude, privacy, and a personal, semispiritual relationship with the object of the gaze. In such cases, the tourist will expect to look at the object privately and thus other visitors intrude on his or her consumption of the object. The collective gaze, by contrast, involves conviviality. Other people are necessary to give atmosphere or a sense of carnival to the place.[26]

With regard to the last point, I am pursuing the thesis that a large part of the publications promoting tourism served to create both the romantic and the collective gaze.

In addition to the narratively and visually constructed character of tourist destinations, however, the concrete regional and supra-regional links in tourism development should by no means be ignored. The investigation of regional production networks in the sense of an industrial district and possible path dependencies are conceptual perspectives by means of which the material background of tourism infrastructures can be traced in their complexity. It is therefore a matter of examining both ideal and material aspects of tourist destinations: "First, any attempt to tell the story of tourism and regional change will fail without the awareness that our study regions are interwoven in complex supra-regional networks of communication, migration, flows of capital and material, and infrastructure. . . . Second, the focus on historical dynamics, social construction and negotiation . . . is not meant to downplay the importance of material 'reality.' Human actors, their perceptions and practices, as well as different forms of material, capital, and infrastructure are interconnected in multiple ways and layers."[27]

A useful framework for basic considerations can also be found in Kathrin Bonackers reference to the ". . . *Bildlore* concept developed by Nils-Arvid Bringéus, which has had a ground-breaking effect in European ethnology since 1981 and clarified in seven points how, in his view, images could be dealt with: He called for a consideration 1. in an international direction, 2. transcending social boundaries, 3. in an uncircumcised temporal perspective (forwards and backwards), 4. freed from qualitative judgments, 5. with the aim of exposing the valuations and attitudes expressed in images, 6. by understanding images as part of and in the context of human action, 7. in their role in influencing people's ideas."[28]

Gateway to Waterways

A predecessor for New Orleans as the "Gateway to the Americas" was the catching phrase of the "Gateway to the Panama Canal." A lot of tourism advertising material used these lines during the twentieth century.[29] Before the Panama Canal was built, ships traveling between the Atlantic and the Pacific oceans had to go around Cape Horn, the southern end of South America. So, the opening of this waterway in 1914, which was controlled solely by the United States of America until 1979, saved two months' time for each journey between the east coast and the west coast of North America.[30] Advertising New Orleans as the United States port city to the most important artificial waterway of the Americas started even before the Panama Canal was completed.

Figure 1: Pamphlet "New Orleans: The Gateway to the Panama Canal", 1912 (Acc. no. 1985.249 (Gift of the Milwaukee County Historical Society), The Historic New Orleans Collection)

The selected advertisement for this contribution depicts New Orleans both in picture and slogan as "The Gateway to the Panama Canal." As an allegory of the "crescent city," a woman is sitting on a sickle moon, pointing toward the city on a map covering most of the Americas. The depiction is decorated with warm colors (two-color print in black and orange on yellowish brown material) and shows the city as directly connected to the sea; both the map and the seagull suggest a coastal city, whilst it is located only near the coast within the Mississippi basin. Created in the Art Nouveau style, the depicted woman's gown is drawn as a quite revealing garment, which is common in this artistic style; nonetheless, it is a reference to the reputation of the city. The woman's hair is decorated with flowers, resembling a more reputable reference to New Orleans: The *fleur-de-lis* (flower of the lily) is a symbol of its French origins. The depiction was printed in 1912 as the front cover of a pamphlet published by the National Folder Company and distributed by Gallagher's Furniture Transfer, a shipping and moving company based in New Orleans. The pamphlet was designed as a postcard with an accordion foldout attached within. The item contains sixteen pages illustrated with New Orleans landmarks, architecture, infrastructures, and a beautifully arranged display of farm products. It is intended to address both possible visitors and immigrants. Whilst showing off architecture, the pamphlet covers educational and cultural issues, public institutions, technical infrastructure, business ventures, several Grand Hotels, and a moving van from the Gallagher's company. Among others, the Tulane University Campus; Canal Street including street cars; the Ursuline Convent and Academy; the Delgado Art Museum; and some of the city's finest hotels (St. Charles, Monteleone, and Grunewald) are depicted.[31]

Mountain Connections

Mountains are physical obstructions; therefore, "it is a considerable paradox of the Alps that this colossal mountain range never formed an insurmountable barrier, but rather a connector between east and west, south and north, a contact zone, a node point of economies, ideas and forms." The Alps served as "cultural bridge between the Mediterranean and northern Europe"; this idea especially was promoted in the nineteenth and even more in the twentieth centuries.[32] The building of railroads in the second half of the nineteenth century allowed much faster and less expensive means of transportation. In the 1880s, the main railroad network in Tyrol was completed; an increase in the number of tourists followed.[33] Soon supplemental railway lines within Tyrol were built. Automobiles became a more important factor and pushed the building of roads. Most traffic routes in Tyrol were built between 1880 and 1914. Mobility was increased and Innsbruck flourished as a trade and tourism center.[34] A major move towards the integration of nature into local urban space was the building of the *Hungerburg* railway and the touristic development of the *Hungerburg* plateau.[35] The funicular railway connecting the city to the area above the city and below the mountain range was built in 1906. Starting in the same year, the few existing structures on the plateau (which had relied on a street connection barely drivable by horse carriage) were rebuilt, expanded, and supplemented. The result was a luxurious recreational area with several fine hotels.[36] One hotel resembled a castle; another one had a terrace overlooking an artificial bathing lake with gondolas, a small ferry, a waterfall, and an observational tower. A network of beautiful hiking paths connected the vicinity.[37]

Figure 2: Poster "Hungerburg-Bahn Innsbruck Tirol führt uns in das Sagenreich der Frau Hitt," 1906 (Acc. no. Pt-45, Stadtarchiv Innsbruck)

The chosen advertisement for this contribution is the most iconic representation of the popular depiction showing the destination in connection to the northern mountain range and its funicular railway. This example is not about the slogan, "*Hungerburg-Bahn Innsbruck Tirol führt uns in das Sagenreich der Frau Hitt*" ("The *Hungerburg* mountain railway leads us from Innsbruck (Tyrol) into the legendary realm of *Frau Hitt*"), which strongly exaggerates the range of the funicular, but the concept of tying Innsbruck to an Alpine massif and a mountain railway. The female allegory in this picture does not refer to Innsbruck directly, but to the legend of *Frau Hitt*, a giant queen who according to lore was turned to stone for sinful behavior (depending on the version either because of cruelty or extravagance); a big rock, (slightly looking like a person on a horse), at the mountain ridge of the *Nordkette* refers to this legendary fate. Art Nouveau is used to depict Alpine symbols. Not just the allegory is drawn in this way: the decorative lines framing the pictures, connecting each flower nest with an eagle, the Tyrolean coat of arms, might represent the rails and rope of the funicular, and the typical flower arrangements draping images of this style are Alpine roses. This colorful promotional poster was designed by the artist Max Schammler (including the work of Paul Tautenhahn) and published by the "*Graphische Kunstanstalt Innsbruck: [Valentin] Fuchs & [Max] Schammler*" in 1906. It contains two views of Innsbruck. The larger image in the center of the poster shows the iconic perspective covering the old center (including the city tower, the church of St. Jakob, the *Stadtsäle* or municipal ballrooms, and the Tyrolean State Theater); the northern mountain range; and its railway. Below it is a smaller picture showing the view of the city from the upper station of the funicular toward the south. All these pictures and symbols are arranged in the form of a heraldic shield, which itself is framed by a black and blue background resembling the texture of stone. The poster's outer frame refers to its geographical context, the shield as an inner main frame shows former political power and aristocratic glory. Pictures and symbols show culture, city, and landscape.[38]

Conclusions

Urbanity defined by tourism advertising often means exaggeration; nonetheless, touristic advertising concepts are one factor in the cultural and economic construction of urban regions. The point is not necessarily the whole advertised concept of hegemonial seafaring or a mystical mountain region, but the perspective. The presented advertisements show far more than the depiction of a city. They emphasize a regional perspective, respectively a water region or a mountain region. The crucial point is not the actual depiction of each advertised concept but the longevity of the idea. Both examples do not show the sole advertising concept of these cities in the Belle Époque era; nonetheless, they present vital ideas that shaped a huge part of both urban identities in terms of advertising and regarding the self-perception of the inhabitants. The selected advertisements depict both cities as gateways, although in the case of Innsbruck in a more symbolic way.

The inclusion of theories from the field of social and cultural studies allows new perspectives into historical research. Kathrin Bonacker's concept of advertising as a cultural concentrate allows the retracing of origins of cultural ideas and historic identities. John Urry's approach of the tourist gaze outlines how tourism consumption is constructed and consumed and how both a collective and a personal gaze are part of the visual experience, which refer to the standards of a tourism era as well as to the narratives of a tourism concept.

Artificial connections based on geographical distinctions allowed for exaggerated regional marketing concepts. In the Belle Époque, the impressiveness of new technologies combined with ideas of local cultural distinctiveness made it even easier to construct these urban spaces as special places and broad concepts of transregional distinctiveness, which also allowed for different, individual interpretations within the conceptional idea. Members of the local communities and visiting outsiders created many different urban identities of one city within the broader concept.

The intention of this article was to show how (urban) tourism can help to construct (supra-urban) regions so that the advertised subject is not the city itself anymore, but a regional concept. In the shown examples, each perspective aims at connectivity and constructs the respective city as a gateway, which creates an identity and implicates an urban relevance transcending far beyond municipal boundaries.

Endnotes

1. An interdisciplinary publication about Innsbruck and New Orleans, discussing a wide range of historic, cultural, social, economic, ecologic, and architectural topographies, from a transnational perspective, already exists: Christina Antenhofer, et al., *Cities as Multiple Landscapes. Investigating the Sister Cities Innsbruck and New Orleans* (Frankfurt am Main: Campus, 2016). The incorporation of natural surroundings into early urban tourism structures in Innsbruck and New Orleans is outlined here: Hester Margreiter, "Urban Destinations within Mountains and Swamps: Landscape and Early Tourism in New Orleans (Louisiana) and Innsbruck (Tyrol)," in *Approaching East-Central Europe over the Centuries*, ed. Marija Wakounig and Ferdinand Kühnel (Berlin: Lit Verlag, 2019), 199–213. Regarding the comparability of Austrian and New Orleanian history, also see Reinhold Wagnleitner, ed., *Satchmo Meets Amadeus* (Innsbruck: Studienverlag, 2006), which analyzes the cultural, economic, social, and political structures behind the creation of music as well as the construction of popular images and myths.

2. Walter Rummel, "Landes- und Regionalgeschichte: Komplementärdisziplinen im gesellschaftlichen Umfeld," in *Methoden und Wege der Landesgeschichte*, ed. Sigrid Hirbodian, Christian Jörg, and Sabine Klapp (Ostfildern: Thorbeke 2015), 29–40 (here 31).

3. Peter Walder-Gottsbacher, *Vom Wirtshaus zum Grand-Hotel: Ein Spaziergang durch Innsbrucks historische Gaststätten* (Innsbruck: Studienverlag, 2002), 26–33; Catherine Donzel, Alexis Gregory, and Marc Walter, *Grand American Hotels* (Paris: Vendome Press, 1989), 102–107.

4. Ueli Gyr, "Geschichte des Tourismus: Strukturen auf dem Weg zur Moderne," *ieg-ego.de* (Dec. 3, 2010), accessed Feb. 12, 2024, http://www.ieg-ego.eu/gyru-2010-de; Rüdiger Hachtmann, "Tourismus und Tourismusgeschichte," *docupedia.de* (Dec. 22, 2010), accessed Feb. 12, 2024, http://docupedia.de/zg/Tourismus_und_Tourismusgeschichte; Elaine Denby, *Grand Hotels. Reality and Illusion. An Architectural and Social History* (London: Reaktion Books, 1998), 33.

5. Philipp Strobl, *Innsbrucker Wirtschaftsgeschichte* (Innsbruck: Studienverlag 2013), 65, 74, 82; Richard Campanella, *Bienville's Dilemma: A Historical Geography of New Orleans* (Lafayette: University of Louisiana at Lafayette, 2008), 249–250; Peggy Scott Laborde and John Magill, *Canal Street: New Orleans' Great Wide Way* (Gretna: Pelican Publishing, 2006), 67–69.

6. Strobl, *Wirtschaftsgeschichte*, 75; Kevin Fox Gotham, *Authentic New Orleans: Tourism, Culture, and Race in the Big Easy* (New York: New York University Press, 2005), 59.

7. Angela M. Lippert, "Focus on Style - Art Nouveau," *Vintage Poster* 2 (Dec. 2019), 6–14 (here 7, 14), accessed Jan. 30, 2024, https://issuu.com/vintageposterivpda/docs/vintageposter_ivpdamagazine_issue2. The author argues that Art Nouveau style was aimed at an elitist clientele and meanwhile understood as bohemian street culture. (Ibid., 10); A brief explanation concerning terminology: "Der neue Stil in Europa: Von 'Modern Style' und 'Art Nouveau' bis

'Jugendstil'," *jugendstilforum.de*, accessed Jan. 30, 2024, https://jugendstilforum.de/der-neue-stil-in-europa-von-modern-style-und-art-nouveau-bis-jugendstil.

8. Shannon Lee Dawdy, *Building the Devil's Empire: French Colonial New Orleans* (Chicago: University of Chicago Press, 2008), 74–95; Ari Kelman, "A River and Its City: Critical Episodes in the Environmental History of New Orleans" (PhD diss., Brown University, 1998), 8, 315. Concerning the complex environment of New Orleans, human adaptations, natural disasters, and the city's most important relationship to its river, see the publication of the aforementioned dissertation: Ari Kelman, *A River and Its City: The Nature of Landscape in New Orleans*, (Berkeley: University of California Press, 2003).

9. For more deeply relevant insight into the foundations of antebellum Southern society and economy, based on the breeding and trading of slaves, see, Ned Sublette, *The World That Made New Orleans: From Spanish Silver to Congo Square* (Chicago: Lawrence Hill Books, 2008), especially chapter 18 "The Slave-Breeding Industry," 220–239.

10. Kirsten Silva Gruez, "The Gulf of Mexico System and the 'Latinness' of New Orleans," *American Literary History* 18, no. 3 (2006): 468–495 (here 468-469).

11. Laborde and Magill, *Canal Street*, 83–85.

12. Anthony J. Stanonis, *Creating the Big Easy: New Orleans and the Emergence of Modem Tourism 1918–1945* (Athens: University of Georgia Press, 2006), 32, 144–146, 152, 156.

13. Sally K. Evans Reeves, William D. Reeves, Ellis P. Laborde, and James S. Janssen, *Historic City Park New Orleans* (New Orleans: City Park Improvement Association and Friends of City Park, 2000), 1–2.

14. Stanonis, *Big Easy*, 15–16, 19–20.

15. Ibid., 104–105, 110–117. For a multifaceted history of societal norms and sexual commerce in New Orleans and its context of race and gender, see Alicia Long, *The Great Southern Babylon. Sex, Race, and Respectability in New Orleans, 1865-1920* (Baton Rouge: Louisiana State University Press, 2004).

16. Alpenverein-Museum Innsbruck, ed., *vertikal: Die Innsbrucker Nordkette. Eine Ausstellung in der Stadt* (Innsbruck: Alpenverein-Museum, 2002), 13–19.

17. Peter Loewit, *Reiseziel Weiherburg: Die Weiherburg im 19. Jahrhundert* (Innsbruck: Universitätsverlag Wagner, 2009, 13; Strobl, *Innsbrucker Wirtschaftsgeschichte*, 73, 83.

18. Michael Forcher, *Zu Gast im Herzen der Alpen: Eine Bildgeschichte des Tourismus in Tirol* (Innsbruck: Haymon, 1989), 92–96, 44–47.

19. Benjamin Türkis, *Innsbrucker Tourismusgeschichte* (Innsbruck: Studienverlag, 2010), 15; Strobl, *Innsbrucker Wirtschaftsgeschichte*, 73.

20. Forcher, *Alpen*, 114.

21. Ibid., 98.

22. Strobl, *Wirtschaftsgeschichte*, 74, 115.

23. Dirk van Laak, "Infra-Strukturgeschichte," *Geschichte und Gesellschaft* 27 (2001): 367–393 (here 393).

24. Dirk van Laak, *Alles im Fluss: Die Lebensadern unserer Gesellschaft: Geschichte und Zukunft der Infrastruktur* (Frankfurt: S. Fischer Verlag, 2018), 30.

25. Kathrin Bonacker, *Illustrierte Anzeigenwerbung als kulturhistorisches Quellenmaterial* (Marburg: Jonas Verlag, 2000), 70.

26. John Urry, "The Tourist Gaze 'Revisited,'" *The American Behavioral Scientist* 36 (1992): 172–186 (here 173).

27. Cédric Humair, Martin Knoll, and Laurent Tissot, "How to Deal with Regional Tourism? Historical (and Interdisciplinary) Reflections," *Zeitschrift für Tourismuswissenschaft* 9, no. 1 (2017): 5–31 (here 9–10).

28. Bonacker, *Illustrierte Anzeigenwerbung*, 38.

29. The Howard-Tilton Memorial Library at Tulane University offers an online exhibit on "Pan-American Life in New Orleans," which showcases the Panama Canal as a crucial point in trade and tourism advertising in the main gallery of the exhibit. See "Pan-American Life in New Orleans," *tulane.edu* (on-site exhibition Nov. 21, 2019 until Aug. 15, 2020), accessed Feb. 15, 2024, https://exhibits.tulane.edu/exhibit/pan-american-life-in-new-orleans.

30. Aileen Cho, Wayne D. Bray, William E. Worthington, Norman J. Padelford, and Burton L. Gordon, "Panama Canal" *britannica.com* (last updated Jan. 28, 2024), accessed Jan. 31, 2024, https://www.britannica.com/topic/Panama-Canal.

31. Pamphlet: New Orleans: Gateway to the Panama Canal, 1912, Acc. no. 1985.249 (Gift of the Milwaukee County Historical Society), The Historic New Orleans Collection.

32. Jon Mathieu, "The Alpine Region" *ieg-ego.de* (March 9, 2017), accessed Feb. 7, 2024, http://www.ieg-ego.eu/mathieuj-2013-en. [Secundary quotes: Mathieu quotes Jean-François Bergier, Pour une histoire des Alpes: Moyen Age et Temps Modernes, Hampshire: Ashgate 1997, Chapter "Le trafic à travers les Alpes et les liaisons transalpines du haut Moyen Age au XVII siècle", 1–2].

33. Forcher, *Zu Gast im Herzen der Alpen*, 44.

34. Adolf Lässer, *100 Jahre Fremdenverkehr in Tirol* (Innsbruck: Universitätsverlag Wagner; 1989), 84–85; and Strobl, *Innsbrucker Wirtschaftsgeschichte*, 65.

35. The place was formerly called "*Mariabrunn*" (Mary's fountain) and got its new name between 1865 and 1880. According to folklore legend, some guests didn't like the menu, argued that they had to leave hungry and called the place "*Hungerburg*" (castle of hunger). See Franz-Heinz Hye, *Vom 'Grauenstain' zur Hungerburg; Geschichte des Stadtteiles Hoch-Innsbruck* (Innsbruck: Interessengemeinschaft Hoch-Innsbruck, Hungerburg-Gramart, 1982), 42.

36. Until today, the plateau remained to be a wealthy village and a tourism hotspot, though some structures (including the lake) did not survive, but in the 1960s a zoo was built. Since 1928, a second railway connects the (modernized) *Hungerburg* railway to the top of the mountain range.

37. Strobl, *Innsbrucker Wirtschaftsgeschichte*, 74–75; Horst Schreiber, '... *in der Schönheit und Ruhe der Hungerburg'. 50 Jahre Bildungszentrum 'Seehof' der Tiroler Arbeiterkammer* (Innsbruck: Studienverlag, 2004), 9–11; and Hye, *Vom 'Grauenstain' zur Hungerburg*, 63–69.

38. Promotional poster: Hungerburg-Bahn Innsbruck Tirol führt uns in das Sagenreich der Frau Hitt, 1906, Acc. no. Pt-45, Stadtarchiv Innsbruck; Peter Adelsberger, *Die Stadtvedute Innsbrucks in der Druckgraphik: Katalog der druckgraphischen Gesamtansichten Innsbrucks von 1470 bis 1980* (Innsbruck: Universitätsverlag Wagner, 2022), 244; Wolfgang Pfaundler, *Innsbruck: Bildnis einer Stadt* (Innsbruck: Verlag Fritz Molden, 1975), 226–227; Meinrad Pizzinini, *Alt-Tirol im Plakat* (Innsbruck: Haymon-Verlag, 1983), 88–89.

The Making of a Regional History Museum: The Case of the Vorarlberg Museum

Markus Barnay and Beat Gugger

It was a major challenge that art historian Andreas Rudigier was faced with when he took up the post of director of the *Vorarlberger Landesmuseum* (Vorarlberg State Museum) in Bregenz at the beginning of 2011. The museum had already been closed for two years at that time because a new building was being constructed in its place. The new building—with slightly more exhibition space than the old one but above all with new rooms for catering and events—was due to open in June 2013. This left just over two years to turn the old state museum into a modern regional museum.

Of course, there was already a paper in 2011 called "Museological Concept for the Reorientation of the Vorarlberg Museum."[1] It came from Rudigier's predecessor Tobias Natter, who surprisingly let his contract expire in the middle of the preparations for the opening of the new museum and decided not to extend it. Quite a few observers saw a connection between this withdrawal and the strong public criticism with which the concept for reorientation (*Konzept zur Neuausrichtung*) was confronted.

It contained only one single exhibition element, the *Schaudepot*, (a museum depot that is open to the public), which was fully developed in terms of content and design. What's more, there were already fixed contracts with an exhibition architect for the *Schaudepot*. The other formats of the "three levels—three approaches" display concept were either still at the brainstorming stage or—under the motto "courage to leave gaps"—simply excluded key themes of Vorarlberg's regional history.

New Formats for a New Museum

Andreas Rudigier therefore had to develop a concept within two years that would meet the requirements of a modern regional history museum. In the discussions between spring 2011 and spring 2012, three formats emerged that were not conceived as special exhibitions with a short duration, but as semi-permanent or even as a kind of "permanent exhibitions":

- A cross-generational exhibition on the Roman history of Vorarlberg or specifically of Brigantium, the former Roman settlement in the area of today's provincial capital of Bregenz.

- An exhibition format with the subtitle *Sichten*, which pursued a specifically participatory approach and undertook an acoustic journey through the country in its first edition (2013-2016) under the title "Sein & Mein."

- A presentation of Vorarlberg's history, known internally as a *Kernausstellung* (core exhibition), with a special focus on contemporary history.

All three formats sought a new, contemporary approach to the history presented. In the "Romans" exhibition, for example, it was already clear from the title that no eternal truths were being proclaimed here, but that current knowledge about the period of Roman rule was to be presented and also critically questioned. The exhibition was called *Römer oder so* (Romans or something) and explored the question of what we actually know about the Roman settlement of the area and where we have to make do with speculation—for example, the question of who was allowed to call themselves "Roman."

The *Sichten* format also took a new approach, with the curatorial team going out into the field to have as many people as possible describe important stages of their lives and thus bring a polyphonic narrative of everyday life, fate, catastrophes, and life lessons into the museum.

Wer bestimmt
über mich?
Who decides my fate?

How Can Regional History Be Conveyed in a Contemporary Way?

However, this article will focus on the third format, as the authors dealt with the question of how the history of a country and a region can be dealt with in a contemporary museum. The starting point was the thesis that in a modern, highly differentiated, and fractionalized society, there is no longer a master narrative about history that applies equally to everyone. Instead, the aim was to find as many points of contact as possible to enable different people to access regional history. The work on this exhibition, which was later given the title *Vorarlberg: A Making-Of*, was carried out in three stages:

1 - The dialog with society: the positioning of the museum in the social environment.
2 - The conception of a new exhibition format: the development of the exhibition in discourse with experts.
3 - The struggle with the collection: the attempt to re-read an existing collection and supplement it with new objects.

Dialogue with Society

"In addition to its system-specific tasks such as the generation and preservation of material cultural heritage and its research and communication, the museum would also like to enter into an exchange with society, because questions of society are also key questions for the museum's work," stated the invitation to the participants of a first major workshop. In a half-day workshop attended by the entire museum team, a selection of experts from a wide range of backgrounds and fields of activity, but all with a high degree of social relevance, were invited to present their views on current social developments and expectations of a contemporary museum.

The thoughts expressed at this event by tourism experts, psychologists, social workers, journalists, business people, musicologists, artists, and energy consultants had a lasting effect and were repeatedly cited in discussions about the exhibition concept in the months that followed. This "dialogue with society" was also continued in the following years. It is now one of the most widely recognized activities of the new Vorarlberg Museum, even beyond the region.

The Conception of a New Exhibition Format

The development of the so-called "core exhibition" was naturally the focus of the work. A team of curators (in addition to the project manager Markus

Barnay, these were the artist and University of Applied Sciences professor Hubert Matt from Bregenz, the museum and exhibition curator Beat Gugger from Switzerland, and the historian Peter Melichar from the museum team) developed an exhibition concept that was committed to the principles of flexibility, interchangeability, and willingness to discuss, among other things, but which was also intended to provide orientation. It turned out that such a concept had many hurdles to overcome. One of these was the lack of objects that could be used to ask or perhaps answer questions about the history of the region. Although the museum was called the *Landesmuseum*, the history of the region, and in particular contemporary history, never played a major role in its collecting activities.

The Struggle with the Collection

The curatorial team had to try to reconcile a collection that had grown over 150 years of museum history with the demands of a modern presentation of regional history. For example, anyone wanting to depict the everyday lives of people over the last 300 years with the help of objects will not find what they are looking for in this collection. Questions of economic activity, coexistence, social structures, and political conflicts may have been key issues in the excavation of earlier cultures, (and archaeology was the defining discipline of the *Landesmuseum* for almost 150 years), but the collection of objects from the period since the museum association was founded does not reflect such questions at all.

It was mainly "valuable" items that were collected, whether paintings, folk art, religious objects, or clothing. Only occasionally did objects that could be described as simple everyday objects sneak in—especially those that were in danger of being lost from a bourgeois point of view, such as agricultural implements. But even these objects have a fundamental flaw: they do not "tell" any stories because nothing is known about them. Normally, the dimensions, material, and external appearance of the objects were registered, (and even meticulously recorded), but not even their exact provenance was known. As a result, they remain symbols for certain activities but hardly objects that can be used to tell concrete stories, for example about people—although this could help visitors to recognize and reflect on more complex contexts.

Flexible, But Expensive

An exhibition that aims to provide comprehensive information about the history of the region now known as Vorarlberg inevitably had to rely on loans and donations. In preparation for the exhibition, the curatorial team visited more than eighty different public and private archives, associations, museums, companies, individuals to find objects for the exhibition and, where possible, to borrow them. On the one hand, this made it clear from the outset that the claim of a flexible and responsive exhibition would not remain merely theoretical but would to a certain extent be forced into practice. After all, many of the loans had to be returned or exchanged after a certain period of time (sometimes one year, more often several years, and usually five to seven years).

Ultimately, it turned out that the attempt to design an exhibition that is constantly changing has its limits. On the one hand, such changeability requires financial and human resources that were not available to the necessary extent, and on the other hand, the question arises as to whether the museum audience will even notice minor changes. During the exhibition's run (which was extended from a planned seven to eight and a half years due to the COVID-19 pandemic), there were several minor revisions, but above all a major "reset" in 2015, during which the scenography was sharpened up.

Key Questions Instead of a Master Narrative

The basic concept remained unchanged, which was not based on a fixed master narrative and did not tell a chronological story, but instead posed four key questions:

- Who decides about me?
- What do I do here?
- Who am I?
- Do I belong?

There were different answers to these questions in all four quarters, as they were called internally. However, it turned out that the key questions offered many starting points for the mediation team to offer individual guided tours that were geared towards the respective needs of the groups to be guided.

Ultimately, the response to the experiment was overwhelmingly positive. Around 80% of the feedback on specially prepared feedback cards was "very positive" or "positive," while around 10% was "negative." The criticism concerned topics that, in the opinion of the respective individuals, were not highlighted enough, complaints about a lack of orientation or a missing central theme, and rightly demanded a multilingual explanation, which only took place in the room texts (in English).

Open Questions

The public also responded very positively to the accompanying events, which were intended to deepen and discuss topics that could only be touched on in the exhibition itself. By the end of 2023, almost 100 events had therefore taken place under the motto "dialogue about history," explaining countless aspects of regional history with expert guests. These discussions were so successful that they were continued even after the end of the *Vorarlberg: A Making-Of* exhibition.

What also remained was a publication that provides a look back at the exhibition using the example of fifty objects (called "scenes" in the book).[2] External authors contributed in-depth essays on the four key questions, and the two authors of this article provided an insight into the internal discussions on the concept and content of *Vorarlberg: A Making-Of*—in the form of an email dialogue, excerpts of which were printed.[3] However, the question also remains as to how the history of a region should be appropriately presented for discussion in the future—in view of a highly differentiated and fractionalized society with different interests and realities of life.

Endnotes

1. Tobias G. Natter, *3 Ebenen - 3 Zugänge: Das museologische Konzept zur Neuausrichtung des Vorarlberg Museums* (Bregenz: Vorarlberg Museum, 2011).

2. Markus Barnay and Andreas Rudigier, eds., *Vorarlberg: Ein Making-of in 50 Szenen. Objekte – Geschichte – Ausstellungspraxis* (Bielefeld: transcript Verlag, 2022).

3. Beat Gugger und Markus Barnay, "*Wir hatten viele Freiheiten – vielleicht waren es auch einige zuviel... "Ein Dialog zwischen Vorarlberg und der Schweiz im März 2021*," in *Vorarlberg: Ein Making-of in 50 Szenen*, Barnay and Rudigier, 286-297.

A Regional History of Migration: South Tyrol in the Throngs of Nationalisms and Capitalism

Eva Pfanzelter

Introduction

The topic of migration fits well into a societal context in South Tyrol that has been marked for over a hundred years by the coexistence of minorities. It builds on stories of immigration and emigration, coexistence or juxtaposition of different ethnicities, cohabitation, and integration that have long predated recent migration movements. Interestingly enough, recent discourses on migration in South Tyrol operate on two distinct levels that rarely intersect: the so-called "new minorities," which relate to recent migration, and that of the "autochthonous minorities," involving members of the Italian, German, and Ladin population groups in the region, and their cohabitation or living side-by-side.

If South Tyrol perceives itself today as a prosperous land thriving despite recurring economic and political challenges, it easily forgets that until a few decades ago, the province was a land of emigration due to sometimes dire economic and/or political conditions. According to the Italian National Institute of Statistics (ISTAT), between 1919 and 1939, almost twice as many people emigrated as immigrated (75,502 and 39,966, respectively).[1] Between 1939 and 1943, during the so-called *Option*, approximately 75,000 German-speaking individuals left the region. After the Second World War, the Province of Bolzano, as the region was called after it's annexation to Italy in 1919, nevertheless experienced a population growth—partly through the return of optants (between 20,000 and 40,000 individuals) and partly due to continuous immigration from other areas of the Italian state since the mid-1920s.[2]

The migration balance remained positive until the mid-1950s. However, the country turned into a land of emigration again until the late 1980s. This time, economic reasons were decisive: job opportunities were scarce, and employment abroad seemed more appealing. On one hand, the "economic miracle," in the form of the now ubiquitous tourism industry, had not yet reached South Tyrol. On the other hand, the tertiary sector remained closed to the German-speaking population until the conclusion of the Second Autonomy Status in 1972, due to a lack of tradition and, especially, ongoing reservations about the Italian-dominated administration. Notably, there are studies from this time on the work migration of South Tyroleans, who were primarily drawn to neighboring German-speaking countries—a trend that persists to this day.[3]

In the 1990s, the migration balance shifted once again. The Province of Bolzano became an area of immigration. However, the number of immigrants remained low. This only changed in the course of EU enlargement in the late 1990s and 2000s. While agriculture and then increasingly tourism became pull factors for labor migration, especially from Eastern Europe, the care sector attracted more and more female migrants from Poland and Romania. After years of steady increase, this influx slowed down considerably in 2015. For the second consecutive time, the migration balance turned negative, and the very modest population growth was almost exclusively due to the positive birth rate among the immigrant population. Despite this positive and much needed contribution to population development, prevalent prejudices persist particularly in the media, revolving around notions of parasitism, poverty-driven migration, and an overpowering inflow of people with foreign passports.[4]

The following chapters will dig deeper into the some of the more prominent migratory movements that accompany South Tyrolean history and collective memory. It will be shown that, to this day, a discrepancy exists in perception, historiography, and commemoration of the history related to "autochthonous" and "new" migration. While the former is often linked to discourses of victimization, the latter is to be positioned in a Europeanized narrative that views migration as both a threat to and a necessity for economic wealth and prosperity.

While many studies on migration history focus on analysis of national migratory movements, the study of regional events and experiences, as will be shown, proves especially fruitful in understanding the complexity of transnational migration and its memorialization, as these more often than not diverge from nationalistic approaches. Thus, regional history offers ways to explore this complexity and enables fine grained studies, giving unique opportunities to understand motives and experiences both from a migrant perspective and from a receiving community perspective.[5]

State of Research on Regional Migration in South Tyrol

The historiography of South Tyrol has extensively engaged in examining past regional events, as the awareness of the constructiveness of history and the changing instrumentalization of historical politics, especially the identity-shaping impact of historical memory, thrives remarkably within the regional-historical context of South Tyrol. The primacy of memory simultaneously revealed the stark differences between the collective memory of the German/Ladin-speaking population and that of the Italian-speaking South

Tyroleans or foreign individuals. Notably, the Germanophone memory witnesses the emergence of a distinctive historiography. This "separate history"[6] of the German-speaking South Tyrol exhibits a specifically regional collective memory, diverging from Italy's national culture of remembrance as well as that of the former homeland, Austria. It questions, as a regional historical memory, the relationships among societal groups—towards, against, and alongside each other—emphasizing the specifics of regional identities. In the juxtaposition between the "Europe of regions" and globalization, this separate historical memory of South Tyrol has consistently served targeted historical-political functions. Within it, the discourse of victimization of the German-speaking minority plays a central role: it reinforces the formation of a distinct identity, in the sense of a "delimiting identity," defined by its own suffering, for which Italy as a nation and Fascism as a regime are held responsible.[7]

Proof for the correctness of this argument is provided by one specific migration movement (although some scholars might shrink from using the term migration for this organized relocation movement[8]) in the interwar period, called the *Option*. In scholarly literature, the *Option* of 1939 is referred to as the "trauma of South Tyrolean society," as a "profound rupture," the most significant societal "dissolidification," a "deep wound" and "lasting weakening" of the minority, as the "most painful chapter in the history written by the people of the region."[9] The scholarly examination of the *Option* has significantly changed in recent decades, although especially the years of commemoration of the events of 1939 allowed the *Option* to be politically instrumentalized over and over again through trivialized and one-sided representations in television documentaries, popular science publications, and on websites and social media. A literature database composed within the project "The Memory of the South Tyrolean Option 1939" lists over 500 contributions to this topic alone,[10] thus showing its prominence in South Tyrolean historiography and migration literature. New angles and detailed analyses continue to be prominent also in recent years. To name only some of the latest publications: Martha Verdorfer, Günther Pallaver, and Leopold Steurer edited a volume focusing on the long reaching consequences of the *Option* in 2019 and Elisabeth Malleier, Günter Pallaver, and Margareth Lanzinger investigated hereditary and larger families of South Tyrolean settlers in the *Reichsgau Sudetenland* in 2021.[11] The project *option-MUDI: Option museal – Option digital* at the University of Innsbruck from 2020–2023 analyzed new pathways both into *Option* and *Return Option* research as well as its public history aspects.[12]

The other migration-related topics referred to in the following chapters are much less researched: The so-called *First Option* of 1919/1920 was mainly analyzed within the assessments of the consequences of the First World War.[13] In contrast to historiography of the *Option*, research into Italian internal migration from southern provinces to South Tyrol has been initiated rather late, from 1999 on by the working group *Für ein Museum in den Semiruarli/ Per un Museo nelle Semiruali* (For a Museum in the Semirurali). Due to the activities of this group, the reappraisal of this migration movement ended in the installation of an exhibition course in Bolzano.[14]

While the South Tyrolean *Option* has been widely researched and has gained continuous attention in the academic community, (and in public discourse), this is not equally true for the *Return Option* topic. Up to today, the history of this specific return migration is to some extent uncertain. The first in-depth research on the return to South Tyrol was carried out by the historian Stefan Lechner in 1989[15] and together with Helmut Alexander and Adolf Leidlmair in 1993.[16] Lechner continued to dedicate some of his future research to this topic, for example with two studies in 2000[17] and 2001[18] and short essays in 2014[19] in 2020.[20] In addition, several degree theses have dealt with these specific historical events.[21] The edited volume *Einmal Option und zurück. Die Folgen der Aus- und Rückwanderung für Südtirols Nachkriegsentwicklung*[22] by historians Martha Verdorfer, Günther Pallaver, and Leopold Steurer brought circular migration processes into the discussion, which by and large increased the perspectives of this remigration. Still, this specific return migration hardly ever gained topicality.[23] Recently, the South Tyrolean *Return Option* has been investigated in a transnational project and a publication on the results is forthcoming.[24]

The time period after the *Return Option* and up to the early 1990s is dominated by two migration related topics: on the one hand, in political and diplomatic history, analyses' focus has been laid on the continuing internal influx of Italian migrants from southern regions.[25] On the other hand, the Germanophone emigration from the Province of Bolzano has been looked into by historian Sabine Falch, who based her study of South Tyroleans searching for better job opportunities in foreign lands during the 1950s and 1960s on an extensive interview tour.[26]

Labor migration is also the focus of studies analyzing the "new migration" from the 1980s/1990s onward. The project *(Arbeits-)migration in Südtirol* (Labor Migration in South Tyrol) at the University of Innsbruck, Austria, 2015–2017,[27] brought forth a bibliography of over 700 titles concerning many different aspects of labor migration in Italy and specifically in South Tyrol that were published from 1990 onwards.[28] Eva Pfanzelter and Dirk Rupnow of the project team also edited a volume on their findings concerning labor migration that was published in 2017 with the title *Einheimisch – zweiheimisch – mehrheimisch. Geschichte(n) der neuen Migration in Südtirol* (One-Native—Two-Native—Multi-Native History(ies) of the New Migration in South Tyrol) and Kurt Gritsch, also a member of the team, published *Vom Kommen und Gehen. Migration in Südtirol* (About Coming and Going: Migration in South Tyrol) that same year.[29] Also, an interview archive resulted from the work in the project.[30]

Besides focusing on the "newcomers" in the Province of Bolzano, the history of migration in recent years has gained widespread interest because the region is experiencing a significant brain drain. Although there is no larger study on this, the media and public administration have paid a lot of attention to the topic recently.[31] Also, since January 2018, South Tyrol's privately funded research institution *EURAC Research* is hosting the project *MigDiv Group* (Migrations & Diversities: diversity of languages, cultures, lifestyles, traditions, and religious beliefs is an integral part of our everyday lives) at the *Zentrum für Migration und Diversität* (Center for Migration and Diversity). This multidisciplinary endeavor has brought forth a series of publications and is hosting webinars as well as (online) seminars.[32] Although only a few of these publications have a specific historic approach, the migration series produced in this context sometimes are based on time series, which can be relevant for historical analyses.

South Tyrolean Migrations during the Interwar Period 1919–1939

South Tyrol came into existence as a result of the First World War, when the border between Italy and the newly erected Republic of Austria was drawn up along the main Alpine ridge, crossing over the Brenner and Reschen passes. Until then, the border between the 500-year-lasting Habsburg Empire and the Italian principalities, and since the mid-nineteenth century the Kingdom of Italy, ran south of the city of Trent, along the northern shore of Lake Garda, and east of the city of Trieste. With the newly erected border at the Brenner Pass, Italy came into possession of the southwestern part of the Germanophone Tyrolean crown land and with it acquired a mostly German-speaking population that subsequently became Italy's German minority. When South Tyrol came to Italy in 1919 without specific provisions in the Peace Treaty of Saint-Germain-en-Laye, it not only meant the establishment of a new border at the Brenner Pass; up until then, predominantly German-speaking South Tyrol had to reorganize itself. Disregarding their previous party affiliations, the German-speaking parties in South Tyrol united under the German Association (*Deutscher Verband*,

DV) to collectively advocate more effectively for the interests of the minority in Italy. Economically, a shift had to occur from the traditional north and east towards the south. Linguistically and culturally, the Germanophones suddenly found themselves a minority, facing an overwhelming majority of Italians. Particularly consequential were also the effects of the world war years, during which there had been a radical anti-Italian war frenzy and propaganda in Tyrol, which had clashed with the Trentino irredentism that had taken on anti-Austrian/anti-German forms, aiming for a radical Italianization of future new state territories. Psychologically adding to the fueled anti-Italian sentiment during the war years for the German-speaking minority was the fact that they considered themselves undefeated losers, as no Italian soldier had set foot on South Tyrolean soil during the war.[33]

Even the initial, relatively liberal years within the Italian state were challenging under these conditions, especially considering the complete takeover and reorganization of the entire administrative apparatus by Italian authorities. This meant, among other things, the expulsion of around 10,000 railway employees, postal workers, and judicial officials who were professionally in South Tyrol but held the so-called *Heimatschein* (certificate of residency) for other parts of the Habsburg Empire. This is also the first migration movement that can be identified in the hundred-year history of the South Tyrol; the emigration or expulsion of Habsburg officials is often referred to as the *First Option.*[34]

South Tyrol, now referred to as Alto Adige or Province of Bolzano in civil administration, came under the *Generalkommissariat für die Venezia Tridentina* (General Commissioner for Venezia Tridentina). Commissioner Luigi Credaro initially pursued a policy considered friendly towards minorities but gradually aligned more with the centralist direction of the government in Rome. Soon, however, these early, hesitant autonomy negotiations and attempts at coexistence would be a thing of the past. On the occasion of the opening of the Bozen Trade Fair on April 24, 1921, "Blackshirts" (the name for fascist thugs) from the south attacked a traditional costume parade. During this incident, Franz Innerhofer, a teacher from the South Tyrolean village Marling, was killed, and there were several injured individuals.

On October 1–2, 1922, fascist thug squads, as if in a trial run for the "March on Rome," organized a "March on Bozen" and deposed Julius Perathoner as the mayor of Bozen. The action provided a preview of the future treatment of the German-speaking minority, which became commonplace after the "March on Rome" on October 28, 1922. The goal of fascism was the Italianization, assimilation, and denationalization of the German-speaking minority. This was to occur in two phases: first, Italianization and Fascistization of the people and the territory prevailed until the second half of the 1920s. Then, when this was unsuccessful, majorization and symbolic land grabbing within the framework of the so-called *conquista del suolo* (conquest of the soil) starting from the late 1920s was at the heart of Italian measures to seize the region.[35]

Building upon a thirty-two-point action plan for the denationalization of the German-speaking population, drafted and proclaimed by Trentino irredentist and fervent nationalist Ettore Tolomei in the spring of 1923, the first decade of fascist dictatorship aimed at Italianization and particularly the Fascistization of the territory. The primary targets of these assimilation measures in South Tyrol were the German language and culture. Fascist directives prompted the replacement of German place names with Italian ones, the dissolution of associations, and the gradual replacement of the German language with Italian in schools. Italian became the sole official language in administration and in court proceedings. From 1925, German-language press was prohibited, municipal autonomy was abolished, and Italian "podesta" were installed instead of mayors. Even the name Tyrol and its variations were banned. To align the population, the Fascists established a tight network of associations and institutions in South Tyrol. Similar to the rest of Italy, they enticed South Tyroleans with perks, free meals, and school uniforms to join youth, women's, leisure, and sports organizations.

The Fascist regime also heavily relied on the symbolic power of monuments and buildings. Particularly in the border regions, the aim was to make the presence of fascism visibly prominent. In the twenties, monumental ossuaries were erected in Gossensaß in the Eisack Valley, Innichen in the Puster Valley, and Burgeis in the Vinschgau. Through arbitrary historical distortion, fallen Italian soldiers were buried here, who had died eighty kilometers further south on the front lines. Even the stone relics of the Austro-Hungarian monarchy came under the scrutiny of Fascist authorities: in 1926, Roman bureaucracy laid the groundwork for the *Victory Monument*, which replaced the partially constructed *Kaiserjägerdenkmal* for the fallen of the First World War. Similarly, other Habsburg monuments were removed from their sockets or replaced by fascist shrines.[36]

This strategy aimed at the architectural presence of fascism was to be interpreted in the context of the *conquista del suolo* and majorization. Besides this, there were certainly modernization efforts, including a push for industrialization through the construction of power plants all over the country and the establishment of an industrial zone in Bolzano, the region's capital. As part of these industrialization measures, there was a massive influx of Italian workers—this too was part of the majorization calculus. Since Italianization or denationalization was not truly successful, the Fascists attempted a massive settlement of people from the South, who were actually lured to the new province by the thousands from the mid-1930s onwards. Most of them came from the main hubs of the industries and settled in South Tyrol, primarily from the impoverished and overpopulated areas around Padua and Venice. Few had proper education, and many were migrating due to existential poverty, not for the first time. Most couldn't be labeled as fanatical party supporters. On the contrary, their dire situation often pushed them toward party membership, as they had few options other than migrating northward. In South Tyrol, having a Fascist party card wasn't necessary; having many children was more important. A building program was initiated for the incoming Italians. This led, for example, to the creation of new workers' residential areas, such as Neugries, today known as Don Bosco, near the Bolzano industrial zone, exclusively housing Italian-speaking worker families. These *semi-rurali* (semi-rural or semi-country) buildings for two to four families with large vegetable gardens were modeled after Benito Mussolini's birthplace. It was this Italian immigration into South Tyrol that became the second migration movement of the territory.[37]

The third, albeit much smaller in its proportions, occurred alongside this industrial influx from the south. In the 1930s, the *conquista del suolo* gained renewed momentum amid the economic crisis. The *Ente di Rinascita Agraria per le Tre Venezie*, (ERA), created for the purpose of taking over auctioned farms in South Tyrol, (and other newly obtained territory), attempted to bring Italian landless farmers as tenants to the acquired farms. However, despite its continuously expanding powers, this land grab partly failed because the German-speaking population managed to weather the crisis years fairly well thanks to financial support from the German Reich. Further, for the farmers mostly originating from impoverished areas in the south, it was sometimes difficult to adapt to the conditions of mountain/Alpine farming. This led to either relatively quick integration or their abandonment of the challenging mountain agriculture, returning to their home villages. The stories these failed farmers brought back to their country of origin did not support this kind of internal migration; hence it never became a popular one.[38]

The South Tyrolean *Option* of 1939: A Case of Coerced Migration

This was not the case with the migration movement known as the *Option* that remained deeply ingrained into the collective memory of the German-speaking minority. Despite the minorities' limited possibilities to counteract the Fascist policies during the 1920s and 1930s, the "South Tyrol question" remained a stumbling block between Italy and Austria during the 1920s and between Italy and Nazi Germany during the 1930s. The radius of action and reaction for the German-speaking population in South Tyrol towards assimilation and majorization was limited, ranging between adaptation, boycott, and occasional resistance. The *Deutscher Verband* had taken over the representation of the German-speaking minority as a political entity in the post-war years. However, with the general ban on political parties in 1926, the official representation of the minority disappeared from political participation. In the following years, there was a sort of detachment among more radicalized, politicized youth sectors and within the ranks of former Alpine clubs and gymnastic associations. They distanced themselves from the *Deutsche Verband*, which was increasingly perceived as conservative and conciliatory—a trend that intensified throughout the 1920s. Additionally, there was a shift among many South Tyroleans away from Habsburg Austria toward Nazi Germany. Within a few years, the former Austro-Hungarian monarchism transformed into a radicalized sense of Tyrolean identity, increasingly aligning itself with the Greater German Reich in the 1930s. Without fascist assimilation and majorization policies, this shift cannot truly be explained. The psychological loss of the homeland and the gradual dissolution of cultural, political, and economic connections within the South Tyrolean society had dramatic effects and led to widespread quests for new directions and identities.[39]

In Germany, after 1918, the revision of the Treaty of Versailles was a primary goal of both domestic and foreign policy. This was intended to be achieved, on the one hand, through diplomatic means and contract policy. On the other hand, especially since Hitler's rise to power in 1933, the reactionary associations of the *Grenz- und Auslandsdeutschtum*, (border-Germans and Germans Abroad), massively supported the promise of a Greater German Reich that would include all the Germanophone peoples within one country. These messages also fueled hopes for the "redemption" of South Tyrol. The Saar referendum in 1935 and especially the Anschluss of Austria on March 12, 1938, were seen as evidence of a future Greater Germany. After the annexation of the Sudeten German territories in September 1938 and the incorporation of the remaining Czech territory into the Protectorate of Bohemia and Moravia on March 15, 1939, enthusiasm of the Border Germans knew no bounds.

During the 1930s, the Third Reich also developed an immense economic attraction for those in South Tyrol who were constantly scraping by due to a lack of professional opportunities. The promise of an unprecedented economic ascent, technological modernity, and an enthralling youth culture soon began to exhibit their propagandistic effects. Under Italian Fascism, these were only attainable by relinquishing one's own ethnic identity and language, whereas under National Socialism, all of this could be achieved while maintaining "Germanness." In this context, a generational rupture became evident. The economic promises, coupled with substantial financial support from Germany, played a significant role in the success of the *Völkischer Kampfring Südtirol* (VKS), the illegal South Tyrolean Nazi movement, during the 1930s. The National Socialist ideology of *Volkstum* (being part of one folk), which promised a unified state for all Germans, seemingly pledged to solve all domestic social and economic problems, including a revanchist program. Against this backdrop, the potency of the Nazi propaganda massively deployed during the 1930s cannot be overstated. It led to intensified anti-Italian, pro-German propaganda on the part of the German-speaking minority.[40]

During the 1930s, the "South Tyrol question" therefore became a stumbling block in the rapprochement policy of the two dictatorships, Fascist Italy and Nazi Germany. One of the solutions seen was for the relocation of the German-speaking minority in South Tyrol. The idea of relocating large population groups was nothing new in the dictatorships of the interwar period. There were ideas and concepts for this on both the Italian and German sides; who ultimately took the initiative is inconsequential. Attempts at forced assimilation targeted several groups in Fascist Italy, such as Slovenes, Croats, Aostans, and Albanians. Since Ettore Tolomei in 1914/15, there were considerations, time and again, for the resettlement also of the German-speaking minority in South Tyrol. Conversely, Nazi Germany, as part of its conquest policy, entered into bilateral resettlement agreements for around one million "ethnic Germans" in the Soviet Union, Estonia, Latvia, Hungary, and Croatia. Such resettlements aligned, on the one hand, with racial-ideological and geopolitical thinking: the "ethnic Germans" were to be "brought home" to the Reich and could, if needed, flexibly settle the conquered "living space" in the east. On the other hand, they also provided the country with abundant "human resources" for the aggression wars in the east, as most male re-settlers were recruited for the Wehrmacht shortly after their arrival in the Reich. Not least, the administration of the German Reich calculated with urgently needed labor force and foreign currency, obtained through exchange—specifically in the case of the inhabitants of South Tyrol—with Italy for the assets of those resettling. For Fascist Italy, the resettlement of South Tyroleans eliminated a constant source of conflict, and the Brenner border, which had been a concern especially since the Anschluss of Austria to the German Reich in March 1938, was thereby guaranteed.[41]

The two dictators, Adolph Hitler and Benito Mussolini, therefore aimed at finding a permanent solution for the South Tyrol problem in a resettlement program. As a result, in June 1939, the so-called *Optionsabkommen* (*Option* agreement) was announced: the German-speaking inhabitants of the South Tyrol would be given the opportunity to opt for an emigration to the German Reich and thus become German citizens, or they could opt to stay in Italy and consequently accept the Italian language and culture. The "voluntariness" of the subsequent migration movement alone would later produce a flood of academic research and publications.[42] After months of bitter debate, around 86% of the eligible voters opted to move north of the Brenner Pass. It remains unclear how many people this concerned, although archival sources indicate a number of roughly 110,000 households or 220.000 individuals. The only indication of the population residing in the province of Bolzano in the 1930s is provided by the census of 1936—a census conducted in a fascist state with deliberate political intentions and limited methods of counting. It states a figure of 277,720 for the people living within the existing boundaries of the province.[43] There is, however, no indication of the language the people spoke. A reconstruction of historical statistical census data by the South Tyrolean statistical institute ASTAT from 2001 concluded that in 1910—before the region's affiliation with Italy—89% of the population declared they used German as their colloquial language, 3-4% used Italian, and 4% used Ladin. By 1961, the numbers had changed significantly: 61% used German, 34% Italian, and 3% Ladin as their spoken language.[44]

The expatriation of *Optants* (the people who had declared a desire to move to the Third Reich) began during the war in 1940 but slowed down considerably when war efforts were reinforced in the following years. After the fall of Mussolini's regime and Italy's change of sides in the War in 1943, the *Option* (as the expatriation came to be called) was stopped. At that point, around 75,000 people had already left their homeland to find an uncertain future in the German Reich—mostly in the neighboring regions of the former Austrian Tyrol, Vorarlberg, Salzburg, and Carinthia.[45]

The *Return Option* Movement 1945–1955

After the war in 1945, the Province of Bolzano remained part of Italy although Austria brought forth a strong plea to the Allies to reincorporate the southern part of the Tyrol.[46] The situation for the inhabitants of South Tyrol at this point was almost dramatic: all those who had opted for the German Reich were stateless. The Italian government treated them as foreigners without civil rights and political representation.[47] Only the

Dableiber (the remainers—those who had declared a desire to remain in Italy) and the *Non-Optants* (those who had refrained from opting at all) possessed Italian citizenship. It took arduous and lengthy negotiations until the *Optantendekret*, the law for the "Revision of the Options of the South Tyroleans" of February 2, 1948, reversed the *Option* agreement and created the legal basis for reassumption of the Italian citizenship for the *Optants* who had remained in South Tyrol.

The situation was more complex for those who had moved abroad; already during the Second World War some South Tyroleans occasionally returned to their homeland, but their number was limited. Immediately after the end of the war, the emigrants faced an uncertain future in their countries of immigration: should they, who had now become stateless, go back to their country of origin or should they try to strengthen their foothold in their country of immigration? In the first few days after the end of the war in May 1945, those who made up their minds quickly had the opportunity to illegally cross the newly emerging borders between the occupying powers and find their way back to the province of Bolzano via the Brenner or the Reschen pass. After a couple of days, this illegal transition was only possible via the mountains, for example via the old smuggler and cattle trails in the Ziller Valley or together with Italian returnees on resettlement trains.[48] Also for those who had moved abroad, the *Optantendekret* of 1948 was essential in deciding their future; now they could apply for the reacquisition or retention of Italian citizenship and eventually move back to their country of birth. If they failed to move back or were denied Italian citizenship, they could then apply for the acquisition of the Austrian or German citizenship.

The *Optantendekret* was a complex legal text distinguishing between three groups of *Optants*: Firstly, the so-called "simple *Optants*," those who had opted for the German Reich but never received German citizenship. This group had the possibility to revoke the *Option* and thus retain Italian citizenship. Secondly, there were the *Optants* who had acquired German citizenship but never emigrated. These persons were able to revoke the *Option* and thus renounce their German citizenship to regain Italian citizenship. Thirdly, there were *Optants* who had acquired German citizenship and emigrated from South Tyrol; whether they had returned to Italy or not, they were now able to request the re-acquisition of Italian citizenship. The application for re-acquisition of Italian citizenship had to include the declaration of revocation of the *Option* and the surrender of German citizenship. However, those who had temporarily resided abroad for reasons of study, business, or military did not fall into this category.[49]

The return, however, was denied if the applicant had been a member of the SS, the Gestapo, the SD, or the SOD (the *Südtiroler Ordnungsdienst* was the South Tyrolean military police installed after 1943). The same applied if they had held a major position at the offices organizing the *Option* resettlement program, the ADERSt (*Amtliche Deutsche Ein- und Rückwandererstelle*, "Official German Immigration and Repatriation Office") or the ADO (*Arbeitsgemeinschaft der Optanten* für Deutschland, "Working Group of Optants for Germany"), or if someone had been convicted of war crimes. Also excluded were those who had demonstrated explicit "Nazi partiality" when making propaganda for the *Option*. This, of course, was a very vague phrasing, which allowed for subjective decisions and personal judgments.[50]

The number of those who were finally allowed and still wished to return is still unknown today. Historian Stefan Lechner estimated that about one-third of the 75,000 emigrants returned to the province of Bolzano after 1948,[51] while more recent research indicates that up to 40,000 of those who had emigrated returned.[52] If they came back, many returnees faced various difficulties and uncertainties, as it was not clear whether they would find jobs and housing and whether integration in their former homesteads would succeed.[53] The question of capital transfer also remained an open one. Simultaneously, those who decided to stay in Austria and Germany often faced no less urgent problems. Here too the question of citizenship remained open for debate until the late 1940s, and it was not clear until then whether the re-settlers would remain on an equal footing with Austrian citizens because by then they had a legal opportunity to return to Italy.[54]

Emigration and Immigration in the Welfare State 1955–1990

In the post-war period, South Tyrol was at the crossroads of people emigrating from Italy to the north and was itself affected by labor emigration. Still, until the mid-1970s, the Province of Bolzano was a land of emigration; many people emigrated, especially to German-speaking countries, due to insufficient economic prospects within the region. During these decades, there were significant differences in the economic development compared to the Austrian federal states of Tyrol and Vorarlberg but especially in comparison with Switzerland or Germany.[55]

In the first post-war decades, the focus of politics and society was primarily on immigration from the south: the so-called "51% policy" promoted immigration from other provinces in Italy. It was referred to as the "death march" in the German-speaking press. People from other linguistic and cultural groups were scarcely noteworthy: in the 1961 census, 281 individuals were recorded in the language category "Other," encompassing "all residents with a different colloquial language." Ten years later, this number had risen to 475, and this time, in the "Other" category, "all residents who did not declare themselves part of any of the three language groups" were included. In both cases, there was no explicit reference to a category of "foreigner," but to some extent, it can be presumed to have included such individuals. Thus, in relation to the total population, at that time there was an immigrant ratio of 0.08 percent (1961) and 0.11 percent (1971).[56]

In South Tyrol, it was only through the political stability established by the Second Autonomy Statute in 1972 and the resulting opening of the so-called "third economic sector" for German and Ladin speakers, along with a delayed but subsequently rapid economic boom, that the processes of emigration came to an end. A very slow and hesitant immigration began in the 1980s, mainly comprising older generations from Germany and Austria. The issue of "overseas" immigration first entered the consciousness of the South Tyrolean public in the late 1980s when so-called *Marocchini*, predominantly male migrants from the Maghreb, sometimes referred to as "carpet traders," arrived in the South Tyrolean valleys to work as seasonal laborers or itinerant merchants.[57]

Within the province, the 1981 census finally showed a different picture. The early 1980s witnessed a significant political and cultural shift, particularly due to the census, since, for the first time, it demanded the declaration of linguistic affiliation. In the liberal spirit in the wake of "1968," the political opposition mobilized against what it defined as "ethnic cages," leading to 9,593 individuals choosing not to affiliate with any of the three language groups (German, Ladin, and Italian).[58] According to the regional statistics office, the ASTAT, this group was defined as "resident locals without a valid declaration of linguistic affiliation and resident foreigners." Based on this information alone, estimating the foreigner quota for these years is not feasible. However, more detailed information comes from the Italian Statistics Institute, ISTAT, which reported that in 1981 there were 4,082 individuals of foreign nationality registered in South Tyrol. Remarkably, these foreigners had a particularly high average age, which was very atypical compared to the migrant population that would arrive later. Nearly three out of ten of these individuals were in the over-sixty-five age group back then, whereas today, this proportion is slightly over 4%.[59]

During the 1980s, immigration of individuals with foreign citizenship slowly increased within the Italian territory. As a result, some official data is also available for South Tyrol. According to a publication by the Italian National Council for Economics and Labor, (*Consiglio Nazionale dell'Economia e del Lavoro,* CNEL), the proportion of foreigners in the

Trentino-South Tyrol region grew from 6,511 to 8,173 between 1982 and 1987. Although some uncertainties remain, it can be presumed that, until this time, these individuals were predominantly from the German-speaking regions because the high average age of the immigrants and because, until 2004, the group holding German citizenship constituted the largest foreigner group in South Tyrol. In fact, among the 649 foreigners who immigrated to the province of Bolzano between 1981 and 1985, around 70% held German or Austrian citizenship (two-thirds were German). Only forty-three individuals (6.6%) migrated from other EU countries to South Tyrol, seventy from other European countries outside the EU, and eighty-two from other parts of the world. Similar figures were recorded in the subsequent five-year period between 1986 and 1990.[60]

Accurate data regarding the composition of South Tyrol's foreign population became available for the first time through the 1991 census. At that time, there were 4,747 foreign nationals residing in South Tyrol (which accounted for 1.1% of the total population). Almost two-thirds (64.5%) of them were German (2,042) or Austrian citizens (1,018). Significantly lower in numbers were individuals from the former Yugoslavia, (totaling 240 individuals, which made up 5%), who had fled prior to the onset of the Balkan Wars.[61]

Interestingly enough, although the 1980s and 1990s slowly brought about a moderate influx of foreign nationals, the focus on migration during these two decades was a different one; finally, after years of silence and downplay, the *Option* became a heavily debated topic in South Tyrolean media and society. It would ultimately change the historical interpretation of the events of 1939 and bring about a flood of literature on the reappraisal of those events.[62]

Internationalization of Migration Flows in the Realm of the European Integration and International (Re-)Settlement since 1990

Compared to previous decades, the migration situation in South Tyrol today is entirely different. This raises the question of when and how this shift from being a land of emigration to one of immigration occurred.

Following the end of the Cold War and the fall of the Iron Curtain in 1989, there was an increasing influx of seasonal laborers, especially in agriculture, to the province of Bolzano: from Poland, (then) Czechoslovakia, and Hungary. Economic hopelessness, escalating violent conflicts, and wars in the 1990s led to mass emigration from former Yugoslavia and immigration or flight to Italy. Larger migrant and refugee groups from Albania also arrived in South Tyrol and were accommodated, for instance, in barracks erected in the villages of the region. This "new" form flight and migration became, at least temporarily, a socially debated issue, sparking the political discussions that, with interruptions, continue to this day.[63] Some of those who arrived in the country at that time returned to their countries of origin. Others settled in South Tyrol and gradually integrated into the work and life environment.

The number of immigrants, however, remained low. This changed only with the EU enlargements in the late 1990s and 2000s. On July 27, 2006, the Italian government informed the EU Commission of its decision to refrain from the temporary regulations on the free movement of workers from eight new member states (Estonia, Latvia, Lithuania, Poland, Slovenia, Hungary, Slovakia, and the Czech Republic). Up until that point, there had been restrictions for the new EU citizens regarding their freedom of movement within the EU. With this decision by the Italian government, these restrictions were lifted.[64]

What followed was a period of immigration and emigration, and only the 2011 census provided a clearer, more concise picture: all present foreigners were registered. According to the census, the number of regularly residing foreigners continued to increase, albeit slowly. As of December 31, 2015, there were 46,454 people with foreign citizenship residing in South Tyrol. This corresponded to a proportion that remained stable at around 8.9% of the total population compared to the previous years.[65] The most recent census of 2021 once more indicates a gradual increase, with 9.7% of the population in South Tyrol considered foreign nationals by the end of that year.[66]

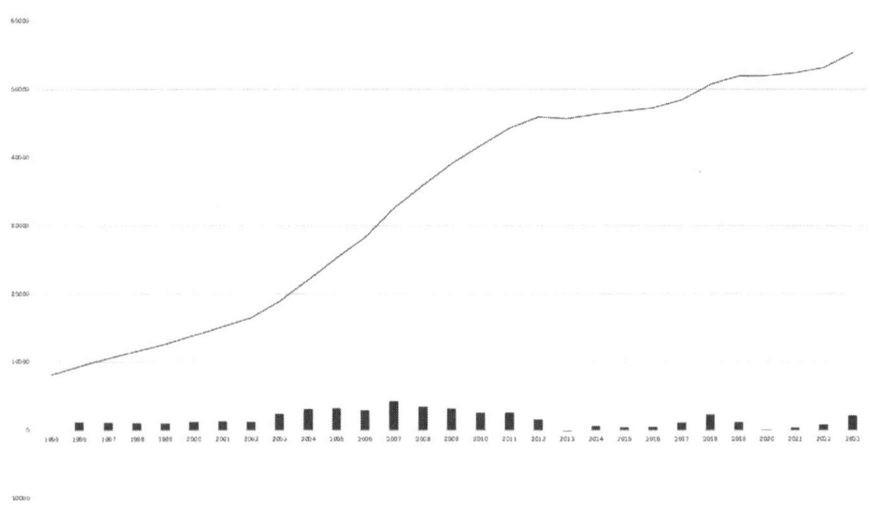

Figure 1: Persons with Foreign Citizenship Resident in South Tyrol, Period 1990–2015[67]

Agriculture, followed by tourism, had become primary sectors attracting labor migration, particularly from Eastern Europe. Concurrently, the healthcare sector increasingly had attracted female migrants from Poland and Romania. The increase in immigration also led to the formation of migrant associations for various nationalities, regions, religious affiliations, and gender in South Tyrol. These self-organizations led to the establishment of civil society NGOs, gradually blurring the seemingly sharp lines between locals and newcomers. Toward the end of the 2000s, these associations became increasingly important as immigration in South Tyrol became statistically relevant for the first time, thus becoming politically interesting. Since then, the emphasis of South Tyrolean regional politics on intercultural mediation, which started earlier compared to the national context, bore fruit.[68] Mediation services were available in the education sector as well as in other public institutions. These services made a significant contribution to fostering dialogue between the migrant population and the host society, especially in recent years when migration increased in scale and complexity.[69]

Conclusion

Today, also in South Tyrol, the education sector is one of the most challenging spaces when talking about immigration and integration. Here linguistic and cultural differences particularly come to the forefront. In transitional and border areas like the South Tyrolean villages Franzensfeste and Brenner, these challenges become visible in school classes that sometimes consist entirely of children whose parents are from abroad. These villages are defined by the (proximity of the) border; they become "non-places," once referred to as global or transnational social spaces, and they thrive on migration. It is precisely in these spaces that opportunities exist for the emergence of something new between foreignness and adaptation.[70]

The interactions between society, politics, and media have been visible in ongoing discourses on immigration and migration for about a quarter century, reflected in the continued unquestioned use of derogatory terms and attributions also in South Tyrol. The progression and changes in these discourses in daily newspapers were examined thoroughly by Sarah Oberbichler in her contribution "Between Benefit and Threat: 25 Years of Migration Discourse in the Newspapers 'Dolomiten' and 'Alto Adige.'"[71] In "Misanthropy 2016? 'Social' Media and Migration," I analyzed the content of some German-speaking Facebook groups from South Tyrol, which, in line with countercultural movements in recent years, have centered on migration.[72] These analyses make it clear that immigration in the media, be it mainstream or social networks, is still perceived and depicted as a threat, perpetuating stereotypes and prejudices between society, politics, and media. Particularly in online discourse, it is evident that due to the algorithms of social media, people find it increasingly difficult to break out of their own echo chambers.

Concurrently, despite South Tyrol being an immigration destination for over thirty years, the trend of emigration among the local population never fully ceased. Economic crisis, the COVID-19-pandemic, and worldwide war and conflicts in recent years also slowed down the South Tyrolean economy, resulting in a decrease in immigration from abroad and an increase in emigration to other countries. Italian citizens definitively emigrating abroad have the possibility to register in the registry of Italians residing abroad (AIRE). As of December 31, 2014, 37,356 Italian citizens with South Tyrolean roots were living abroad, a number that has been on the rise since 2007. Among the places of origin for emigrants, the larger cities of the Province of Bolzano stand out—particularly the capital, Bolzano, followed by Meraon, Bressanone, Brunico, and the municipality of Appiano as well as the villages in the Vinschgau valley.[73]

The primary destination for South Tyrolean emigrants are German-speaking countries. By the end of 2009, 10,957 South Tyrolean emigrants were residing in Germany (which constitutes 37%), 5,688 in Austria, and 4,914 in Switzerland. Less frequent destinations include Central and South America (867), the USA and Canada (570), Great Britain (460), France (427), and Spain (285). In 2013 alone, another 2,892 South Tyroleans, mostly from the capital city of Bolzano, emigrated abroad. In two out of three cases, these were men. The most popular destination countries remained those within the German-speaking region: Austria (1,042), Germany (681), and Switzerland (464). However, citizens from nearly all South Tyrolean municipalities also emigrated. Determining the reasons for emigration among South Tyroleans is complex. According to ASTAT, "a large part of South Tyrolean emigrants moved away from home to start a new family abroad," yet starting a family abroad could also indicate the stabilization of their residence elsewere. Indeed, many young individuals choose to study at foreign universities, and more students are favoring Austrian universities while fewer are choosing Italian ones. Some of these students opt to stay abroad for various reasons after completing their studies. Additionally, migration motives for many are likely similar to those in the rest of Italy: among the approximately 4.6 million highly qualified Italians living abroad, the majority do so due to better job opportunities. This is why London's financial center is often referred to as the third-largest Italian city.[74]

The resulting "skilled labor shortage and acute brain drain" has been a constant concern of local politics, economic development agencies and the media in South Tyrol without having any concrete ideas on how to counter this particular challenge.[75] In a study of 2020 the *Wirtschaftsförderungsgesellschaft* (WIFO, the Chamber of Commerce of Bozen) estimated that around 2,500 highly qualified individuals, often with a university degree, emigrate annually. Current immigration from the south and east does not compensate for this brain drain, mainly because low-skilled workers are the ones who come to South Tyrol. This is partly due to the structure of the South Tyrolean economy, which is not particularly friendly toward academics.[76]

Thus, South Tyrol remains a region with a high migration dynamic. What remains striking is how discourses on immigration differ from those regarding emigration.

Endnotes

1. Serie Storiche ISTAT, ed., "online-Archiv Aus- und Zuwanderung nach Region und geografischer Aufteilung, table 2.10.1," *seriestoriche.istat.it*, accessed Sep. 13, 2019, http://seriestoriche.istat.it/index.php?id=7&user_100ind_pi1%5Bid_pagina%5D=45&cHash=5c2d5f8f6a763461de405ca2f03fcd69.

2. Eva Pfanzelter, *Option und Gedächtnis, Erinnerungsorte der Südtiroler Umsiedlung 1939* (Bozen: RAETIA, 2004), 11–15.

3. For more on the quantitative aspects of South Tyrolean migration, see Rainer Girardi and Eva Pfanzelter, "Migration in Zahlen: Ein- und Auswanderung in Südtirol in den amtlichen Statistiken," in *einheimisch – zweiheimisch – mehrheimisch, Geschichte(n) der neuen Migration in Südtirol*, ed. Eva Pfanzelter and Dirk Rupnow (Bozen: RAETIA, 2017), 43–66 (here 43–44).

4. Eva Pfanzelter and Dirk Rupnow, Einleitung, in *einheimisch – zweiheimisch – mehrheimisch, Geschichte(n) der neuen Migration in Südtirol*, ed. Eva Pfanzelter and Dirk Rupnow (Bozen: RAETIA, 2017), 9–19.

5. This can, for example, be also seen in various articles in CAS Volume 26: Günter Bischof and Dirk Rupnow, eds., *Migration in Austria* (New Orleans: UNO Press; Innbruck: Innsbruck University Press, 2017).

6. Georg Grote coined this term; see Eva Pfanzelter, "The (Un)Digested Memory of the South Tyrolean Resettlement in 1939," in *A Land on the Threshold. South Tyrolean Transformations, 1915–2015*, ed. Georg Grote and Hannes Obermair (Bern, et al: Peter Lang, 2017), 119–43.

7. More on memorialization and identity in South Tyrol: Eva Pfanzelter, "Die (un)verdaute Erinnerung an die Option 1939," in *Option und Erinnerung/La memoria della opzione,* Geschichte und Region/Storia e Regione 22, ed. Eva Pfanzelter (Innsbruck: Studien Verlag, 2013), 13–40 (here 13–14).

8. Renowned migration scholars Dirk Hoerder, Jan Lucassen, and Leo Lucassen, however, argue that also this "induced" or "forced" settling of co-ethnics is an essential part of the migration regime of the twentieth century: Dirk Hoerder, Jan Lucassen and Leo Lucassen, "Terminologies and Concepts of Migration Research," in *The Encyclopedia of European Migration and Minorities: From the Seventeenth Century to the Present*, ed. Klaus J. Bade, Pieter C. Emmer, Leo Lucassen and Jochen Oltmer, (Cambridge: Cambridge University Press, 2011), 15–42 (here 32–33).

9. The terms used in this paragraph come from multiple authors, in detail; see Pfanzelter, *Option und Gedächtnis*, 11–15.

10. Projekt: Die Erinnerung an die Südtiroler Option 1939, ed., "Literaturverzeichnis Option und Erinnerung, Stand 2015," *optionunderinnerung.org*, accessed Dec. 28, 2023, http://www.optionunderinnerung.org/wp-content/uploads/2014/11/Literaturliste-Option-und-Erinnerung.pdf.

11. Martha Verdorfer, Günther Pallaver and Leopold Steurer, eds., *Einmal Option und zurück: die Folgen der Aus- und Rückwanderung für Südtirols Nachkriegsentwicklung* (Bozen: Edition RAETIA, 2020); Elisabeth Malleier,

Günther Pallaver, Margareth Lanzinger, eds., *Erbgesund und kinderreich Südtiroler Umsiedlerfamilien im „Reichsgau Sudetenland"* (Bozen: Edition RAETIA, 2021).

12. "optionMUDI: Option museal – Option digital," *uibk.ac.at*, accessed Dec. 28, 2023, https://www.uibk.ac.at/zeitgeschichte/optionmudi/.

13. Stefan Lechner, "Die Erste Option. Die Vergabe der italienischen Staatsbürgerschaft an die Südtiroler in Folge der Annexion 1920," in *Regionale Zivilgesellschaft in Bewegung/Cittadini innanzi tutto. Festschrift für/Scritti in onore di Hans Heiss*, ed. Hannes Obermair, Stephanie Risse and Carlo Romeo (Bozen: Folio, 2012), 219–236; Stefan Lechner, "Annexion. Schock der Entfremdung," in *Das 20. Jahrhundert in Südtirol, Bd. 2: 1920–1929. Faschistenbeil und Hakenkreuz*, ed. Gottfried Solderer (Bozen: Edition RAETIA, 2000), 12–39; Andrea Di Michele, *Die unvollkommene Italianisierung. Politik und Verwaltung in Südtirol 1918–1943* (Veröffentlichungen des Südtiroler Landesarchivs 28), (Innsbruck: Wagner'sche, 2008).

14. Stadt Bozen/Assessorat für Kultur und aktives Zusammenleben, ed., *Ausstellungsparcours Semirurali*, (Bozen: Stadt Bozen 2015); Arbeitsgruppe Für ein Museum in den Semirurali, ed., *Nicht nur Semirurali* (Bozen: Stadt Bozen, 2013).

15. Stefan Lechner, "Rückoption und Rücksiedlung nach Südtirol," in *Die Option. Südtirol Zwischen Faschismus und Nationalsozialismus*, Innsbrucker Forschungen zur Zeitgeschichte vol. 5, ed. Klaus Eisterer and Rolf Steininger (Innsbruck: Studien Verlag, 1989).

16. Helmut Alexander, Stefan Lechner, and Adolf Leidlmair, eds., *Heimatlos: Die Umsiedlung der Südtiroler* (Vienna: Deuticke, 1993).

17. Stefan Lechner, "Zwischen den Landesteilen. Südtirols Optanten 1945–1948," in *Südtirol - Stunde Null? Kriegsende 1945–1946*, Veröffentlichungen des Südtiroler Landesarchivs vol. 10, ed. Hans Heiss (Innsbruck: Studien Verlag, 2000).

18. Stefan Lechner, "Alles retour. Rückoption und Rücksiedlung nach 1945," in *Das 20. Jahrhundert in Südtirol: 1940–1959*, ed. Gottfried Solderer and Helmut Alexander (Bozen: Edition RAETIA, 2001).

19. Stefan Lechner, "Auf der Suche nach der Heimat Südtirol: Rückoption und Rücksiedlung," in *Le Opzioni rilette: Die mitgelesenen Briefe*, ed. Ulrike Kindl (Bolzano: La fabbrica del tempo, 2014).

20. Stefan Lechner, "Rückfahrkarte statt Selbstbestimmung," in *80 Jahre Option: Das dunkelste Kapitel der (Süd-)Tiroler Zeitgeschichte,* Schriftenreihe Studien zur Zeitgeschichte vol. 115, ed. Andreas Raffeiner (Hamburg: Verlag Dr. Kovac, 2020).

21. For instance, Ivan Stecher, "Die Rücksiedlung Von Südtiroler Optantinnen und Optanten. Genese, Ablauf und Reintegration Anhand Ausgewählter Fallbeispiele sowie fachdidaktische Ausarbeitung der Thematik für den Schulunterricht" (Master's Thesis, Universität Innsbruck, 2020).

22. Martha Verdorfer, Günther Pallaver and Leopold Steurer, *Einmal Option und zurück: Die Folgen der Aus- und Rückwanderung für Südtirols Nachkriegsentwicklung* (Bozen: Edition Raetia, 2019).

23. More on the state of the art: Eva Pfanzelter, "Digital Historical Remigration: The Example of the South Tyrolean Return Option," in *Return and Circular Migration in Contemporary European History*, Migrations in History, ed. Sarah Oberbichler, Eva Pfanzelter, and Valerio Larcher 18-40 (Berlin: De Gruyter, 2024).

24. Sarah Oberbichler, Eva Pfanzelter, Valerio Larcher, eds., *Return and Circular Migration in Contemporary European History*, Migrations in History (Berlin: De Gruyter, 2024). https://doi.org/10.1515/9783111186016.

25. For example, Rolf Steininger, *Südtirolvom Ersten Weltkrieg bis zur Gegenwart* (Innsbruck, Vienna: Studien Verlag, 2014).

26. Sabine Falch, *Heimatfern. Die Südtiroler Arbeitsmigration der 1950er und 1960er Jahre,* Innsbrucker Forschungen zur Zeitgeschichte vol. 17 (Innsbruck: Studien Verlag, 2002); concerning the labor market situation in South Tyrol during these years, see also Evi Brigl, *Das Kuckucksei im Eisacktal. Die Continental-Debatte in Brixen 1969–1972* (Bozen: Edition RAETIA, 2009).

27. "(Arbeits-)migration in Südtirol," 2015–2017, *uibk.ac.at*, accessed Dec. 28, 2023, http://zeitgeschichte-suedtirolmigration.uibk.ac.at/.

28. "Literaturliste: Migration (in Südtirol)," ed. Project (Arbeits-)migration in Südtirol, *uibk.ac.at*, accessed Dec. 28, 2023, http://zeitgeschichte-suedtirolmigration.uibk.ac.at/wp-content/uploads/2016/04/literatur-migration-in-sudtirol.pdf.

29. Eva Pfanzelter and Dirk Rupnow, eds., *Einheimisch – zweiheimisch – mehrheimisch. Geschichte(n) der neuen Migration in Südtirol* (Bozen: Edition RAETIA, 2017); Kurt Gritsch, *Vom Kommen und Gehen. Migration in Südtirol* (Bozen: Edition RAETIA, 2017).

30. "Datenarchiv der Migration in Südtirol," 2015–2017, *uibk.ac.at*, accessed Dec. 28, 2023, https://zeitgeschichte-suedtirolmigration.uibk.ac.at/omeka/.

31. Südtiroler in der Welt. Arbeitsstelle für Heimatferne VFG, ed., "Arbeitsmigration. Rund 1000 junge Menschen verlassen jährlich Südtirol. Arbeitsmigration ist immer noch ein großes Thema," *suedtirolerinderwelt.org*, accessed Dec. 28, 2023, https://www.suedtirolerinderwelt.org/news/arbeitsmigration/.

32. "MigDiv Group. Zentrum für Migration und Diversität," *eurac.edu*, accessed Dec. 28. 2023, https://www.eurac.edu/de/institutes-centers/institut-fuer-minderheitenrecht/projects/migdiv-group.

33. An extended version of this part has been published in the following chapter: Eva Pfanzelter, "Die Option – Vorgeschichte, Ablauf, Folgen," in *Option und Gedächtnis: Erinnerungsorte der Südtiroler Umsiedlung 1939*, Eva Pfanzelter (Bozen: Edition RAETIA, 2014), 15–45.

34. Ibid., 16.

35. Ibid., 17.

36. Ibid., 18–19.

37. Ibid., 19-20.

38. Ibid., 21.

39. Ibid., 22–25.

40. Ibid.

41. Ibid., 22–23.

42. "Literaturverzeichnis Option und Erinnerung," *optionunderinnerung.org*, accessed Dec. 28, 2023, http://www.optionunderinnerung.org/wp-content/uploads/2014/11/Literaturliste-Option-und-Erinnerung.pdf. For more details on the procedures and results, see, Pfanzelter, *Option und Gedächtnis*, 25–32.

43. "Elenco dei comuni del Regno e loro popolazione residente al 21 aprile 1936," 28–29, *ebiblio.istat.it*, accessed Dec. 28, 2023, https://ebiblio.istat.it/digibib/Censimenti%20popolazione/censpop1936/IST0005666ElencocomuniRegnoepopres21Apr936.pdf.

44. "Südtirols Bevölkerung – Gestern, Heute, Morgen – Von 1936 Bis 2010," in *Quadro Demografico Della Provincia Di Bolzano – Dal 1936 Al 2010*, ASTAT-Schriftenreihe vol. 85, ed. by Landesinstitut für Statistik – ASTAT (Bozen: ASTAT, 2001), 42–43.

45. Concerning the history of the Option, see *in extenso*, Eva Pfanzelter, *Option und Gedächtnis*; also Eva Pfanzelter ed., *Option und Erinnerung*, Geschichte und Region/storia e regione 2013 (no. 2) (Innsbruck, Vienna, Bozen: Studien Verlag, 2014). For an extended list of publications, see *Literaturverzeichnis Option und Erinnerung*.

46. An extended version of this subchapter and more citations can be found here: Pfanzelter, "Digital Historical Remigration."

47. Stefan Lechner and Helmut Alexander, "Die Rücksiedlung" in *Heimatlos. Die Umsiedlung der Südtiroler*, Helmut Alexander, Stefan Lechner and Adolf Leidlmair (Vienna: Deuticke, 1993), 181–273 (here 191).

48. For the situation at the end of the war, see Eva Pfanzelter, *Südtirol unterm Sternenbanner. Die amerikanische Besatzung Mai–Juni 1945* (Bozen: Edition RAETIA, 2005).

49. "Legislative decree of 2 February 1948, no. 23 – Revisione delle opzioni degli alto atesini," *gazzettaufficiale.it*, accessed Sep., 19, 2023, https://www.gazzettaufficiale.it/eli/id/1948/02/05/048U0023/sg.

50. Ibid.

51. Lechner, "Alles retour," 76–87.

52. "Return Migration as an Interdisciplinary Research Area Using the Example of the South Tyrolean 'Return Option,'" *uibk.ac.at*, accessed Dec. 28, 2023, https://www.uibk.ac.at/zeitgeschichte/remigra/archiv/index.html.de.

53. Ivan Stecher, "The Decision-Making Process and Re-Option of the South Tyrolean Optants from the Perspective of Contemporary Witnesses," in *Return and Circular Migration*, ed. Oberbichler, Pfanzelter and Larcher.

54. Lechner and Alexander, "Die Rücksiedlung," 250–259.

55. An extended version of this subchapter can be found here: Pfanzelter and Rupnow, *einheimisch*, 9–19.

56. Details on the statistics and detailed citations can be found here: Girardi and Pfanzelter, "Migration in Zahlen," 43–66.

57. Pfanzelter and Rupnow, *einheimisch*, 9–19.

58. Oskar Peterlini, *Autonomie und Minderheitenschutz in Trentino-Südtirol: Überblick über Geschichte, Recht und Politik* (Bozen: Präsidium des Regionalrates Trentino-Südtirol in Zusammenarbeit mit der Regionalregierung, 2000).

59. ISTAT, ed., "Popolazione straniera residente in Italia per classi di età, sesso e regione ai censimenti 1981, 1991, 2001 e anni 2002–2009," *seriestoriche.istat.it*, accessed Nov. 27, 2023, http://seriestoriche.istat.it/index.php?id=7&user_100ind_pi1%5Bid_pagina%5D=46&cHash=d39ba72c3edae259ecb657f1819aea71.

60. Girardi and Pfanzelter, "Migration in Zahlen," 43–66.

61. ASTAT, ed., *13. Allgemeine Volkszählung 1991* (Bozen: Landesstatistikinstitut ASTAT, 1995) 52–53.

62. For more concerning these decades, see Pfanzelter ed., *Option und Erinnerung.*

63. ASTAT, ed., *Immigration in Südtirol. Lebensumstände und Sichtweisen der in- und ausländischen Bevölkerung. Autonome Provinz Bozen–Südtirol* (Bozen: Landesstatistikinstitut ASTAT 2012); ASTAT, ed., *Info 16/2001, 11/2002, 17/2003, 20/2004, 14/2005, 17/2006, 22/2007, 19 und 21/2008, 35/2009, 27/2010, 26/2011, 41/2012, 45 und 71/2013 und 29/2015.*

64. "Rundschreiben des Innenministeriums und des Ministeriums für soziale Solidarität," no. 1 (January 4, 2008).

65. ASTAT, ed., *Info 71/2013, 45/2014, 30/2016.*

66. ASTAT, ed., "Bevölkerung, 2024," *astat.provinz.bz.it*, accessed Dec. 28, 2023, https://astat.provinz.bz.it/de/bevoelkerung.asp.

67. ASTAT, ed., for the data 1990–2010, ISTAT ed., for the data 2011–2015.

68. Kurt Gritsch, "Migrationsnetzwerke in Südtirol: Organisationen von und für Migranten. Eine zeithistorische Bestandsaufnahme," in *einheimisch – zweiheimisch – mehrheimisch, Geschichte(n) der neuen Migration in Südtirol*, ed. Eva Pfanzelter and Dirk Rupnow (Bozen: RAETIA, 2017), 211–227; Julia Tapfer, "Südtiroler Migrantinnen und ihre Vereine: Entstehung und Handlungsräume von Frauenorganisationen," in Ibid., 233–247.

69. Fernando Biague, "Interkulturelle Mediation in Südtirol: Gesetzliche Regelungen, Ausbildung und Diversifizierung" in Ibid., 257–274.

70. Hans Karl Peterlini, "Lebenswelten im Zwischen. Ansichten der Migrationsgesellschaft an Schnittstellen von Öffnung und Schließung: Franzensfeste/Fortezza, Brenner/Brennero," in Ibid., 283–304.

71. Sarah Oberbichler, "Zwischen Nutzen und Bedrohung: 25 Jahre Migrationsdiskurs in den Tageszeitungen Dolomiten und Alto Adige,in Ibid., 163–178.

72. Eva Pfanzelter, "Menschenhass 2016? Soziale Medien und Migration," in Ibid., 183–202.

73. Girardi and Pfanzelter, "Migration in Zahlen," 43–66.

74. Ibid.

75. "Afi-Erhebung: Job-Studie: Arbeitsklima wichtiger als Karriere," *rainews.it/tgr/tagesschau* (April 11, 2019), accessed Dec. 28, 2023, https://www.rainews.it/tgr/tagesschau/articoli/2019/04/tag-Arbeit-Jobstudie-f8a62f4d-570b-4305-a5af-a568b0ca7be0.html.

76. Stefan Perini, "Ohne Migration wird es nicht gehen," *zum Beispiel* no. 2 (2020) (= Beiträge zur Jugendarbeit in Südtirol und Tyrol): 10–11; Christian Pfeifer, "Haltet die Digital Natives!," *Südtiroler Wirtschaftszeitung*, February 7, 2020; Hanspeter Staffler, "Brain Drain - jetzt ist es amtlich," *SALTO.bz* (May 26, 2023), accessed Dec. 28, 2023, https://salto.bz/en/article/26052023/brain-drain-jetzt-ist-es-amtlich.

Caritas and Migration in the State of Tyrol and South Tyrol[1]

Marcel Amoser

Introduction

There is currently a wide range of counseling and support services for migrants in the federal state of Tyrol and in South Tyrol. These institutions play a crucial role in mitigating the social disadvantages faced by migrants. However, political authorities were initially hesitant in establishing support and counseling organizations. In Tyrol, as in South Tyrol, it was therefore mainly church institutions that provided support for migrants, partly out of ideological convictions and partly out of practical needs. The Caritas, in this context, emerged as a key player, engaging early on in the areas of migration and asylum. However, there is a lack of regional-historical studies addressing the work of the Caritas in this field. This is probably also due to the fact that contemporary historical migration research itself has only been dealing more intensively with the history of Tyrol and South Tyrol for a few years.[2] Such studies represent a modern regional history that also considers migration beyond urban centers. They thereby overcome the often prevailing spatial container thinking along with notions of ethnic homogeneity inherent in traditional regional history. This makes migration and diversity visible as constitutive elements of coexistence in Tyrol and South Tyrol. They open up transnational perspectives that incorporate interactions between global processes and local conditions, and inquire into their social, economic, political, or cultural conditions and consequences.

This essay builds upon that and focuses on church-based support centers for migrants in the federal state of Tyrol and in South Tyrol since the 1960s. Due to their shared history, but distinct migration stories in North and East Tyrol as opposed to South Tyrol after 1945, a comparative perspective is warranted.

The comparison helps, reflecting different historical conditions, to explain specifics as well as similarities in counseling and support for migrants.[3] A comparison of these two regions is obvious due to their common history. Additionally, there is often a lack of comparative studies on migration in Tyrol and South Tyrol.[4] Since immigration played a varying role at different times historically in Tyrol and South Tyrol, any comparison can only be time-shifted.[5] In Austria in the 1960s, extensive full employment resulted in bilateral agreements with Spain (1962), Turkey (1964), and Yugoslavia (1966). Many people, in this context known as *guest workers*, traveled to Tyrol. Relevant counseling and support services were established there much earlier than in South Tyrol, where immigration only became a significant issue in the 1990s—especially in connection with the collapse of the Soviet Union and the Yugoslav Wars.[6]

This article primarily focuses on the early days of relevant institutions. In Tyrol, the *Gastarbeiterseelsorge*, (pastoral care for guest workers), financed by Caritas of the Diocese of Innsbruck, was already active in 1967, addressing mainly to Croatian-speaking labor migrants. In South Tyrol, the Caritas of the Diocese of Bolzano-Brixen institutionalized support services in the 1990s, which soon expanded to other communities after the year 2000.

The question arises as to why these centers were established, under what structural conditions they began their work, and what areas of activity they covered. The organizational focus on the church directs attention to the ideological positions formulated in connection with counseling activities and how migrants were addressed. The comparison not only reveals regional specifics and differences but also highlights temporal changes in the ideological orientation and justification of care activities. It is evident that, for support activities in South Tyrol, profane economic logics were more relevant to a greater extent than in the primarily religiously motivated guest worker pastoral care in North and East Tyrol, which resonated primarily with Croatian Catholic labor migrants. Before delving into the similarities and differences of counseling and support facilities in the federal state of Tyrol and in South Tyrol, the source situation will first be discussed.

Sources and Archives

The starting point for this research involved documents and interviews at the contemporary historical *Dokumentationsarchiv Migration Tirol* (DAM, Documentation Archive Migration Tyrol) at the *Zentrum für MigrantInnen in Tirol* (ZeMiT, Center for Migrants in Tyrol).[7] Additionally, materials from two archives, the *Diözesanarchiv Innsbruck* (DAI, Diocesan Archive Innsbruck) and the Archive of Caritas Bolzano-Brixen (CABB), form the basis for this work. The DAI primarily houses records related to the activities of the *Gastarbeiterseelsorge*. These records are available fragmentarily from the initial phase of pastoral care in 1966 until the Yugoslav Wars in the 1990s, including protocols, activity reports, and correspondence. The archive also contains relevant materials on public relations, such as press releases, posters, and flyers, as well as articles from newspapers and Catholic journals.[8]

In the CABB, there are primarily printed works. The magazine *Caritas.info* (also known as *Helfen*) is aimed at donors and interested members of the public. It provides information in German and Italian about the organization's positions, institutions, and activities and is published quarterly. *Caritas io&du,* a magazine with a similar focus, is aimed specifically at volunteers and parish Caritas employees and is published six times a year. Additionally, there are annual reports from Caritas and its sub-organizations as well as an extensive collection of media observations and press releases.[9]

Furthermore, five expert interviews with former officials of the organizations are included. The interviews serve to fill existing gaps by providing insights into certain details and contexts that cannot be reconstructed from the archival materials alone. They also provide information about personal motivations and retrospective evaluations of counseling activities. However, due to the temporal discrepancy between experienced and narrated history, oral history is only considered supplementary in this work. To contextualize the material, data from the *Landesinstitutsfür Statistik der Autonomen Provinz Bozen* (State Institute of Statistics of the Autonomous Province of Bolzano) and association records in the *Tiroler Landesarchiv* (TLA, Tyrolean State Archives) are also consulted.[10]

Historical Overview

The care of migrant workers in Tyrol is closely linked to the recruitment agreement between Austria and Yugoslavia in 1966. While in Austria, this agreement aimed to meet the demand for labor through an *industrial reserve army*, especially in the construction industry, textiles, and gastronomy, the Yugoslav leadership, through a liberal approach, hoped to alleviate pressure on its own labor market and acquire additional foreign currency. In 1973, 10% of the employed population in Tyrol were foreign nationals, 70% of whom were from Yugoslavia.[11] The exact number of Croatian-Catholic migrant workers among them cannot be determined precisely. However, the Yugoslav census of 1971 indicates that 39% of all Yugoslavs working abroad came from the Croatian republic.[12] Political scientist Othmar Haberl estimated their overall share in Austria to be 15% in his 1978 study on the emigration of workers from Yugoslavia.[13] A breakdown by individual federal state is still missing. The number of those who migrated for political reasons can only be speculated upon. Numerous supporters of a Croatian-Catholic nation state and sympathizers of the *Ustasha* fled as early as 1945 after the regime's fall. Motives for political emigration from the Croatian republic in the years that followed included the challenging situation of the Catholic Church in Yugoslavia and

Tito's repressive course following the *Croatian Spring*.[14]

By contrast, South Tyrol was still a land of emigration around 1965. The strongly agrarian economy with limited jobs in industry and public services, a low level of education, and an unstable political situation prompted many people to move to the Federal Republic of Germany (FRG), Switzerland, or Austria—despite South Tyrol's relatively good economic situation. For the German-speaking population in South Tyrol, opportunities for public housing and employment in public services and industry were often limited.[15] Finally, some re-settlers—who had used the option of returning to South Tyrol since the first Statute of Autonomy in 1948—felt alienated and left the country again. According to the highest estimates, around 1970 there were between 15,000 and 18,000 so-called *Heimatferne* (South Tyrolean emigrants). That was about 10% of the total population. However, the majority emigrated again in the 1970s.[16]

In addition to emigration, South Tyrol experienced significant internal migration from other Italian provinces since the 1950s, particularly in the industrial sector in Bolzano.[17] Although immigration increased in the 1970s due to the expansion of the service sector driven by tourism and the political stabilization through the Second Autonomy Statute, a positive immigration balance only occurred from the 1980s onwards. In the 1990s, immigration became more noticeable and publicly discussed. In addition to cities with a large Italian-speaking population, such as Bolzano or Merano, migration by harvest workers and migrant traders from Eastern Europe and the Maghreb also became visible in German-speaking valleys.[18] From the 1990s onwards, there was a positive migration balance in South Tyrol. However, immigration only increased more significantly after 2000. According to the Statistical Yearbook for South Tyrol in 1999, 12,667 people did not possess Italian citizenship, whereas in 2009, the number rose to 39,152 individuals. As of December 31, 2016, there were 46,794 foreign citizens living in South Tyrol, which is 8.9% of the total population.[19] Apart from immigration from Germany and Albania, there was substantial migration within the framework of the EU eastward expansion from countries such as Slovakia, Romania, and Bulgaria to South Tyrol.[20]

Tyrol and South Tyrol have undergone similar developments in many respects. Both regions are shaped by exchange processes along the important Brenner Transit route. Over the past decades, they have experienced economic growth accompanied by infrastructure projects, a tourism sector boom, and a decline in the significance of agriculture. Additionally, there has been an expansion in education, with the University of Innsbruck playing a significant role in training students from Tyrol and South Tyrol. Similarities are also evident in the societal and political dominance of conservative Catholic conditions. Despite a certain decline observed in both regions in the influence of traditional mainstream parties and the Catholic Church, these majority conditions likely contribute to the relevance of religious institutions, which early on engaged with migration alongside various social issues. Finally, similarities are seen in the gradual integration of both regions into the European Union, which institutionalized in 2011 as the European Region Tyrol-South Tyrol-Trentino, building upon a shared history in a modernized form.

Care Facilities in the Federal State of Tyrol and in South Tyrol

In Tyrol and in South Tyrol, the increased number of migrants and the increased public attention were pivotal factors that led to the involvement of church institutions in addressing migration issues. In North and East Tyrol, this occurred as early as the 1960s, while in South Tyrol, it began in the late 1980s.[21] Consequently, church institutions in both regions were the first to engage in the care and counseling of migrants. This stance may be associated with an ideological understanding that will be examined in more detail below. Church institutions also had an already established global infrastructure, not least due to colonial expansion, which probably also enabled early awareness of migration movements and rapid implementation of support services.[22]

Tyrol had a long tradition of informal pastoral care for migrants. Even before the Second World War, Croatian-speaking migrants came to Innsbruck, and some of them studied theology there. This led to the development of unofficial pastoral centers where Croatian-language masses were celebrated.[23] After 1945, the topic of migration also became more present in the Vatican. The apostolic constitution *Exsul Familia* of 1952 first outlined pastoral work for migrants, further articulated during the Second Vatican Council. *Cura pastoralis pro emigrantibus croatis,* established as a coordination center for pastoral work, was part of the *Supreme Council for Emigration* in Rome. By 1965, there were only twenty so-called *Ausländerseelsorger* (foreign pastoral workers). By the end of the 1980s, there were already around 150 guest worker chaplains active in Western Europe.[24]

The Yugoslav leadership approved the controlled departure of Catholic priests as a positive signal to the Catholic-oriented wing of the Non-Aligned Movement and to maintain some influence over migrant workers, especially considering tensions with Catholic and Croatian-national oriented groups in Yugoslavia. Concerns about reinforcing an anti-Yugoslav stance in pastoral positions led the Yugoslav secret service to closely monitor foreign pastoral workers.[25] Associations like *Bratstvo*, established in Innsbruck in 1972, served as a counterbalance to potentially separatist sentiments, focusing on cultural events to strengthen a pan-Yugoslav identity. It is probably no coincidence that the emergence of Yugoslavian-oriented associations in Austria correlated with the activities of the *Croatian Spring* national movement in Yugoslavia. Croatian-Catholic support for migrant workers in the destination countries had already been problematized by the Yugoslav government in the late 1960s. In 1969, the FRG was urged to employ secular organizations for the care of migrant workers and to promote the establishment of Yugoslav rather than Croatian centers.[26] Upon the directive of Paulus Rusch—the first bishop of the Diocese of Innsbruck, founded in 1964 (until 1968 the Diocese of Innsbruck-Feldkirch), which until then had been an Apostolic Administration of the Diocese of Brixen—the *Katholische Arbeiterjugend* (KAJ, Catholic Workers' Youth), emerging from the *Catholic Action*, took over the administration of the *Gastarbeiterseelsorge* in Innsbruck. As early as 1966, committed individuals in the KAJ in Innsbruck were working on the issue of migration. To bundle the previous initiatives, a separate working group for guest worker care was set up in cooperation with the bishop and the Caritas. It met for the first time at the beginning of October 1966 in the *Haus der Begegnung* (House of Encounter, Catholic center for meetings, events etc., in Innsbruck).[27] Rusch promoted lay organizations and was actively involved in the founding of the KAJ and the Catholic Workers' Movement.[28] His aim was probably to bring workers closer to the Catholic faith and thus keep them away from influences such as communism.[29]

While these international contexts were relevant for establishing a guest worker pastoral care in North and East Tyrol, Caritas work in South Tyrol was influenced by different dynamics. The present-day Caritas of the Diocese of Bolzano-Brixen traces its roots back to the merger of Caritas in Brixen (established in 1946) and Caritas in Bolzano (established in 1950). This fusion was prepared in 1958 with a joint statute of the Caritas Association of Bolzano-Brixen and implemented in 1964 with the establishment of the new Diocese of Bolzano-Brixen.[30] Due to the multilingual situation in South Tyrol—in 1961, 34.3% of the population declared Italian as their first language, 62.2 % German, and 3.4 % Ladin—the employees worked in two separate sections, each with its own management.[31] For the German-speaking area, there was the *Stiftung Diözesancaritas* (Diocesan Caritas Foundation) and for the Italian-speaking area, there was the *Opera Diocesana di Assistenza Religiosa* (ODAR, Diocesan Assistance Religious Work Foundation). In 2012, the German-Ladin and Italian sections were merged. Caritas aimed to better coordinate the previously fragmented network of welfare organizations in South Tyrol and provide efficient assistance to people in social distress.[32]

The Caritas of the Diocese of Bolzano-Brixen currently offers over thirty counseling and support facilities, covering a broad spectrum of social services, including areas such as poverty, drug addiction, homelessness, development cooperation, youth work, men's counseling, as well as migration and asylum.[33]

The oldest Caritas facility in South Tyrol that focused on supporting migrants was the *Erstaufnahmestelle für Einwanderer* (Reception Center for Immigrants) in Bolzano, established in 1990. In the 1990s, the Italian Caritas section set up the *Beratungsstelle für Nomaden und Einwanderer*, (Counseling Center for Nomads and Immigrants), intended for non-EU citizens and nomads who received no support from the state. In addition to advisory services, it provided emergency assistance with material aid, such as clothing, transportation tickets, and medicine, funded through donations. In the wake of the war in Yugoslavia, Caritas' refugee counseling service was set up in 1993. The services range from counseling and support in the asylum process and family reunification to assistance in finding accommodation.[34] In the 1990s, Caritas had already established a differentiated network of locations and covered a wide range of services for migrants. In the 2000s, Caritas expanded its support network, with the founding of *Chance* in Merano (2005, operated since 2012 as *Moca*) and *InPut* in Brunico (2005), extending care to municipalities outside of Bolzano. [35]

Gastarbeiterseelsorge in Innsbruck

The organization of the *Gastarbeiterseelsorge* in Innsbruck underwent several significant developments. Until the end of 1966, pastoral care and social assistance were informal. With the establishment of a working group at the end of 1966, the church's engagement in various initiatives was consolidated. From 1967, there was an official position with Marian Kopić as a full-time Yugoslav guest worker pastor. The center was located at Falkstraße 27.[36] Between 1966 and 1968, the care was institutionalized and expanded. The funding for the facility came from Caritas of the Diocese of Innsbruck, and the remuneration of the pastor was the responsibility of the Finance Department of the Episcopal Ordinariate.[37] Since there was no other similar facility in Innsbruck, the church assumed not only pastoral but also social and cultural responsibilities, filling a gap in state care. Pastoral care included masses, confessions, weddings, funerals, baptisms, first communions, and confirmations.[38] Posters in Serbian, Croatian, and Slovenian drew attention to the events.[39] In addition to German and handcraft lessons, the cultural offerings included materials such as musical instruments, a projector, national costumes, soccer press, toys, records, newspapers, and books. There were also two soccer teams.[40] The soccer club *Bratstvo,* founded in Innsbruck in 1967, was presided over by the guest worker pastor Kopić.[41] St. Nicholas celebrations were particularly popular. In 1966, around 250 Yugoslavian migrant workers attended one such celebration in the *Haus der Begegnung*.[42] In addition to such events, the KAJ repeatedly tried to raise public awareness and break down prejudices. In May 1967, for example, they dedicated a special issue of their monthly magazine *Der junge Arbeiter* to the topic of guest workers. As a sign of considering migrant workers as part of society and expressing solidarity with them, the first page was designed in four languages (German, Turkish, Slovenian, and Serbo-Croatian).[43] In the same year, the KAJ also carried out a poster campaign.[44] In addition to media outreach, study days were organized to discuss the situation of migrants.[45]

Beyond the deemed necessary pastoral care and awareness-raising public relations, the initial scope of the *Gastarbeiterseelsorge* included translation services, assistance with bureaucratic processes, job-related advice, and housing mediation. The activity report for the period 1970/71 documented significant assistance in areas such as job counseling, consular services, document preparation, clothing distribution, interventions with companies, and job placement, totaling 1,940 counseling cases.[46]

These tasks were carried out with a small staff. In the early days, it consisted of a full-time pastor (two from 1969 onwards); a KAJ official (Herbert Bucher), who was responsible for administrative and accounting tasks; and, from 1968, a Yugoslavian social worker. The support of migrant workers in East Tyrol was entrusted to Ivan *Olujić* of the Salzburg Diocese.[47] As the number of migrant workers steadily increased, and the work of the *Gastarbeiterseelsorge* became more widely known among the recruited people, the organization of the support center was debated from 1968 onwards. The discussion was driven by Caritas, among others. The Caritas director of the Innsbruck diocese, Josef Steinkelderer, emphasized the financial burden on his organization. Therefore, he demanded greater involvement from the Finance Department of the Diocese and set a lump sum of 86,000 schillings for social care.[48]

In addition to financial resources, the limited spatial infrastructure was also a recurring issue. The influx of people attending masses necessitated additional space, and space was also needed for the leisure activities of migrants. Many of them, including those who did not profess the Catholic faith, used church facilities as social meeting points. The space problem intensified when the *Gastarbeiterseelsorge* initiated German courses for migrants from 1967; at times, they were held in the *Haus der Begegnung*. According to the pastoral care activity report, up to 140 people participated in these courses in 1967. They were conducted by aspiring theologians from Yugoslavia studying in Innsbruck. When the seminar rooms in the *Haus der Begegnung* were needed for other purposes, the guest worker pastor held the courses privately in his apartment.[49] Due to the high demand, this could only be a temporary solution. German courses were discontinued in 1968 due to the space problem.[50] The infrastructural issue was also discussed at a conference of the eight pastoral workers for migrants in Austria on March 9, 1968, at the *Haus der Begegnung*.[51] By no later than 1969, there was finally a dedicated guest worker center in Hofgasse 2, which served as a social meeting place and venue for cultural events. Inspired by Marion Kopić, works of art by migrant workers were exhibited there, for example.[52] Although the space problem persisted in the years that followed, the situation of the pastoral care office improved from the early 1970s onwards.[53]

Initially, the responsibilities of the guest worker office in Innsbruck were reorganized. As of July 20, 1971, guest worker pastoral care fell under the Pastoral Care Office, with the KAJ remaining responsible for technical-organizational tasks.[54] On July 1, 1972, the *Gastarbeiterseelsorge* was elevated to a Mission, with all the rights and duties of a personnel parish.[55] The restructuring brought about the greater involvement of the Episcopal Ordinate, as demanded by Caritas, and allowed for an increase in staff. As a result, the number of interventions rose to 3,120 in the reporting period of 1971/72.[56]

In the early 1970s, other actors began to address the issue of migration as the number of migrant workers continued to rise, and it became apparent that many of them would stay in Austria for an extended period. In this context, the term "integration" first appeared in the media. Establishments such as the *Betreuungsstelle für Gastarbeiter des Landes Tirol* (Support Center for Guest Workers of the State of Tyrol) from 1972 and the Austrian-Turkish and Austrian-Yugoslav Societies, supported by companies and the *Handelskammer* (Chamber of Commerce), reflected initial signs of integration policy.[57] However, funding and scope were modest.[58] For the *Gastarbeiterseelsorge* in North and East Tyrol, these bodies initially achieved a focusing of their areas of responsibility. From the end of 1971 onwards, the responsibilities of the Church in migration matters were also discussed nationwide. In a comprehensive program, migration was treated as a cross-cutting issue that affected all levels of the church. To provide the best possible care, it was also important to strengthen cooperation between the Dioceses.[59] *The überdiözesane Arbeitsgemeinschaft für Gastarbeiterfragen in Österreich* (ÜDAG, Inter-diocesan Working Group for Guest Worker Issues in Austria), was established for this purpose in 1972. It consisted of Diocesan working groups, representatives of the Austrian pastoral offices,

Catholic Action, Caritas, the bishops, and others. The ÜDAG was based in Vienna. Its function was to network and raise awareness of the situation of migrants in Austria. However, the response in the parishes remained muted. [60]

Erstaufnahmestelle für Einwanderer and *Migrantes* in Bolzano

The oldest Caritas facility in South Tyrol dedicated to supporting migrants was the *Erstaufnahmestelle für Einwanderer*, founded in 1990 at Latemarstraße 3 in Bolzano. It was managed by the ODAR Foundation on behalf of the Bolzano Social Services. Since the opening of the *Migrantes* building at Romstraße 85a, it has been relocated there.[61] The Center is designed for individuals with residence permits, assisting them with job and housing searches, as well as addressing financial, material, and health emergencies. From an integration policy perspective, the facility aids with bureaucratic processes, provides information on Italian legislation, and organizes language courses to help "immigrants ... adapt to the social and cultural conditions in South Tyrol."[62]

The facility also offers emergency accommodation for up to one hundred people. Some of these are used by people who have been living in Bolzano for decades and are in financial difficulties. In recent years, an increasing number of people entitled to asylum have also had to make use of emergency accommodation, as many end up "on the street" after completing their asylum procedure.[63] Beyond sleeping arrangements, the counseling services are of particular interest. In 2016, 2,148 people made use of these services, primarily seeking housing assistance, legal advice, and support in job searches. Most people came from Morocco, Pakistan, India, Afghanistan, and Bangladesh.[64] The counselors not only assist with bureaucratic matters but also strive to contribute to the self-sufficiency of migrants.[65] This motif of *helping people to help themselves* also appears at other Caritas facilities (see below).

Don Tonino Bello, *Chance* and *Moca* in Merano

The institutionalization of counseling and support services in South Tyrol followed a specific commitment in individual parishes. In Merano, for instance, the local pastor responded to the increasing number of primarily male seasonal workers from Africa and female caregivers from Eastern Europe by establishing a space for Stay and Pray. He was supported by two mediators who provided social work. This initiative later evolved into the *Centro di Ascolto e di prima Accoglienza Don Tonino Bello* in 1994, financed by the ODAR

Foundation.[66] From 2004, *Don Tonino Bello*, located at Romstraße 11, also offered special services for immigrant women. In the afternoons, the center opened exclusively for women, who were supported by a female employee from Ukraine. This service was co-financed by the municipality of Merano.[67]

At the same time, Caritas, in cooperation with the District Community of *Burggrafenamt*, set up an office called *Chance* at Passeiergasse 26 in 2005, financed by the European Social Fund and the Autonomous Province of Bolzano.[68] While *Don Tonino Bello* mainly provided low-threshold services such as rooms, showers, books, magazines, and a television, and thus primarily carried out cultural work, the two employed *Chance* advisors offered professional career advice, job search support, placement services for language, and further education courses and intercultural projects.[69] According to the press release accompanying the founding of *Chance*, the project was aimed at immigrant women, as they require special support due to multiple specific burdens.[70] In practice, it soon became apparent that men also wanted to take advantage of the advice offered in Merano. Therefore, *Chance* was de facto a general facility for migrants. When the ODAR and Caritas foundations merged in 2012, *Don Tonino Bello* and *Chance* also fused under the name *Moca*. This consolidation had been prepared since 2008, when both entities began working under the umbrella of *Gemeinsam für Integration* (Together for Integration).[71]

Since the merger, the facility has been located at Verdistrasse 10 in Merano. *Moca* is run by Caritas in cooperation with the municipality. *Moca* continues the low-threshold offerings of *Don Tonino Bello*, providing showers mainly for male seasonal workers and homeless individuals. Additionally, it maintains the employment-related counseling and support previously offered as *Chance*, complemented by awareness-raising efforts through various intercultural projects. A dedicated space for migrants is also established to facilitate exchange.[72]

Migrant Consultation Service *InPut* in Brunico

The Migrant Consultation Service *InPut* in Brunico has been in existence since winter 2005. It is run by the Caritas Diocese of Bozen-Brixen and the *Sozialsprengel Bruneck/Umgebung*, an institution of the Puster Valley district community financed by the state. Initially located at Europastrasse 8, it then moved to Sternbach-Strasse 6. *InPut* is financed by the European Social Fund and the Autonomous Province of Bolzano.[73] Since 2005, two local counselors have been working part-time for the facility.[74] *InPut* is therefore a smaller facility compared to *Moca*. It caters to newcomers with valid residence or work permits seeking employment in the Puster Valley, as well as the longer-term residents interested in information about migration. At the time of the official opening of the office, this amounted to 1,889 people, around 6% of the total population of the Pustertal district community.[75] Like *Moca*, *InPut* can be described as an integration and intercultural facility. Accordingly, its activities include support for bureaucratic processes, housing and job searches, career counseling, as well as the facilitation of language courses and various intercultural events.[76] This orientation is evident in the name *InPut*, where the abbreviation stands for *Integration in the Puster Valley*.[77]

Areas of Activity and Developments in Comparison

When comparing the organizations, it is initially noticeable that for a long time there was only the *Gastarbeiterseelsorge* in the federal state of Tyrol, which also provided social and cultural support. Only in the early 1970s, when the integration debate flared up for the first time, did state and economic entities (albeit less impactful) come into play. This may be because the issue of migration was more strongly perceived in the media, politics, and civil society during this time, and the prevailing notion was that the so-called guest workers would only stay in the country for a short period.[78]

Pastoral care centers were also established in other parts of Austria and in many other countries in the 1960s, primarily to support Croatian migrant workers. Caritas financed these centers but did not initiate their establishment. The KAJ was also responsible for the local administration. This may have been a reason why Croatian pastoral workers operated relatively independently from the local church and Caritas repeatedly questioned its share of the funding.[79]

In South Tyrol, the facilities were structurally more closely integrated into Caritas. In the 1990s, Caritas already established several positions for the areas of asylum and migration. This network was expanded in the 2000s and extended to additional municipalities beyond Bolzano. In 2004, *Don Tonino Bello* was founded in Merano, and in 2005, the *Chance* facility was added. In the same year, *InPut* started its activities in Brunico, and since 2006, the *Erstaufnahmezentrum für Einwanderer* in Bolzano has been operating in the newly built house *Migrantes*. The activities in these years are also a consequence of the EU enlargement in 2004. The funding usually comes from public tenders (EU, regional government, and municipalities). Financially and personnel-wise, the institutions in South Tyrol were better equipped from the start compared to the *Gastarbeiterseelsorge* in North and East Tyrol. The latter was only subsidized by the Caritas of the Diocese of

Innsbruck and the diocesan finance chamber and repeatedly had to struggle with infrastructural problems.

This situation is also linked to the different historical contexts. The so-called guest worker system in Austria was established in the 1960s during a time of full employment, high growth rates, and optimism about progress, and it was regulated through social partnership negotiations and bilateral agreements. The systematic use of labor occurred against the backdrop of the rise of tourism, industrial mass production, and consumption. The conditions contributing to the increasing relevance of migration in South Tyrol since the 1990s, on the other hand, included factors such as the collapse of socialism; the expansion of European integration leading to a common internal market and labor potential; and increased globalization characterized by economic interconnections, intensified competition in the global market, and developments in transportation and communication technologies that facilitate higher mobility of people. Additionally, the role of refugee and migration movements from Africa and Asia has become more significant in this context. While in the 1960s in North and East Tyrol, the situation of migrants was hardly present in the public consciousness, and the prevailing idea was that guest workers would only temporarily stay in the country, South Tyrol could build on the experiences of neighboring countries. Under integration policy perspectives, both in the state of Tyrol and in South Tyrol, there is now a broad field of specialized state, church, and non-governmental organizations working in the areas of asylum and migration.

There are also differences in the field of activity. In Innsbruck, social and cultural activities were offered in addition to pastoral care due to the practical work and lack of other facilities. With the establishment of a care center by the state of Tyrol, the areas of responsibility were defined, and the institution concentrated primarily on pastoral care and social support. Social counseling and support were increasingly taken over by the NGO *Ausländerberatungsstelle Tirol* (Foreigner Advisory Center Tyrol, now ZeMiT) from 1985 onwards. During the Yugoslav Wars, social assistance in the *Gastarbeiterseelsorge* was scaled back. While the institution now primarily focuses on pastoral care tasks, the Caritas of the Diocese of Innsbruck is currently particularly active towards refugees.[80]

In contrast, the offerings of Caritas of the Diocese of Bolzano-Brixen were specialized from the beginning, and the areas of responsibility were much clearer. While the *Gastarbeiterseelsorge* gradually specialized and lost significance over the years, the structures of Caritas for labor market policy and social support for migrants in South Tyrol remain important institutions. Services such as assistance with job and housing searches, legal advice, intercultural projects, and language courses do not fundamentally differ from non-religious NGOs specializing in this area. Caritas Bolzano-Brixen, which dealt with migration very early on, simultaneously had structures to offer social support and counseling for migrants.

Ideological Positions

With the establishment of an office dedicated not only to pastoral but also social care for migrant workers, the Catholic Church in Austria took up this issue very early on compared to state institutions. There are many reasons why the Church took on this task. Its ideological self-image was not an insignificant factor. Stuart Hall defined ideology in 1986 as "mental frameworks—the language, concepts, categories, images of thought and systems of imagination—that different classes and social groups develop in order to make sense of the workings of society, to define it, to shape it, to make it understandable."[81]

It can then be stated that ideology does not have to be understood as a false consciousness that conceals the underlying real conditions. Rather, a neutral concept of ideology can encompass "all organized forms of social thought."[82] They become effective by shaping ideas of the world, producing forms of representation, positioning subjects, flowing into social practices, and being reflected in material infrastructures. Ideologies also have a historical dimension, as they have grown historically and are subject to change. They connect to existing traditions and provide an interpretive repertoire for the past, present, and future. Ideologies usually operate implicitly in everyday life, appearing as unquestionable normality. This everyday understanding, *Alltagsverstand* as Antonio Gramsci referred to it, is, however, a constantly contested terrain of different interest groups and ideologies.[83]

These brief remarks make it clear that the support centers cannot be read independently of ideology, which made the necessity of their establishment plausible and justified the activities. Their effectiveness was evident not only in the establishment of the centers, the organizational structure and the composition of the staff, but also in the way in which migrants were addressed. The aim of the following discussions will therefore be to outline, in a comparative perspective, the ideological traces and the subject positions expressed in the support centers in the state of Tyrol and in South Tyrol.

Christian Archives and Migration

In the materials related to the *Gastarbeiterseelsorge* in North and East Tyrol, frequent reference is made to a *Christian archive.*[84] The way in which migration was discussed was therefore essentially shaped by content from the Bible. This can already be seen in the Apostolic Constitution *Exsul Familia* from 1952, which was central to the Catholic Church's stance on migration. Pope Pius XII declared in it:

"The exiled family of Nazareth, Jesus, Mary and Joseph, fleeing the wrath of the godless king, rises above all times and spaces both through their migration to Egypt and through their refugee life in Egypt, serving as a parable, model and protection for every kind of emigrant, foreigner and refugee who, for fear of persecution or under the pressure of need, are forced to leave their homeland, their dear parents and relatives, their dear friends and move to a foreign land."[85]

Furthermore, the support of migrants is part of an "all-encompassing mission of salvation entrusted by Christ," which also grants "spiritual care" to "strangers, new arrivals, displaced persons, emigrants."[86]

The outlined ideological positions reappear in the documents related to the *Gastarbeiterseelsorge* in Tyrol. A significant function was assigned to the task of *Christian charity*. From this, the equivalence of all people was derived, and support for migrant workers was declared a Christian program. An article in the *Gastarbeiter* supplement of the magazine *Wende* from March 28, 1971, for example, entitled *Social* "*Outsider.*" "The Fate of Christ—the Fate of Guest Workers," for example, draws analogies between the marginalization experienced by Jesus Christ and that of migrant workers. Supporting them would therefore ensure that "the Lord comes to resurrection in them."[87] This article was explicitly addressed to Catholic believers to raise awareness of migrants' situation and provide assistance from a Christian perspective. Another article in the magazine *Aktivist* of the KAJ stated boldly: "The guest worker is also your brother." With reference to the intended Catholic readership, it denounces the fact that migrant workers are treated as second-class citizens "by us Christians." Those who want to identify as "Christians" should not see them as "strangers" but must see them as "brothers." This call was explicitly directed at dealing with people of other faiths. Especially towards them, one should show so much "brotherhood" to break down "old prejudices."[88] This statement claims authority over the true interpretation of Christianity and connects it with the concept of *Christian charity* to demand the correct approach to migration. The media attention around the organized St. Nicholas celebrations also served as an opportunity to advocate for the social equality of migrant workers.[89] In doing so, the church officials distanced themselves from reducing people to their labor force.

However, the ideological positioning is also characterized by a missionary mandate. Sociologist Bernhard Giesen describes this sense of mission as characteristic of communities that carry out boundary drawing processes through universalistic coding. In this logic of interpretation, outsiders are potentially future members. The task for current members is therefore to recruit more people for the group. According to Giesen, such communities "start with the special idea of salvation or Parousia [that] presupposes a tension between a transcendent realm of the sacred, sublime, or transcendent and a mundane realm that needs to be transformed in the name of the sacred."[90]

This coding becomes evident in an article written in 1970 by Herbert Bucher, the secretary of the *Gastarbeiterseelsorge* in North and East Tyrol, in the magazine *Aktivist* of the KAJ. There, migrant workers were portrayed as victims of xenophobia, a circumstance that should be countered in the spirit of *Christian charity*. By setting such a good example, even people from "Mohammedan and communist countries" would be brought closer to Christianity, simultaneously providing "development aid and missionary work."[91] *Charity* becomes a missionary tool benefiting the Church and the fight against communism. Although the Vatican had already distanced itself from its fundamental opposition to communism in the 1960s, opting instead for diplomacy,[92] a critical stance persisted. The reality of a communist threat was demonstrated not least by events such as the violent suppression of the Hungarian uprising in 1956 and the Prague Spring in 1968.

If we follow Stuart Hall's understanding that representations receive their meaning in relational contexts, in which concepts and images are historically linked in a certain way to form a discourse, then the outlined explanations have a further dimension of meaning.[93] The linking of missionary work and development aid thus takes on a specific connotation against the backdrop of Christianity's colonial past. It actualizes a discourse of the *West and the rest*.[94] *Exsul Familia* already suggested that a colonial legacy and a missionary logic of interpretation were inscribed in the handling of migration. To justify support for migrants, the argument was made that, historically, the Church had always distinguished itself through pastoral care for strangers. The Christianization was affirmatively referred to as evidence:

"The joyful exuberance of the bishops and priests, who endeavored to bring the benefits of the true faith and humane forms of community to the inhabitants of the new territories, as well as to bring the incoming barbarian tribes, who were won over to the Christian religion and education in one go, into contact with the indigenous population, also shines.... When new lands were discovered in the other hemisphere of the earth, there was no lack of priests of Christ, who immediately set themselves to accompany those who founded settlements in those regions, on the one hand so that they would not lose Christian customs and so that presumption would not arise from the acquisition of earthly goods, and on the other hand so that suitable and willing messengers of the faith would be at hand to teach the natives, still completely unfamiliar with the divine light, the Gospel and to proclaim the duty to treat them as brothers."[95]

Based on the premise that the Christian faith has a universal claim to truth, it is implied that the spread of one's own ideology is obligatory and to be advocated. After all, it brings others a more human community, even the "divine light." Priests had a pioneering role in this, as they kept believers away from corrupting influences and saved those who were previously unbelievers. The fact that Christianity was used as a violent instrument of civilization in colonial contexts was ignored at this point. It fulfilled the function of legitimizing claims to power and at the same time forming a supposedly superior Western Christian identity.[96] The discourse on development aid and missionary work aligns with this context. In Bucher's updated way of speaking, a Eurocentric idea of development also coincides with a self-defined paternalistic pioneering role of Christianity. The postcolonial theorists Nikita Dhawan and María do Mar Castro-Varela argue that today the imaginary space of Europe, formerly occupied by the colonized, is now occupied by migrants. Migrants thus function as *the Others* in the construction of Western/European superiority.[97] In this context, *the Others* are people specifically with Muslim beliefs who are supposed to be convinced by Christianity and its superiority. The methods used in this context include good deeds, specifically solidarity with and support for migrant workers.

The colonial traces of this asymmetrical relationship can be seen even more clearly in paternalistic arguments. In an internal activity report from 1967, for example, the guest worker chaplain emphasized the need for a meeting room, stating that migrant workers should not be forced to go to the pub and "suspicious places" to expose themselves to corrupting influences. The general concern for the working class mentioned above and the aim of preventing them from leading a materialistic life through the Catholic faith is specified for migrants. Drunkenness, gambling, brawls, crime, (especially among men), but also unwanted pregnancies, (among women), are therefore the specific problems faced by migrant workers from the pastor's point of view.[98] In this paternalistic depiction, the migrant subject is a victim of social structures and morally corrupting influences. The Church, in this argumentative figure, assumes the self-defined vanguard role of protecting and guiding migrant workers onto the right path. It thus engages in sociopolitical work under a religious interpretive primacy.

The ambivalence of this ideological positioning becomes clear from the explanations outlined above. On the one hand, the *Christian archive* offers points of reference to motivate and legitimize social assistance through the concept of *Christian charity*. On the other hand, a missionary awareness and paternalism are inherent to it, which reproduces an asymmetrical discourse between the *West and the rest*.

Interplay of Integration Policy and Economic Rationality

The ideological reference point for Caritas' engagement in South Tyrol can initially be associated with (Catholic) Christianity. At its core was the universalistic concept of humanity. From this, Caritas derived the mission, in the spirit of *Christian charity*, to support all people in need. Caritas positioned itself as an "advocate for the disadvantaged," aiming to provide social assistance to migrants and raise awareness in the public about the social situation of immigrants. Accordingly, Caritas of the Diocese of Bolzano-Brixen was commissioned by the bishop in the 1990 statutes to ensure that "Christ's commandment of love remains alive in the attitude of the individual Christian and in the parish and diocesan community and is expressed in contemporary works that serve the overall human development of those in need." The service to the needy was explicitly justified "from faith," aiming to awaken "solidarity," the "readiness for charity," and the willingness for "service to the needy" among the "people of God." The service to the "needy" was also understood as an "expression of a Christian way of life."[99] In addition to the religious rationale for social assistance, the collaboration with the Mission Office of the Diocese, as stated in the statutes, indicated a missionary consciousness associated with charitable activities.

In contrast to pastoral care for migrant workers in the province of Tyrol, however, a profane service orientation plays a much greater role in South Tyrol. This is currently also reflected in other Caritas facilities. The gap between religious mission and pragmatically oriented assistance also led to tensions with the Vatican in this context. These came to the fore, for example, in a 2012 decree by Cardinal Tarcisio Bertone, Secretary of State, which reorganized the legal framework of *Caritas Internationalis*. To ensure the transmission of church messages, the Caritas umbrella organization was directly placed under Bertone and the papal council *Cor Omum*. As reported by *Dolomiten*, the most widely circulated German-language daily newspaper in South Tyrol, in 2012, tensions had long existed between Caritas and the Vatican regarding whether the spread of religious faith or concrete social assistance should take precedence.[100]

The secular orientation of Caritas was also evident in the sources examined in South Tyrol. In contrast to the *Gastarbeiterseelsorge*, professionalism was an essential criterion for justifying their work. The associated terminology, together with the relevant experience in supporting migrants, offered semantic points of reference for public funding. Although the ideological references of Caritas Bolzano-Brixen in the 1990 statutes are anchored in the Catholic Church, they are scarcely mentioned in the media's self-descriptions. The self-positioning is shown pointedly in a press release sent out in 2005 on the occasion of the launch of the *Chance* project. Regarding the specific target group of foreign women, it stated:

"It is important to us that the social situation of immigrant women . . . is improved. Many live in precarious situations . . . . She [a counselor, author's note] develops individual projects together with the women and in cooperation with the social assistants. These are intended to help the women enter the job market, find further training opportunities or language courses. [The counselor] gives career advice, provides support in the job search and helps with the preparation of CVs. The women are given tips for successful job interviews and receive information about further training and language courses. The foreign women are also given the opportunity to exchange ideas and support each other. Each measure focuses on the specific skills and abilities of the individual woman. . . . The women need a network that catches them and in which they are integrated. Then integration can succeed."[101]

This communication is marked by a secular rhetoric. Professionalism is presented to the outside world through the factual description of the status quo, the listing of a wide range of *target group-oriented* advisory services, the emphasis on a *cooperative* work process, *individually* tailored measures and the linking of specific *competences*[102] all presented with an integration policy agenda. The service orientation also appeals to the initiative of migrant women. The institution sees itself as a platform that aims to promote exchange between women. The advisors therefore work *with* them and support those who are willing to continue their education in the sense of *lifelong learning*.[103]

The central claim is to promote the individual skills of those willing to perform and to integrate migrant women as effectively as possible into the working world. Furthermore, the embedding of the institution in the Catholic Church was particularly evident on a symbolic level when *Chance* was officially opened on September 16, 2005, in the St. Nikolaus parish hall in Merano.[104]

The positioning aligns with the guidelines outlined in the project's announcement, creating a semantic framework.[105] Adherence to these guidelines is necessary to successfully attract funding. Accordingly, the Caritas service concept for a tender in Merano also included primarily profane wording. The title "individual, flexible, rational" was followed by references to the "Universal Declaration of Human Rights," the "Italian Constitution," and "humanist ideals." The company's own professional standards were also set out. Criteria such as "orientation towards participation and independence," "connection to resources and learning potential," "creativity and flexibility," "goal orientation," "competence," "willingness for further training," "supervision," and consideration of feedback from "clients" are not only used as reference points in the field of social work to legitimize activities and obtain project-related funding.[106] Instead, they can be understood against the broader background of the *economization of the social* and the accompanying restructuring of social work from a business perspective.[107]

Using the example of Caritas in South Tyrol, it is therefore possible to trace the historical shifts that have taken place in recent decades. First of all, there has been a redefinition of state tasks. Non-state actors have increased in importance. Many new organizations were founded and dedicated themselves to specialized areas of responsibility. Funding is mostly obtained through projects that must be reapplied for regularly and can therefore be handled flexibly. Due to their financial dependency, NGOs are also forced to align their rhetoric and project orientation with the criteria of funding bodies. The assumption of state tasks and the necessary orientation towards the tender texts can be read, with Michel Foucault, as a specific government rationality that shifts disciplinary forms of external management to the *self-management* of institutions and individuals.[108] The shift from external to self-governance through project calls and proposals is accompanied by the adoption of specific ways of thinking and acting that are reflected in the way migrants are addressed. While they were *sheep worthy of protection* in the Tyrolean *Gastarbeiterseelsorge*, they now represent an economic resource that should be integrated into the work cycle by means of "help for self-help."[109] In this context, the support offered can also be read as a form of *activation* of migrants in the sense of *self-government*.

Conclusion

The care of migrants played a role in the state of Tyrol and in South Tyrol at different times. In connection with the demand for labor in Austria in the 1960s, the number of migrant workers from Yugoslavia and Turkey also increased in Tyrol. As early as 1967, a *Gastarbeiterseelsorge* was set up there, mainly targeting people from the Yugoslav Republic of Croatia. The KAJ in Tyrol was responsible for the local administration. It was one of the lay organizations that were upgraded by the Second Vatican Council.

In addition to pastoral support, the KAJ also engaged in the social and cultural care of migrants. It was not until the 1970s, in connection with the integration debate at the time, that state and economic agencies were also founded, but these met with little response.

Towards the end of the 1980s, Caritas of the Diocese of Bolzano-Brixen began to deal with migration in South Tyrol and, from the 1990s onwards, set up a network of support services. One of the facilities was the *Erstaufnahmezentrum für Einwanderer/Migrantes. Don Tonino Bello* and *Chance* in Merano (run as *Moca* since 2012) and *InPut* in Brunico were added in the 2000s, particularly in the wake of the EU's eastward expansion. In contrast to the initial phase in the province of Tyrol, South Tyrol already had a differentiated and specialized range of support services right from the start. This is not surprising, as migration did not play a major role in South Tyrol until much later, and it was possible to build on experience from surrounding countries.

Both in the province of Tyrol and in South Tyrol, church institutions were the first to take on the care of migrants. This may have various reasons, but, according to my thesis, the ideological self-concept played a significant role. Here, substantial differences between the compared regions can be observed, explained by specific historical circumstances. While religious justifications were relevant in North and East Tyrol to justify engagement with migrants, institutions in South Tyrol positioned themselves as professional service providers. Accordingly, Christianity served as a crucial ideological reference point in the *Gastarbeiterseelsorge*. This references took a back seat at Caritas facilities in South Tyrol. There, it was primarily the positioning as a professional service provider and the recourse to general human rights that served to justify their own activities. Where missionary tasks and paternalism seemed evident in the *Gastarbeiterseelsorge*, fitting into a discourse of the *West and the rest*, the offer in South Tyrol focuses on *activating* migrants for economic and integration policy purposes.

The comparison showed that, although church support centers in North and East Tyrol and South Tyrol were similar in their services, offering cultural events as well as language courses and support in dealing with authorities and in finding work and accommodation, they differed greatly in many areas. These differences point to specific forms of development and social conditions in the state of Tyrol and in South Tyrol. However, they also provide an insight into different temporal contexts in which the outlined ideological traces can be located.

Endnotes

1. This paper is an updated and shortened version of a previously published German-language contribution: Marcel Amoser, "Caritas und Migration im Bundesland Tirol und in Südtirol," *Tiroler Heimat* 82 (2018): 333–364.

2. On contemporary migration research in Austria, see Dirk Rupnow, "Migration," in *Österreichische Zeitgeschichte - Zeitgeschichte in Österreich. Eine Standortbestimmung in Zeiten des Umbruchs*, ed. Marcus Gräser, and Dirk Rupnow (Vienna: Böhlau, 2021), 236–262. On the more recent history of migration in Tyrol and South Tyrol, see for example, Marcel Amoser, Sarah Oberbichler, and Eva Pfanzelter, *Von Zugewanderten, Weggegangenen und Dagebliebenen. Beiträge zur Migrationsgeschichte Kufsteins 1930–2000* (Kufstein: self-published, 2022); Sarah Oberbichler, *Autochthone Minderheiten und Migrant*innen. Mediale Argumentationsstrategien von 1990 bis 2015 am Beispiel Südtirols* (Innsbruck, Vienna: StudienVerlag, 2020); Gerhard Hetfleisch, "Migration in transnationalen Kontexten. Die Anwerbung von Filipinas in den 1970er-Jahren durch Missionare der St.-Josefs-Missionsgesellschaft von Mill Hill zu Brixen und Absam," *Tiroler Heimat* 82 (2018): 301–332; Eva Pfanzelter, and Dirk Rupnow, eds., *einheimisch - zweiheimisch - mehrheimisch. Geschichte(n) der neuen Migration in Südtirol* (Bolzano: Raetia, 2017).

3. Hartmut Kaelble, *Der historische Vergleich. Eine Einführung zum 19. und 20. Jahrhundert* (Frankfurt, New York: Campus, 1999), 13.

4. For the exceptions, see for example, Laura Volgger, "Integration und Emanzipation durch Selbstorganisation" (diploma thesis, Innsbruck University, 2019); Kurt Gritsch, "Migration und Migrant_innennetzwerke in Südtirol: Spezifika einer historischen Sonderentwicklung," *Tiroler Heimat* 82 (2018): 269–300; Roberta Medda-Windischer, Gerhard Hetfleisch, and Maren Meyer, eds., *Migration in Südtirol und Tirol. Analysen und multidisziplinäre Perspektiven* (Bolzano: Athesia, 2011).

5. Historical studies are usually devoted to comparisons of different (especially national) territories in the same temporal context. A time-shifted comparison, on the other hand, looks for similarities and differences between territories at different times. Especially when certain processes took place in different areas at different times, this form of comparison can make sense in order to find out how the processes were dealt with in the respective units of investigation. This method is particularly useful when comparing institutions, (in this case, church support centers for migrants), whose development is closely linked to processes that occurred at different times (in this case, increasing immigration). On this basis, more general ways of dealing with and interpreting the situation can be worked out, but also the view for specifics can be sharpened. However, this approach also requires that the respective historical contexts are carefully considered. Kaelble, *Der historische Vergleich*, 15–16, 144–145.

6. Eva Pfanzelter, and Dirk Rupnow, "Einleitung," in *einheimisch - zweiheimisch – mehrheimisch*, Pfanzelter and Rupnow, 9–18.

7. Interviews not yet recorded by the *Dokumentationsarchiv Migration Tirol* (DAM)

and the *Datenarchiv der Migration in Südtirol* (DAMS). On the DAMS, see, "Datenarchiv der Migration in Südtirol," https://zeitgeschichte-suedtirolmigration.uibk.ac.at (2016), accessed Dec. 28, 2023, https://zeitgeschichte-suedtirolmigration.uibk.ac.at/omeka/collections/browse; on the DAM, see, Marcel Amoser, Karl C. Berger, Gerhard Hetfleisch, and Christina Hollomey-Gasser, "Migration sammeln, vermitteln, ausstellen und archivieren. Das Beispiel einer Kooperation aus Tirol," *Austrian Journal of Historical Studies* 29, no. 3 (2018): 202–214.

8. Not yet indexed holdings on the *Katholische Arbeiterjugend* and the *Gastarbeiterseelsorge*. Diözesanarchiv Innsbruck (DAI).

9. Unlisted holdings of Caritas of the Diocese of Bolzano-Brixen. Caritas Archive of the Diocese of Bolzano-Brixen (CABB).

10. Landesinstitut für Statistik. Autonome Provinz Bozen-Südtirol, "Statistische Jahrbücher für Südtirol des Landesinstituts für Statistik (ASTAT)," *astat.provinz.bz.it* (2022), accessed Dec. 28, 2023, https://astat.provinz.bz.it/de/statistisches-jahrbuch.asp; Sicherheitsdirektion Tirol, Vereinsakten, 1221–1222, Tiroler Landesarchiv (TLA).

11. Gerhard Hetfleisch, "Auf vielen Wegen nach Tirol: Aspekte der Zuwanderungsgeschichte Tirols in der Zweiten Republik," in *einheimisch - zweiheimisch - mehrheimisch*, Pfanzelter and Rupnow, 117–132 (here 121). On the significance of remittances for transnational migration processes, see Claudius Ströhle and Silke Meyer, eds., *Remittances as Social Practices and Agents of Change. The Future of Transnational Society* (Cham: Palgrave Macmillan, 2023).

12. Kurt Buchenau, *Orthodoxie und Katholizismus in Jugoslawien 1945–1991*, (Wiesbaden: Harrasowitz, 2004), 275.

13. Othmar Nikola Haberl, *Die Abwanderung von Arbeitskräften aus Jugoslawien. Zur Problematik ihrer Auslandsbeschäftigung und ihrer Rückführung*, (Munich: Oldenbourg, 1978), 279.

14. Buchenau, *Orthodoxie*, 99–103, 272–276.

15. Sabine Falch, "Heimatfern. Die Südtiroler Arbeitsmigration der 50er und 60er Jahre" (PhD diss., Innsbruck University, 2001), 9–16.

16. Falch, "Heimatfern," 32–33, 42.

17. Siglinde Clementi, "Conservative Renewal. Von den Hilfspaketen zur Stillen Hilfe," in *Das 20. Jahrhundert in Südtirol*, vol. 3, ed. Gottfried Solderer (Bozen: Raetia, 2001), 130–155 (here 136).

18. Kurt Gritsch, "Migrationsnetzwerke in Südtirol: Organisationen von und für Migranten. Eine zeithistorische Bestandsaufnahme," in *einheimisch – zweiheimisch – mehrheimisch*, Pfanzelter and Rupnow, 211–226 (here 212).

19. *ASTAT* (2000), 99; *ASTAT* (2010), 111; *ASTAT Info*, no. 5 (2017), 1.

20. Rainer Girardi, and Eva Pfanzelter, "Migration in Zahlen: Ein- und Auswanderung in Südtirol in den amtlichen Statistiken," in *einheimisch - zweiheimisch - mehrheimisch*, Pfanzelter and Rupnow, 43–66 (here 47).

21. Bericht über die Gastarbeiterseelsorge in Tirol, 21.12.1966, 3, DAI; Interview

Julia Tapfer with Franz Kripp (former director of Caritas Diocese of Bolzano-Brixen), Bolzano Pastoral Center, Feb. 11, 2015, 2, DAMS.

22. An overview of the role of the Catholic Church and its relationship to colonial expansion: Jürgen Osterhammel, *Kolonialismus. Geschichte – Formen – Folgen* (Munich: C. H. Beck, 1995), 101–107.

23. Rudo-Smiljan Radić, "Der Kroatische Gastarbeiter in Tirol" (diploma thesis, Innsbruck University, 1973), 15–16.

24. Frano Prcela, "Kroatische katholische Missionen in Westeuropa," *G2W – Glaube in der 2. Welt. Ökumenisches Forum für Glauben, Religion und Gesellschaft in Ost und West*, no. 5 (2011): 16–18; Buchenau, *Orthodoxie*, 286.

25. Ibid., 288.

26. Ibid., 291, 355–359.

27. Bericht über die Gastarbeiterseelsorge in Tirol, December 21, 1966, 3–4, DAI.

28. Helmut Alexander, "Bischof DDr. Paul Rusch (1903–1986). Eine biographische Skizze," in *Bischof Paulus Rusch. Wächter und Lotse in stürmischer Zeit*, ed. Helmut Alexander and Bernhard Kriegbaum (Innsbruck: Verlag Kirche, 2004), 9–31 (here 21–23). Tyrol was not a special case with the establishment of such pastoral care centers. Similar developments were reconstructed for Styria by the historian Verena Lorber: Verena Lorber, *Angeworben. GastarbeiterInnen in Österreich in den 1960ern und 1970ern* (Göttingen: V&R, 2017), 174–182.

29. In this context, Rusch advocated cooperation based on social partnership and moderate socialism as early as the 1950s. He was therefore called "the red bishop" by both conservative opponents and supporters. Alexander, "Bischof," 23-24. Annemarie Fenzl, "Der rote Bischof", in *Bischof Paulus Rusch. Wächter und Lotse in stürmischer Zeit*, ed. Helmut Alexander, and Bernhard Kriegbaum (Innsbruck: Verlag Kirche, 2004), 32–49 (here 38–42).

30. Birgit Pomella, "Die historische Entwicklung der Südtiroler Caritas" (diploma thesis, Innsbruck University, 2014), 141.

31. *ASTAT* (2016), 118.

32. Pomella, "Historische Entwicklung," 126–139.

33. "Caritas Diözese Bozen-Brixen," https://caritas.bz.it (2023), accessed December 28, 2023, http://www.caritas.bz.it/.

34. Die Hoffnung auf Glück, *Caritas-Sonntag. ArMut, etwas dagegen tun*, 2000, 16, CABB.

35. 110 Freiwillige setzen sich für Flüchtlinge ein, *Das andere Südtirol. Wirkungsbericht 2015*, 2016, 8, CABB.

36. Bericht des Arbeiterseelsorgers Marijan Kopic, Nov. 2, 1967, 1; Bericht über die Gastarbeiterseelsorge in Tirol, Dec. 21, 1966, 3–4. Schreiben an Johann Grieser betreff Hilfsfond für jugoslawische Theologen, Nov. 29, 1968, DAI.

37. Offizieller Bericht des Seelsorgers der jugoslawischen Gastarbeiter in der Diözese Innsbruck, January–March, 1968, 3, DAI.

38. Bericht des Arbeiterseelsorgers Marijan Kopic, November 2, 1967, 2; Offizieller Bericht des Seelsorgers der jugoslawischen Gastarbeiter der Diözese Innsbruck, November–December, 1967, 2–3, DAI.

39. Bericht über die Gastarbeiterseelsorge in Tirol, January–February, 1967, 2, DAI.

40. Offizieller Bericht des Seelsorgers der jugoslawischen Gastarbeiter in der Diözese Innsbruck, January–May, 1969, 2, DAI.

41. Offizieller Bericht des Seelsorgers der jugoslawischen Gastarbeiter in der Diözese Innsbruck, November–December, 1967, 4, DAI.

42. "Nikolausfeier für jugoslawische Arbeiter," *Tiroler Tageszeitung*, December 6, 1966, 3, DAI.

43. "Die Lösung des Gastarbeiterproblems: ‚Junger Arbeiter' viersprachig," *Kathpress*, April 29, 1967, DAI.

44. "Gastarbeiter," *Aktivist*, August–September, 1967, 23, DAI.

45. Offizieller Bericht des Seelsorgers der jugoslawischen Gastarbeiter in der Diözese Innsbruck, January–March, 1968, 3, DAI.

46. Bericht für die Gastarbeiterbetreuung, August 1, 1970–May 30, 1971, DAI.

47. Schreiben der Caritas an Olujić betreff Spesenbeihilfen, July 16, 1971, DAI.

48. Bericht des Gastseelsorgers Marijan Kopic aus der Tätigkeit der Gastarbeiterseelsorge, April–September, 1968, 1; Gastarbeiter-Seelsorge in unserer und anderen österreichischen Diözesen (Auflistung anlässlich der Besprechung betreffend die Gastarbeiterseelsorge), December 16, 1969, DAI.

49. Offizieller Bericht des Seelsorgers der jugoslawischen Gastarbeiter in der Diözese Innsbruck, November–December, 1967, 4, DAI.

50. Offizieller Bericht des Seelsorgers der jugoslawischen Gastarbeiter in der Diözese Innsbruck, January–March, 1968, 4, DAI.

51. "Wir kommen doch nicht aus der Wildnis," *Tiroler Tageszeitung*, March 9, 1968, DAI.

52. Offizieller Bericht des Seelsorgers der jugoslawischen Gastarbeiter in der Diözese Innsbruck, January–May, 1969, 1, DAI.

53. Tätigkeitsbericht über das abgelaufene Arbeitsjahr, May 15, 1971–May 15, 1972, 2–3, DAI.

54. Schreiben von Msgr. Hans-Joachim Schramm an Pater Pero Skopljak OFM, September 1, 1971, DAI.

55. Schreiben des Seelsorgeamtsleiters an Guido Mark betreff Gastarbeiterseelsorge, June 26, 1972, DAI.

56. Tätigkeitsbericht über das abgelaufene Arbeitsjahr, May 15, 1971–May 15, 1972, 2, DAI.

57. On the beginnings of the integration discourse in Austria: Dirk Rupnow, "Ausländerforschung. Frühe Studien zu den Gastarbeitern in den 1970er Jahren," in *Wandlungen und Brüche. Wissenschaftsgeschichte als politische Geschichte*, ed.

Johannes Feichtinger et al. (Göttingen: Vienna University Press, 2018), 363–372; Stefanie Schmiderer, "Integration: Schlagwort - Zauberwort - hohles Wort. Eine historische und begriffliche Auseinandersetzung im Kontext der österreichischen Immigrationsgeschichte (1970–2000)" (diploma thesis, Vienna University, 2008). On the institutions and the integration policy orientation, see, "Öffentlichkeit erinnert sich nun an Gastarbeiter," *Tiroler Tageszeitung*, February 26, 1972, DAM; "Höchste Zeit für Integration der Gastarbeiter," *Tiroler Nachrichten*, April 22, 1971, DAI; Statuten der Österreichisch-Türkischen und der Österreichisch-Jugoslawischen Gesellschaft in Tirol, Sicherheitsdirektion Tirol, Vereinsakten, 1221–1222, TLA.

58. On the lack of resonance, see Ligia Staudinger, *Die Gastarbeiterbeschäftigung in der Eisen- und Metallindustrie Tirols* (Innsbruck: Wagner, 1974), 87–89; Interview Marcel Amoser with Peter Koller (former head of the *Betreuungsstelle für Gastarbeiter des Landes Tirol* and member of the KAJ), ZeMiT Innsbruck, October 7, 2015, line 256–280; Interview Marcel Amoser with Peter Reiter (former head of the *Gastarbeiterreferat der Handelskammer* and co-initiator of the *Gesellschaft zur Betreuung von Gastarbeitern in Tirol*), ZeMiT Innsbruck, June 3, 2015, line 207–240, DAM.

59. Maßnahmenkatalog und Protokoll der Arbeitstagung, November 15, 1971, Vienna, DAI.

60. Lorber, *Angeworben*, 72–74, 174–182.

61. "Eröffnung des Aufnahmezentrums Migrantes für Einwanderer," *sozialbetrieb.bz.it* (February 15, 2006), accessed Dec. 28, 2018, http://www.sozialbetrieb.bz.it/de/1063.asp.

62. Die Hoffnung auf Glück, *Caritas-Sonntag. ArMut, etwas dagegen tun*, 2000, 16, CABB.

63. Interview Julia Tapferer, and Kurt Gritsch with Danilo Tucconi (former head of Migrantes Bolzano), Migrantes Bolzano, August 6, 2015, 1–3, DAMS.

64. *Gli utenti del servizio Consulenza,* in: *Migrantes. Servizio di consulenza e accoglienza migranti. Relazione annuale 2016*, 2017, 7–8, CABB.

65. Interview Tucconi, 3, DAMS.

66. Technisches Angebot der Caritas zur Durchführung des Dienstes Betreuung und Beratung von Personen mit Migrationshintergrund sowie allgemeiner Informationsdienst in Ausländerfragen in Meran, undated, CABB.

67. Ausländische Frauen im Blick, *Caritas-info*, no. 3/5, 2005, 9, CABB.

68. Presseaussendung Beratung für arbeitslose ausländische Frauen, September 16, 2005, CABB.

69. Memorandum Fusione Chance – Don Tonino Bello Insieme per l'inclusione, November 9, 2010, CABB.

70. Presseaussendung Beratung für arbeitslose ausländische Frauen, September 16, 2005, CABB.

71. Technisches Angebot der Caritas zur Durchführung des Dienstes Betreuung

und Beratung von Personen mit Migrationshintergrund sowie allgemeiner Informationsdienst in Ausländerfragen in Meran, undated, CABB.

72. *Consulenza per migranti Moca. Relazione annuale 2012*, 2013, 11–16, CABB.

73. *Jahresbericht Sozialsprengel Bruneck/Umgebung 2005*, 2006, 33; Presseaussendung Einladung zur offiziellen Eröffnung der MigrantInnenberatung InPut, April 13, 2006; "Hilfe für Beratung," *Südtiroler Tageszeitung*, Jan. 10, 2012, CABB.

74. *Jahresbericht InPut 2016*, 2017, 9, CABB.

75. "InPut für unsere Gesellschaft," *Dolomiten*, April 22/23, 2006, CABB.

76. *Jahresbericht InPut 2016*, 2017, 9, CABB.

77. "InPut für unsere Gesellschaft," *Dolomiten*, April 22/23, 2006, CABB.

78. The *guest worker* concept did not provide for long-term immigration. Employment permits were issued for a maximum of one year based on quota agreements negotiated by the social partners for specific sectors with a need for workers. However, the system soon became obsolete in practice, as many people stayed in Austria permanently and brought their families to join them. Schmiderer, "Integration," 18–24.

79. Lorber, *Angeworben*, 38.

80. As this article focuses on the early days of church-organized counselling and support for migrants, it is not possible to go into more detail about the current work of Caritas in Tyrol. A comparison of current Caritas work in North-East and South Tyrol would certainly be promising to analyze how and whether a profane service orientation now dominates over religiously based assistance in the state of Tyrol as well.

81. Stuart Hall, "Ideologie und Ökonomie. Marxismus ohne Gewähr," in *Ideologie, Identität. Repräsentation (Ausgewählte Schriften 4)*, ed. Stuart Hall, fourth edition (Hamburg: Argument, 2013), 8–33 (here 10).

82. Ibid.,11.

83. Ibid., 28–31.

84. In this context, I use the term archive in a metaphorical sense. It describes a powerful epistemic order or a traditional repertoire of interpretation. For an insight into post-structuralist-inspired archive theories, see, Marlene Manoff, "Theories of the Archive from Across the Disciplines," *Libraries and the Academy* 4, no. 1 (2004): 9–25.

85. Papst Pius XII, "Apostolische Konstitution Exsul familia über die geistliche Betreuung der Auswanderer," *kathpedia.com* (August 1, 1952), 1, accessed Dec. 28, 2023, http://www.kathpedia.com/index.php?title=Exsul_familia_(Wortlaut).

86. Pius XII, "Apostolische," 4.

87. "Soziale Outsider. Schicksal Christi – Schicksal Gastarbeiter," *Wende*, March 28, 1971, 11, DAI.

88. "Auch der Gastarbeiter ist dein Bruder!," *Aktivist*, December 1966–January

1967, DAI.

89. "Nikolausfeier für jugoslawische Arbeiter," *Tiroler Tageszeitung*, December 6, 1966, 3, DAI.

90. Bernhard Giesen, *Kollektive Identität. Die Intellektuellen und die Nation 2* (Berlin: Suhrkamp 1999), 54.

91. Herbert Bucher, "Austria nix gut! Erfahrungen mit Gastarbeitern," *Aktivist*, December 1967–January 1968, 21–22, DAI.

92. Roland Verny-Werner, and Rainer Gries, "Der Vatikan und der Ostblock im Kalten Krieg," *bpb.de* (December 18, 2008), accessed Dec. 28, 2023, http://www.bpb.de/apuz/32272/der-vatikan-und-der-ostblock-im-kalten-krieg?p=all; Thomas Bremer, *Kleine Geschichte der Religionen in Jugoslawien. Königreich – Kommunismus – Krieg* (Freiburg: Herder, 2003), 44–47; Buchenau, *Orthodoxie*, 309–317.

93. Stuart Hall, "Cultural Studies, Postmoderne und Artikulation. Ein Interview mit Stuart Hall," in *Cultural Studies. Ein politisches Theorieprojekt (Ausgewählte Schriften 3)*, ed. Stuart Hall (Hamburg: Argument, 2002), 52–77.

94. Stuart Hall, "Der Westen und der Rest: Diskurs und Macht," in *Rassismus und kulturelle Identität (Ausgewählte Schriften 2)*, ed. Stuart Hall (Hamburg: Argument, 2016), 137–179.

95. Pius XII, "Apostolische," 6–8.

96. Hall, "Der Westen," 137–179; Iman Attia, and Mariam Popal, "Antimuslimischer Rassismus dekolonial. Kontrapunktische Lektüren westlicher Islamdiskurse," *Das Argument* 319, no. 5 (2016), 651–660.

97. Nikita Dhawan, and María do Mar Castro Varela, "Migration und die Politik der Repräsentation," in *Re-Präsentationen. Dynamiken der Migrationsgesellschaft*, ed. Paul Mecheril, and Anne Broden, (Düsseldorf: self-published, 2007), 29–46.

98. Bericht des Arbeiterseelsorgers Marijan Kopic, November 2, 1967, 2–4 u. 7.

99. Pomella, "Historische Entwicklung," 165–169.

100. "Caritas soll ‚katholischer' sein," *Dolomiten*, May 12/13, 2012, CABB.

101. Presseaussendung Einladung zur offiziellen Einweihung von Projekt "Chance," September 13, 2005, 1–2, CABB.

102. The educational scientist Bernd Lederer has worked out the implications of the term and interpreted it as a sign of the economization of the social. Bernd Lederer, *Kompetenz oder Bildung? Eine Analyse jüngerer Konnotationsverschiebungen des Bildungsbegriffs und Plädoyer für eine Rück- und Neubesinnung auf ein transinstrumentelles Bildungsverständnis* (Innsbruck: Innsbruck University Press, 2014), 265–268, 390–421.

103. On the governmental logic of the concept of *lifelong learning* using the example of adult education, see, Daniela Rothe, *Lebenslanges Lernen als Programm. Eine diskursive Formation in der Erwachsenenbildung* (Frankfurt, New York: Campus, 2011).

104. Presseaussendung Einladung zur offiziellen Einweihung von Projekt "Chance," September 13, 2005, 1–2, CABB.

105. Lastenheft für die Vergabe des Dienstes Betreuung und Beratung von Personen mit Migrationshintergrund sowie allgemeiner Informationsdienst in Ausländerfragen in Meran, 2011, CABB.

106. Technisches Angebot der Caritas zur Durchführung des Dienstes Betreuung und Beratung von Personen mit Migrationshintergrund sowie allgemeiner Informationsdienst in Ausländerfragen in Meran, undated, CABB.

107. Michael Buestrich, and Norbert Wohlfahrt, "Die Ökonomisierung der sozialen Arbeit," *bpb.de* (March 6, 2008), accessed Dec. 28, 2023, http://www.bpb.de/apuz/31339/die-oekonomisierung-der-sozialen-arbeit?p=all.

108. Ulrich Bröckling, Thomas Lemke, and Susanne Krasmann, eds., *Gouvernementalität der Gegenwart. Studien zur Ökonomisierung des Sozialen* (Frankfurt: Suhrkamp 2000).

109. *Jahresbericht Migrant(innen)beratung InPut 2012*, 2013, 6, CABB.

US Intelligence in Austria: A Provincial View[1]

Duncan Bare and Siegfried Beer

Introduction

This article examines the activities of US intelligence in postwar Austria from a regional perspective. Intelligence, particularly in the modern era, is often understood in geopolitical terms and/or as it impacts (inter)national security; however, it does have regional and local contexts. Despite its small size, regional differences in Austria are pronounced owing to the specific historic role played by the *Provinz* vis-à-vis the erstwhile imperial center and capital city, Vienna. For any intelligence service to have focused exclusively on the Austrian capital or other significant urban areas in Austria would have neglected large swathes of the populace and country. Then, as now, intelligence services needed to be vigilant of local, regional, national, and international phenomena, particularly since they were attached to the occupational forces. As such, this article seeks to shed light on how US intelligence applied and operated regionally in Austria during the immediate postwar period, and not merely in Vienna or other large cities. In so doing, our approach is one of intelligence historians examining the regional aspects of their area of expertise, and not the converse (regional historians examining intelligence).

In an organizational sense, our focus encompasses the Office of Strategic Services (OSS), Strategic Services Unit (SSU), and Central Intelligence Group (CIG)/Office of Special Operations (OSO). Chronologically, the period from May 1945 up to May 1946 and October 19, 1946, is discussed. While this overlooks the considerable efforts of other US intelligence agencies active in Austria, such as the Counter-Intelligence Corps (CIC), US Army G-2, and US Military Intelligence Division (MID)/Military Intelligence Service (MIS), as well as the State Department, it allows more attention to be devoted to Austria as a region itself.[2]

This approach was chosen since OSS/SSU records are believed entirely declassified up to October 19, 1946.[3] As OSS operated in Austria from shortly after the end of hostilities in May 1945, (and had several intelligence teams in Austria at that time), an exploration of its efforts provides a continuous picture of the intelligence situation within the whole country. Nevertheless, it is prudent to divide this into several periods of activity.

This first stage, which started in May 1945, drew to a close at the beginning of October that year with OSS's (earlier than anticipated) liquidation and subsequent division into SSU (consisting largely of OSS's Secret Intelligence or SI, and Counter-Intelligence, or X-2 branches) and Interim Research and Intelligence Service (IRIS—entailing OSS's Research and Analysis, R&A branch). SSU became the War Department's charge, whereas IRIS was situated within the US State Department and largely ceased operation outside of the United States, signaling a second stage in our study.

In the spring of 1946, the third stage began, as SSU's SI and X-2 branches were reorganized into the Foreign Reports Branch (FRB) and Security Control Branch (SCB), both of which formed the Foreign Security Reports Office (FSRO).[4] According to a CIA historical survey, this "placed the personnel of these two branches in physical juxtaposition in each geographic and country area" and was a precursor to the Central Intelligence Group's (CIG) Office of Special Operation (OSO).[5]

For the purposes of this article, the bulk of OSS Austria became SSU Austria in October 1945 before undergoing a reorganization and name change in the middle of June 1946 into "OSO Austria."[6] By October 19, 1946, field- and headquarters-based components of SSU were *pro forma* dissolved, with all personnel terminated and many rehired on the following day to CIG/OSO.[7]

Despite the frequent and confusing changes in organization within a relatively brief period, the personnel, approaches, and methods remained largely consistent from October 1945 until October 1946. Continuity with both OSS Austria and its predecessors (Secret Intelligence Central Europe's German-Austria desk and the Vienna City Unit) extending back to the summer of 1944 allows our approach to present a nearly unbroken view of field-based US intelligence on Austria from the summer of 1944 until October 1946.[8]

A second clarification concerns the meaning of "provincial." In an Austrian context, this includes everything outside of Vienna a lá "*Wien ist nicht Österreich, und Österreich ist nicht Wien.*"[9] Approached in a more scientific manner, the country's regional capitals (eight, excluding Vienna) or statutory cities (thirteen as of 1938, again excluding Vienna) might serve as a useful criterion for differentiation. However, here too there are complications; only six have populations above 100,000 (Vienna, Graz, Linz, Salzburg, Innsbruck, and Klagenfurt), and even then, despite their sizes, some, like Klagenfurt and Innsbruck would be seen by few as "cosmopolitan" in character. Several of the remaining cities are regional centers with populations in the low tens of thousands.

From the perspective of an urbane thirty-year-old US intelligence officer, likely university-educated, most, if not all, of Austria would seem "provincial" outside of Vienna and (possibly) Salzburg. Luckily (or unluckily) for the purposes of this study, OSS intelligence gathering in Austria was initially organized into branches that bore responsibility for different parts of the country, large swathes of which both then and now would be seen almost entirely as "provincial."[10]

At the same time, the regional approach of OSS/SSU intelligence in Austria means that no single branch or mission was exclusively responsible for "provincial" areas. SI, X-2, and R&A operated in or gathered intelligence on the *Provinz* at various times, as will be demonstrated below. As an example, the Salzburg office did not initially address the "Land" of its namesake (for which a separate office was created), but rather coordinated several different desks and branches, many of which operated outside of Austria's modern borders. Thus, although tempting, it would be incorrect to state that, upon consolidation in October 1945, SSU Austria used its presence in Vienna to handle "high-level" or international intelligence and its Salzburg facilities for "provincial" matters. On many occasions, the reverse was true.

To fix our spatial dimensions, apart from their role as headquarters or bases for operating in the province and gathering intelligence there, cities, either as operational areas or where intelligence targets could be pursued, shall not be discussed here in depth. This relates primarily to Vienna, Salzburg, Linz, Innsbruck, Zell am See, and Klagenfurt, as OSS and SSU maintained offices in each at various times.[11]

We intend to examine US intelligence *am Land* i.e., in and on the countryside, as it would likely have been seen by US intelligence officers of the period (and almost certainly remains to this date). In this way, this section's approach follows the urban/rural and center/periphery cleavage(s) more common to political science or sociology.

The third approximation relates to the final word, "perspective." Here, we intend to discuss both what sort of information US intelligence received on the "provincial" areas of Austria as well as how it conducted intelligence activities there that, under "normal" conditions, would likely not have occurred. A good example of the latter is offered by the large numbers of displaced persons (DPs) and non-Austrians who could be found throughout the Austrian countryside in the immediate aftermath of the Second World War. Among them, forced laborers, concentration and death camp survivors, non-Germanic soldiers of either Nazi Germany or its allies, no-longer accredited foreign (Axis) diplomats, and others added noticeable non-provincial flairs to the Austrian countryside and, on occasion, became entangled (either willingly or unwillingly) in US intelligence matters.

Coupled with this, several early OSS reports from Austria concerned small towns that had been occupied and subsequently relinquished by the Red Army or discussed OSS teams that had been overrun by Soviet forces. These provide a unique and largely unfettered glimpse into the brutality of the Red Army and the Soviet Union. One can convincingly argue that, just as had been the case in Romania (as witnessed by Lt. Cmdr. Frank G. Wisner) and Bulgaria (as witnessed by Lt. Harry H. Harper) earlier in 1944 and 1945, OSS interactions with the Red Army in Austria, and the reports they generated, quickly helped many field-based OSS officers identify the limits of their Soviet ally's "goodwill" and get a healthy, first-hand dose of their cynicism and brutality.[12] These insights, gained in the autumn and winter of 1944, would be further sharpened over the course of 1945 as many Mediterranean-based OSS veterans shifted to Austria, bringing with them their past experiences and informed biases. Any remaining hopes for rapprochement with the Soviet Union/Red Army were quickly dashed within SSU Austria (and likely, most of the other US intelligence agencies operating in Austria) by early 1946, at the latest.[13]

In addition, the winter of 1945/46 saw large amounts of tactical and order of battle intelligence on both the Soviet and Yugoslav armies gathered by SSU Austria (from March 1946, these were its first and second priorities, followed as a third by "high-level Austrian political reporting").[14] This too necessitated access to the *Provinz*, since military units were then, as now, mainly based on the outskirts of cities or in remote areas, outside of public view. Along the Yugoslav-Austrian border, this issue was even more precarious as partisan incursions into modern-day Styria were common. To resolve this "spatial" issue, an example of each perspective is offered: intelligence activities in the *Provinz* (oriented at "non-provincial" targets) as well as reflective reports on the *Provinz* itself.

Finally, a few words are due about our structure. We begin by briefly examining OSS Austria's intelligence-gathering efforts (SI, X-2, and R&A) in Austria before providing a summary of provincial activities from May–October 1945. After that, the same is done for SSU and OSO Austria (SI/FRB and X-2/SCB).

OSS Austria (May[15]–October 1945)

As various elements of OSS trickled into Austria in May 1945, three of its five intelligence gathering branches (SI, X-2, and R&A) established themselves on its territory. Most personnel congregated around Salzburg and would remain there for the majority of OSS Austria's (brief) existence. Satellite offices were established in Innsbruck (closed in July 1945), Klagenfurt (closed in June 1945), Linz (closed in October 1945), and Zell am See (closed in

October 1945), largely conforming to the (C) Variant of the FREEBORN plan, which had been developed earlier in the year.[16] As the summer of 1945 wore on, however, most OSS personnel were (predictably) attached to the Salzburg, and later Vienna, "offices."[17] By the middle of October 1945, except for a small station in Trieste, which is outside the scope of this study, SSU Austria's personnel were based entirely in Salzburg and Vienna.

The primary responsibilities of SI and X-2 personnel in the immediate postwar period were denazification, the hunt for Axis war criminals, and ascertaining the existence of an *Alpenfestung*, along with any stay-behind "*Werewolf*" groups, even though the likelihood of the latter two had largely been written off by the time the first OSS units entered Austria. In these areas, SI and X-2 rarely collaborated, and X-2 worked closer with CIC in Austria, particularly in Salzburg, Zell am See, and Linz, where X-2 maintained small branch offices alongside the larger SI and later R&A components.[18] As an additional postwar responsibility, OSS Austria's SI personnel needed to establish contact with the eleven teams they had operating in Austria at the end of hostilities.[19]

SI's denazification efforts were primarily realized within two different frameworks: The first was the search for those who had committed war crimes against US personnel, specifically members of OSS.[20] As many OSS Austria personnel had been or still were part of SICE, there was no shortage of desire to seek out those who had executed colleagues and friends, particularly from the ill-fated Dawes group, which had been captured in the Slovak hinterland and summarily executed at Mauthausen.[21] The second and related denazification focus SI pursued was undertaken by SICE's Hungarian Desk and its chief, Martin Himler. These efforts centered on identifying, interrogating, and turning over to Hungarian authorities the large number of prospective Hungarian war criminals and Nazis who were in Austria at the end of the war.[22] In addition, SI pursued a range of other intelligence gathering activities intended to gain insight into the political and economic landscape of postwar Austria.

R&A, the last of the three branches to physically arrive in Austria, (towards the end of May 1945), set to work almost immediately on supporting the military government in economic and agricultural matters, the most pressing of which was the food situation in Vienna.[23] However, R&A also became involved in denazification efforts as well as the assessment of scientific and technical intelligence from various Nazi research institutes and related economic and political topics. By the time it shuttered in November 1945, R&A Austria had produced around forty reports, many of which concerned political, social, and economic matters in Austria and approximately half of which pertained to Vienna.[24] Nevertheless, of the three branches, R&A Austria likely spent the most energy (prior to

September 1945) evaluating the Austrian *Provinz*.[25]

By June 1945, all three intelligence-gathering branches had established themselves in Austria and were operating as part of Detachment A, under the command of Lt. Col. Abram G. Flues.[26] A total of 107 OSS personnel were then in Austria (this figure would grow to 194 before declining to 37 a year later). In addition to their headquarters at Salzburg, OSS maintained small groups in Linz (two, set to grow to fifteen by the end of the month), Innsbruck (ten), and Klagenfurt (ten, who returned to Salzburg by the end of the month).[27]

Table 1 below shows the approximate strengths of OSS Austria's various stations and offices from the end of May 1945 until the end of September 1945. As noted above, the selection of locations largely followed the April 1945 overall program for Austria under FREEBORN conditions.[28]

	May 1945[29]	June 1945	July 1945	August 1945[30]	September 1945
Salzburg	85	Unknown[31]	Unknown[32]	137	Unknown
Vienna	-	30[33]	15[34]	32	8[35]
Klagenfurt	10	Closed[36]	-	-	-
Innsbruck	10	10	Closed	-	-
Linz	2	8[37]	Unknown	18	6[38]
Zell am See	-	-	-	8	8[39]
Trieste	-	-	1[40]	2[41]	2[42]
Total	107	Unknown	Unknown	195	121[43]

Table 1: OSS Austria Field Stations and Staff (May–October 1945)

Between May and the beginning of October 1945, OSS Austria's SI, X-2, and R&A branches produced an estimated 415-427 intelligence reports on Austria.[44] Broadly speaking, most intelligence reports (~80%) were SI products with X-2 and R&A each contributing around 10% of OSS Austria's total.[45] R&A Austria's reports, while fewer in number, were significantly longer and more detailed than those produced by either of the other branches.[46] X-2, in its defense, was not an intelligence-producing branch of OSS (or SSU) per se but did report on its activities and operations.[47] Although many of these occurred in the Austrian *Provinz*, they did not necessarily refer to its conditions. Any resulting positive intelligence from X-2's counterintelligence work was shared with SI, however.

Owing to the relative autonomy of the SI and X-2 branches within both OSS and SSU, each forwarded its reports directly to its branch headquarters in Washington as well as the chief of OSS Austria.[48] Field-based R&A detachments, particularly in the Mediterranean and especially Austria, were gradually amalgamated into SI and submitted their reports together through the SI Reports Office.[49] As noted above, X-2 Austria and its successor, SCI/A, do not appear to have tallied the reports they produced in any of its monthly summaries, let alone indicated their geographic origin.

Region	Number of Reports
Burgenland	2[50]
Carinthia	10-13[51]
Lower Austria	18
Upper Austria	56-59[52]
Salzburg	79-82[53]
Styria	7
Tyrol	81-84[54]
Vienna	105
Vorarlberg	4
Austria General	53

Table 2: OSS Austria Reports by Region (May-September 1945)

Table 2 shows the approximate number of intelligence reports issued by OSS Austria's SI Reports Office from May 1945 until the end of October 1945 and represent the number of reports produced by OSS Austria's SI and R&A branches.

There are several important factors to keep in mind when viewing the above chart. First, for May 1945, there are no regional statistics, as the SI Reports Office's thirty-three reports are divided topically into "sixteen on Austrian political subjects, eight on international economic subjects, and nine on Austrian economic subjects." As such, of the thirty-three reports, twenty-five focused on Austria but cannot be attributed to a *Land*. These are therefore categorized as "Austria General," a term that would be used throughout the period under observation.

Second, we can see that OSS Austria was most active in Vienna, Salzburg, and the Tyrol, followed by Upper Austria and Lower Austria. Salzburg, the Tyrol, and Upper Austria were occupied by US forces at various times, as were parts of Vienna, all of which helps explain the amount of coverage each received.[55] However, the Tyrol is something of an outlier: OSS left Innsbruck at the beginning of June, one month before occupation duties were officially transferred to the French. Further, records strongly suggest that OSS coverage of the Tyrol *increased* after OSS rebased from Innsbruck to Zell am See, reaching a highpoint in September 1945 with thirty-four reports on the province.[56] The lack of reports on the more remote and smaller *Länder*, such as Burgenland[57] and Vorarlberg, is not particularly surprising, nor is the paucity of activity in the British zones in Carinthia and Styria (both around ten reports each).[58]

Equally telling is the significant number of reports on Lower Austria, within the Soviet occupation zone, however, for the opposite reason. There, the high point, so well as can be determined, was reached in October 1945 (eighteen reports), clearly showing the growing importance OSS personnel attached to intelligence from the Soviet zone.[59] Indeed, OSS and later SSU used their Upper Austrian base as a forward operating post into Lower Austria and Vienna before they formally established themselves in the Austrian capital.[60] All of this provides further evidence buttressing earlier statements both authors have made that OSS and SSU Austria were well ahead of their counterparts and contemporaries in accurately gauging and monitoring the Soviet threat.[61] This is underlined in the shift of focus and targeting priorities, with SSU Austria focusing on Yugoslav OB, Red Army OB, and only then high-level Austrian politics.[62]

Taken together, OSS Austria did direct a considerable amount of attention to the *Provinz* and was not fixated on Vienna or Salzburg. One of its earliest intelligence reports, of the Hungarian "LH" series from May 1945, provides significant insight into conditions in the Styrian countryside.

Case Study 1: LH-24

Capt. Burton B. Lifschultz of SI, working under the source name "Tilden," submitted an intelligence report based on interviews he had conducted near the end of May 1945 in and around Salzburg with two different sub-sources, rated C-3 ("doubtful reliability; information unsupported but considered probably true") and F-3 ("cannot be judged; information unsupported but considered probably true.")[63] Source A (C-3), a German communist who "had spent years in concentration camps" escaped during a forced march from Wiener Neustadt and "hid with friends in Selzthal." His remarks, reported in cable form were:

> Russians entered latter town [Selzthal] about 13 May. Immediately wholesale looting [of] homes and stores. Disorderly and drunk Russ soldiers in streets. Much rape. Russ authority did not

> interfere with disorderliness. Local communists treated as other natives. Subsource who has scars to show his mistreatment lost suit of clothes, bicycles, and accordion on first day of Russ occupation. Home of subsource's communist friends looted. Practically all Russ appointed town officials are communists. SS-men and Nazi bigwigs are being shot. People and especially communists very disappointed in Russians. Subsource ascribes Russ excesses to flourish of victory after memory of what Nazis did in Russia. Subsource still convinced Communist.[64]

Sub-source B (F-3), a "childhood friend of subsource A whom he met recently in Selzthal" was "a former businessman, soldier since year three nine. Deserted in year four four when scheduled for front." Capt. Lifschultz rated him as an "opportunist and not as reliable as subsource A." However, he had experienced the Soviet occupation of Graz and saw:

> Looting, rape. All bicycles requisitioned. Press and radio ordered all native men sixteen to sixty and women eighteen to fifty report to local labor offices for work permits and assignment to cleaning squads. Many of such laborers assigned to Donawitz Werke, Alpine Montaine [sic!], Steyr, and Puch Werke to dismantle machinery. Subsource saw many trainloads machinery and bicycles in Foitsberg [sic!]. West of Graz Russ is building fortifications. Armored vehicles and heavy guns in area. Many Russ troops between Leoben and Hiflau [sic!]. Austrians/Germans not permitted cross into American zone.[65]

As Capt. Lifschultz notes:

> Subsource B ascribes food shortage Graz and Selzthal to pillage and indiscriminate slaughtering by Russ troops and former slave laborers. For weeks now no meat, no milk, no potatoes, bread only occasional. All stores closed since about 22 May. German speaking Russ soldiers say that Jerry nationals will be treated like Jews were handled by Nazis. Proclamation in Graz: Marriages between Austrians and Germans with latter Nazi partner must be annulled or Austrian partner will be shipped Russ occupied Germany where all Germans will eventually go.[66]

The above report presents a wealth of information of intelligence value (if verifiable) about the activities of the Red Army both *am Land* (Selzthal, Hieflau, and Voitsberg) as well as the city of Graz. Economic information, regarding both the now well-known systematic Soviet stripping of factories and industrial equipment, as well as the poor state of food supply in Austria's second largest city, is also present.[67] Tactical information, concerning the building of fortifications as well as the movement of artillery and mechanized vehicles, would also have been highly welcome to US military OB specialists in Austria. Finally, the social component, while the most disturbing, cannot be ignored, particularly considering nearly identical atrocities committed in recent times by soldiers of the Russian Federation in Ukraine.[68]

At the same time, LH-24 offers so much and varied information that it exemplifies the "scattershot" nature of some early postwar OSS reporting in Austria. This wartime approach, otherwise referred to as "strategic intelligence," signifies the methodology and mindset instilled into OSS intelligence specialists; every crumb or morsel of information was scooped up, evaluated, and catalogued, in the belief that the small pieces would eventually, when assembled, create a collage that would yield some tactical or strategic advantage.[69] While this worked during the war and led to a number of brilliant successes, in the postwar period it lacked accuracy and depth, with the trend toward more focused and insightful reporting, referred to in both official documentation as well as theoretical writings as "national policy intelligence," which would inform decision-making rather than reveal a particular secret or weakness. The latter would come to reflect the type of intelligence produced and pursued by R&A and the SI branch of OSS Austria as the summer progressed and, eventually, by SSU Austria.[70]

SSU Austria & the *Provinz*

SSU Austria's relationship with the *Provinz* began similarly, but ultimately diverged sharply, from that of its predecessor. Even prior to the liquidation of OSS at the end of September 1945, its Austrian-based personnel were progressively focusing on what might now be termed the "big picture" and concentrating their efforts on Salzburg and especially Vienna. In the aftermath of OSS's liquidation, the divorce of R&A from SI and X-2 saw SSU Austria lose a major driving force in provincial intelligence on political, social, and economic matters. At the same time, as noted above, R&A Austria's final reports were fixated on Vienna from September 1945, signaling yet a further shift away from the *Provinz* compared with the situation that prevailed prior to the entrance of OSS into the city. SSU Austria's SI component, responding to customer needs, prioritized order of battle intelligence and high-level political reporting, neither of which had much topical connection to the *Provinz*. In the January 1946 progress report, shortly before taking over the position of chief, Al Ulmer reflected how:

> . . .it is becoming more and more likely that the bulk of our political reporting on Austria can be done by making close contacts with strategically placed representatives from all the Laender. The section has firm friends in all of the political parties, important labor unions, and semi-public societies, though lack of available qualified operational personnel prevents complete exploitation of our opportunities. In general, it may be said that the political parties look upon the organization as an unofficial liaison body to which they can speak frankly and have their propositions reach a fairly high-level audience.[71]

In terms of basing, the first casualties of OSS's liquidation were the provincial out-stations in Zell am See and Linz, which closed by the "first 10 days of October 1945."[72] The bulk of SSU Austria's provincial capabilities remained in Salzburg, in the form of the Western Austria Intelligence Unit, under Maj. Burton B. Lifschultz; however, his desk also operated intelligence chains into Poland, Hungary, and beyond while Vienna, once active, peered into Burgenland, the more rural areas of Lower Austria, and even Styria on occasion.[73] The proverbial other shoe dropped in March 1946 when SSU Washington informed SSU Austria of its revised priorities, striking "provincial coverage" from among them:

> With notification from Washington to cease coverage of the provinces, this zone office [Western Austrian Intelligence Unit] has taken a drastic cut. The unit is now completely under cover and will concentrate almost exclusively on operations eastward. Certain lines into the Tyrol and Carinthia are being severed, and the unit is being officially closed out. Remaining under cover in the American zone as a secure rear base will be sources Dundalk [Oliver von Schneditz, better known as "Oliver Rockhill"[74]], Connemara [believed to be Victor H. Ross], and Athlone [believed to be Joseph M. Rzonca], three steady producers of quality reports.[75]

Complicating matters further, within a month, SSU Austria's coverage of its titular country declined by nearly two-thirds, dropping from thirty-six reports on Austria in March 1946 to eleven by the following month, and thirteen in May 1946, the last month for which comprehensive statistics have been found.[76] The figures available strongly suggest that overall Austrian coverage hovered around ten reports per month throughout the summer of 1946. Thus, the issue at that juncture was not so much whether the *Provinz* was being covered, but Austria itself.

Region	Number of Reports
Burgenland	21[77]
Carinthia	10[78]
Lower Austria	58[79]
Upper Austria	9[80]
Salzburg	30
Styria	21[81]
Tyrol	22[82]
Vienna	52[83]
Vorarlberg	1
Austria General	108

Table 3: SSU Austria Reports by Region (October 1945 to April 1946)

Table 3 shows that the discrepancy between *Länder* gradually slackened during the first several months of SSU's existence, with only Vienna and Lower Austria the subject of significantly more reports. One cause for this might be the general trend within SSU Austria to condense multiple smaller reports into larger and more comprehensive ones.[84] Also of note are the increases in reports from zones not occupied by the US Army, such as the Soviet zone (Burgenland and Lower Austria, seventy-nine reports), the British zone (Carinthia and Styria, thirty-one reports), and the French zone (Tyrol and Vorarlberg, twenty-three reports). While those into Burgenland and Lower Austria clearly centered on the Red Army and had been requested specifically by US military intelligence in Austria, the reports from the British zone in the south can be seen as a by-product of Anglo-American assessment of the Yugoslav threat and intelligence sharing.[85]

Nevertheless, as conditions on the countryside were largely known after a year in Austria, the *Provinz*'s role shifted for US intelligence, becoming the backdrop rather than showplace for geopolitical intelligence operations that were entirely foreign to it, one example of which, the Macy Project, is discussed below.

Case Study 2: Macy Project, Salzburg Land[86]

Robert Cunningham joined SSU Austria on December 21, 1945, after serving with CIC during the war and operating alongside OSS and SSU with USFA in and around Salzburg throughout the summer and fall of 1945.[87] He was thrown immediately into the action and told to "cut his teeth" on the Macy project shortly after Christmas 1945. Started in October 1945 by Lt. Gerhard Nellhaus and Henry C. Fleisher, it was one of SSU Austria's most ambitious and audacious projects.[88] Its trio (and later pair) of principles had been found on a tip-off in neighboring Bavaria, happily writing about their wartime experiences.[89] Two Soviet citizens, Georgii Alexandrov[90] and Dmitri Moltshanov,[91] both with military/intelligence backgrounds, as well as a German signals intelligence officer, Max Bleschke, were to work the Viennese black market and hopefully set up intelligence chains into the Soviet zone and penetrate Soviet security forces and, eventually, the USSR itself.[92]

Although the project would operate in Vienna, its roots and operationalization were entirely provincial.[93] The three men were collected from Prisoner of War Enclosure (PWE) 29 in Dachau as well as PWE Bad Aibling and brought to Salzburg.[94] While at first they were briefly held in the *Landesgericht*, arrangements were soon made to prepare and debrief them, with the three residing for several weeks in the "Gasthaus Neuhausel" in Salzburg/Koppel and having semi-regular meetings with their US handlers there.[95] Bleschke asked to be removed from the project by the middle of December, having volunteered all of the information he allegedly had about Soviet codes and ciphers, as well as the inner workings of German military signals intelligence. Desirous of returning to his wife and child, and not having received the assurances about his family's safety that he sought from the Americans, he was ultimately returned to Germany and told to make himself scarce at the PWE for the coming six months.

Together with Cunningham, "Mason" and "Alberts," wearing US Army uniforms, travelled to Vienna by train on the night of 12–13 January 1946. The trip was "uneventful" and the two agents were set up in Spitalgasse 29/12, in the Ninth District (Alsergrund).[96] However, once in the big city, the project floundered. In February 1946, it had yet to deliver any results, was believed to require additional (Polish) language instruction for its principles (who were themselves Russian and did not speak the language of their cover identities) and was renamed "Calomel."[97] The following month's progress report notes that Calomel too had been "abandoned because of language difficulties, difficulties in obtaining the proper civilian papers, and the security dangers inherent in carrying out such risky operations within

Vienna."[98] It is not believed that a fate like that of the *Caviar* operation befell its principles, however, apart from a few leads among disaffected young communists in Vienna, there is nothing further on *Macy/Calomel* in the available archival files, and it appears to have simply fizzled out.[99]

Conclusion

As can be seen, throughout 1945 and 1946, the *Provinz* played a significant role both in US intelligence about Austria as well as, later, a staging area for intelligence operations with potential geopolitical ramifications. The differentiation is not clearcut: OSS Austria pursued international war criminals around the Austrian countryside and SSU Austria collected information on developments *am Land* concerning politics, the economy, society, and almost all other matters. Nevertheless, there is a general shift in the *Provinz*'s role as OSS became SSU.

We have attempted to provide a regional overview of how OSS and SSU Austria conducted intelligence on Austria in the *Länder* themselves. While Austria's importance in and of itself declined sharply in late fall and winter of 1945 as more pressing international matters took center stage, if only for its geographic location, the Alpine country remained a significant staging area for both West and East to points further afield.

Endnotes

1. Significant amounts of archival documentation found in this work were gathered thanks to a generous grant from the Botstiber Institute for Austrian-American Studies (BIAAS) that Duncan Bare received for the 2022–2023 period.

2. CIC records can be found in National Archives and Records Administration, Building II [hereafter, NARA II], Record Group 319, Entries UD-1075, UD-1076, UD-1077, UD-1079, UD-1080, UD-1082, UD-1083, UD-1084, UD-1085, UD-1087, and UD-1089. Siegfried Beer has written extensively on CIC's activities in Austria between 1945 and 1950. See: Siegfried Beer, "Monitoring Helmer. Zur Tätigkeit des amerikanischen Armeegeheimdienstes CIC in Österreich 1945–1950. Eine exemplarische Dokumentation" in *Geschichte zwischen Freiheit und Ordnung. Gerald Stourzh zum 60. Geburtstag*, ed. Emil Brix, Thomas Fröschl, and Josef Leidenfrost (Graz: Styria, 1991), 229–259, as well as "'Planned Communist Insurrection in Austria.' Ein CIC-Dokument zur Putschgefahr im Herbst 1947," in *Bananen, Cola, Zeitgeschichte. Oliver Rathkolb und das lange 20. Jahrhundert, Bd. 2*, ed. Lucile Dreidemy, Richard Hufschmied et al (Vienna: Vandenhoeck & Ruprecht, 2015), 681–691. MID was replaced by MIS in 1942; however, the earlier name continued to be used up until 1945. Records for both are available in RG 165. G-2, NARA II. Records for Austria can be found in RG 319, E 82 and 82A. Entry 82 contains "P" or "Publications" files, which were part of the G-2 Intelligence Library. State Department records, including those of the Interim Research and Intelligence Service (IRIS), which replaced OSS's Research and Analysis (R&A) branch in October 1945, as well as those of its various successors (Office of Intelligence Coordination and Liaison, the Office of Research and Intelligence (ORI), the Office of Intelligence Research (OIR), and the Bureau of Intelligence and Research (INR), the current manifestation, can be found in RG 59, E 448- E451, NARA II. For a general overview of all US intelligence activities in Austria during and immediately after the Second World War, see Siegfried Beer, "Target Central Europe: American Intelligence Efforts Regarding Nazi and Early Postwar Austria, 1941–1947," Working Papers in Austrian Studies 97/1, Minneapolis 1997.

3. As elements of SSU were attached to CIG and OSO, the availability of primary sources noticeably declines. This is reflected below, for example, in the lack of detailed progress reports and statistics for Austrian reporting from May 1946 onwards. It is interesting to note the number of once-classified reports released pursuant to the Interagency Working Group's (IWG) efforts in the late 1990s and early 2000s, (seen primarily in entries 210-224 of Record Group 226 for OSS records), for which unclassified versions exist elsewhere in the same record group. This highlights the varying character of Agency reviewers from the 1960s-1980s. See Interagency Working Group, Nazi War Crimes & Japanese Imperial Government Records Final Report to the United States Congress, April 2007, (College Park, MD: Office of Records Services (NW), 2007).

4. From May 1946, SSU intelligence on Austria was no longer differentiated by province, but simply lumped together as "Austrian." In addition, the authors have not yet found comprehensive statistics for June, July, and September 1946.

Monthly evaluations prepared in Washington do not list the specific number of reports pertaining to Austria (or individual *Länder*) but only sporadically refer to those that were particularly good or poor. It would be possible to manually review reports and categorize them; however, for expediency and temporal accuracy, we have relied instead upon SSU/CIG/OSO self-reporting.

5. See OSO from July, 1946 to December, 1946, EFH to ABD, May 8, 1952, *cia.gov*, accessed Dec. 13, 2023, https://www.cia.gov/readingroom/docs/CIA-RDP84-00499R000500110004-6.pdf.

6. Complicating matters further, for cover purposes, ties to CIG were disavowed, and OSO missions were instructed to operate as "External Survey Detachments." OSO Austria was renamed "External Survey Detachment 22." See Col. William S. Quinn, "Detailed Procedure for Liquidation of SSU Activities Overseas," September 13, 1946, RG 226, E 210, B 314, WN 10846, NARA II. For an example of usage, see John G. Heyn to Lt. Col. George Rochman, LSX-457, Mary Fluise Baum Revesz, November 13, 1946, RG 226, E 108, B 459, NARA II. At the time, Heyn was head of OSO Austria's SCB, having succeeded Maj. Edward 'Phil' Barry earlier in the summer.

7. Although outside the scope of this study, OSO was something of a misnomer, as it was primarily concerned with intelligence gathering and analysis, not operational activities. This is discussed in greater detail in the co-author's forthcoming doctoral dissertation. David Rudgers, for example, notes that OSO "was primarily an intelligence collection unit." See David Rudgers, *Creating the Secret State: The Origins of the Central Intelligence Agency, 1943-1947* (Lawrence, KS: University Press of Kansas, 2000), 171. Peter Sichel, of SSU and later OSO's Berlin detachment, writes how "The gathering of intelligence by clandestine means (my area) and the proactive OPC [Office of Policy Coordination] functions of political and paramilitary action were at that stage [1948] still in two ostensibly separate silos." See Peter Sichel, *The Secrets of My Life: Vintner, Prisoner, Soldier, Spy* (Bloomington, IN: Archway Publishing, 2016), 222-223.

8. This is likewise outside the scope of this study; however, more information can be found in: Duncan Bare and Siegfried Beer "Building a Presence Along the Danube: A Fresh Look at OSS and SSU Austria in 1945 and 1946," *Journal of Austrian-American History*, No. 5/2 (2021): 122–156. For an earlier overview of US intelligence activities in occupied Austria, see Siegfried Beer, "Rund um den 'Dritten Mann': Amerikanische Geheimdienste in Österreich 1945-1955," in *Österreich im Frühen Kalten Krieg 1945-1958. Spione, Partisanen, Kriegspläne,* ed. Erwin A. Schmidl (Vienna: Böhlau, 2000), 73-99.

9. *Austria Is not Vienna and Vienna Is not Austria*. Florian Gasser, writing for *Die Zeit* in 2019 added "Wer wissen will, was das Land wirklich bewegt, findet die Antworten in der Provinz," (Whoever wants to know what really drives the country will find the answers in the Provinz.) See Florian Gasser, "Provinz in Österreich: Innsbruck die Treue," *zeit.de* (November 15, 2019), accessed Dec. 7, 2023, https://www.zeit.de/2019/47/innsbruck-provinz-oesterreich-einwohner-leben-heimat.

10. OSS and its successors in Austria were not staffed by "Indiana farm boys," a phrase Howard Chapin used when writing from Washington in his role as

Chief of the Scandinavia-Central Europe SI desk (SC-CE, later, FBM) to SSU Austria's first CO, Col. Charles W. Thayer in December 1945. He was referring to the inability of said "farm boys" to penetrate the Vatican and Central Europe. See Howard M. Chapin to Col. Charles W. Thayer (USFA, SSU-Austria), December 10, 1945, RG 226, E 215, B 6, WN 26165-26170, NARA II.

11. Zell am See became the Tyrol Intelligence Unit's new base after the unit left Innsbruck in July 1945 and served as headquarters for the Western Austria Intelligence Unit, which would cover all of Tyrol along with Land Salzburg.

12. Lt. Harry H. Harper, who would become OSS Austria's SI reports officer, served in both Cairo and later Istanbul alongside Lt. Alfred C. Ulmer, SSU Austria's second chief. In the winter of 1944, he was slated to head the Sofia City Unit and tried on several occasions to enter and operate in Bulgaria from neighboring Turkey. His experiences with the Red Army were not positive and he was ultimately removed from the country under Red Army escort. He subsequently became Balkan SI Reports Officer within the 2677th OSS Regiment and gained a unique glimpse into developments across the region. For a report of Lt. Harper's first stint in Bulgaria, see J-010-930, Col. Edward J.F. Glavin to Director OSS, Semi-Monthly Report, October 6, 1944, RG 226, E 99, B 20, F 106, NARA II. A survey from the beginning of January 1945 states: "The Sofia unit has been twice withdrawn under pressure; the Tirana unit has been unable to arrange its entry despite the fact that Albania has been liberated for nearly two months; and the Budapest unit (with problems akin to those of the Balkan units) has still been unable to obtain necessary clearance from Moscow. On the other hand, the Bucharest unit under Lt. Cmdr. Wisner has done an extremely creditable piece of work. Likewise, Lt. Col. Thayer, operating under somewhat different conditions in Belgrade, has performed service of considerable value... It is evident that no really effective SI work can be done in territories under Soviet control, or influence, so long as OSS is identifiable as such. The truth is that we have not engaged in genuine SI work. In nearly every city the situation has gone, or may be expected to go, through two phases: the pre – and post diplomatic." See Lt. Col. William P. Maddox to CO, SI Branch MEDTO at beginning of 1945, January 1, 1945, RG 226, E 165, B 250, F 29, NARA II. See also, H.H. Harper, Acting Reports Officer: REPORTS OFFICE FROM PERIOD 16-31 DECEMBER, January 3, 1945, RG 226, E 99, B 29, NARA II; and, OP-23 MEDTO, 1-15 April 1945, RG 226, E 99, B 33, F 1, NARA II.

13. This coincides with the so-called "Shanghai Incident," during which Red Army intelligence officers and repatriation officials were caught *in flagrante* impersonating US military personnel and wearing US Army uniforms in the US zone and attempting to kidnap the vaunted German spymaster, Richard Kauder aka "Klatt," the Abwehr source "Max." Gen. Mark Clark was notified, as was Marshal Tolbukhin, and the Soviet intelligence officers/thugs were returned the following day to prevent further scandal. Media coverage of the incident was squashed, but the SSU reports of it provide a nearly hour-by-hour summary of the events. They can be found in: LSX-174, Shanghai Incident: Project Cactus, March 5, 1946, RG 226, E 213, B 2, WN 20640-20649, NARA II. This is also discussed by Alvarez and Mark, in David Alvarez and Eduard Mark, *Spying*

Through a Glass Darkly: American Espionage against the Soviet Union, 1945–1946 (Lawrence: University Press of Kansas, 2016), 171-176; as well as Ralph W. Brown III, "Making the Third Man Look Pale: American-Soviet Conflict in Vienna During the Early Cold War in Austria," *Journal of Slavic Military Studies* 14, no. 4 (2001): 85. On Richard Kauder's spying career, see especially Winfried Meyer's authoritative work: *Klatt: Hitlers jüdischer Meisteragent gegen Stalin* (Weimar bei Marburg: Metropolis, 2015). Klatt's activities with US signals intelligence leading up to the incident, including the so-called "Mount Operation" also largely played out in the Austrian countryside (at the so-called "Hoettl Central" near Steyrling).

14. See 1098 to CO, SSU Austria, Progress Report for February 1946, March 1, 1946, RG 226, E 210, B 177, WN 8862, NARA II.

15. OSS Austria was not officially constituted until August 21, 1945, with OSS disbanded barely a month later (September 30, 1945). The genesis of the various units that came to form OSS Austria exceeds the scope of this article; however, they can be roughly divided between Secret Intelligence Central Europe and the Vienna City Unit. For the first weeks of its existence, what would become OSS Austria was based around several military detachments. Detachment A, commanded by Lt. Col. Abram G. Flues, was the largest of these. Lt. Col. Howard M. Chapin, SICE's CO, filled a similar role, while Lt. Col. Charles W. Thayer was designated the CO of OSS Austria in April 1945 by OSS Director Brig. Gen. William Donovan. For expediency, the May–October 1945 period here is referred to that of "OSS Austria." For more on this period, see Siegfried Beer, "Salzburg nach dem Krieg: Beobachtungen des US-Geheimdienstes OSS/SSU über Österreich 1945/46," *Mitteilungen der Gesellschaft für Salzburger Landeskunde* 139 (1999): 117–221; and Bare and Beer, *Building a Presence Along the Danube*.

16. Maj. Flues said the following of the period: "The intelligence obtainable in the Tyrol and Oberdonau has been attacked by sub-detachments sent respectively to Innsbruck and Linz." See Maj. Flues to CO 2677th Regiment OSS through CO, OSS Austria, Monthly Report, Detachment A, 1-31 May, June 15, 1945, RG 226, E 210, B 58, WN 2319, NARA II. This report can be found in other entries that were not withheld by CIA and provides a good example of the inconsistency in classification among OSS records.

17. For more on FREEBORN, see Lt. Col. Peter G.S. Mero (Commanding, Acting) for CO, 2677th Regt OSS to A.C. of S., G-2 AFHQ, OSS Forecast Plan for US Occupational Zone, Austria, February 16, 1945, RG 226, E 99, B 31, NARA II.

18. The May 1945 X-2/SCI/A progress report notes an "excellent working agreement" with CIC, which is believed to have been maintained for the entire period under study. See SCI/A Preliminary Report, 15-31 May, 1945, undated, RG 226, E 108A, B 276, NARA II. See also John H. Richardson, *My Father the Spy: An Investigative Memoir* (New York: HarperCollins, 2005).

19. By the end of May 1945, Lt. Ulmer, the new chief of SICE's German-Austrian Desk, noted that eight had been contacted. See Lt. Alfred C. Ulmer Jr.,

Chief SI to CO, Detachment A, 2677th Regt. OSS, Monthly Report for May 1945, May 31, 1945, RG 226, E 190, B 127, F 676, NARA II.

20. A separate War Crimes branch was activated in Austria near the end of July 1945, but this branch worked closely with the other sections of OSS Austria, in particular SI. For its activation, see 1st Lt. Hart Perry, Chief, SI, 1. August 1945 Progress Report SI Branch, undated, RG 226, E 99, B 34, F 2, NARA II.

21. One of the first acts of SI personnel on Austrian territory in May 1945 was the retrieval of Lt. Jack Taylor from Mauthausen. See Maj. Flues to CO 2677th Regiment OSS through CO, OSS Austria, Monthly Report, Detachment A, 1-31 May, June 15, 1945, RG 226, E 210, B 58, WN 2319, NARA II.

22. 1st Lt. Hart Perry, Chief, SI, 1. August 1945 Progress Report SI Branch, undated, RG 226, E 99, B 34, F 2, NARA II.

23. Secretariat to Director; Progress Report Detachment A, OSS Austria, July 1945, September 4, 1945, RG 226, E 99, B 34, F 2, NARA II.

24. The "Vienna R&A Reports" subsequently renamed "Vienna R&A Field Reports" focused exclusively on the Austrian capital. The first was disseminated in September 1945. See R&A Progress Report, 1 September–15 October 1945, October 17, 1945, RG 226, E 99, B 33, NARA II. For a listing of these intelligence reports on Austria, see Siegfried Beer, "Research and Analysis about Austria, 1941-1949. American Intelligence Studies on the Reconstruction of Central Europe," in *Wiener Beiträge zur Geschichte der Neuzeit 24* (Vienna: Verlag für Geschichte und Politik, 2000), 192-210 (here 204-210).

25. Many of these R&A reports were already published in 1985; see *Gesellschaft und Politik am Beginn der Zweiten Republik. Vertrauliche Berichte der US-Militäradministration aus Österreich 1945*, ed. Oliver Rathkolb (Vienna: Böhlau, 1985).

26. As noted above, OSS Austria's command structure is outside the scope of this project; however, there existed three de facto chiefs: Lt. Col. Howard M. Chapin, CO of SICE (from which OSS Austria drew most of its personnel); Maj./Lt. Col. Abram G. Flues, CO of Detachment A (which encompassed all of OSS Austria, apart from its Vienna Headquarters Unit); and Col. Charles W. Thayer, CO of OSS Austria from April 1945. Col. Thayer was first not in Austria, and thereafter, preoccupied with translation duties for Gen. Mark Clark and other US occupation authorities. In addition, his command was not officially constituted until August 21, 1945. Documentary evidence strongly suggests that Chapin and Flues were primarily responsible for the leadership of OSS Austria until the end of August 1945, and Col. Thayer only took an active leadership role from that time forward. All three men behaved cordially and respectfully with one another—upon his return to the US in September 1945, Thayer recommended Chapin for a State Department posting. Cf. Siegfried Beer's 1996 interview with A. Gilmore Flues: Siegfried Beer, "From Ohio, via North Africa, the Middle East and Yugoslavia to Austria, 1942-1945," *Journal for Intelligence, Propaganda and Security* 5, no. 2 (2011): 117-137.

27. See Lt. Col. Howard M. Chapin, Chief SICE to Commanding Officer,

2677th Regiment OSS (Prov); Progress Report, Period 1 May 1 June 1945, June 4, 1945, RG 226, E 99, B 33, F 4 OP-23, MEDTO, May 1945, NARA II.

28. This too foresaw a largely provincial deployment with Innsbruck (38), Salzburg (50), and Linz (53), each to receive significantly more personnel than Vienna (37). This contingent would have been supplemented by a reports office (5), communications and secretarial staff (9), and a detachment for the US zone under Col. Suhling (26) for a total strength of 218. See OSS Unit for Austria under Freeborn Conditions, April 15, 1945, RG 226, E 99, B 28, F 135, NARA II.

29. See Lt. Col. Howard M. Chapin, Chief SICE to Commanding Officer, 2677th Regiment OSS (Prov); Progress Report, Period 1 May to 1 June 1945, June 4, 1945, RG 226, E 99, B 33, F 4 OP-23, MEDTO, May 1945, NARA II.

30. See Monthly Report OSS Austria, September 13, 1945, RG 226, E 99, B 34, F 3, NARA II.

31. Unfortunately, neither Maj. Flues nor Lt. Col. Chapin provided personnel figures for June 1945. See Maj. A.G. Flues (Commanding) to CO HQ 2677th Regt. OSS, Monthly Report, 1 to 30 June 1945, July 10, 1945, RG 226, E 190, B 127, F 6, NARA II. Lt. Col. Chapin's June progress reports only cover several weeks and not the entire month. See Howard M. Chapin (Lt. Col, AUS, Acting S-2) to D/AC of S, G-2, Report on Intelligence activities 9 June to 16 June 1945, June 16, 1946, RG 226, E 125, B 49, F 602, NARA II; and, Howard M. Chapin (Lt. Col, AUS, Acting S-2) to D/AC of S, G-2, Report on Intelligence Activities, 16 June–23 June 1945, June 23, 1945, both in: RG 226, E 125, B 49, F 602, NARA II.

32. The July 1945 progress report (dated September 1945) likewise does not provide any personnel statistics. See Secretariat to Director, Progress Report Detachment A, OSS Austria, July 1945, September 4, 1945, RG 226, E 99, B 34, F 2, NARA II.

33. This is an estimate for the Vienna unit's eventual size provided by Col. Maddox at the end of June 1945—this figure would not be reached until the end of August 1945. See, William P. Maddox to D/AC of S, G-2, June 30, 1945, RG 226, E 125, B 49, F 602, NARA II.

34. According to the July 1945 progress report, Lt. Col. Thayer, 1st Lt. John W. Gardner (Executive Officer), and S/Sgt. Laverdure (a driver) made up the first OSS contingent to arrive in Vienna on a permanent basis. They were joined on July 31, 1945, by "the first echelon of the OSS intelligence unit," which consisted of "Schryver, Fromson, Kaplan, and Lowenstein, a small services unit under Capt. Steinhope, and the communications team," the majority of whom (except Lowenstein) were OSS R&A. By the end of July 1945, the Vienna unit likely comprised some fifteen OSS personnel (assuming three services personnel under Capt. Steinhope, and an equally small communications team). See Secretariat to Director, Progress Report Detachment A, OSS Austria, July 1945, September 4, 1945, RG 226, E 99, B 34, F 2, NARA II.

35. This is based on an SI personnel roster from September 6, 1945. Figures would change dramatically over the following weeks. See LS-003-906: SI Personnel Roster, September 6, 1945, RG 226, E 215, B 6, WN 26165-26170, NARA II.

36. Major A.G. Flues, AC, Commanding to CO 2677 Regiment (Prov.), Monthly Report, Detachment A, 1-31, June 15, 1945, RG 226, E 108A, B 276, NARA II.

37. This is based on an SI estimate. It is known that two X-2 personnel were also active in Linz in the summer of 1945 and that Linz was used as a forward operating base for Salzburg and a staging area pending OSS Austria's move to Vienna. See Draft of SI, Austria Organization, June 23, 1945, RG 226, E 210, B 223, WN 9894, NARA II.

38. This is based on an SI personnel roster from September 6, 1945. Figures would change dramatically over the following weeks. See LS-003-906: SI Personnel Roster, September 6, 1945, RG 226, E 215, B 6, WN 26165-26170, NARA II.

39. As Zell am See was a purely SI office, this figure corresponds to that of the previous month. Zell am See merged with the Vienna HQ Unit in October 1945. Two deserter volunteers, "Norman Greene" (real name: Siegfried Scheibl) and "Herman Kirby" (real name: Herman Kinzell), were also part of this outfit. See LS-003-906: SI Personnel Roster, September 6, 1945, RG 226, E 215, B 6, WN 26165-26170, NARA II.

40. Lt. Col. F.A. Lindsay to CO, 2677th Regt. OSS, Trieste Activities, August 27, 1945, RG 226, E 190, B 125, F 637, NARA II.

41. See, LS-003-906: SI Personnel Roster, September 6, 1945, RG 226, E 215, B 6, WN 26165-26170, NARA II.

42. Ibid.

43. This estimate is based on the September 1945 progress report, which supplies numbers of personnel for each of OSS Austria's sections. SI, X-2, and R&A accounted for roughly half of the total figure (thirty-seven, fourteen, and eleven, for a total of sixty-two, respectively). See OSS-Austria September 1945, undated, RG 226, E 99, B 125, F 8, NARA II.

44. The War Crimes and Medical Intelligence branches of OSS Austria likely also contributed a handful of reports (around two to three per month); however, these are not accounted for owing to their specificity and the (small) size of those detachments.

45. For June 1945, the first full month for which detailed statistics are available for OSS Austria, the SI Reports Office sent 146 reports to Washington, 9 of which were from R&A. See, Progress Report for June 1945, 1st Lt. Harper to CO, Company A, July 3, 1945, E 99, B 25, RG 226. The X-2 Austria (SCI/A) progress report for June 1945 does not provide any insight into how many reports the branch published, let alone their geographic/regional focus. See Maj. E.P. Barry, CO, SCI/A, X-2 Branch report for June 1945, June 30, 1945, RG 226, E 108A, B 276, NARA II. In July 1945, the situation was as follows: SI Austria: 138,

R&A Austria: 8; X-2 Austria: unknown. See Secretariat to Director, Progress Report Detachment A, OSS Austria, July 1945, September 4, 1945, RG 226, E 99, B 34, F 2, NARA II.

46. Lt. Harper noted how R&A Austria's 8 reports for July were "perhaps the most uniformly high quality" of that month's "take." Progress Report for July 1945, 1st Lt. Harper to CO, Detachment A, August 1, 1945, RG 226, E 99, B 34, RG 226, NARA II.

47. Although lamentably far outside the scope of this study, "Chief OSS Austria [believed to be Col. Charles W. Thayer] requested that X-2 divorce itself from the OSS organization in general since X-2 activities do not entirely fit into the overt picture of OSS and may hinder a more complete liaison with the Russians, British and French." See Secretariat to Director, Progress Report Detachment A, OSS Austria, July 1945, September 4, 1945, RG 226, E 99, B 34, F 2, NARA II. This issue is discussed in greater detail in the co-author's pending dissertation.

48. Al Ulmer remarked in the summer of 1946: "The two branches [SI and X-2/SCI/A] are working harmoniously in Austria and a great deal of cooperation is extended on a reports level, but in all other aspects, the branches go their separate ways. . . .[This] followed in the policy of my predecessor, Lt. Col. Thayer, in giving X-2 almost complete freedom of operation and a great deal of administrative autonomy. It has been supposed that the X-2 operations have been cleared by X-2 Washington, and that the Chief of Mission was not expected to take responsibility for them." See Al Ulmer, Relationship between SI and X-2, June 3, 1946, RG 226, E 210, B 509, WN 19051, NARA II.

49. This topic is discussed in the authors' previous article. See Duncan Bare, Siegfried Beer; "Being a 'Solomon' in Washington: Evaluating and Processing OSS and SSU Intelligence from Austria, 1945–1946," *Journal of Austrian-American History* 7, no. 2 (2023): 169–212.

50. There is not any definitive confirmation of OSS reports on Burgenland. Lt. Harper notes for June 1945 how two reports came from the Soviet zone, but were not from Vienna, leaving Lower Austria and Burgenland as the possible sources. See Progress Report for June 1945, 1st Lt. Harper to CO, Company A, July 3, 1945, RG 226, E 99, B 25, NARA II.

51. In the June 1945 Reports Office summary, Lt. Harper states that "7 to 10" reports came from Carinthia, in addition to Upper Austria, Salzburg, and Tyrol. See Ibid.

52. In the June 1945 Reports Office summary, Lt. Harper states that "7 to 10" reports came from Upper Austria. See Ibid. For a wider selection of OSS and SSU reporting on Upper Austria, see Siegfried Beer, "Oberösterreich nach dem Krieg. Vertrauliche Berichte des amerikanischen Geheimdienstes OSS aus dem Jahre 1945. Eine exemplarische Dokumentation" in *Oberösterreich, April bis Dezember 1945: ein Dokumentarbericht*, ed. Gerhart Marckhgott (OÖ, Linz: Landesarchiv, 1991), 177-232.

53. In the June 1945 Reports Office summary, Lt. Harper states that "7 to 10" reports came from Salzburg. See Ibid.

54. In the June 1945 Reports Office summary, Lt. Harper states that "7 to 10" reports came from Tirol. See ibid. On OSS in the Tyrol cf. Siegfried Beer, "Tirol nach dem Krieg. Erkundungen des US-Geheimdienstes OSS vom Mai bis Juli 1945. Eine exemplarische Dokumentation," *Das Fenster. Tiroler Kulturzeitschrift* 29, no. 60/61 (1996): 5763-5776.

55. Several of these reports on Vienna are accessible in Siegfried Beer, "Wien in der frühen Besatzungszeit. Erkundungen des US-Geheimdienstes OSS/SSU im Jahre 1945. Eine exemplarische Dokumentation," *Studien zur Wiener Geschichte. Jahrbuch des Vereins für Geschichte der Stadt Wien* 51 (1995): 35-92.

56. As late as March 1946, the "Political Adviser" (of the US State Department) was keenly interested in "requisitions in the French zone" and tasked SSU Austria with providing intelligence in this direction. See 1098 to CO, SSU Austria, LS-010-331, Progress Report for March 1946, April 1, 1946, RG 226, E 108B, B 76, NARA II.

57. Notwithstanding, Burgenland may be the only province of Austria on which digitally collected FOIA- and CREST-materials from the CIA Archives have been analyzed: Martin Krenn, "Das Burgenland in Akten der Central Intelligence Agency," *Burgenländische Heimatblätter* 79, no. 1-2 (2017): 61-80.

58. For more documentation of OSS and SSU reporting on the British zone in Carinthia and Styria, see Siegfried Beer, "Schlaglichter auf Kärnten 1945. Observationen und Berichte des US-Geheimdienstes OSS/SSU. Eine exemplarische Dokumentation," *Carinthia I* 185 (1995): 415-437; and Siegfried Beer, "Von der russischen zur britischen Besetzung der Steiermark. Berichte des amerikanischen Geheimdienstes OSS aus dem Jahre 1945," *Blätter für Heimatkunde* 59 (1985): 14-26.

59. A June 1945 progress report from MEDTO notes that "Linz was the principal source of information on the Russian zone of occupation." See, MEDTO Report June 1945, undated, RG 226, E 99, B 34, F 6, NARA II.

60. OSS Austria's Security Branch report for July 1945 states: "At the moment our Linz installation (in addition to its regular function) is being employed as a staging and holding area for our move into Vienna." See Monthly Report, Capt. Frank Fortunato, Security Section to CO, Detachment A, OSS Austria, August 1, 1945, RG 226, E 99, B 34, F 2, NARA II. See also Siegfried Beer, "Niederösterreich unter der Roten Armee. Erkundungen des US-Geheimdienstes OSS/SSU im Jahre 1945," *Niederösterreich 1945-Südmähren 1945*, ed. Ernst Bezemek, Willibald Rosner (Vienna: NÖIL, 1996): 125-182.

61. See, for example, Bare and Beer, *Building a Presence Along the Danube*.

62. Although officially set in April 1946, these had become OSS and SSU Austria's foci much earlier. See, for example, Lester C. Houck, Reporting Board SI to Lt. Harry Harper, Salzburg Austria, LS-038-907, BS-4, September 7, 1945, RG 226, E 108B, B 77, NARA II.

63. See Grading of Reports, October 19, 1942, RG 226, E 147, B 7, F 103, NARA II.

64. Salzburg to Caserta, #77, 301440B, Spielman to Harper, May 29, 1945, RG 226, E 108A, box number unknown, NARA II. The intelligence report number is LH-24, which can be found in RG 226, E 108, B 186, NARA II.

65. Ibid.

66. Ibid.

67. One of R&A Austria's first tasks upon arriving in the country was to assess the state of food supply to Vienna. See Secretariat to Director, Progress Report Detachment A, OSS Austria, July 1945, September 4, 1945, in Ibid.

68. One feature common to most OSS reporting about Soviet zones of occupation is the element of rape. An excellent and accessible overview of the historical roots of this can be found in Daina Eglitis, "The Soviet Legacy of Rape and Denial," New Eastern Europe, *eurozine.com* (May 13, 2022), accessed Dec. 6, 2023, https://www.eurozine.com/the-crimes-of-bucha-have-a-long-history/. Conditions in Styria during the Soviet occupation were also addressed by other OSS-reports. These have been translated into German and published as "Zustände in der russisch besetzten Steiermark" (Report 139 624, 22.6.1945), in: Blätter für Heimatkunde 59/4 (1985) 107-109 and "Zustände in der Steiermark während der russischen Besatzung" (Report XL 14114, 4.8.1945), in: Informationen für Geschichtslehrer 6/85, 15-22.

69. George S. Pettee, an early US "philosopher of intelligence," differentiated these in his seminal text: "Strategic intelligence" is that which is conducted in wartime, while "national policy intelligence" was gathered in peacetime. See George S. Pettee, *The Future of American Secret Intelligence*, (Washington, Infantry Journal Press: 1946): 65-66. By early 1947, this shift would be institutionalized as OSO Stations were instructed to "abandon their current commitments to provide 'tactical' intelligence to the occupation forces and the local legations, and instead concentrate on priorities set in Washington." See: Michael Warner and Kevin C. Ruffner, "Moving Up to the Big Leagues, The Founding of the Office of Special Operations," Studies in Intelligence, Vol. 44, No. 2, 2000, 1-17. Here, 9. Available at: https://www.cia.gov/readingroom/document/05374892.

70. Already in September 1945, Capt. Else of the SC-CE, wrote to Col. Thayer how, based on the "thin" customer evaluations they had received, "we draw the tentative conclusion that customers in general like complete, survey-type reports better than fragmentary, spot information. [T]hey [customers] tend to prefer the R&A type to the SI type of report, but it still seems to us an attitude which should be borne in mind in SI reporting as well, particularly for areas which are not regularly or systematically covered by R&A." See Capt. G.F. Else to Lt. Col. Charles W. Thayer, USFA, OSS, Austria, Attn. Lt. Col. Chapin and Lt. Ulmer, September 12, 1945, RG 226, E 108B, B 75, NARA II.

71. This often quoted passage attests to the centralization of US intelligence efforts in Austria, away from the countryside and toward the (major) cities. "Representatives" seems to indicate those regional or provincial leaders based or frequently found in Vienna. See LS-010-1231: Alfred C. Ulmer Jr. (Chief SI) to CO SSU Austria: Progress Report December 1945, January 2, 1946, RG 226, E 215, B 6, WN 26190, NARA II.

72. Vienna to Washington, #0017, Vien-2417 (In 26822), October 20, 1945, RG 226, E 88, B 659, F In Plain Vien 001-099, NARA II.

73. See LS-010-103-SI; Alfred C. Ulmer (Chief, SI) to CO SSU Austria; Progress report for October 1945, November 2, 1945, RG 226, E 108B, B 76, NARA II.

74. See, in particular, Florian Traussnig, *Militärischer Widerstand von außen. Österreicher in US-Armee und Kriegsgeheimdienst im Zweiten Weltkrieg* (Vienna: Böhlau, 2016), 264-300.

75. Although von Schneditz was Austrian, Ross and Rzonca both focused primarily on non-Austrian targets, specializing in Hungary and Poland, respectively. See 1098 to CO, SSU Austria, LS-010-331, Progress Report for March 1946, April 1, 1946, RG 226, E 108B, B 76, NARA II.

76. For March 1946, see Ibid. For April 1946, see Reports Officer (James G. Cate; SSU Austria) to CO (SSU Austria): Progress Report for the Month of April 1946, May 1, 1946, RG 226, E 211, B 33, WN 20132-20137, NARA II. For May 1946, see FSRO-21, LS-010-531, William S. Mackenzie for the Chief of Mission to the Director, SSU, Washington, Monthly Progress Report for period of May 1–31, 1946, June 1, 1946, RG 226, E 210, B 310, WN 10831, NARA II.

77. In February 1946, these were "7 combined with Lower Austria." See Theodore Cohn, Reports Officer to CO, SSU Austria, Progress Report for February 1946, March 1, 1946, RG 226, E 108B, B 76, F 625, NARA II.

78. In February 1946, there was "1 combined with Styria." See Ibid.

79. In November 1945, there were "18 combined with Vienna." In February 1946, there were "7 combined with Burgenland"; and in March 1946, there was "1 combined with Upper Austria." See Robert D. Brewster (Capt. CAC, Reports Officer) to CO, SSU Austria, Progress Report for November 1945, December 1, 1945, RG 226, E 210, B 177, WN 7790, NARA II; Theodore Cohn, Reports Officer to CO, SSU Austria, Progress Report for February 1946, March 1, 1946, RG 226, E 108B, B 76, F 625, NARA II; 1098 to CO, SSU Austria, LS-010-331, Progress Report for March 1946, April 1, 1946, RG 226, E 108B, B 76, F 625, NARA II.

80. In March 1946, there was "1 combined with Lower Austria." See Ibid, Progress Report for March 1946, in: Ibid.

81. In February 1946, there was "1 combined with Carinthia." See: Ibid.

82. In April 1946, there was one report on South Tyrol, which is included here. See Reports Officer (James G. Cate, SSU Austria) to CO (SSU Austria): Progress Report for the Month of April 1946, May 1, 1946, RG 226, E 211, B 33, WN 20132-20137, NARA II.

83. In November 1945, there were "18 reports combined with Lower Austria." See Robert D. Brewster (Capt. CAC, Reports Officer) to CO, SSU Austria, Progress Report for November 1945, December 1, 1945, RG 226, E 210, B 177, WN 7790, NARA II.

84. Reid Denis, Executive Officer to the Chief of SI/FRB in Washington, and a former OSS Austria R&A man, wrote Ulmer in June 1946: "We have noted the tendency that you comment on to increase your selectivity as to the material deemed suitable for re-printing, and to combine a number of brief reports into an overall one. We approve of both of these tendencies, and are of the opinion that they are trends which should be continued, even upon the return of your missing staff members you will lighten the work load that you are carrying. This trend I think is a general one throughout the organization, which represents the first steps toward our ultimate goal of putting out fewer but better reports, and making those that we put out really first rate pieces of clandestine intelligence." See Mr. Reid Denis to Mr. Alfred C. Ulmer Jr., LS-005-731, Intelligence Reports, July 31, 1946, RG 226, E 108B, B 75, NARA II.

85. The March 1946 SSU Austria progress report states: "G-2's continued plea for tactical information is being met with increasingly thorough coverage of military developments and maneuvers in Lower Austria, the Burgenland, and Hungary." See 1098 to Commanding Officer, SSU Austria, Progress Report for March, 1946, April 1, 1946, RG 226, E 108B, B 76, NARA II.

86. The Macy Project has been discussed in print and greater detail elsewhere. See Alvarez and Mark, *Spying Through a Glass Darkly*, 155f.

87. John H. Richardson, another CIC veteran, as well as James G. Cate were also hired to SSU Austria in December 1945. See SASAC VIENNA to TOFTE and YORKER WASHINGTON, #2365, VIEN #6125, In 30463, December 28, 1945, RG 226, E 88, B 655, NARA II. See also Richardson, *My Father the Spy*.

88. The term "audacious" is not an exaggeration. At various times, the (Russian) principles expressed their willingness to buy Red Army officer uniforms on the black market, circulate in the Soviet zone while wearing them, and attempt to penetrate the NKVD. Their first case officer, Lt. Gerhard "Gerry" Nellhaus, agreed that this was a good idea. Henry Fleisher, who served as a sort of interpreter/case officer along with Nellhaus appears to have had the most level head, noting in November 1945 that "there is an indication of slippery storytelling and it is strongly advised that their actions be closely controlled and supervised." See H.C.F, Comments on Biography, for Macy File, November 23, 1945, RG 226, E 210, B 264, WN 10983, NARA II. For the uniforms comment, and the ease with which they could be obtained, see 1st Lt. Gerhard Nellhaus to Mr. Alfred C. Ulmer Jr, Chief SI, SSU Austria, December 6, 1945, in Ibid.

89. 2nd Lt. Gerhard Nellhaus, Memorandum, October 2, 1945, in Ibid.

90. Alexandrov ("George Alberts," later "Tadeusz Piotrovski") had allegedly fought in the First World War (he had been aboard a torpedo destroyer that had sunk, subsequently fought in the Imperial Russian cavalry, and was deployed in 1916 to France); the Russian Civil War (he was a liaison officer to the "French Marine Infantry" and had fought alongside French and American soldiers against the Bolsheviks); and evacuated to France in 1919, but returned to fight with the "First Tank Division of the Don Army" against the Red Army in 1920. He returned to Petrograd, but his family was "liquidated by the Tscheka" so he fled first to Finland in 1923 and subsequently Holland, completing his education as

an "electrical engineer in Liege" (Belgium). Unable to find work, he moved in 1926 to Serbia (Yugoslavia) before returning home to the Soviet Union in 1929, owing to his homesickness. The wartime biography of Alexandrov is not nearly as fantastic: As of 1941, he was again in "Serbia" (Yugoslavia) and sent by the German occupation forces to Germany. In 1944, he volunteered for the "Vlasov Army" and "was put in charge of organizing the Third Grenadier Regiment." Once deployed along the Oder Front, his division refused to fight and relocated to Prague, where it came into contact with anti-German groups and organized resistance. His division surrendered to the US Army on May 12, 1945. See Unknown to Mr. Alfred C. Ulmer Jr, Macy Project Biographies, November 20, 1945, in Ibid.

91. Moltshanov, "Molitshanov," or "Moltshavov" had allegedly served in the NKVD/OGB from 1927–1934 before dismissal. Thereafter, in 1941, he was recalled to military service as a Captain and fought in the Red Army until capture by the Wehrmacht that same year. He was given the unimaginative codename "Danny Mason" and the slightly more plausible Polish cover identity "Stefan Konopczak" although he could not speak Polish. See Ibid.

92. Sonderführer Max Bleschke (born in Białystok, present-day Poland) was a cryptanalyst and signals officer from the OKH's *Inspektion 7 Gruppe VI* who led *Referat 5 (Russisch)*. He was allegedly relieved of duty after the failed July 1944 assassination plot against Hitler but without prejudice or bias. He withdrew his bid of participation in Macy shortly after Cunningham took over the project. See Ibid.

93. Ulmer remarked in January 1946 that "Macy will be based in Vienna and will have as its target intelligence from high military figures." See LS-010-1231: Alfred C. Ulmer Jr. (Chief SI) to CO SSU Austria: Progress Report December 1945, January 2, 1946, RG 226, E 215, B 6, WN 26180-26199, NARA II.

94. Robert J. Cunningham to Mr. Alfred C. Ulmer, Chief, SI, SSU WD Mission to Austria, Macy Project, January 15, 1946, RG 226, E 210, B 264, WN 10983, NARA II.

95. The address given is "Grazer Reichsstrasse 85," which is currently "Grazer Bundesstrasse 85" along the B 158. There is no longer a Gasthaus at the given address, and B 158, an old post route, does not terminate in Graz, but Bad Ischl (in Upper Austria)..

96. Robert J. Cunningham to Mr. Alfred C. Ulmer, Chief, SI, SSU WD Mission to Austria; Macy Project, January 15, 1946, RG 226, E 210, B 264, WN 10983, NARA II.

97. See 1098 to CO, SSU Austria, Progress Report for February 1946, March 1, 1946, RG 226, E 210, B 177, WN 7790, NARA II.

98. See 1098 to Commanding Officer, SSU Austria, Progress Report for March 1946, April 1, 1946, RG 226, E 108B, B 76, NARA II.

99. Caviar was an attempt by the Salzburg-based SCI/A to play back Georgian nationalists to the Soviet security forces and led to the disappearance/death of around twenty people. See Bare and Beer, *Building a Presence Along the Danube*. It is also discussed in Alvarez and Mark, *Through a Glass Darkly*, 161-165.

Forum

The World War II Bombing War Over Austria and Archeology: The Case of Matrei am Brenner

The Air War in the Tyrol: The Case of Matrei am Brenner

Günter Bischof

Introduction

This roundtable presents a regional history of the bombing war over Tyrol during World War II.[1] More specifically, the three essays deal with the bombing war over the village of Matrei in the *Wipptal*, north of the Brenner border. The railroad line from Innsbruck in the Tyrol through Verona in Italy was subject to relentless bombing by the Americans and the British in the final months of the war. Their objective was to interrupt the supply of the Southern Front in Italy from Nazi Germany. After the surrender of Italy to the Allies in September 1943, the Nazis opened a new front in Italy that needed to be supplied. The Allies pushed this frontline north in the final months of the war and tried to interrupt the supply of this frontline through the "Brenner railroad line."

In the final months of the war (from November 1944 to April 1945), the Brenner line experienced severe bombings. The little village of Matrei was bombed five times by American bomb squadrons. In spite of the American notion of "precision bombing," the bombs often failed to reach their exact target, as Emily Hanish explains in her paper.

Harald Stadler and D. Ryan Gray present an overview in their paper of archeological excavations of aircraft crash sites from World War II. This is a relatively new branch of archeological work. Much of it has been furthered by the Defense Department Accounting Agency of the U.S. Defense Department. This organization is responsible for finding "missing in action" soldiers from all wars. Contracting with Dr. Gray at the University of New Orleans, a number of archeological digs have been organized in the Austrian Alps, where American aircraft went down in the final months of the war. Dr. Gray, in turn, contracted with Professor Stadler from the University of Innsbruck, who has worked on World War II crash sites previously. Thus the broad institutional partnership between the Universities of New Orleans and Innsbruck was put to good use. The most spectacular success story of this archeological partnership was the identification of Captain Dickson, a famed Tuskegee airman whose P-51 was shot down over Hohenthurn in Carinthia, late in the war near the Italian border.

More recently, Stadler and Gray have been digging in Germany, in Carinthia, and on the grounds of Castle Trautson, near Matrei, to establish the exact amount of destruction. It was bombed by the Americans on April 2, 1945. The thirteenth century castle towered on a hill over a railroad tunnel. The tunnel on the "Brenner line" was the target, but the castle was destroyed.

In her paper, Elisabeth Waldart, who joined the team digging at Castle Trautson, looks at a number of castles destroyed by Allied bombs in World War II in the Tyrol (North and South). She is interested in "how ruins of old buildings can become symbols of suffering and loss." These buildings might be subject to "removal, recycling, repair, reconstruction replication, replacement, curation." She concludes that World War II archeology "can be used as a means of remembering."

Emily Hanish also was part of the archeological team digging on the grounds of Castle Trautson in the summer of 2020. She subsequently wrote her Masters thesis in the History program of the University of New Orleans on the bombing of *Matrei am Benner*.[2] In her paper in this roundtable, she is concentrating on five bombing raids of Matrei (March 22, April 2, April 5, April 17, April 25, 1945). The raid on March 22, when thirty-six tons of bombs were dropped on Matrei, killed fifty-six people. The railroad tunnel was the target, but the town was hit and would never be the same. After the deaths of so many people, including entire families, Hanish is interested in the strategy of the US Air Force but also what the bombs can wreak on the "receiving end." Ever since the historian Jöerg Friedrich castigated the destructiveness of Allied bombing on the civilian population of Nazi Germany, this perspective has not been popular.[3] Americans rather dwell on the "bombing war" from the perspective of the Eighth and Fifteenth air forces out of England and North Africa/Italy. Donald Miller's popular book on the Eighth Air Force, *Masters of the Air: America's Bomber Boys Who Fought the Air War against Nazi Germany*,[4] now turned into a much-watched miniseries by Apple+, attests to this.

Endnotes

1. For a history of the bombing war over Tyrol, see Thomas Albrich, *Luftkrieg über der Alpenfestung 1943-1945: Der Gau Tirol-Vorarlberg und die Operationszone Alpenvorland* (Innsbruck: Wagner, 2017).

2. Emily Hanish, "20,000 Feet Between: The Experiential Disparities of Precision Bombing in Austrian Bomb Victims and American Bombardiers, 1945," (M.A. Thesis, University of New Orleans, 2023).

3. Jörg Friedrich, *Der Brand: Deutschland in Bombenkrieg 1940-1945* (Berlin: Propyläen, 2002); Jöerg Friedrich, *The Fire: The Bombing of Germany, 1940-1945*, transl. Allison Brown (New York: Columbia University Press, 2008).

4. Donald Miller, *Masters of the Air: America's Bomber Boys Who Fought the Air War against Nazi Germany* (Berlin: Propyläen, 2020).

Missing in Action Reports and Reality: On the Archaeology and Taphonomy of Downed World War II Aircraft in Austria

Harald Stadler and D. Ryan Gray

Introduction

The archaeological excavation of aircraft crash sites from the Second World War, guided by and intended to address scientific research questions, does not have a very long tradition in Austria. The first investigations of such sites were made by Karl Kaus in the Burgenland region of eastern Austria during the 1980s. They were carried out as part of a rescue operation by the Federal Monuments Office (the *Bundesdenkmalamt*) on two German Messerschmitt 110 aircraft crash locations.[1] Since 1998, the Lienz lay researcher Roland Domanig has been researching the fate of pilots on both the German and Allied sides in North, South, and East Tyrol.[2] In addition to him, there are a number of interested people who have approached the topic in a semi-professional manner and have also presented it in publications, as shown by the example of Ster's account of the Pilot Midshipman Treher, originally from Hamburg-Altona, whose death in Fischamend is memorialized on ninety-three A4 printed pages.[3] For Styria, the commendable work of Christian Arzberger,[4] who investigated two plane crashes in detail, should also be mentioned. This form of archaeology only became part of university curricula and training at the University of Innsbruck at the Institute for Prehistory and Early History and Medieval and Modern Archaeology, now the Institute for Archaeology, in 2002. A special form of underwater archeology involving complex technical applications (side-scan sonar, remote-operated vehicles, etc.) for locating aircraft was undertaken by Wolfgang Falch, who then achieved his greatest success by recovering a P-47 Thunderbolt with the nickname "Dottie Mae" at a depth of 72 m in the Traunsee, a lake in Upper Austria, in 2005.[5] In 2016, a crash site of an Me109 in East Tyrol was included in pre-scientific work at the high school in Volders, Tyrol.[6] A particular challenge was the recovery of a German Ju-52 transport aircraft, which resurfaced seventy years after an emergency landing on the Umbalkees glacier, Prägraten am Grossvenediger, East Tyrol (Figure 1).[7]

The utilization of both historical documents and local knowledge in research is especially important in the study of World War II crash sites.

After a U.S. aircraft was lost, a "Missing Air Crew Report" (or MACRs) normally had to be prepared within forty-eight hours of the aircraft being shot down. This document contains eyewitness accounts from crew members of other aircraft who had witnessed the loss, often with detailed geographic coordinates. However, these "MACR" reports only reflect the position of the aircraft at its last sighting, and, as several examples have shown, there may be many kilometers between this location and the actual crash site. The correlation of wreckage scatters with historical losses through intensive modern research is an essential element of the study of crash sites. Such research is often undertaken as something of a labor of love by independent researchers, who conduct interviews and collect local accounts that may be shared with scholarly researchers. Particularly noteworthy in this regard is Reinhard Samitz, Klagenfurt, who has worked intensively on crash sites in Carinthia and neighboring Slovenia since 2005 and has achieved some notable successes in the search for missing American bomber aircraft crews.

Research on the taphonomy of aircraft crashes is also a necessary part of the archaeological investigation of aircraft crash sites, as there is a wide variety of options for reusing aircraft parts after crashes even without melting them down for manufacturing. This ranges from the re-use of aluminum for school lessons in the high schools of East Tyrol in the 1950s, which were lacking in such materials after the War, to the incorporation of parts for roofing material in alpine or hay huts, to the use of metal for covering wooden summit crosses. The latter is something that has been passed down from the *Bettelwurf* in Absam in 1948, which was covered with aluminum sheeting from the "Powder Anne," an American aircraft that crashed on the Largozalm in Volders in 1943 and is now located at the Bettelwurfhütte.

Also important to understanding the taphonomy of aircraft crash recoveries are the requests made by the American Graves Registration Command, based in Bad Tölz, Bavaria-Germany, to local gendarmerie offices after the war. These contain very detailed information about crashes, including witnesses, locations of graves, and information about officials and other people who were at the crash site, along with detailed descriptions of the shortest route to the site. This information was to be reported by telephone dispatch in 1947. The reporting protocols from local gendarmerie posts or from locations like the Innsbruck-Hötting airfield command show that the crash site was immediately secured and guarded after crashes took place. Written evidence from these reports suggests that, as far as the topography permitted, all material important to the war effort was transported away and put to use. But there were also cases where this did not take place. For example, in Obernberg, after a crash in which the machine guns from an aircraft were brought into the valley, the order was made to bury the aircraft parts or, as happened at Obernberger Lichtsee, Tyrol, to simply throw them into the lake in order not to endanger the grazing animals with the jagged metal parts.[8] To this day, many aircraft parts are still in private hands, either as trophies or as memorabilia.

DPAA Partnership MIA Recoveries in Austria

In 2016, the United States Defense POW/MIA Accounting Agency (DPAA) began a new effort to fulfill its mission of making the fullest possible accounting of missing in action American military personnel. The Strategic Partnerships initiative, as it was then known, built upon the DPAA's "Hub and Spoke" program, in which academic institutions hosted research fellows to help fulfill the accounting mission. This program, since renamed and placed under the Partnerships and Innovation Directorate, has expanded enormously since 2016. While the DPAA has previously been (and continues to be) responsible for supporting its own "organic team" investigations in Central Europe, the Partnerships and Innovation Directorate has built further capacity for recovery excavations in Austria. In the remainder of this article, we will focus specifically on the partner efforts of the University of New Orleans (UNO) and the Leopold-Franzens-Universität Innsbruck (UIBK); a similar partnership program involving the University of Maryland and the University of Vienna is not considered here, though it has produced comparable results, as has work conducted by Geoscope Services Limited, a UK-based organization under the direction of Tim Fletcher. These investigations have both resulted in identifications of lost US air crews and in the expansion of our understanding of World War II aircraft crash locations as archaeological sites. The UNO/UIBK cooperation has now brought together international teams to investigate other sites with World War II connections as well (see Waldhart and Hanish, this volume).

The first archaeological investigation done in collaboration with the DPAA as a result of the UNO/UIBK partnership was located in the vicinity of Hohenthurn, Carinthia, Austria. The National World War II Museum provided technical support for the effort, and UNO's long-standing Innsbruck Summer School provided the academic and administrative structure for an archaeological field school at a location identified previously as the possible crash site of a P-51D Mustang piloted by Capt. Lawrence Dickson, one of the famed Tuskegee Airmen of the 100th Fighter Squadron, 332nd Fighter Group, 15th Air Force. A team including students, archaeologists, metal detector technicians, and a curator from the Museum began excavations at the site in the summer of 2017, and, in part due to the considerable interest in the Tuskegee Airmen, the project received considerable media attention afterwards.[9]

Figure 1: Umbalkees, East Tyrol. The parts of the Ju52 Transport Aeroplane turned up after seventy years in the glacier. Photograph by Alpine rescue group Prägraten a. Großvenediger

Figure 2: Students from UNO and UIBK mapping on steep mountain slope. Photograph by D. Ryan Gray, University of New Orleans, Department of Anthropology and Sociology

Figure 3: Photomontage of artifacts from mountain crash site, including a nineteenth century climbing crampon, a mining hammer, a 1980s beer can, and a 1944 Reichsmark

The Hohenthurn case, even though relatively straightforward, provided a glimpse on a small scale of the complexities of the investigations of aircraft crash sites. On December 23, 1944, Capt. Dickson and 2nd Lt. Robert Martin had been on an aerial reconnaissance mission to Prague, but Capt. Dickson developed engine trouble and radioed his intent to bail out while returning to Ramitelli Air Force Base. In the Missing Air Crew Report filed afterwards, 2nd Lt. Martin stated that he saw the P-51's canopy jettisoned, and that it then rolled over, part of the manual process involved in bailing out. However, he also never saw a parachute, speculating that this could have been because the snow cover on the ground obscured it. He estimated their location at the time as between the towns of Malborghetto and Tarvisio, but an American search team working in the vicinity in 1946 had no success in locating Capt. Dickson's P-51. German records seized after the war contained information about the crash of a P-51 near Hohenthurn, Austria, just across the border from the Italian towns mentioned in the Missing Air Crew Report, stating that it was almost completely destroyed. Further investigation by the Austrian Detachment, First Field Command, American Graves Registration Command, during which local police chiefs and civil officials were interviewed, seemed to confirm that wreckage from the P-51 had been transported to Arnoldstein, Austria, by the German military, and Capt. Dickson's remains were declared unrecoverable in 1949.[10]

Roland Domanig, a researcher from Lienz, Austria, contacted the US Defense Prisoner of War/Missing Personnel Office (DPMO) in 2012 with information about the location of Dickson's P-51 crash site. A team from the DPMO and the Joint POW/MIA Accounting Command, now consolidated as the DPAA, visited the site and interviewed local eyewitnesses. While there were some inconsistencies with those stories, including one supposed eyewitness who later went to the local press in Austria with a dramatically different account of the incident,[11] there appeared to be considerable corroborating evidence that the crater location Domanig had identified was associated with the Dickson loss. Of the recollections that witnesses shared, some of the most intriguing were by Mr. Hermann Kandutsch. While not witnessing the crash himself, he recalled visiting the site as a boy in the 1950s to collect .50 caliber shells, but he said that he quit after finding what appeared to be human remains in the crater. He had kept an interest in the site through all of the subsequent years, and he was eager to see it excavated. Finding that the historical evidence, a visible possible crash crater, and surface finds of aircraft wreckage made the site a good candidate for potential investigation, the DPAA recommended it for excavation. While a full account of the UNO/UIBK excavations in 2017 is outside the scope of this article, the project resulted in the identification of Capt. Dickson and the return of his remains to his family for interment in Arlington National Cemetery. A number of examples of what the DPAA terms "material evidence" (items that facilitate the identification of missing individuals) were recovered, with the most dramatic example being a ring engraved with his and his wife's initials along with a heart pierced by an arrow and the date of his birthday in 1943.[12]

Since the successful Hohenthurn mission, UNO has worked with the DPAA Partnerships team in recovery efforts funded through grants with the Henry Jackson Foundation for Naval Medicine. More recent projects have been focused on recovery efforts at B-17G crash sites in Central Europe. One of these, conducted in 2019 at a B-17 crash site near Kimratshofen, Germany, has now resulted in the identification of two missing air crew, Staff Sgt. Edgar Mills and Tech. Sgt. William Leukering.[13] After a suspension of efforts during CoVID-19-related shutdowns in the summer of 2020, UNO has continued to partner with Harald Stadler and the University of Innsbruck and local researcher Reinhard Samitz in a multi-year excavation effort at another B-17 loss site in Carinthia, Austria.

Both of the excavations of B-17 loss sites were complex projects. The one in Germany involved a massive crater created by the explosion of the aircraft's bomb payload after its impact; this had been subsequently filled by a farmer due to safety concerns. In this investigation, UNO partnered with the Task Force Dagger Foundation, a non-profit working with US Special Operations veterans, who provided technical expertise and participated in the excavations. The recovery site in Carinthia was located in a high altitude, steep-slope setting, requiring mountaineering experts to provide training and support in excavation in conditions that made access difficult (Figure 2). The site itself was distributed over an extensive linear area, with wreckage strewn essentially from the peak of the mountain down to its base through a network of erosional drainages.

Even as the DPAA's efforts to fulfill its recovery mission have continued, resulting in a greater and greater body of archaeological data, scholarly investigations of other World War II era crash sites in Europe have increased.[14] This has led to notable attempts to synthesize data to create taxonomies of crash sites and to standardize methodologies more broadly[15] in addition to specific considerations of crash sites as archaeological sites and attempts to apply contemporary theoretical perspectives to aviation archaeology.[16]

The Social Life of Crash Sites

The work of organizations like the DPAA has resulted in considerable additional information about both the taxonomy and taphonomy of crash sites, adding to that being accumulated during research-driven investigations by scholars within Austria. Different types of losses produce different distributions of wreckage on the ground. Presumably, if these can be classified and identified in a typological system, then this information may be used to predict where specific portions of the aircraft would be located in a wreckage field. Post-depositional taphonomic processes then alter that "ideal" distribution, as both natural and cultural processes affect the crash site. Within organizations like the DPAA, in which the primary goal of the archaeological investigations of such sites is fulfilling the goal of accounting for missing air crew, both of these are seen as factors influencing that search: presumably, if one knows the position on an aircraft that a missing crew member occupied (e.g. pilot, navigator, tail gunner), and then one can reconstruct the type of loss and the relevant post-depositional factors influencing the distribution of wreckage, one can more accurately locate the area in a debris field in which remains of the missing person might be found.

The DPAA's evidence-driven approach has been productive in fulfilling its mission of recovering those lost in action, and the DPAA through its partnership program has been working to bring together those who are interested in using the evidence-driven methodologies of DPAA's style of forensic archaeology to address broader archaeological research questions about World War II sites. This often involves examining where data collected during DPAA-supported excavations overlaps with those collected during other types of research on World War II sites, whether conducted through academic institutions or through the efforts of independent researchers and wreck hunters.

One of the things that rapidly becomes apparent across all of the crash sites that the UNO/UIBK teams have excavated in Austria and Germany is that they are continuous productions of the intersection of past and present, moments of rupture into the everyday that eventually become part of it. In crashes, the aircraft involved violently intersect with a social and physical world in which they are foreign, and the sites and debris fields left behind then reveal evidence of multiple visitations, even as they are gradually incorporated into local landscapes. Witnesses see the site and pull bodies from the debris; soldiers look for intelligence and survivors, and partisans look for usable armaments; metal is salvaged and enters into commodity chains or is converted into useful household objects. Crash sites of US aircraft are visited again after the war by personnel from the American Graves Registration Command, who search sites for identifiable bodies by excavating or sorting through wreckage; or by local searchers, attracted by promises of rewards for finds of dog tags. After they leave, craters and wreckage fields become part of the social landscape for local populations. Young people hunt for souvenirs or unspent machine gun shells, perhaps hiding a few under a stump for retrieval later; crash hunters look for wreckage, buttons, unique items; hunters pass through, noting the odd bit of metal projecting from the ground. Eventually, a farmer may fill in a crater or haul away remnants of metal, hoping to restore land to cultivation or eliminate a safety hazard from his fields. Local stories of the crash circulate and pass down in local lore; moments of trauma are replayed, embellished, or lost with the passing of age.

All of these are social processes that we have observed in the sites we have investigated, and many of these moments of intersection are crystallized in the archaeological record of the crash site (Figure 3). While Arjun Appadurai certainly wasn't thinking of aircraft crash sites in the introduction to his seminal volume on "the social life of things,"[17] the consideration of crash sites as active products that themselves create a new kind of social life around them provides a productive mechanism for interpreting the myriad non-incident material—artifacts from earlier eras and uses; visitations to the site for intelligence gathering, for salvage, or for past searches for missing soldiers; site alterations and subsequent reuse—that is inevitably produced during excavation efforts at crash sites. And while Appadurai might certainly provide some perspective on how post-incident aircraft wreckage enters into and out of commodity flows, the work of Kopytoff on the cultural biography of objects particularly gives some useful questions to bring to a site.[18] What are the significant periods in the site's life? How are each of those periods marked materially? What kinds of "value" are being extracted from the site? What is being commoditized from it, and how do those doing this work see its importance? All of these things ultimately impact the potential for recovery of human remains and where they might be found, but they also provide a deeper understanding of how traces of war on the landscape are remembered or forgotten.

Of course, archaeologists are usually asking these questions, whether implicitly or explicitly, and drawing upon historical research, interviews, and present-day interactions to help decode the site's taphonomy. It is our suggestion here that the intersection of scholarly work on aviation archaeology with the DPAA mission provides an opportunity to operationalize these questions by highlighting the social and cultural production of sites as an explicit research agenda in contemporary archaeological practice.

Conclusions

As is clear from the discussion here, the scientific research of plane crashes from the Second World War in Austria is still a very young branch of historical archaeology. However, the professionalization of the work is progressing, particularly as universities such as Vienna and Innsbruck have undertaken research in cooperation with American universities. Collaboration between the DPAA and academic institutions works very well in and of itself even with some divergence between their ultimate goals. The DPAA prioritizes the identification of its war dead as its focus, and it has its own procedures for assessing whether this goal has been met; however, the complexity of crash sites will always raise ethical questions about the exhaustiveness of efforts in this regard. If one follows the rules of the institution responsible for the war dead in Austria, the Österreichisches *Schwarzes Kreuz* or Austrian Black Cross, the location of the discovery of any human remains is still legally a war grave that is subject to special protection.[19] In contrast, there are other questions in archaeology too, such as the reconstruction of the social history of the crash site and the taphonomic processes that created it, which form a continuous narrative up to the point of excavation. There is still much to be done in this field, although the authors already have experience in recovering aircraft from various environments such as water, earth, and glaciers, and a manual for archaeological aircraft recoveries is being prepared.

While the events of the Second World War took place almost eighty years ago, crash sites like those discussed here are not only still of scientific interest to archaeologists, historians, and government agencies like the

DPAA, but they also continue to be important to those affected by the air war, including the family members of lost air crew. This is underlined by the contacts made in recent years between generations of great-grandchildren who ask about guided visits, like those who now go to the crash site of the B24 "Powder Anne" on the Largozalpe in Volders-Tyrol. It will be the task of the future to maintain the memory of these tragedies of young men in the fight against National Socialism, and, above all, to preserve and protect sites associated with crashed World War II aircraft in Austria. They are not only archaeological sites but also places of remembrance.

Endnotes

1. Karl Kaus, "Zwei Messerschmitt BF110 – Zeugen des Luftkrieges über dem Burgenland," in *Das Burgenland im Jahr 1945: Beiträge zur Landes-Sonderausssstellung 1985*, ed. Stefan Karner (Burgenland: Amt der Burgenländischen Landesregierung, Abteilung xii/2, Landesarchiv-Landesbibliothek, 1985), 119–122.

2. See Roland Domanig, "Flugzeugabsturz? Wer erinnert sich? Wer hat Informationen?" in *Nußdorf-Debant Gemeindekurier*, Nr. 78, 2014, 12. Unfortunately, this significant research is mostly only accessible through newspaper reports. A comprehensive publication is still a desideratum for aircraft archaeology research, and not just in East Tyrol. See also Nicole-Melanie Goll and Georg Hoffmann, *Missing in Action, Failed to Return. Die Todesopfer der amerikanischen und britischen Air Forces im Luftkrieg über dem heutigen Öesterreich (1939-1945): ein Gedenkbuch* (Vienna: Republik Österreich/Bundesminister für Landesverteidigung und Sport, 2016).

3. Rudolf Ster, Das Bergeprojekt Treher Messerschmitt Bf109D-1 (Fischamend 2012).

4. *Mein Bezirk,* Aug. 3, 2015, Memorial plaque unveilings in Strallegg and Ratten, Styria.

5. Wolfgang Falch, "Gesucht, aber (noch) nicht gefunden: ein amerikanisches Jagdflugzeug, das während des Zweiten Weltkrieges in einem österreichischen See versank," in *Archäologie Österreichs* 13 (2002), 77–80; at this point, the aircraft was not yet identified with certainty, but it was later raised unharmed. cf. Wolfgang Falch, "Aviation Archaeology in the Alps," in *Historical Archaeology in Central Europe*, ed. Natascha Mehler, 2013, 325–338; *Flugrevue*, Jan. 19, 2017; Sabine Falch, dissertation in preparation; Sandra Falch-Lindner bachelor´s thesis in preparation.

6. Article in the *Tiroler Tageszeitung* from Monday, Dec. 19, 2016, and pre-scientific work by Simon Stadler, "Luftkrieg in Tirol während des 2. Weltkrieges," VWA-2017 Volders, 56 pages.

7. Harald Stadler, "Abstürze und Notlandungen mit Todesfolge während des Zweiten Weltkrieges in Tirol und Vorarlberg. Ein flugzeugarchäologischer Beitrag," in *Sterben in den Bergen. Realität - Inszenierung – Verarbeitung*, Michael Kasper, Robert Rollinger, and Andreas Rudigier (Vienna: Böhlau, 2018), 271-287.

8. This continued later when hobby divers discovered objects from the aircraft, including a sighting mechanism, and brought them to the surface, kindly communicated by Reinhard Kinzner, Aldrans-Tyrol.

9. Claudia Felsberger, "Auf der Suche nach totem Kriegspiloten," *Kleine Zeitung*, July 23, 2017; Adam Norris, "Dig of a Lifetime," *Silver and Blue Magazine,* Fall 2017. In addition to numerous articles that circulated in US media about the case, an episode of the PBS *Nova* program, entitled "The Last B-24," made reference to the Dickson search. The National World War II Museum hosted a screening of this program in which Capt. Dickson's family, excavation team members, and DPAA representatives were all present.

10. Michael Ruane, "Pentagon Identifies Tuskegee Airman missing from World War II," *The Washington Post*, July 27, 2018, accessed March 31, 2024, https://www.washingtonpost.com/news/retropolis/wp/2018/07/27/pentagon-identifies-tuskegee-airman-missing-from-world-war-ii/; Missing Air Crew Report (MACR) 10734, Missing Air Crew Reports of the U.S. Army Air Forces, 1942-1947; National Archives Microfilm Publication M1380, Record Group 92: Records of the Office of the Quartermaster General, National Archives: College Park, Maryland.

11. An article in the *Kleine Zeitung* from April 8, 2012, by Jochen Bendele publicized an account by an additional purported eyewitness who came forward after others had been interviewed and who claimed that she had been fired upon by an American fighter pilot while on the ground before he crashed. This narrative was at odds with every other contemporary account of Capt. Dickson's crash.

12. Michael Ruane, "A Tuskegee hero is buried 75 years after his death in World War II," *The Washington Post,* March 22, 2019, accessed March 31, 2024, https://www.washingtonpost.com/local/a-tuskegee-hero-is-buried-75-years-after-his-death-in-world-war-ii/2019/03/22/cb5046cc-4a4b-11e9-9663-00ac73f49662_story.html#:~:text=Local-,A%20Tuskegee%20hero%20is%20buried%2075%20years,death%20in%20World%20War%20II&text=Nearly%2075%20years%20after%20his,daughter%20and%20grandchildren%20looked%20on.

13. DPAA press releases dated March 27, 2023, and Feb. 6, 2024.

14. Stadler 2018, cf. Claudia Theune, *A Shadow of War: Archaeological approaches to uncovering the darker sides of conflict from the 20th century* (Leiden: Sidestone Press, 2018).

15. Christopher R. Eck, "Broken Wings, Recovered Souls: Understanding Site Formation Processes and Developing a Lexicon for Terrestrial Military Aircraft Crash Site Types Associated with the Recovery of Missing Personnel Remains," in *Strides Towards Standard Methodologies in Aeronautical Archaeology*, ed. Hunter Whitehead and Megan Lickliter-Mundon (Cham, Switzerland: Springer, 2023), 25–50.

16. Michael Deal, Lisa M. Daly, and Cathy Mathias, "Actor-Network Theory and the Practice of Aviation Archaeology." *Journal of Conflict Archaeology* 10, no. 1 (2015): 3–28; Phil Marter et al. "The Excavation of WWII RAF Bomber, Halifax LV881-ZA-V," *Journal of Conflict Archaeology* 12, no. 1 (2017): 29–45.

17. Arjun Appadurai, "Introduction: Commodities and the Politics of Value," in *The Social Life of Things*, ed. Arjun Appadurai (New York: Cambridge University Press, 1986).

18. Igor Kopytoff, "The Cultural Biography of Things: Commoditization as Process," in Ibid., 64–92.

19. Barbara Hausmair, Claudia Theune, and Harald Stadler, "Handling 'war graves': The current situation in Austria," *Forensic Science International,* vol. 318, January 2021.

Creating Ruins: The Repercussions of the Air War on Monuments in Tyrol

Elisabeth Waldhart

Introduction

Upon my initial visit to Castle Trautson (Matrei a. Brenner, Tyrol, Austria) in 2020, the site presented itself as a stereotypical ruin of an old building: a meadow, surrounded by remains of decaying walls, with some loose building elements partly covered by the high grass. Only weeks later, archaeological excavations by the universities of Innsbruck and New Orleans exposed the remains of the destruction through aerial-bombing in the last days of the Second World War. These digs made visible formerly hidden traces of wartime destruction as well as processes of levelling and rebuilding in the post-war years. The latter hid the traces of war and finally left the building in the state of a "romantic ruin" in which I first encountered it. The example of Castle Trautson demonstrates how an archaeology of the World War II strategic bombing can lead to detailed and localized views on the destruction of specific places. It not only tells the story of the bombing itself but also reflects practices of dealing with the destruction in the years and decades following the war as a process that is still ongoing. I use the excavations at Castle Trautson and the wartime history of six other castles within northern and eastern Tyrol, Austria, and southern Tyrol, Italy, to explore how these buildings were impacted by the war and especially air bombing and what strategies were implemented to deal with the destruction. An archaeological perspective on such bomb-damaged sites shows how the destruction of the Second World War is still visible in Europe's urban and rural landscape.[1]

Castle Trautson: History and Archaeological Findings

Today, the remains of the castle are a well-curated ruin as efforts have been made since 2018 to transform the site into public space. Kicked off by an association and with approval by the owners, the community of Matrei am Brenner renovated the persisting buildings and completed a new building in 2023. These interventions were accompanied by archaeological work in different areas of the northern part of the castle, where a series of research questions (from building history and material culture of former inhabitants to the impact of World War II bombing) were followed up by an international and interdisciplinary team from 2020 to 2023 led by Harald Stadler (University of Innsbruck) and D. Ryan Gray (University of New Orleans).

With the oldest parts dating back to the thirteenth century and a rich number of annexes, Castle Trautson represented from the middle of the nineteenth century until its destruction in 1945 and the post-war years a well-equipped castle with extensive buildings, a mighty defensive tower, and a chapel. The first serious damage to the masonry occurred already in 1868 as the result of construction work for a railway tunnel directly beneath the castle. The same railway line would ultimately also contribute to the near total destruction of Trautson, when it became the target of a series of eight air raids by the Allied Air Forces (15th USAAF) in the last days of the Second World War, conducted between February 14 and April 21, 1945.[2] Only one building, the southernmost part of the western wing, was not destroyed beyond repair and could be rebuilt in the post war years around 1949. (See Figure 1) Further reconstruction work was prevented by financial means, as Castle Trautson had not been the only castle owned by the family Auersperg that was hit by bombs. After reusable building material had been taken from the site and frescoes that had survived the destruction were secured,[3] the whole northern part of the building was levelled with construction machinery. The remaining building was repaired and inhabited until a rockslide event in the 1970s occurred at the southern edge of the castle rock. Afterwards, it was still used as a summer residence by a member of the family. The air raids destroyed not only the castle complex but also hit the nearby villages of Mühlbachl und Matrei am Brenner, where more than thirty-five buildings—including historical ones—were destroyed, and over fifty people died.[4]

Figure 1: Trautson Castle, Matrei am Brenner; degree of destruction after the bombing on April 2, 1945. Source: Bundesdenkmalamt Tirol, Verein Schloss Matrei-Trautson

During the excavations, a layer containing bricks; stones from the walls; and fragments of ceramic, glass, stove tiles, and iron parts that could be identified as various structural/architectural elements were discovered beneath the topsoil in all cuts. Based on the composition—a mixture of different building materials—this layer can be linked to the bombings and subsequent levelling work. A comparison with historical photographs shows that parts of the building had remained intact after the bombing and were later demolished. At the plateau, the former rooms are backfilled with approximately eighty to ninety centimetres of rubble from the floor to the crowns of the remaining walls (see Figure 2). The walls themselves are quite evenly dismantled. On the east side of the castle, a several-meter-thick cone of debris was located where the eastern wall and rock bottom plunged several meters to where the former garden had been. Within this debris, more massive parts of the building, like a large part of a former concrete staircase, were also recovered. These findings indicate that the rubble was moved heavily during the levelling work. The remains of a window are another finding that might be related directly to the events of 1945. Here the bricks that lined the window opening as well as the windowsill—a slab of concrete—were found in a tilted position. This formation could probably be a direct result of the high-explosive bombs or a further consequence of the levelling of the building. Settlement cracks found in the area of the walls could also be a result of the bombing. Although a historical inventory made in 1947 for the purpose of showing where bombs hit the castle area[5] helps to locate possible areas where traces of destruction might be visible in the archaeological record, the details of the wartime destruction are hard to track. Overall, the later levelling event seems to superimpose many of the direct traces of the destruction through bombs.

Figure 2: The remains of the kitchen stove and a remnant of a wall. Trautson Castle, Matrei am Brenner; Cut 4, SE 21, view from the southeast. Source: E. Waldhart, 2020, Department of Archaeologies, University of Innsbruck

Destruction Of Castles during the War in Tyrol

Castle Trautson was not the only castle in the region of Tyrol (north, east, and south) that was impacted by war damage. Of seven affected buildings, three were directly hit by bombings, although one of them already had been in a ruined state. The Kienburg (Matrei in East Tyrol Austria) had been abandoned in the seventeenth century and resembled a ruin by the Second World War. The main tract including the tower was hit by a US bomber that was part of pattern bombing of the area. In recent years, restoration work has been done there to prevent further deterioration.[6] At Sprechenstein Castle (Sterzing, South Tyrol, Italy), dating from the thirteenth century, severe damage was inflicted by bombing in April 1945. The nearby railway line (*Brennerbahn*) seems to have been the target again. The building was rebuilt and, with parts of the remaining debris, reconstructed from 1947 to 1954. It is still inhabited.[7]

The Trostburg (Waidbruck, South Tyrol, Italy), with origins in the twelfth century, was used as a residence up to September 1943. It was then accidentally hit by artillery fire from German troops, which destroyed large parts of the building. Renovation works started in 1967, and it now houses the *Südtiroler Burgenmuseum* (the South Tyrolean Castle Museum).[8] The Kehlburg (Gais, South Tyrol, Italy), whose origin lies probably in the twelfth century, tells another story of destruction and reuse. After having been confiscated by the Italian state in 1929, it was neglected in the following years. A fire in 1944 damaged the complex and large parts of the inventory. After the war, the remains were saved from further damage by new roofing. In the course of riots in 1964, the castle was targeted by the police as an explosives depot and hiding place affiliated with a militant group advocating for South Tyrolean self-determination. As a result of the police sweeps, the castle remained open and was subsequently completely looted. The building was then restored in 1997.[9]

Due to a concussion caused by a bomb explosion, a palace wall of Kropfsberg Castle (Reith im Alpachthal, Austria) ruins collapsed in 1945. During the invasion of the Allied troops in the last days of the war, the roof of the north wing of Tratzberg Castle (Jenbach, Austria) caught fire from incendiary grenades. However, this was brought under control, and only damage to the roof was reported.[10] A single bomb that hit the eastern part did not detonate.[11]

Dealing with the Damage

The excavated rubble made the vast scale of destruction tangible at Castle Trautson. This devastation is a characteristic of the twentieth century and to this degree only conceivable through modern means like bombs and bulldozers.[12] But beyond that, the archaeological perspective shows the processes of how people dealt with the impacts of bombing and the destruction of monuments during the war in general. Archaeologist Gabriel Moshenska discusses on a more general basis how ruins of bombed buildings can become symbols of suffering and loss; how these structures are curated; and how they can take on different and complex meanings over time, serving different parties and interests. He identifies several different approaches to post-war buildings—removal, recycling, repair, reconstruction, replication, replacement, curation—of which several can be found in the discussed castles.[13]

In 1947, the demolished buildings had a symbolic character for the local community, as short press notes demonstrate in the case of Castle Trautson: “However, the historically valuable buildings still bear all the dreadful war wounds: the new Gasthaus zur ‘Uhr’ and the landmark of Matrei: Trautson Castle”[14] In contrast, an article on the progress of the work of the Antiquities and Monuments Office mentions the progress in 1949: “Trautson Castle was partly rebuilt in its unfinished state. In its old form, however, this landmark of Matrei will no longer be resurrected, but the dominant hill now has an architectural centrepiece again…”[15] Also Oswald Trapp, the head of the regional Monument Trust, bemoans the the terrible “wounds” that aerial warfare had inflicted to historic monuments in Tyrol in a small booklet from 1947, where he lists all the monuments in the Tyrol that were impacted by the war.[16]

Of all the mentioned castles, the ones that were inhabited up to the Second World War were—at least partially—rebuilt or even reconstructed after their destruction. For Trautson, this is visible in the levelling as a measure to make the space safe to inhabit. The sites that were not inhabited or were already in a ruined state often were neglected in the first post-war years—also due to financial means. In the second half of the twentieth century, starting in the 1960s, these structures were reconstructed or curated as historic monuments, but mostly without a focus on their history in the Second World War.

Conclusion

While Castle Trautson is listed as one of five “total losses” of historic monuments in Tyrol,[17] it became a lively place of the local community in the last decade. It is also an example of how archaeology can be used as a means of remembering. The archaeological work at Trautson laid bare the rubble as a palpable trace of the bombings and the destructions of war. During the digs, the romantic view on ruins as part of the cultural landscape overlapped with the ruin as a testament to the destruction of the Second World War. Furthermore, the excavation itself was practical memory work: in 2021 and 2022 the dig was led by the University of Innsbruck as well as the University of New Orleans, with students from New Orleans doing excavation work. Also, local people visiting the site used this occasion to talk about their memories of the place. Another meaning attached to the ruin became obvious in the local newspapers: the way it used to be a site of representation for the local communities, it is regaining this function today. This resonates with Gabriel Moshenska's analysis of the term destruction as "wounds."[18] Found in the contemporaneous newspapers, it inflicts ideas of damage that can be healed. The same thought of the disappearance of the visible traces of damage and the easing of a traumatic memory is repeated in the practical memory work onsite and the covering of the rubble after the work was completed. Now the traces of damage are only visible in selected ways and in curated spots on site.

Acknowledgements

I would like to thank my supervisors Harald Stadler and D. Ryan Gray, who constantly discussed the themes presented in this essay on site and helped me develop the ideas for this text.

Endnotes

1. David Capps Tunwell, David G. Passmore, and Stephan Harrison, "Second World War bomb craters and the archaeology of Allied air attacks in the forests of the Normandie-Maine National Park, NW France," *Journal of Field Archaeology* 41, no. 3 (2016): 312–330; Gabriel Moshenska, "Resonant Materiality and Violent Remembering: Archaeology, Memory and Bombing," *International Journal of Heritage Studies* 15, no. 1 (2009): 44–56; Jonathan Gardner, "Gainig Ground: Bomb Rubble, Reclamation and Revenance," *Journal of Contemporary Archaeology* 10, no. 1 (2023): 25–48.

2. Leo Unterrichter, "Die Luftangriffe auf Nordtirol 1939–45," *Veröffentlichungen des Tiroler Landesmuseum Ferdinandeum* 26–29 (1946/49): 555–581.

3. Martin Bitschnau and Oswald Trapp, "Matrei Trautson," in *Tiroler Burgenbuch, vol. III. Wipptal,* ed. Oswald Trapp and Magdalena Hörmann-Weingartner (Bozen: Verlagsanstalt Athesia, 1974), 35–39.

4. Konrad Egg, "Brand-Chronik von Matrei, Bombardierungen," in *Beiträge zur Heimatkunde von Matrei am Brenner. Schlern-Schriften 84,* ed. Raimund von Klebelsberg (Innsbruck: Universitäts-Verlag Wagner, 1950), 54–55.

5. Bitschnau and Trapp, "Matrei Trautson," 43.

6. Wilfried Beimrohr and Magdalena Hörmann-Weingartner, "Kienburg," in *Tiroler Burgenbuch, vol. IX. Pustertal*, ed. Magdalena Hörmann-Weingartner (Bozen: Verlagsanstalt Athesia, 2003), 485–494.

7. Adelheid Zallinger, "Sprechenstein," in *Tiroler Burgenbuch, vol. III. Wipptal,* ed. Oswald Trapp and Magdalena Hörmann-Weingartner (Bozen: Verlagsanstalt Athesia, 1974), 101–140.

8. Adelheid Zallinger, "Trostburg," in *Tiroler Burgenbuch, vol. IV. Eisacktal,* ed. Oswald Trapp and Magdalena Hörmann-Weingartner (Bozen: Verlagsanstalt Athesia, 1978), 258–324.

9. Julia Hörmann, "Kehlburg," in *Tiroler Burgenbuch, vol. IX. Pustertal,* ed. Magdalena Hörmann-Weingartner (Bozen: Verlagsanstalt Athesia, 2003), 229–248.

10. Oswald Trapp, *Die Kunstdenkmäler Tirols in Not und Gefahr: Bericht des Landeskonservators über die Geschehnisse in den Jahren 1938–1945* (Innsbruck: Rohrer, 1947), 74–91.

11. Personal communication by the owner Graf Ulrich Goëss-Enzenberg, 2023.

12. Alfredo González-Ruibal, *An Archaeology of the Contemporary Era* (London: Routledge 2018), 42–47.

13. Gabriel Moshenska, "Curated Ruins and the Endurance of Conflict Heritage," *Conservation and Management of Archaeological Sites* 17, no. 1 (2015): 77–90.

14. "Rund um Innsbruck, Matrei a. Br., Bauliches und Erbauliches," *Tiroler Bauern-Zeitung*, December 20, 1947, 8. Quoted text in German: "*Aber die historisch wertvollen Häuser tragen noch all die schaurigen Kriegswunden: das neue Gasthaus zur Uhr und das Wahrzeichen von Matrei: das Schloß Trautson.*"

15. J. G., "Arbeiten des Landesdenkmalamtes in der zweiten Jahreshälfte 1948," *Bote für Tirol*, February 4, 1949, 6–7, here 7. Quoted text in German: "*Die Burg Trautson konnte zum Teil im Rohbau wieder errichtet werden. In seiner alten Form wird dieses Wahrzeichen von Matrei allerdings nicht mehr erstehen, aber der beherrschende Hügel besitzt nun wieder einen architektonischen Abschluss.*"

16. Trapp, *Die Kunstdenkmäler Tirols in Not und Gefahr*, 71.

17. Ibid., 90.

18. Moshenska, *Resonant Materiality and Violent Remembering*, 49–50.

American "Precision Bombing" and the Destruction of Trautson Castle in the Tyrolean Village of Matrei am Brenner, Spring 1945

Emily Hanish

Introduction

Beginning in the summer of 2020, the University of Innsbruck's Archaeology Department partnered with the University of New Orleans to create what is now known as Operation Trautson Castle—a multidisciplinary, collaborative effort to establish the historical and archaeological record of Trautson Castle in Matrei am Brenner, Austria. Much of this effort was facilitated by the fact that the owners of Trautson Castle are currently refurbishing the castle and nearby grounds in order to re-solidify its place as a cultural staple for the town and region. All of that said, the need to refurbish, and the overall memory of Trautson Castle for many of the residents in Matrei am Brenner, directly correlates to the village's experience during the Second World War.

Analyzing the events, causes, and effects of the Second World War in Austria is a complex undertaking with several layers and perspectives to understand; though the country was very active in the political sphere and in aiding the German war effort, the battles themselves did not significantly impact the Alpine country until the end of the war due to the nature of the Allied war effort. Though aerial activity above Europe began as early as 1942, the American and British capabilities to fly over Central Europe and achieve their goals was incredibly limited. Furthermore, it would not be until the Allies penetrated the "soft underbelly" of Europe that the Allies would find Austria in reach, both via land and air.

In early spring and early summer of 1945, the United States Army Air Force bombed Matrei am Brenner in five distinct instances resulting in death and destruction throughout the village. The bombing of the Brenner line, otherwise known as the "Battle of the Brenner," took place over seven months from November 5, 1944, through May 2, 1945. From Innsbruck, Austria to Verona, Italy, the campaign covered 168 miles of attacks and included 370 attacks on 70 rail targets.[1] Brigadier General Robert D. Knapp and his 57th Bombardment Wing executed these missions with the belief that if they could knock out 50% of the line at a minimum then they could seriously impede the German war effort by thwarting troop and supply movements.[2] As fate would have it, Matrei am Brenner possessed two Brenner Railroad bridges, thus making it a suitable target for the Mitchell bombers. One of these bridges was and is still situated directly below Trautson Castle, and if there is one lesson to learn from World War II American Bombardment theory, it is that precision-bombing is anything but precise.

Western historiography covering the topics of the Second World War and the subsequent bombing theory and campaigns rarely, if ever, covers the air war over Austria; should Austria find itself in the index of a book or article discussing the bombing war during the Second World War, one could flip a coin and be correct—heads, it refers to the Anschluss; tails, it refers to the bombing of Vienna. In regard to Austrian and German histories of the war, Austria is covered in much greater detail overall and in relation to the bombing war, especially the histories covering the war in Tyrol. However, the Battle of the Brenner is completely neglected by name and context in both Western and European World War II histories; this is more than likely due to the fact that the 57th Bomb Wing was much smaller than the 8th and 15th air forces, causing it to be left out of general histories of the Second World War and popular histories of the air war. Additionally, the Battle of the Brenner occurred after the race to Berlin was on.

While the story of Matrei am Brenner and subsequent destruction of Trautson Castle in 1945 raises several questions relating to a variety of historiographical issues, such as bombing morality, American air war theory, Austria's role during the Second World War, and the list goes on, this article will focus on the story of the Battle of the Brenner over Matrei and illuminate the short- and long-term effects on the civilians and village.[3]

Figure 1: Photograph of a postcard picturing Trautson Castle and the Brenner Railroad tunnel after 1868 but prior to the Second World War. Courtesy of the Gemeindearchiv in Matrei am Brenner, Austria

Missions over Matrei am Brenner

In February 1945, the Battle of the Brenner hit a turning point as the upper Brenner line was finally in sight. Two months later, on April 25, the 57th Bomb Wing's 12th United States Army Airforce flew its last mission of the Battle of the Brenner. Within this two-month period, the 57th Bomb Wing targeted Matrei am Brenner a total of ten times, yet it only bombed the village on five separate days.[4] Of the 57th Bomb Wing, the 310th, 321st, and 340th bomb groups directly attacked the village all six times to debilitate the North and South rail bridges. Targeting the bridge system is what essentially led to the destruction of Trautson Castle and known deaths of forty-eight civilians in one day, as the North Bridge spawned into the tunnel underneath Trautson Castle and the South Bridge paralleled the *Altstadt.* For the purpose of this paper, the attacks on March 22 and April 2 will be the primary focus, while the remaining three attacks on April 5, 17, and 21 will be supplementary. The trauma from the dozens of deaths within a single hour and destruction of Trautson Castle define much of the bombing war in 1945 for Matreiers.

Date	Bomb Group	Bomb Squadron	Sorties	Tonnage	Target	Result
22-Mar-45	310th	379th	16	72 x 1000 lbs	South Br.	Target missed with hits in town.
2-Apr-45	321st	446th / 447th	9 / 18	? x 1000 lbs	North Br.	"All bombs in close concentration covering bridge."
5-Apr-45	310th	381st	18*	?	South Br.	100% of bombs hit in the target area with probable direct hits.
17-Apr-45	340th	488th	18	65 x 1000 lbs	North & South Br.	Direct hits and near-perfect accuracy reported. Damage inflicted on rail-road bridges.
21-Apr-45	340th	488th	6	24 x 1000 lbs	North Br.	Successful attack

Table 1: Bombing Missions Against Village of Matrei am Brenner

At 1:00 p.m. on March 22, 1945, citizens walked along the main road carrying out their conventional Thursday duties while their children studied at school. At 1:00 p.m. on March 22, 1945, sixteen Mitchell bombers from the 379th Bomb Squadron, 310th Bomb Group, attacked the South Railroad Bridge with thirty-six tons of bombs. Lacking a prompt alarm warning,

Matrei citizens were sitting ducks as the heaviest bombing attack engulfed their village, destroyed their homes, and killed fifty-six of their neighbors, friends, and family members.[5] American bomb crews bombed Matrei am Brenner's South Bridge, almost entirely missed their targets, and instead hit the main village killing dozens and injuring several more. Josef Hörtnagel, a young boy at the time, sat with his father on the top of a nearby slope. Here he remembered seeing American planes open their bomb bays and unleash their payloads on the castle and the "cloud of dust [covering] Matrei."[6] Of all attacks on the village during World War II, this was by far the heaviest, most chaotic one. Survivors remember piles of rubble and ash, bomb craters in the middle of town, and even the sight of entire families as large as eight in a row of coffins in the church square. Josef Offer, an eyewitness to several bombing raids in Tyrol, recalled images of his fellow Matreiers "digging after buried people and [finding] dead people again and again." According to Offer, Matrei did not have enough coffins; those not placed directly into a coffin were "mutilated" and laid on the floor of the fire department where his father was the chief.[7]

Fortunately, residents of Matrei did not experience the degree of death and destruction on par with that of March 22 again. But two weeks later, on April 2, the 321st Bomb Group bombed Matrei am Brenner once again. This time, the 446th Bomb Squadron targeted the North Railroad Bridge and Tunnel while the 447th Bomb Squadron attacked Matrei's South Railroad Bridge. In total, 36 planes carried 72,000 pounds of bombs and dropped almost all of it on their targets.[8] Per the "446th Bombardment Squadron Historical Records," there was an accuracy of 86.1% as all bombs fell "in close concentration" covering the bridge. What Major Smedley and the 446th Bomb Squadron presumably did not know was that the bridge directly rested underneath Trautson Castle.[9] Had precision bombing been an actual reality of the time, this detail might not have carried any weight. However, bombing at this day and age was not precise, and the USAAF destroyed all but one building of Trautson Castle, a 724-year-old castle with historical and cultural meaning for Matrei am Brenner and her neighboring villages.[10]

Additionally, two civilians died during these attacks, and the priest was severely traumatized as he remained in the chapel of the castle during the bombings.[11] Results of raids in the Battle of the Brenner were categorized as damaged, blocked, hit, or not hit. The raid of April 2 deemed the North Bridge as blocked and South Bridge as damaged within the larger 57th Bomb Wing report, but at the squadron level nothing suggests whether or not the mission was a success.[12] USAAF raids over Matrei am Brenner on April 2 and the calamities associated with this day clearly exemplify the failures of precision bombing and realities of area bombing missions. Trautson Castle is not mentioned at all in any of the official AAF or Office of Strategic Services reports. While this absence is highly concerning in regard to the level of intelligence and amount of planning that went into missions on transportation lines, it does suggest that Trautson itself was not an American target. Based on the strategic bombing evolution in terms of the leading figures calling the shots, the lack of research suggests that the war was accelerating at a pace where sloppy mistakes, blatant omissions, and a severe decline in planning was acceptable. After the debris settled and the initial feelings of bedlam dissipated, Matreiers, relieved that no one was killed, still found themselves surrounded by despair and destruction. American bombing completely decimated fifteen out of ninety-four houses, ruined nine almost beyond repair, and wrecked the remaining residences to varying degrees. Simultaneously, the market was largely leveled along with the *Rathaus.*[13]

Recalling the April 2 attacks on the North Bridge, the sheer proximity of Trautson Castle to the North Bridge and rail tunnel automatically placed it in the line of fire whether the US airmen and their superiors intended to target it or not. On April 17 and April 21, Trautson Castle was further damaged, especially considering that the April 17 attack did not hit its target at all. In the wake of the fifth and final bombing, only the baroque chapel endured the Second World War.

Experiencing the Battle of the Brenner

Throughout the entirety of the Second World War, Allied bombing killed approximately 800,000 civilians; more than half of these civilians died in Europe.[1] Bombing missions differed in the end results based on the weaponry used, size of the bomber force assigned to attack the particular target, and even how embedded the target was in its surrounding environments, i.e., cities. However, it is important to realize that, as individuals in varying backgrounds assess traumatic events in history, one should not downplay their own experiences at the hands of others. In terms of World War II bombardment, as Jörg Friedrich describes, for the individual person, aerial attacks were not mentally categorized into varying levels of destruction or specific military reasons for the attack.[15]

All civilians knew was that enemy, Allied planes were attacking their livelihoods, and they were at the mercy of the uncontrollable fate in the "annihilation zone" they found themselves in.[16]

First-hand accounts of bombardment are rare for a variety of reasons. For instance, survivors grappled with their feelings in a decimated post-war environment surrounded by occupiers. Processing the pain and devastation around them overwhelmed many Austrian and German natives to the point that many of their perspectives were never shared. Those who managed to put pen to paper to tell their stories did so at the risk of being associated with the trends of victimization that existed in far-right circles. There were also individuals whose memories of the war followed them as they lived out their lives only to later be released to the public, such as Matrei am Brenner's own Konrad Plank. Plank began writing his memories down in the 1980s, and the amount of detail he recounted decades later is beyond impressive.[17]

On the morning of March 22, 1945, residents of Matrei am Brenner woke up and went about their normal day—parents prepared for their wartime jobs, and children made their way to school. At this point, there had already been one shocking attack on the village's train station, but no major damage resulted from this event. It is rumored today that the alarm system at the Rathaus had been disconnected due to the impish children and their pranks, but there is no documentation in the archives that suggests as much. However, what is definitive is that, on March 22, the air raid sirens sounded ten minutes too late to promptly signal the sixteen Mitchell bombers targeting the South Railroad Bridge. In those moments "all [one] could hear [was] the roar of the bombs."[18]

Few civilians found themselves with a perfect view of the bombings and watched from above as their friends and family lost all autonomy of their livelihood.[19]

Matreiers rushed indoors for shelter, but for many, "the heavy air pressure tore their lungs."[20]

Even if individuals were fortunate enough to safely make it to the bomb shelters, there was no guarantee that they would suffer no damage. Bomb shelters were dangerous places to be depending on the construction methods, materials, and location; many of these supposed spheres of safety turned into annihilation zones themselves. People could become trapped under the collapsed structure, cellars could significantly increase in temperature if incendiary bombs were mainly used, and there was even a change in air pressure and quality. Air raid cellars could be both "a shelter and a grave," yet no one had the power to choose which one their space would turn to.[21]

Konrad Plank's family, which consisted of his pregnant wife, grandmother, and three children, sought protection in the basement of their home.[22]

The March 22 raid proved to be the most destructive for Matrei am Brenner. Shortly after residents like Plank's family, schoolteachers and their students, and other business owners and families made it indoors, the bombs began hitting their targets and destroying their hideaways. With "rubble up to the first floor" all of their belongings in pieces, "the house[s] looked terrible." Those who stayed in their homes found themselves buried beneath the rubble and ruins. Plank's wife and family sustained varying degrees of injury in their buried state but made it out alive. Others who stayed in their home "were killed in the stairwells by falling beams and collapsing masonry."[23]

Spaces traditionally filled with warmth and safety turned to skeletons, cold and gray, after the USAAF dropped their bombs and missed their target.

Directly after the bombing, disoriented citizens had no choice but to come together and assess the damage. Collapsed roofs, damaged water and electrical systems, and mountains of rubble replaced the once colorful *Altstadt*. The infrastructural decimation in Matrei am Brenner plagued the residents for decades, though eventually all of the business owners rebuilt, the water lines were repaired, and the electricity was restored. However, the fifty-six innocent people killed by the 379th Bomb Squadron's bombs could not be brought back.[24]

In the hours and days after the attacks, surviving members of the community searched for missing friends and family in the architectural remains. The fire department served as the point for post-bombardment search and rescue, meaning that those volunteering or employed experienced an unimaginable level of misery. When digging through the debris, survivors "found dead people again and again" and were then responsible for bringing the bodies to the fire station to be identified.[25]

There were not enough coffins for those who perished, so many of the bodies were laid on the ground.[26]

Those searching for the missing did so in their own states of grief; the fire chief was seen standing on a pile of rubble amid the search with tears streaming down his face as he was processing the loss of his wife and three of his children.[27] Among the dead were women and children along with prisoners of war, foreign workers, and refugees from across the Reich. Most devasting, though, is due to Matrei am Brenner's small population and village size, whole families, some including eight or more, were essentially "exterminated."[28]

Even though the attack on March 22, 1945, rendered the most death and destruction, the missions following also produced their own traumatic results. An obvious blow at the hearts of many Matreiers, Trautson Castle's destruction during the April 2 attack was severely traumatic for Kaplan Wilhelm Stolz, being that he sought cover in a crevice in the Baroque-styled St. Euphemia Kapelle on castle grounds. "The time-honored castle was no more," but thankfully many of the cherished historic and religious items had been sent to Castle Sprechenstein in South Tyrol. When Plank looked, he noticed that "the landscape from the castle to the Brennerstrasse resembled a lunar landscape, one crater after the other."[29]

Figure 2: Pictured to the left is the "lunar landscape" Plank described; on the rightmost hill is the remains of Trautson Castle. Date of photo unknown. Photo courtesy of the Gemeindearchiv in Matrei am Brenner, Austria

Not only were the surviving residents worried about bombs falling from the sky—sometimes four chained together at once—but there was an ever-present fear of *zeitzunders*, timed bombs, going off after the initial bombardment. Along with worries of another bombardment, Plank and his community wondered when they would finally have access to water and electricity. On April 7, there was still no electricity or heat, and it began snowing. Citizens laying in their beds barely slept as they laid under a blanket of snow.[30] During the day, POWs stationed in Matrei am Brenner filled the craters even though the threat of another attack still lingered. With little material and manpower, fixing dilapidated homes was extremely difficult. To make matters even more sinister, Austrian *Gauleiters* and German newspapers traversed through the village spouting propaganda prepared by Goebbels and the Nazi Propaganda Ministry. In Matrei, the newspaper utterly ignored the devastation and instead insisted that "now all the more, until the final victory, defense of the homeland."[31] Between Nazi propaganda and American precision bombing, the lines between civilian and soldier no longer existed.

Through the end of the bombing war in Matrei, Plank and others tasked with cleaning up the streets continued to find mutilated body parts. As the Allies closed in on the Third Reich and Germany, both the fight for building material and tensions between Austrians and foreign workers increased exponentially. When the international war ended and the first American tanks rolled through town, the war in Matrei am Brenner was nowhere near over.[32] Not only did Matreiers have to deal with cleaning up their town, securing food and supply transits, and mourning the loss of their friends and family, but they also found themselves at the mercy of American occupiers' demands. On May 9, American soldiers demanded food and supplies for a feast and working men to repair the roads. Matreiers were expected to procure new identification, participate in routine blackouts, and aid the Americans in their de-Nazification campaigns. At the same time that parents were dealing with the frustrating requests of American men, their children were entertaining the more charismatic sides of American soldiers: chocolate bars and grenades. In the first week of American occupation, US grenades injured three children and kill one child.[33]

These events occurred daily through snowstorms and torrential downpours and thunderstorms while many Matreiers still lacked a roof over their head. The American occupation of the Tyrol region for the most part bettered the Austrian post-war recovery experience, but they still managed to add to the already traumatic conditions.

Figure 3: View of Matrei am Brenner in 1946 still showing much of the wartime destruction. Photo courtesy of the Gemeindearchiv in Matrei am Brenner, Austria

During the last six months of the Second World War, 15,000 tons of bombs were dropped on Matrei am Brenner and the neighboring villages of Mühlbachl and Pfons; four hundred and twenty of these bombs were of the heaviest caliber and often found themselves bound together with "four-piece chains," leaving enormous craters wherever they landed.[34] In 1946, as seen in Figure 4, the city of Matrei was far from being fully repaired. Matrei was one of the most destroyed cities in all of Tyrol—27 businesses destroyed and 112 families homeless. With little manpower, material, or money, it was unclear how the rebuilding process would or even could commence. Furthermore, 112 families were without a roof over their heads. These conditions were not exclusive to the residents of Matrei am Brenner—Germans, Bulgarians, Italians, the French, and countless other countrymen and women found themselves facing eerily similar situations. Ten years after the war ended, millions of Austrians still needed support. Austria was now home to four thousand war widows and five thousand war orphans. For civilians in Matrei am Brenner, Austria and the rest of Europe, the Second World War lasted until the 1950s and 1960s.[35]

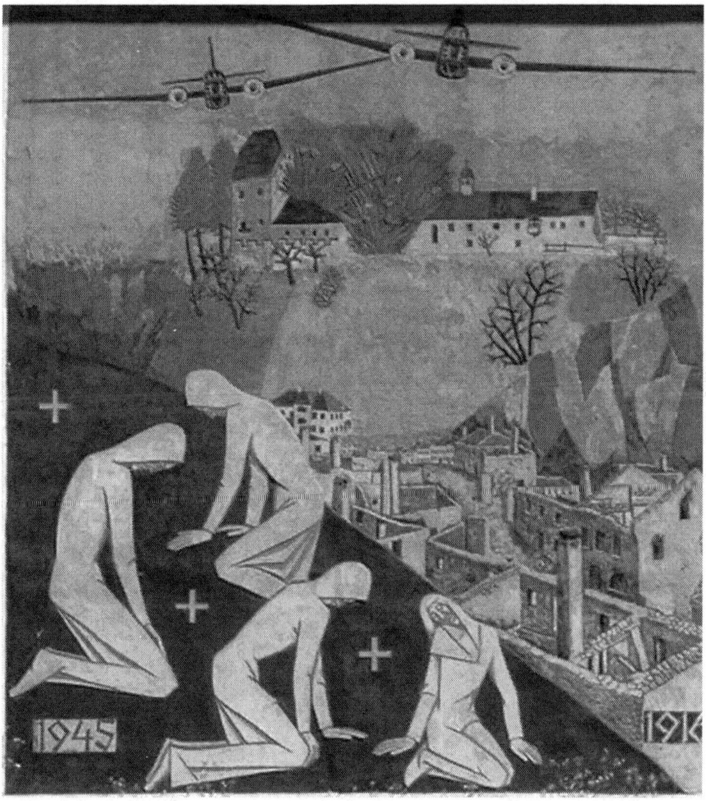

Figure 4: Fresco painting on the Volksschule in Matrei am Brenner, Austria. Courtesy of the Gemeindearchiv in Matrei am Brenner

Conclusion

After a year-long delay due to the COVID-19 pandemic, University of New Orleans archaeologists and a single historian traveled to Austria to begin their collaborative work with the University of Innsbruck on Operation Trautson Castle. The summer was spent excavating the site of the St. Euphemia *Kapelle*, destroyed in the World War II bombings, learning of the post-excavation plans for the site, and building relationships with local residents and government officials—an incredibly worthwhile experience for the single historian from the University of New Orleans, as many of the primary sources used in this article and more extensive research would have stayed buried in the *Gemeindearchiv*. In constructing this history and postulating the short- and long-term impacts of the Battle of the Brenner, but specifically when exploring the reasons why the story of Matrei am Brenner still matters seventy-nine years later, the image above frequently comes to mind. Every day, students, parents, and teachers arrive at the *Volksschule* in Matrei am Brenner and are reminded of the horrors of 1945. *Schloss Trautson* will never be restored to the former architectural glory that the "Pearl of the Wipp" once had, but its place in history is solidified via historical efforts, such as this article, and international initiatives like Operation Trautson Castle.[36]

Endnotes

1. 57th Bomb Wing, "Battle of the Brenner," 1945, WG-57-SU-OP, reel B0998, Air Force Historical Research Agency (AFHRA).

2. Brig. Gen. Robert D. Knapp, interview by Dr. Judd Katz, August 26, 1991, transcript, United States Air Force Oral History Program, AFHRA, Montgomery, AL.

3. As explained, Matrei am Brenner's experience during the Second World War is absent in the historiography, as are the other smaller Tyrolean villages impacted by the Battle of the Brenner. While this article's sole focus is to give a voice to these traumatic encounters with the US Army Air Force, Matrei am Brenner's story is also part of a larger narrative questioning the veracity of the US precision-bombing doctrine. In "20,000 Feet Between: The Experiential Disparities of Precision Bombing in Austrian Bomb Victims and American Bombardiers, 1945," this author has conducted a deeper dive into the historical record and historiography to study precision-bombing as advertised by the US Military and as experienced by those on the ground and in the skies in order to argue that Matrei am Brenner and other cities in Europe bombed post D-Day were truly done in the name of area-bombing. For further reading, see Emily Hanish, "20,000 Feet Between: The Experiential Disparities of Precision Bombing in Austrian Bomb Victims and American Bombardiers, 1945," unpublished paper, University of New Orleans, May 2022.

4. Although the village was targeted a total of ten times, this thesis will only focus on the five attacks executed via bombardment from B-25 Mitchell medium bombers because it was in targeting the bridges that Trautson Castle and civilian lives were destroyed. The remaining four missions either did not occur for various reasons or included one or two fighter planes in a direct attack on the train cars or train station.

5. "Trautson Castle – Pearl of the Wipp Valley," *wipptalblog Tirol* (Nov 19, 2019), accessed May 3, 2024, https://www.wipptal.at/en/blog/Schloss%20Trautson~40.

6. Reitmair, "Die Brennerschlacht," 2015.

7. Wolfgang Ingenhaeff and Johann Bair, *Die Erinnerung bleibt: Tirol im Bombenkrieg 1943 bis 1945* (Vienna: Berenkamp, 2004), 79, 83.

8. Headquarters 321st Bombardment Group (M) AAF, "Historical Records," May 1945, box GP-321-HI (BOMB), file 6486-7, AFHRA; Bad weather delayed the flights on this day and caused extreme turbulence. Additionally, the bad weather and immense cloud coverage interfered with actual payload deployment.

9. "446th Bombardment Squadron – Historical Records," April 1945, box SQ-BOMB-446-HI, file 6486-9, AFHRA.

10. Thomas Albrich, *Luftkrieg über der Alpenfestung 1943-1945: Der Gau Tirol-Vorarlberg und die Operationszone Alpenvorland,* (Innsbruck: Universitätsverlag Wagner, 2014); Reitmair, "Die Brennerschlacht," 2015.

11. Reitmair, "Die Brennerschlacht," 2015.

12. 57th Bomb Wing, "Battle of the Brenner," 1945, WG-57-SU-OP, reel B0998, AFHRA.

13. Reitmair, "Die Brennerschlacht," 2015; the Rathaus is the main city hall in all Austrian cities and municipalities.

14. A.C. Grayling, *Among the Dead Cities: The History and Moral Legacy of the WWII Bombing of Civilians in Germany and Japan* (London: Walker Books, 2007), 6; Richard Overy, *The Bombers and the Bombed: Allied Air War over Europe, 1940-1945* (New York: Penguin Books, 2015), 437.

15. Austrian civilians, along with their German compatriots, understood why they, the country, underwent heavy bombardment. However, the specific reasonings did not change their or their loved ones' fates, and explanations did not make death or destruction any easier to comprehend.

16. Jörg Friedrich, *The Fire: The Bombing of Germany*, 1940-1945, translated by Allison Brown (New York: Columbia University Press, 2006), 325; Jörg Friedrich describes an "annihilation zone" as any space where bombardment is experienced whether that be a military target, a bomb shelter, or residential buildings. He is clear that each bombardment can produce multiple annihilation zones. The author chose to use this wording as it describes the sheer horror associated with experiencing bombardment regardless of the bomber's intent or intended target. It also emphasizes just how terrible the consequences were on the ground for civilians as will be described later.

17. Konrad Planks's post war diary is impactful yet slightly evocative of Jörg Friedrich's own writing. As a local source, Plank adds niche details to the historical record that historians can appreciate regardless of the inherent biases. Plank's diary as a source for the bombing war in 1945 must be taken with a grain of salt because it was completed forty years after the event. Lengthy lapses in time naturally allow for gaps in memory and even hardened feelings to develop. In the future, a further study into Konrad Plank and his diary must be undertaken to fully grasp its role as a primary source for World War II studies in Austria.

18. Plank Diary, 7; "Squadron History for the Month of March 1945 of the 379th Bombardment Squadron (M) 310th Bombardment Group (M) AAF," March 1945, box SQ-BOMB-379-HI, file 6325-2, AFHRA.

19. Reitmair, "Die Brennerschlacht," 2015.

20. Plank Diary, 7.

21. Friedrich, *The Fire*, 337.

22. Plank Diary, 7.

23. Reitmair, "Die Brennerschlacht," 2015; Plank Diary, 8.

24. Ibid.

25. Ingenhaeff and Bair, *Die Erinnerung bleib*t, 79.

26. Ibid., 83.

27. Ibid., 79; Frau Plank, once she recovered from her own injuries from being buried, had no choice to aid in recovery even though she was eight months pregnant.

28. Plank Diary, 8; "einige Familien sogar ausgerottet" in German translates to "Some families were even exterminated."

29. Ibid. 9; Reitmair, "Die Brennerschlacht," 2015; throughout the war, Trautson Castle and Sprechenstein Castle transferred important artifacts between one another in order to protect religious memorabilia from destruction. The author was assigned to excavate in the area where the chapel once stood and where Wilhelm Stolz hid from the bombs.

30. Plank Diary, 10; although for some citizens "blanket of snow" was just the roof of their unheated house, many actually slept with snowflakes as their homes were unroofed or severely damaged.

31. Reitmair, "Die Brennerschlacht," 2015.

32. The Americans liberated Tyrol and initially occupied the country. In July, the French moved into their assigned Occupation Zone—the Tyrol and Vorarlberg. See, Klaus Eisterer, *Französische Besatzungspolitik: Tirol und Vorarlberg 1945/46* (Innsbruck: Studienverlag, 1991).

33. Plank Diary, 15.

34. Reitmair, "Die Brennerschlacht," 2015.

35. Ibid. Reitmair, "Die Brennerschlacht," 2015. The United States developed the Marshall Plan to assist European countries with anti-communist intentions in their post-war comebacks. This aid was first offered to Austria and reached Matrei am Brenner in 1948.

36. "Trautson Castle – Pearl of the Wipp Valley," wipptalblog.Tirol (Nov. 19, 2019), accessed May 3, 2024, https://www.wipptal.at/en/blog/Schloss%20 Trautson~40.

Historiography Roundtable on John Boyer's Austria 1867–1955

John Boyer, *Austria 1867–1955* (Oxford History of Modern Europe) (Oxford: Oxford University Press, 2022)

Günter Bischof

Introduction

John Boyer's *Austria 1867-1955*, published in the prestigious Oxford History of Modern Europe series edited by Lord Bullock and Sir William Deakin, promises to be the definitive history of Austria for a generation. Its thoroughness, covering the history of the late Habsburg Monarchy, World War I, the First Republic, World War II, and the beginnings of the Second Republic, is unsurpassed. As the four reviewers of the book in this roundtable observe, it is a bold new interpretation of a long stretch of Austrian history, covering the political and administrative history of the late Dual Monarchy and the transition to small Republican Austria after World War I. Ernst Hanisch was the last scholar to write an ambitious history of Austria in the twentieth century some thirty years ago. His was largely a social and political history; Peter Berger wrote a short history of Austria in the twentieth century for students.[1] For all his long and productive academic life, John Boyer has studied the emergence of political parties, especially the Christian Social movement/Party, in the late Habsburg Monarchy.[2] And it shows in his massive volume, as he returns frequently to the main political camps as mass movements.

The reviewers are mostly experts in the late Habsburg Monarchy and are covering that era with great erudition. I will therefore mainly look at the three chapters of Austria's post-Habsburg Republican history (chapters eight through ten). This is not the area of Boyer's principal expertise, but he presents the history of Austria 1918 to 1955 magnificently. He again looks at Austria's political camps in the 1920s and finds that Ignaz Seipel and Otto Bauer were radical in their respective approaches (972–73). To Seipel the Catholic church was important: "... he was a Catholic priest—his estimation of the role of Catholicism in public affairs was much more ambitious than the defensive-oriented Catholic politicians of the 1870s and 1880s" (669). Boyer is very impressed with the accomplishments of "Red Vienna": "This dual identity of the Socialist project in Vienna [Bauer's anti-bourgeois and Karl Renner's 'evolutionary investment within the existing legal order'] made it all the more fascinating, for the history of Vienna between 1919 and 1934 was one of successful utopian ambition confronting grueling social realities" (703). And he concludes: "Red Vienna's most signal achievement was not its ubiquitous rhetorical proclamations about social transformation, however, but its quiet assumption that with steady administrative interventions, meaningful social change was possible without a second revolution." (717).[3]

Boyer spends considerable time with the violent events of July 15, 1927, (684-689), as a turning point in the fortunes of the First Republic. For the Socialists, the violence of that day got out of hand. Seipel "played confrontational politics" by supporting the Heimwehr. Their "counterrevolutionary populism unleashed by the July 1927 riots and Seipel's subsequent coquetry with the Heimwehr led to serious tensions within the Christian Socials. (689). It spelled the end of the "Seipel coalitional paradigm of and alliance between the Christian Socials and the Greater Germans" (767). By late 1934 Engelbert Dollfuß repudiated both the 1920/9 constitutional order and this Seipel coalition paradigm (Ibid).

Similarly, Boyer gives considerable attention to "February 1934 and the Conquest of Vienna" (778-789) and the subsequent "launching of the Catholic dictatorship" (788-797). He is not too impressed by Kurt Schuschnigg, who was a "stiff, inflexible, and stubborn leader, lacking the charismatic skills that Dollfuß possessed, respected but not admired by many in his own camp and often given to indecision and inconsistency" (797-98).[4] Boyer opens a new chapter in the historiography of Austrian history by including "The Attack on the Jews" after the Anschluss of March 1938 in an extensive separate subchapter (820-834). Similarly, he also covers Austrians' "gutter anti-Semitism" (835) and war crimes in the subchapter "Täter versus Opfer: Austrian Society under Nazi Rule, 1938-1945" (834-851). By including the "Catholic dictatorship" in a chapter with the Nazi years of Austria (1934-1945), he makes a clear statement that one led to the other. But on the other hand, he refuses to dive into the "nomological debate," deeply dividing Austrian historiography between left and right, whether the Dollfuß-Schuschnigg regime ought to be termed "Austrofascist" (759-60). He comments on the Allied bombing war of Austria and Vienna only briefly (850).[5]

His final chapter on the "Reconstruction of a Republican Political System" during the four-power occupation of Austria after World War II ends on the positive note that the moderate Conservative-Socialist grand coalition led to a more successful democratic Austria than after World War I. Boyer continues to follow the Christian Catholic camp, what became known as the ÖVP (People's Party) after the war (885-888), and observes that "the party styled itself as non-confessional, in the sense of avoiding an organic connection with the Church" (885). At the same time, he looks at the reconstitution of the Socialist camp, where older social Democrats and Revolutionary Socialists made up the SPÖ after the war (888-891). The left-wing socialist émigrés, many of whom were Jews, were not invited back after 1945 (891-92). And then Boyer makes this shrewd observation: "[N]o longer was the state an exclusive instrument of class hegemony by the bourgeoisie. Rather, the class state had been altered by the fascist horrors of 1938 to 1945 into a democratic administrative state of opportunity to which the working classes should join and dedicate themselves" (892). Austrians voted on November 25, 1945. The ÖVP won an absolute majority. The SPÖ came in second. But the big surprise was that the Communists scored only 5% of the vote—not the expected 30%. Women voters outnumbered men 2:1 (many former "Nazis" were not allowed to vote, and men still lingered in prisoner-of-war camps all over the world). Boyer concludes: "Communists paid a heavy price for the rapes perpetrated by Russian soldiers earlier in the year and their ongoing economic depredations" (893). The three parties formed a coalition government, which the Communists left in late 1947. The ÖVP-SPÖ "great coalition" would last until 1966 and helped stabilize democratic governance in postwar Austria. The British and American government put much pressure on the two parties to continue cooperation in the great coalition, and Boyer adds that "both parties cast off much of their previous Klassenkampf and Kulturkampf posturing" (898). So, the great coalition continued after the 1949 elections and Chancellor Figl soon would have to contend with the general strike of September 1950 (902-03) as well as economic pressures due to the Korean War. Moreover, the Americans no longer wanted to subsidize coal, coke, and foodstuffs like bread with Marshall Plan funds, which increased the cost of living (902).

Boyer does go into the difficult denazification process and also does not shy away from the "victim's doctrine" defining postwar memory. In his conclusions, he does argue that "the use of the innocent victim argument created a cocoon in which the legitimacy of the new state could thicken." He adds: "This came at the cost of equivocation (the famous *Opferthese*) about the deep involvement of many Austrians in Hitler's genocidal empire." Boyer concludes, "from a realpolitik perspective the ethical gap was probably inevitable, given that any state-led, moral-stocktaking about the past could only become fully institutionalized once the republican state proved itself competent as a manager of economic security and social welfare in the eyes of the great majority of its citizens, viewed as a collective civic audience, and was no longer subject to hostage-taking by extremist electoral minorities" (962). In his support, he cites Gerald D. Feldman's observations on postwar Germany: "a genuine purge would have been tantamount to a civil war" (962n2)[6]. While Gerald Stourzh argues for the "*Geist der Lagerstrasse*," Boyer argues against it. Based on Robert Knight who "scoff[ed] at the idea that Red and Black collaboration after 1945 was hatched out of the egg of joint suffering in Nazi concentration camps." (971). Earlier Boyer notes that Figl claimed in American intelligence report that "not a single of the Social Democrats in the Renner government ever was to [a] concentration camp" (877). In other words, postwar cooperation between ÖVP and SPÖ had "more to do with the fact that many of these men had known each other as being moderates or centrists in their respective political camps in the early 1930s and having a shared ambivalence about extremism before 1934, this enabled them to make deals after 1945" (877). And then he goes into this fascinating counterfactual thought—had Seipel and Bauer, "brilliant Viennese extremists surrounded by a coteries of devoted younger radicals," been more moderate and "prepared to cooperate with the other camp and at the same time engage in rigorous rivalries within their own camp," like Renner and Figl did after the war, the state might not have been pushed "into high levels of structural stress," and the history of the First Republic might have been very different.

In his conclusions, Boyer brings the story up until the end of the Kreisky era in 1983. He reflects upon the fact that between 1955 and 1966 the Great Coalition "survived, but with increasing tensions, as each side chafed under the constraints that came with consensual policy management, without the a priori need to secure a state treaty" (963). One would need to add that the Great Coalition survived also despite the lack of pressure of the British and the Americans to hold it together. And at the end this thought: "After twenty years of being forcibly tethered to the oxygen tube of Red-Black cohabitation, the Austrian polity was resilient enough to sustain the most venerable of democratic practices, namely, a respected and legitimate majority, even if the ÖVP leaders believed that the Socialists did everything possible after 1966 to discredit Klaus" (975).

What is most impressive about this admirable work is the extent of scholarship that went into it. Not only does Boyer cite almost 100 pages of secondary literature; he has looked at thirty-three *Nachlässe* (personal papers) along with other collections in some twenty archives, not to speak of twelve pages of printed primary records and contemporary sources. Boyer's acute considerations on political Catholicism, for example, have been greatly enriched by the *Nachlässe* of Theodor Innitzer, Otto Maurer, Ignaz Seipel, and Friedrich Rennhofer (a Seipel biographer who collected most of Seipel's papers for his biography), all collected in the diocesan archives of the archdioceses of Vienna; these papers are rarely cited in any other scholarly treatises.

The reviews by four prominent scholars that follow are all full of praise for John Boyer's astounding scholarship. But they also see some specific issues that he fails to engage in. Gary Cohen would have liked to see more treatment of social and economic changes. Pieter Judson is missing a discussion rather than a dismissal of the idea of "national indifference," a concept that he pioneered. Maureen Healy notes that "glimpses of female actors are fleeting"—she would have liked Boyer to include more gender history in his account. To this one could add that Austria's rich cultural history is missing too in Boyer's long treatise. If one considers that the Austrian Foreign Office likes to speak of Austria as a "cultural superpower," this is no small matter.

Endnotes

1. Ernst Hanisch, *Der lange Schatten des Staates: Österreichische Gesellschaftsgeschichte im 20. Jahrhundert* (Vienna: Ueberreuter, 1994); Peter Berger, *Kurze Geschichte Österreichs im 20 Jahrhundert* (Vienna: WUV, 2007).

2. John Boyer, *Political Radicalism in Late Imperial Vienna: Origins of the Christian Social Movement, 1848-1897* (Chicago: University of Chicago Press, 1981); John Boyer, *Culture and Political Crisis in Vienna: Christian Socialism in Power, 1897-1918* (Chicago: University of Chicago Press, 1995); John Boyer, *Karl Lueger: (1844-1910): Christlichsoziale Politik als Beruf* (Vienna: Böhlau, 2010).

3. Also see Richard Cockett, *Vienna: How the City of Ideas Created the Modern World* (New Haven, CT: Yale University Press, 2023).

4. The diplomat Heinrich Wildner's recently published wartime diary, confirms this lowly view of Schuschnigg among conservative high civil servants, see Gertrude Enderl-Burcel, ed., *Heirich Wildner Taqebücher, 1938-1944: "Heute geht es gegen die Juden, morgen kann es gegen die anderen gehen…"* (Vienna: Böhlau, 2022). In an entry on May 30, 1938, Wildner considers him "as the gravedigger (*Totengräber*) of Austria [...]," 79.

5. Heinrich Wildner, who also served as an air raid warden, gives the Allied bombing attacks of Vienna and their massive destruction regular attention in his diary; in late February 1944, he notes that the air war was getting closer to Vienna. See *Tagebücher, 1938-1944,* 436-494, passim.

6. Boyer could also have cited Gerald Stourzh in support of his argument, who has said that the postwar politicians had no other choice but use the Moscow Declaration to "advocate" against the victim's doctrine; moreover, the victim's doctrine matched with the personal experience of people like Figl. See Gerald Stourzh, *Um Einheit und Freiheit: Staatsvertrag, Neutralität und das Ende der Ost-West-Besetzung Österreichs 1945*-1955, 5th ed. (Vienna: Böhlau, 1998), 25-6.

John Boyer's Achievement

Gary B. Cohen

By any fair measure, John Boyer's *Austria 1867–1955* is a magnificent achievement. It examines the development of politics, government, foreign policy, and civil society over the period with greater depth and insight than any other synthesis on modern Austrian history in English or German known to this reader. Of course, no study of such ambition and magnitude can be perfect, and one can imagine other approaches to the project. Nonetheless, Boyer presents an extraordinary work of historical research and interpretation. It is no conventional survey, since the scholarly literature, published primary sources, and also archival documents that he cites for each major topic, and his in-depth analyses of events and processes with their previous historical interpretations match or even surpass what many monographs in the field offer. To accomplish this for a period of nine decades that saw massive political, governmental, and social changes represents a unique achievement—and explains why presenting the results has required 1,100 densely printed pages.

In candor one must say that the book's length, richly detailed narrative, and highly nuanced analyses make it inappropriate for general readers who might seek a readable overview of modern Austrian history. This volume will have the greatest value for people with serious interests in Austrian history who can bring to it a basic familiarity with the general course of events. The many untranslated German terms included in the text suggest that the author and editors expected as much. As in Boyer's earlier writings, the depth of his reading and thinking about the issues has generated a wealth of important insights. Here, as before, the writing includes many notably long sentences, which—together with their accompanying footnotes—are often so packed with interesting observations that they must be carefully pondered and savored.

Anyone familiar with Boyer's two great volumes on the development of the Christian Social movement in Vienna and the Habsburg Alpine lands before 1918 will not be surprised at the focus in this new book on high-level political decision-making, the major political actors and forces, and government policies. The series editor for Oxford University Press, Lord Alan Bullock, set as the primary goal for this study a historical rendering of the political dynamics of the two Austrian Republics up to the signing of the State Treaty in 1955 with their roots in the politics and governance of the German-speaking lands of the Habsburg Monarchy during its last half century. Boyer declares at the outset that, in fulfilling these purposes, he gives particular emphasis in treating the late Imperial era to "the state-level politics and administration in and around Vienna as the key elements" (2).

The book offers such a fulsome discussion of major developments in politics, governance, and public policy over the last half century before 1918 that readers might begin to think that this is really a general political history of the Austrian half of the monarchy. Boyer deliberately gives disproportionate attention, however, to the Christian Social movement, the rise of the German-speaking segment of the Social Democratic Party, and politics in Vienna and shorter shrift to other political parties and the non-German-speaking crown lands in order to set the stage for what will follow in his accounts of the First and Second Republics. This enables him to present with great insight critical continuities across the divide of 1918 in laws, government administration, and political forces in the territory that became the Austrian Republic—and to reduce to some extent the inherent asymmetries between his treatments of the pre-1918 and post-1918 eras.

Eighty to ninety percent of the book is devoted to a chronological political narrative, but it is a uniquely rich and thoughtfully analyzed presentation. Boyer dives deeply into the processes that brought to power each new minister-president or later federal chancellor and their respective councils of ministers and produced major policy initiatives, political crises, and constitutional changes. Societal interests and economic developments come into the story as critical elements of context, but larger changes in social and economic structures during the late Imperial decades and the 1920s and 1930s typically get no more than brief mention, although such comments are always pithy and well-informed. The critical changes in society and economic structures after World War II call for greater attention, and they get it. As in much of Boyer's earlier writing about nineteenth and twentieth century Austria, he repeatedly points to the importance of the state administration in the functioning of governance, which, although seldom foregrounded in the narrative, always hovers in the background.

Particularly welcome are Boyer's deftly drawn portraits of leading figures and their political values, goals, and leadership styles, whether it be Emperors Franz Joseph and Karl; the Ministers-President Eduard Taaffe, Casimir Badeni, Ernest von Koerber, and Karl Stürgkh; Archduke Franz Ferdinand; or party leaders, ministers, and Federal Chancellors in the republican era such as Karl Renner, Otto Bauer, Ignaz Seipel, Engelbert Dollfuß, Leopold Figl, Julius Raab, and Bruno Kreisky. Where historians have disagreed on the interpretation of specific events or the performance of major figures in particular crises, Boyer addresses the interpretive questions and offers his own judicious assessments based on wide reading of the scholarship and primary sources as well. He always does this economically so that the narrative does not bog down. Many accounts of political crises here depend on insider accounts. Experts on one or another such event may well disagree with Boyer on how to weigh conflicting sources, but one cannot easily dismiss his well-reasoned conclusions. He does break the narrative of high politics with some well-chosen excursions into topics of special interest such as the waves of intellectual and cultural modernism around 1900, the changing political role of the Austrian aristocracy, Jews' social place and experience, the political role of the Catholic Church, changes in public schooling and the universities, and economic reconstruction and development in the post-1945 era.

The chapters on the last half century of the monarchy offer an informative and highly persuasive account of politics and statecraft. Eduard Taaffe emerges as someone who, behind his self-deprecating description of his work as minister-president as a matter of "muddling through," (*fortwursteln*), brought to the effort the outlook of a fundamentally conservative nobleman and accomplished career state official who applied great skill and flexibility to develop a legislative program that maintained a disparate parliamentary majority over a remarkable fourteen-year tenure. One finds in the book similarly insightful treatments of the ministries of Badeni, Koerber, Beck, and Stürgkh and the challenging political crosscurrents through which they navigated. Boyer gives great attention to the *development* of the Imperial Austrian state, its constitutional principles, laws, and civil society over the half century after 1867. He sees no stagnation or paralysis here even if some of the political contention that arose from society presented enormous challenges, the Czech-German nationality conflict in Bohemia in particular. One finds here no speculative argument that those conflicts would—or would not—have inevitably brought down the Imperial state without the impact of a long, devastating war—nor any of the frequently repeated meta-narrative of the Imperial state being ineluctably doomed by nationalist aspirations for total independence.

The treatment of state politics, popular political action, and ideology during the First Republic offers a fresher viewpoint and, if anything, more sweeping generalizations about patterns and structures than in the discussion of the late Imperial era. This sense of greater freshness owes perhaps to Boyer having written little previously on the First and Second Republics, and this also brings some more easily flowing prose. The recent vintage and notably high quality of much of the best historical scholarship on the

First and Second Republics helps here. In this account, the basic unwillingness of both the Christian Social and Social Democratic parties to accept the other's opposition as legitimate and the doctrinaire ideological commitments and hyper-partisan stances of major leaders such as Seipel and Bauer doomed Austrian parliamentary democracy to failure long before Dollfuß carried out his coup in March 1933 and inaugurated the dictatorial *Ständestaat.* Boyer refers aptly at various points to the "blockade tactics" and partisan "gang warfare" that the two major parties used against each other intermittently in the 1920s. He joins with other scholars in modifying Adam Wandruszka's well-known portrait of Austrian political life in the early twentieth century as divided fundamentally into three equally well-articulated camps, since the loss of the German-speaking regions of Bohemia and Moravia after 1918 deprived Austria's German nationalist forces of their primary and most influential political base until the rise of support for Nazi Germany and the Austrian Nazi Party after 1933. Surprisingly, beyond the contention over the border between Austria and Czechoslovakia after autumn 1918, Boyer does not discuss the concurrent disputes over the new borders with Hungary, Italy, and the Kingdom of the Serbs, Croats, and Slovenes.

The book concludes with a summation of the arc of development in political life and governance from the late Imperial period to the present, which draws together all the important thematic threads in masterly fashion. If there are weaknesses in this book worthy of note, they are largely matters of omission. In light of Boyer's emphasis on the long-term importance of the state administration in Austria's Imperial and Republican history, one wishes that he had done more to discuss systematically the development of the administration and how it worked in society. The scattered observations in the text about demographic changes and evolving social and economic structures during the last decades of the monarchy and the First Republic, together with the more penetrating treatment of society and economics in the Second Republic and copious references to scholarship on social and economic history, indicate that Boyer is well informed on those matters. Still, the strong focus on the development of the state, high politics, and political movements during the late Imperial period and First Republic has effectively precluded more systematic treatment of economic and social changes. Readers must look elsewhere for synthetic discussions of subjects such as the final stages of peasant emancipation and its consequences, the advance of market agriculture, rural-urban migration, overseas emigration, industrialization and urban growth, the expansion of the commercial and the service sectors, the growth of new middle- and lower-middle-class strata, everyday life, and the changing social experience of the laboring classes in Austria before and after World War II. To an extent, Ernst Hanisch's excellent *Österreichische Geschichte 1890–1990: Der lange Schatten des Staates* (Vienna, 1994) offers a treatment complementary to Boyer's that fills some of these gaps for the decades after 1890 and under the First Republic, but historians of society and economy in nineteenth and twentieth century Austria have produced an excellent body of new work over the last thirty years that should inform any broad synthesis. One can hope that other scholars will take inspiration and incentive from the wisdom and many insights offered by John Boyer in this volume and produce their own syntheses on the modern Austrian experience to complement his.

John Boyer, *Austria 1867–1955*

Pieter M. Judson

For historians of the late Habsburg Monarchy and of the Austrian Republics, John Boyer's work has been critical to developing modern interpretations of how politics and the administration functioned and, crucially, to the ways in which political parties gained considerable influence in running the Imperial state. As a political and administrative history of the Austrian states during the period 1867–1955, this book constitutes an extraordinary achievement. I am not an historian of administration, nor of high politics, despite my ongoing fascination with liberals of all kinds in nineteenth century Imperial Austria. My own work does wrestle with politics, but I try to approach this topic more from regional or local perspectives than at the highest state level. I do, however, appreciate good political narrative, and in this regard, Boyer's new history of Austria offers a thousand-page feast for political junkies like me. It may not be an easy read, but it is immediately the go-to reference book on the subject, and I have already recommended it to several PhD researchers here at the European University Institute.

One of the challenging elephants in the room for such a work is the question of the geographic, social, or cultural location of this Austria. A study that starts in 1867 (really 1848) and ends in 1955 (with material going up to the 1990s) must wrestle with the question Ernst Hanisch posed a quarter of a century ago in his own history of Austria in the twentieth century: "What does Austria mean before 1918?" Hanisch answered that in "public usage, it mostly meant the western half of the Habsburg Monarchy" while acknowledging that even this definition was too broad for a twentieth-century history. Nevertheless, he also argued perceptively that it was "important always to keep an open perspective, and not to limit one's field of vision too hastily to the narrow territory of the small republic." Hanisch, for example, left Galicia and Austria's littoral out of his history, a sensible choice in the days before global history has encouraged us rethink the geographic spread of states, nations, and citizens beyond classic state borders.[1]

Boyer's dilemma is more challenging, since his history spans a period that sits longer in the Imperial epoch than in the Republican, a fact of which the book's surprising cover design reminds us.[2] Like Hanisch, Boyer too focuses on what are often called the Austrian *Kernländer* although with significant forays into other regions where the political narrative requires it, especially the Bohemian lands. Ultimately, however, given Boyer's main interests, his is an unapologetically Vienna-centered history, a fact that gives his narrative considerable coherence. Yet it is also a choice that may seem odd for a history of what became a federal state after 1918 and 1945 and which has been described persuasively as federal in character well before 1918, most recently by Jana Osterkamp.[3] The centrality of Vienna to this story is often a strength, especially given the book's political and administrative focus. But it does mean that some critical episodes even in post-1918 Austrian history go unmentioned. I was surprised, for example, to find no discussion of the Carinthian plebiscite of 1920, an incident that even today provokes strong political reactions in some Austrian circles. And while Boyer does pay close attention to the critical relationship between Vienna and those German nationalists in Bohemia and Moravia who saw their future within a new German Austrian state in 1918–19, there is no mention of the precarious situation in the south, which also remained highly unstable for some months in 1918–19 until the Treaty of St. Germain, and then the 1920 plebiscite determined Austria's final border with the new Kingdom of Serbs, Croats, and Slovenes.

One strength of this account from beginning to end is Boyer's rich characterization and analysis of so many important political figures from the 1860s through the 1950s. One has to marvel at Boyer's deep knowledge not only of their actions but also of the personal foibles that occasionally drove critical historic developments, from the failure of a Czech Settlement in 1871 to the fall of the liberal party in 1879 over the occupation of Bosnia Herzegovina, to mention just two of countless examples. Not surprisingly, Boyer's nuanced interpretations of Francis Joseph's actions play a central, if not the central, role in a remarkable and colorful cast of characters. And for the period after 1918, Karl Renner, despite his many mistakes, is for Boyer the decent realist who, more than anyone else, made both Austrian republics possible. Ignaz Seipel and Otto Bauer, meanwhile, become the radical antagonists whose determination not to engage with each other's parties in any effort at compromise renders politics in the 1920s disastrously polarized and foretells the many catastrophes of the 1930s. By the way, I doubt whether anyone alive has a command of both the archival and secondary sources equal to Boyer's for the period 1880–1920, and he is also most generous in flagging the critical contributions of many of his fellow historians.

That said, Boyer (291-96) strongly disagrees with what some historians including myself refer to as "national indifference," (or in my preferred version, "indifference to nationhood"). Here, I will take a moment to explore this question—which plays a very minor role in Boyer's account—because it sheds some light on how Boyer conceptualized and organized his history.

Boyer disputes the importance of this category, which originated as a tactic for understanding Imperial society in some new and non-nationalist ways twenty-five years ago. He writes that those who argued strategically for its relevance greatly exaggerated its significance. Although I disagree with this assessment, and with his idea that indifference somehow presumed an outright refusal of nationhood, I do understand how Boyer arrived at this view. If we examine Austrian history from the perspectives of state administration, state institutions, and political parties, it will render indifference to nation invisible, and the concept will seem irrelevant to the account. Boyer contends that in the nineteenth century people increasingly faced situations that demanded they choose a nationality for themselves, the decennial census or local elections being the most important examples. From the point of view of the state and high politics, this was the case. But from the point of view of local conditions and social life, the evidence for the importance of this particular choice to daily life is murky at best. Moreover, one of the arguments for national indifference was precisely the ways in which citizens recognized that they were being forced to make a choice, and how they made use of this demand to choose for their own benefit.

From the point of view of regional, local, or legal histories, indifference to nation—along with practices of multilingualism and strategic "side switching"—remains a critical factor for understanding Imperial Austrian history and one that has influenced many of the best recent studies, at least according to their authors. It developed most notably out of US readings of very different kinds of works by historians Gary B. Cohen and Gerald Stourzh.[4] It has helped us especially to understand one conundrum for which the "nationality conflict" lens has always failed to account: how exactly did linguistic and regional nationalisms combine with Imperial patriotism to reinforce each other, and especially how did those intimately related factors work in Habsburg society during the First World War? As I and many others (among them James Bjork, Gábor Egry, Jeremy King, Claire Morelon, Dominique Reill, Máté Rigó, Rok Stergar, and Tara Zahra) have argued from very different perspectives, indifference characterized daily life when larger state political issues were not in question—which was most of the time. And as mentioned above, the evidence shows that the "choice" to which Boyer refers could often be ignored or instrumentalized to the point where it no longer reflected the views and desires of those who had posed it in the first place. Strangely, too, Boyer ends up largely confirming the existence of a strong Austrian *Staatsidee* (293) as put forward by most of those who have written about indifference.

Boyer's dismissal of this way of thinking about Austrian history reinforces the Vienna-centricity of his account and ultimately helps to explain some other limits to his analysis of Austrian society. These have to do with the place of social and economic developments in his narratives. Boyer does provide richly contextualized accounts of social phenomena that provide background to some key political decisions or their legacies. He cites and clearly knows well the relevant literature in the fields of economic and social history. Nevertheless, without making views from the provinces and localities more fundamental to the story, without a more explicit focus on factors such as regional economic development, social change, and especially interregional mobility and its rapidly changing conditions, his narrative remains focused on the political history of a specifically Viennese-German kind of Austria.

These points do not suggest that Boyer's *Austria 1867-1955* is in any way a flawed account. Many of us know first-hand the terrific challenges that face the historian who writes a big comprehensive history like this.[5] Each of us who attempts this task chooses to emphasize different approaches and different narratives, and each of us will fail to include what others consider to be important. We make these choices to encourage others in the field to consider familiar histories in new ways and to allow for the consideration of new perspectives and new actors. This book is, as I have argued, a magnificent handbook of administrative and political history. It especially complements the more decentered approaches historians have pursued of late by emphasizing the core and its central administration. Students of Austrian history from undergraduates to professional scholars should once again be profoundly grateful to Boyer for his extraordinary contribution to our field.

Endnotes

1. Ernst Hanisch, *Der lange Schatten des Staates. Österreichische Gesellschaftsgeschichte im 20. Jahrhundert* (Vienna: Ueberreuter, 1994), 15–16.

2. The book's cover features portraits of three Habsburgs: Emperor-King Francis Joseph, Archduke Francis Ferdinand, and Emperor-King Charles. Given the arc of Boyer's narrative, I would have expected to see Francis Joseph perhaps juxtaposed to Karl Renner rather than to the other two ill-fated Habsburgs.

3. Jana Osterkamp, *Vielfalt Ordnen. Das föderale Europa der Habsburgermonarchie (Vormärz bis 1918)*, Veröffentlichungen des Collegium Carolinums Band 141 (Göttingen: Vandenhoeck & Ruprecht, 2020).

4. Gary B. Cohen, *The Politics of Ethnic Survival. Germans in Prague, 1861–1914*, revised edition, (Indiana: Purdue University Press, 2006); Gerald Stourzh, *Die Gleichberechtigung der Nationalitäten in der Verfassung und Verwaltung Österreichs 1848–1918* (Vienna: Verlag der österreichischen Akademie der Wissenschaften, 1981).

5. Most recently on the late Empire, Steven Beller, *The Habsburg Monarchy 1815–1918* (Cambridge, UK: Cambridge University Press, 2018); Pieter M. Judson, *The Habsburg Empire. A New History* (Cambridge, MA: Harvard University Press, 2016).

Reading John Boyer at the Beach

Maureen Healy

John Boyer's *Austria 1867–1955* has a handsome but misleading book jacket. An amalgam of three portraits—Kaiser Karl, Franz Ferdinand, Kaiser Franz Joseph—the cover leads a reader to guess this is a Habsburg-era study, perhaps in line with Steven Beller's *The Habsburg Monarchy* (2018) or Pieter Judson's *The Habsburg Empire* (2016). An alternate book jacket—say with portraits of Franz Joseph, jurist Hans Kelsen, and a double-headed profile of Ignaz Seipel staring down Karl Renner—would more accurately capture the hundred years of Austrian political history that Boyer is reconstructing. The chronological timespan covering 1867–1955 is ambitious, even radical. It threads together the temporal divisions of Austrian history that in English-language scholarship are nearly always treated separately: the huge multi-national empire and the tiny Alpine republics that followed. Barbara Jelavich's *Modern Austria: Empire and Republic, 1815-1986* (1987) covers Boyer's terrain and time period, but in textbook fashion and without an argument. To my mind, the great benefit of uniting the Imperial and Republican histories in one study is apparent only if the historian presents a compelling new *interpretation* that allows us to see both periods in a new light. This is a great accomplishment of the book. Writing a synthetic history, Boyer does not offer an easily portable "new take" on modern Austria, and he pragmatically sidesteps the "national indifference" discourse that has shaped Habsburg historiography for the last decade. He tells a story, one with a surprisingly optimistic conclusion, about a resolution of clashing worldviews. German-speaking Austrians, once fiercely opposed ideological partisans organized in mass parties born in the late nineteenth century learned after 1945 to govern themselves "with consensual, democratic methods" (39). There is a (sort of) happy ending.

Before exploring the approach and some key themes of the work, we should pause to consider the appearance of a hardcover book, 1,147 pages long (including front matter), weighing 3lbs. 2 oz. (on my kitchen scale), at this particular historical moment. As undergraduate readers grow increasingly resistant to the suggestion that they should buy "an actual book," and some publishers try to cut costs by offering only digital copies of their books for review, *Austria 1867-1955* might soon constitute an historical artifact in its own right. Given our current moment of technological transition, might Boyer have written the last "big book" on Austria? Over the course of several months, I held the book as a thing in hand. Not a book to skim, it asks a commitment of the reader. As I lugged this "summer reading" to the beach, on camping trips and on airplanes, I was reminded of my own early introduction to the thrill of historical research as a graduate student under the supervision of John Boyer. Boyer's footnotes in this volume, as in his earlier monographs on Christian Socialism, are glorious, decadent. They reveal an intimacy with his sources and historical actors that is unmatched. The present book draws extensively on the *Nachlässe* of major and minor figures housed across twenty archives and libraries. The very first time I walked into the Austrian *Staatsarchiv* in the 1990s, I was clutching an archival citation I had copied from a Boyer footnote. I passed it to the archivist, and, miraculously, a file soon appeared. A note to future scholars: there are dissertations waiting to unfurl from the footnotes of this monumental book.

Austria 1867-1955 does not have a subtitle. In lieu of summarizing its ten chapters I have organized my thoughts into four imaginary subtitles. Each presents a key theme or set of questions that stand out in the whole or, in the case of the last, an angle I wish Boyer had devoted more space to.

1 - A Tale of Two Parties

Two features of Austrian Liberalism emerge in the first 400 pages of the book: its "capacity to create institutional frameworks for the general people—the allgemeine Volk in its totality—and at the same time its inclination to assume that that Volk would want to be (and would allow itself to be) ruled by" those same German-speaking Liberal elites (167). Liberals had *capacity* and *inclination*. The two newly emergent mass parties, the Social Democrats and the Christian Socials, were born of these capacious "institutional frameworks" and forcefully outgrew the Liberals' assumptions about the body politic. Boyer's tenacity in pursuing the rise, contests between, ideological incompatibility of, demise and resurrection of, and eventual truce between the "Reds" and the "Blacks" is epic and forms the core of the study.

2 - The Little Constitution that Could, or ". . . how to (finally) make the Constitution of 1920 work" (26)

One way to read the book is as a constitutional history of Austria. Boyer structures the study around three constitutional moments: 1867, 1920, and 1945. These constitutions are reformed and even jettisoned along the way, but each stood as a founding document for its era. For the Liberals of 1867, "Law had to stand, almost float, above . . . powerful social and ideological impulses, constraining them and organizing a political society as a general mechanistic structure that would be self-sustaining and self-replicating" (107). Boyer's masterful analysis of a gradually expanding franchise stressing and eventually exploding this rather "apolitical" view of Law is magnificent and opens the way for the "Tale of Two Parties" above.

If there is a fulcrum point in this long book, it is the 1920 constitution. If there is a "hero," it could be the drafter of this document, Hans Kelsen. Drawing on Imperial Austrian jurisprudential traditions, he developed a framework of a "pure theory of law." Kelsen reasoned that "in a state 'which comprehended so many groups that differed by race, language, religion and history' it was impossible to impute state unity on social psychological or socio-biological affinities or similarities, but only as a legal entity" (635). Of Kelsen's work, Boyer writes, "Rarely in the history of constitution writing in modern European history did high theory and murky politics more serenely cohabit the same political space" (635). While the murky and murderous politics of the next twenty-five years swamped and eventually swallowed this text, it reemerged in 1945 as a "core legitimating document" of the Second Republic. We can almost imagine Karl Renner and Leopold Figl, shaking mud off the damaged document, looking into the eyes of the Allied Powers, and shrugging, "shall we try again?"

3 - The "Jewish Spirit"

Austria 1867-1955 includes a thoughtful and deeply researched chapter titled "The Catholic Dictatorship and the Nazi Occupation, 1933-1945" that examines both policies enacted against Jews and Jews' reactions as they faced increasingly dire circumstances. It goes without saying that these are topics exceedingly difficult to summarize in a synthetic history. There were around 170,000 Jews living in Vienna in 1934; in 1944, only about 6,200 Jews remained there (739, 820). The book's index alone serves to underscore the prevalent hatred of Jews in wide sections of Austrian society. Under "anti-Semitism," subcategory "among" we find in alphabetical order: "academics, artisans, Austrian students, Catholics, Christian Socials, German Nationalists, Greater Germans, middle class, public officials, right wing." Other named individuals and incidents appear throughout the list (1092). Even after the decimation of this community, postwar antisemitism lingered, "latent and widespread." Western diplomats reported the comments of Viennese clerics who "insisted that they did not hate the Jews but only the 'Jewish spirit'" (918). Boyer offers several interwar factors that exacerbated the Austrian antisemitism that had grown endemic during the First World War. Among them, severe impoverishment and high unemployment among gentiles after 1919 "stressed the emotions of many individuals and families who were all the more inclined to fall prey to Christian Social scapegoat rhetoric to explain away their own miseries." Additionally, in the climate of Red Vienna, many *kleinbürgerlich* voters equated "Reds" with "Jews" who imposed taxation and "strange modernist values on traditional private communities" (740-41). And yet, despite cataloging the antisemites and offering these carefully considered explanations for the persistence and growth of the phenomenon of antisemitism, Boyer's political history approach somehow doesn't fully capture the *Austrianness* of it all. Or maybe the awfulness of it all. For this, perhaps one must look beyond both administrative and constitutional history and party political instrumentalization of antisemitism and deeper into the realm of culture. To my mind, Boyer's survey could be strengthened with reference to Lisa Silverman's exploration of "Jewish difference" as a category against which to measure an imagined "Austrian" identity in *Becoming Austrians: Jews and Culture Between the World Wars* (2012).

4 - A History of Men

Twenty-five years ago, French historian Lynn Hunt declared, "Gender history is here to stay." This assertion has never really applied to Austrian history, where political history as "general history" has remained seemingly immune to the gender currents that have shaped French and British historiography. In this sense, Boyer's history of "state-level politics and administration in and around Vienna" (2) seems quite "Austrian"; at heart, political history can still be written as the history of men. A sub-section on "New Micro-Communities in Search of Full Citizenship Rights: The Fin-de-siècle Women's Movement" traces efforts of women who sought "to create new laws redefining civic agency for women within the Rechtsstaat and thus to change a political system that was fundamentally anti-feminist" (430). Beyond these dozens or so leaders of the turn of the century bourgeois and socialist women's movements, glimpses of female actors are fleeting. The ill-fated Mary Vetsera and the equally ill-fated Countess Sophie Chotek are named as are Maria Theresa, Rosa Luxemburg, and Henriette von Schirach, wife of the Gauleiter of Vienna, whom Hitler dismissed for her "sentimentalities" (838). Margarete Kahane, a Gestapo spy posing as a Communist agent, was one of two infiltrators "responsible for 800 arrests and the deaths of over 100 of their compatriots" (841). Jewish mother Helene David, who pleaded for help abroad to leave Austria in late 1938, was murdered in Riga four years later (832). In over a thousand pages of Austrian history, these are (by my count) the only named women. Women appear in the aggregate in discussions of two other topics: suffrage and marriage laws. After 1919 they formed a majority of the electorate, and voting envelopes were color coded by gender "so that the parties could keep track of the impact of the enfranchisement of women" (663). Women's most overt influence on Austrian politics in the book comes in 1945. Having endured mass rapes by Soviet soldiers, they constituted nearly two-thirds of the electorate and dashed Soviet hopes for Communist popularity in the Nationalrat elections (853). Now, it may seem beside the point to count women, because after all, this is a political history, and women in fact did not occupy leading positions in the Austrian government or political parties. But what strikes me is how impervious this account of Austrian political history remains to *gender*. Boyer's men of Austria have multiple identities—they are situated as creatures of class, they have national and ethnic affiliations, they have religious beliefs and animosities, they are urban or rural. Boyer has a gift for sketching lively, three dimensional portraits of Austria's leading men. Differentiated in myriad ways, their maleness nevertheless evades inquiry.

Surely, there is manhood at stake, masculinity being performed, in the complex scenes of dizzying political subterfuge that Boyer so brilliantly reconstructs throughout the book. Take this gem of a sentence (context is enlargement of the parliamentary franchise in the early 1880s):

Taafe's motives in encouraging Lienbacher's initiative remain somewhat murky: was he trying to destabilize the Liberals, or was he acceding to pressure from the feudals and the clerical Conservatives who gambled (rightly) that kleinbürgerlich voters could be put into play in ways more adverse to Liberal interests than their own, as well as throwing Lienbacher a bone after the latter's attempts to water down the imperial School Law had been blocked by Liberal members of the Herrenhaus in 1881? (215).

We have men jockeying, second guessing each other, putting each other into play, gambling, throwing bones, seeking redress for past grievances. To *not* consider the role masculinity played in such scenarios is to miss ways that power operated in the Austrian past. Every named and unnamed participant in the above scenario owes his very position, in some measure, to his status as an Austrian man.

5 -Will There Be a Volume II?

In the spirit of exchange, I will pose a question for John Boyer (perhaps tongue in cheek) about what a volume II of his *Austria* might look like. The current volume concludes with the "Construction of a New Political

Culture, 1955-1983." In this coda, "the governance problems of the First Republic, a heritage of the bitter ideological and class conflicts of the late Empire, were finally resolved . . ." (962) The Black and Red *Lager* learned to share the state; a "national and democratic maturation" (975) took place, with "each side claiming resources within the given and shared democratic legal order—rather than seeking to dominate the general political system solely for their own purposes" (977). Directly following the exile and extermination of Austrian Jewry, this post-1945 resolution was achieved in Austria's period of most extraordinary religious and cultural homogeneity. But labor agreements with Turkey in 1964 and Yugoslavia in 1966 initiated the process by which the homogenous little Alpine republic would eventually become again an Austria of diversity. Over decades, new religious/cultural minorities (this time Muslims/Turks rather than Jews) and Slavic minorities (Yugoslavs rather than Czechs) came to figure centrally in discourses of what constituted being "Austrian." This labor migration has only recently been included in Austrian historians' own accounts of their postwar history in the fledgling subfield of *Migrationsgeschichte*. It seems to me that post-1945 Austrians recycled late Imperial and interwar techniques of negative self-definition, with these various newcomers serving as a foil against which Austrians could be crafting a useable "national identity." This happened alongside the socio-economic compromises and constitutional maturation recounted in the last chapter and conclusion of the book. What historical similarities exist between management (through law) of late Imperial and interwar national/ethnic/religious diversity and management (through law) of diversity in the contemporary Second Republic? In Kelsen's words, modern Austria has again become a state "which comprehend[s] so many groups that diffe[r] by race, language, religion and history."

John W. Boyer *Austria, 1867–1955*. Oxford: University Press, 2022

Peter Becker

This is a truly remarkable book, which will provide guidance and inspiration for the next generations of scholars. It provides a political history at its best and covers a time period known for its turmoil and ruptures. With his impressive control of an extensive body of literature, Boyer integrates research that is rarely brought together into one overarching argument. He skillfully connects the history of the Habsburg monarchy with the history of two Austrian Republics and of the Nazi occupation. In my remarks on this exquisite piece of scholarship, I will start with a brief look at the regional foci of Boyer's argument and then reflect on the way he pursues his main analytical interest, i.e., the history of democratic nation building in Central Europe.

The book looks at democratic nation building in the singular. This means Boyer follows the political ruptures in 1918, 1938, and 1945 from the perspective of the Austrian republic exclusively and disregards similar attempts of building a democratic state from the remains of the Habsburg monarchy by other successor states. This restricted focus is responding to the brief of the editors of the series *Oxford History of Modern Europe* who wanted "a book that would provide a political and institutional history of Austria for the century between 1867 and 1955, with Austria explicitly referring to the German-speaking lands of the former Empire and especially Vienna, but to set that story within the crucible of dynastic, administrative, and parliamentary institutions in the general state and imperial system."

The demand of the editors is met brilliantly. The result is a narrative that does not build on a stable geographic space. When discussing Austrian history after the Great War, Boyer reduces his focus to the territory of Austria as one of the successor states of the monarchy. The reduction is necessary because he diverts from the editors' brief for good reasons and also includes some, but not all, of the monarchy's non-German speaking lands into his analysis. Which part of the monarchy is covered and what logic can be identified for his choice? To answer this question, I turned to basic lexicometric tools. Through this lens, I see a strong dominance of Vienna (5,349) as the power center of the monarchy and the two republics. Among the lands of the monarchy, Bohemia plays the leading role (609). It surpasses by far the references to Galicia (85). But also Lower Austria (111) and Styria (62) are given much less attention, even though they remain in the focus of the argument after the end of the Great War.

The prominent position of Bohemia results from Boyer's interest in far reaching changes that redefined the "institutional and ideological context for the practice of politics in the Western half of the Empire" in the 1880s (189). He relates these changes to the rise of the Young Czechs, the Christian Socials, and the Social Democrats as three new political movements and to the demise of liberalism. Bohemia is assigned an important, but certainly not the exclusive, role in Boyer's reflections on the decline of Austrian Liberalism "into a cluster of heavily regionalized and ethnically self-conscious power groups" (326). The German liberals and their political heirs in Bohemia are being portrayed as a political force focused on the defense of their national *Besitzstand* since the 1870s and incapable of a constructive engagement with their Czech counterparts. This uncompromising attitude culminated in the political turmoil around the language ordinances of Count Badeni and led to a lasting crisis, which Boyer characterizes as "domestic civil war within and among the regions that formerly comprised the old Hereditary Lands (essentially, the interests of Bohemia and Moravia set against the interests of Vienna and the Alpine Crownlands)" (189).

The importance of the crisis of liberalism in Boyer's reflections on the political development in the Habsburg monarchy can be learned from another quick look at statistics. The lemma *liberal* has a towering presence of 1,342 appearances, exceeding by far the references to the Christian Socials and the Social Democrats. Boyer traces the crisis of liberalism also to the transformation of the political system in Vienna—an argument that is well known from his earlier publications. From this perspective, the imperial capital appears as "a crucible of mass political action led by the Christian Socials and the Social Democrats" (344) since the mid 1890s.

Boyer analyzes the reframing of politics under the influence of the two new, highly disciplined party machines in great detail, especially when discussing the role of Lueger. He combines a detailed reconstruction of political strategies and policies with a more theoretical perspective, though. A constant shift in levels between the detailed narration and the conceptual reflection is one of the main intellectual attractions of this book, as it allows the readers to follow Boyer's engagement with the vast amount of empirical evidence that he is able to master when developing his argument. When he takes a step back to gain more analytical depth, he uses either a comparative perspective, usually referring to Germany, or introduces a theoretically informed viewpoint. To explain the rapid ascent of mass parties in the late nineteenth century, he uses, for example, the concept of the *shock city*, which had been developed by Harold Platt on the basis of a comparative study of

Manchester and Chicago.[1] Boyer does not take on the entire conceptual package, though, as he uses *shock city* to capture the massive demographic, industrial, and political transformation without including the environmental side of the story, which is so dear to Platt.

Boyer uses Platt's concept wittily to break the ground for developing a central tenet of his argument. Democratic nation building was not simply a question of politics and thus of new political institutions; it is closely linked in his argument to a new political culture. He strongly emphasizes this point in the conclusion, referring to the American political scientist Charles Merriam,[2] whom he introduces as a friend of Hans Kelsen's, and quotes with the notion that "democracy had to become 'a way of life'" (972). In which institutional practices does Boyer locate the emergence of this new political "way of life"? Focusing on the emergence of mass politics in Vienna as the *shock city* of the fin-de-siècle, he sees competitive urban politics as "a decisive step forward in the learning curve of the European . . . political imaginations" (345). This quote is a fine example of Boyer's profound thinking about political developments within a broad comparative perspective and with an interest in long term effects of the transformation of political practices. Still, the bird's eye view leaves the reader with some open questions. Which institutions and practices actually initiated and accelerated this learning curve? Were they restricted to the imperial capital or did they exist also in smaller industrial cities? Boyer does not divert into this anthropological perspective on political practices and culture and therefore does not provide guidance for our curiosity. Were the grassroot organizations of the two mass parties, which he refers to at another instance, responsible? Were new forms of participation in decision making processes, as in newly established accident insurance organizations, the site where a few persons became socialized into a new political rationale and acted as influencers for a wider politically active population?

Boyer covers an almost breathtaking breadth of interconnected historical developments. He presents a political history in a more traditional sense with a lucidity of argument and a complexity of thought that have characterized his writings for a long time already. To focus on the *political* in his narrative has the clear advantage that Boyer is able to look at the history of Austria across several substantial political transformations with an interest in rupture and continuity regarding personnel, institutions, and political culture. In doing so, his narrative is guided by his interest in the emergence of a stable democratic system, which characterizes Austrian politics in the aftermath of the Second World War. While his book goes far beyond a mere political genealogy of the Second Republic, his analysis of the political struggles during the Habsburg monarchy and the First Republic provide the building blocks for a fresh look at the rebuilding of the Austrian republic after the catastrophes of Austrofascism, Nazi occupation, and the Second World War.

My reference to Boyer's interest in ruptures has pointed already at a key feature of his narrative. He characterizes the processes leading towards a fragile and, finally, stable democratic system as "hard, tortuous, and fraught with great difficulties" (345). This quote is taken from his reflections on changing political systems and cultures in Europe and America. It nevertheless captures well the general thrust of his argument about Austria's political development. Changes in its political system are not presented as an evolutionary process, as a kind of morphing of old practices into new ones, but rather as the result of political crises, which destabilized the existing system and opened the way to the emergence of new forms of political organization and practices.

Crisis plays an important role in Boyer's argument. This can be learned from another look at statistics. "Crisis" and its derivatives appears 246 times, related mainly to political, financial, and social problems in the Habsburg monarchy. Boyer uses this concept in a manner that is well established in our field. This can be illustrated with a look at the concluding chapter, where he summarizes the political transformation after the Great War: "The crisis of 1914/18 eliminated the imperial order, with the Crown self-destructing in the face of military defeat, chronic domestic unrest, and bitter national partisanship. But this crisis also accelerated the emergence of new structures of democratic self-governance, enshrined in the republican Constitution of 1920" (976).

It is a strength of Boyer's narrative that he looks closely at political actors and their political context. When discussing political crises in the Habsburg monarchy, Boyer ascribes the emperor an important role—not as the authoritarian voice enforcing a solution but rather as the skillful manager of political networks using his political and cultural capital to engender a compromise. Building political capital and increasing the legitimacy of the dynasty through successful conflict management was the bright side of the coin. Failing to achieve a compromise in the Badeni crisis in 1897, as Boyer argues, was the dark side of the coin, as it left the emperor tainted; Francis Joseph "found his credibility challenged as a leader who could preserve the delicate balance of equity among the rival nationalities" (35).

Managing crisis moved exclusively into the hands of the Chancellor after the end of the Habsburg monarchy. If we follow Boyer's argument about the solution of the most serious financial crisis of the early years of the Republic, we are faced with a narrative in which Chancellor Seipel is given the key role. In his argument, Boyer follows a long tradition of conservative historiography, which has been questioned recently, however. A study by Nathan Marcus uses the rich archival holdings of the League of Nations and develops a different perspective. He points out, that "credit for drafting the League scheme and overcoming international political difficulties in its realization in August 1922 should go to Arthur Balfour and his French colleague Gabriel Hanotaux, who jump-started the League's Austrian reconstruction work."[3]

Marcus's remark introduces two points that I would like to raise in my concluding remarks. First, Boyer is an ardent reader and engages with a broad range of scholarship. He uses the work of Marcus to build part of his argument on the Geneva loan, but the assessment of Seipel's role remains part of his narrative, opening the view onto an older layer of his engagement with the history of the First Republic. Second, it is not a shortcoming of Boyer's book that it resists the temptation to pursue the many themes related to the history of democratic nation building into all their historiographical and archival ramifications. It will be the task of further research to use this excellent book as a starting point to looking beyond its regional focus and, for example, study the democratization and state building processes of different successor states from a comparative angle. Having Boyer's masterpiece available as guidance will make this task much easier to accomplish.

Endnotes

1. Harold L. Platt, *Shock Cities: The Environmental Transformation and Reform of Manchester and Chicago* (Chicago: University of Chicago Press, 2005).

2. Charles E. Merriam, *The New Democracy and the New Despotism* (New York: Whittlesey House, 1939).

3. Nathan Marcus, *Austrian Reconstruction and the Collapse of Global Finance, 1921–1931* (Cambridge, MA: Harvard University Press, 2018), 5.

Response to the Reviewers Who Contributed to the CAS Roundtable on *Austria 1867–1955*

John W. Boyer

I am grateful to my distinguished colleagues for their insightful and thoughtful commentaries. Coming from different scholarly perspectives, their own work has been of fundamental importance to creating the rich texture of current scholarship on Austrian history. Let me offer some thoughts about the book, about my personal background, and then respond to some of the salient points raised. The book was commissioned as part of a series of major studies edited by Lord Alan Bullock and Sir William Deakin for Oxford University Press, the Oxford History of Modern Europe series. The series consisted of several important and even classic thematic books on international and diplomatic history, (those by A.J.P. Taylor, Paul Schroeder, and Zara Steiner), but it primarily privileged major books with national and state frameworks: Gordon Craig's and James Sheehan's histories of Germany, Theodore Zeldin's two volumes on France, Raymond Carr's book on Spain, Hugh Seton Watson's volume on Imperial Russia, Keith Hitchens on Romania, E. H. Kossmann on the Low Countries, and so on. When Lord Bullock offered me the commission to write the book on Austria, he reported that he intended to commission parallel studies on Hungary, the Czech lands, Poland, and the south Slavs (none of which, unfortunately, have been published). Hence Bullock took the devastating ruptures of 1918 and 1945 as preordained realities, and he wanted to understand the nineteenth century through the clear and transparent view of the mid-twentieth century. When I asked Bullock what he understood by "Austria," he observed that one could view Austria from 1848 forward, or from 1955 backward, and in his mind the latter option was the most realistic way to proceed. This two-way, linear focus was obtained not because Bullock felt the nineteenth or even eighteenth centuries to be tendentious or irrelevant, but because in the case of the old Empire, he thought that the Revolutions of 1918 were fundamental in confirming the bias toward independent national states that defined the launch of the short twentieth century.

Hence, my book begins with the Empire, but it deliberately emphasizes those people, places, and institutions in the old Empire that resulted in the creation of the two Austrian Republics. In doing so, it seeks to traverse but also straddle the turning point of 1918, connecting the world of political institutions and parties up to 1918 with those that came after 1918 and even after 1945.

The book also reflects the fact that my initial engagement with Austrian history came through the lens of the history of the Catholic "Right" in Austria—the Christian Social party—and the history of modern antisemitism and in the context of comparative urban politics, with a special interest in mass politics. These vantage points gave me a particular sensibility to the *Sonderweg*-like assumptions about continuity as opposed to change that one could or should impose on Austrian history—for example, how was one to think about Karl Lueger in light of the careers of Ignaz Seipel and Engelbert Dollfuß, not to mention the sometime disgruntled resident of Imperial Vienna, the young Adolf Hitler?[1] Given my early interest in the history of the Catholic Church, and its imperial ambitions up to 1918, I also came to have a very palpable sense of the functioning of a large, semi-public corporation that defined its identity as a supra- and trans-national agent of cultural transmission. The Church was not the state, and its often-fraught struggles with the Imperial administrative state in the name of its own claims to freedom gave me a deeper appreciation of the power and success of civil society institutions in the Monarchy to defend their prerogatives and privileges.

If the Church was not the state, then what about the city? Was Vienna the state? For an American scholar interested in the history of mass politics in my own country, the parallels between urban mass politics in Chicago and in Vienna were quite fascinating. By 1900, huge cities like Vienna and Chicago constituted realms of enormous demographic and economic power, so large that they had outgrown the roles that the constitution writers of the nineteenth century imagined for them. As they grew in size and authority, they were bound to prove challenging to the liberal or liberal-authoritarian state systems installed in Europe and America over the course of the nineteenth century. Both cities—Vienna and Chicago—served between 1890 and 1930 as immense schools of civic participation and political identity formation, based on what we call in US history the patronage and clientage relations of "machine politics." I have always found it charming that, during the national election campaign in Austria in October 1990, the Freedom Party launched their advertising campaign with a poster that read "*Wien darf nicht Chicago werden*" or "Let's not let Vienna become like Chicago." In fact, looking at structures of urban governance, Vienna long ago became like Chicago and vice versa. Given such parallels, it is not a surprise, as Pieter Judson rightly notes, that I have written a very "Viennese" book. It reflects the inescapable fact that the central administrative governing institutions of both the Empire and the republics were located in Vienna, and it traces how the two major political forces—Catholicism and Socialism—that shaped much of the terrain of Austrian history in the twentieth century were born in Vienna.

During the course of writing of this book, I also assumed a senior administrative role at my university (serving as Dean of the College for thirty-one years), which gave me a range of practical experiences in managing complex budgets, political-structural changes, administrative-regime transitions, jurisdictional and personnel conflicts, and institutional legal problems. Like the churches, universities are also supra- and trans-national institutions, seeking to influence human life from a variety of identity points and with a large store of myths, rituals, traditions, and even occasional dogmas. Like the churches, they depend on effective leadership to protect their claims to enduring continuity, while in fact being forced to manage inevitable pressures for structural change and (in our time) to defend themselves against external pressures that seek to undercut their independence and ideological neutrality. These experiences, in retrospect, influenced my sense about both the durability and the fragility of institutional structures, about how social and political change comes (or does not come) about, how individuals and groups react to uncertainty and to crisis, and how effective leaders learn to use bureaucratic structures to their own advantage. My experiences in university governance thus impacted my thinking about the crucial role of leaders in crisis management and in guiding and shaping large-scale social and political change in Austrian history.

The thematic focus of the book, in the largest sense, is the emergence of political movements and constitutional structures around the turn of the century (1890 to 1910) that led, with great drama, to the project of democratic nation-building after 1945. These movements and institutions flowed through the crisis points of 1918 and 1945, and they were able, after substantial internal and external struggles, to create many of the elements of the political culture that has come to define the modern Austrian Republic. The telos (and origin) of the book is the renewed Republic as it came to exist in 1955. As the restored Republic gained public credibility and legitimacy, the idea of an Austrian civic or cultural nation (re-)emerged, and by the 1960s and 1970s public opinion polls began to show a clear trend of popular confidence in the conception of an admittedly still somewhat ambiguous Austrian national identity. The democratic Republic of 1918 was now joined with public acceptance of an Austrian cultural nation, concluding what I have called the project of democratic nation-building that began with the electoral reforms of 1907.

Seen from the vantage point of the 1970s, of all of the so-called successor states who came into existence in November 1918, modern Austria had the most fortuitous circumstances. Not only had it escaped Soviet domination, establishing a neutral state under international law whose independence was guaranteed by the four occupying powers, but it presumed an implicit normative "neutrality" within the state itself. If each party could not "own" all of Austrian society separately—as each had aspired to do in the 1920s—perhaps they could own it together. This calculation of parity control was a silent but critical motive undergirding the Austrian neo-corporate state after 1945.

Pieter Judson and Maureen Healy raise valuable and justifiable issues about cultural identity and social interaction in public and private spaces. The concept of national indifference has proven both attractive and fruitful, and it has garnered much attention in recent historiography. It is part of a larger arsenal of concepts having to do with personal and group identities in the old Empire, and as such it is certainly worth discussing and debating, particularly in those Crownlands or even subordinate administrative units that had mixed ethnic populations. But if we seek to understand a general political system that rested on publicly validated elections, I do think that we must pay great attention to the consequences of voting choices, whatever the private or personal attitudes of the voters outside of the voting booth. Most Czech-speaking (or perhaps more accurately, "Czech-identifying") citizens who voted in Bohemia and Moravia voted for Czech candidates after 1880, and most German-speaking (or "German-identifying") voters voted for German candidates of some kind. Some ethnic cross-over voting in regional and national elections up to 1914 may have occurred, but it seems to have been negligible in terms of final aggregate outcomes. The reasons and motivations why voters behaved in this way can be debated, and their own private/personal relations with fellow citizens who had different primary languages may have been more complex, but these electoral outcomes licensed the formation of strong ethnic political parties who claimed a holistic legitimacy and a special entitlement to group representation that was deeply influential, and these patterns would certainly flow through the revolutions of 1918.

For the Alpine crownlands, where the population was predominantly German-speaking, the issue of ethnic multiversity even on private levels was less relevant or, perhaps, relevant in different ways. Regional and class identities and religious identities played formidable divisive and unifying roles in these areas as much or much more than "national" concerns in generating electoral choices. For Vienna itself, the issue was similarly relevant, but in a different sort of way, for Vienna was a city of many different ethnic streams, all of whom had to come to terms with what Karl Lueger insisted were the overarching assimilationist claims to loyalty of the *Vaterstadt*, under the guise of which Viennese voters of all sorts of ethnic backgrounds were strongly encouraged to set aside any possible ethnic and even class differences to unite against the Social Democrats and the pan-Germans.

My book assumed that elections do have consequences, and that the struggle for citizen rights that defined modern Central European history in the middle and later nineteenth century meant that, if one took power from the Dynast and gave it to the plebs, then the structural policy choices by which the plebs governed itself had enormous consequences for all dimensions of the lives of the citizens, even their most private concerns. Elections became the main plumbing system through which the newly legitimated coercive powers of the administrative state and the exercise of popular sovereignty began to flow after the 1870s. If Aristotle's *Politics* asserted the teleological essence of the classical polis as the end and the fulfillment of all individual proclivities, since the mid-nineteenth century the modern polis has demonstrated that such unifying work was hard to achieve and even harder to sustain in the face of increasingly complex structures of voter preferences. However fascinating private identities may be, when they are rolled up into public power via popular elections based on mass political parties, the civic stakes become very high indeed. Since elections ultimately involve allocations of resources and the use of coercive state power, politics leave a deep imprint on private life that one really cannot overlook. This is ultimately why political history is so important and, to make a digression to present-day America of 2024, it is why the act of citizens voting in elections (as opposed to not showing up to vote on election day) is of extraordinary importance in our time as well.

Perhaps the most interesting feature of the national identity issue for "small" Austria is that of imperial and republican continuities. For the situation by the 1970s had become striking in creating a new kind of nationality, not one beholden to language per se, but to a slow combination of traumatic fate, upended history, multiple Cold War anxieties, and shared cultural sensibilities about who Austrians were "not" as much as who they "were." The work of Karl Renner may be relevant here. The elderly Renner's admiration for cultural cohesion beyond class warfare and for a culturally integrationist rhetoric that might be exploited by the modern administrative state was a formidable factor in his strategies as State Chancellor of the provisional republican government after April 1945. Indeed, Renner postulated the idea of a distinct Austrianness in his declaration of April 1945—in addition to being a state whose population were anti-Fascists and who belonged to the collective social categories of "*Arbeiter, Bauern und Bürger*," Austria also had an "*österreichisches Volk*."[2] As is well known, Renner began his political career as a young intellectual who studied law at the University of Vienna and who then worked in the library of the central parliament. Renner first made his name by publishing books and essays on the Habsburg nationality problem. Renner believed nations were essentially cultural communities developed on the basis of voluntary accession, not communities based on coercive will and legal domination and that they could not be defined as territorial states but only on the basis of what Renner called the "personality principle." Renner thus emerged as a forceful proponent of a new way of approaching the now enshrined "nationalities problem" by trying to contain it as a substantially "cultural" issue. He also believed that the state was called upon to fulfill several different functions that would be better and more efficiently served by reconceptualizing its internal boundaries, hence his notions of double networking the multinational state with agencies for economic and fiscal services and with parallel organizations supporting the "cultural" interests of formally defined, but voluntary, national communities. Renner's theories were fascinating but went nowhere under the Empire. In a surprising way, however, the conjuncture of genuine democratic political practices and economic stability and the slow maturation of cultural attitudes of "Austrianness" in the Second Republic was a remarkable coming full circle of Renner's most earnest aspirations for the Empire. What was impossible under a multi-"ethnic" Empire, eventually, with considerable drama and fierce struggle, came to be plausible under a republican, democratic, and neutral small Austria—a democratic administrative state, bounded by and supported by a cultural nation (but not an "ethnic" nation). After many decades of living in and then beyond the multi-national Empire, after becoming "free" in 1918, "unfree" in 1938, and again "free" in 1945, Austrians finally united the concepts of democratic republicanism on the one hand and cultural nationalism on the other.

As to the issue of masculinity raised by Maureen Healy, the book is a history of party politics, constitutional institutions, and administrative decision-making, and the individuals playing such roles were very substantially men until well into the 1960s. That said, I do discuss the goals of women's political and labor organizations in the 1890s and 1900s as well as changes to educational resources for women and to marriage law. I agree that it would be fascinating to think about the identities of key male leaders in a more three-dimensional way, through the lens of gender, but I found little in the actual documentary record that would have given me sound and defensible evidence to do so. As Peter Becker rightly states, there remain a host of fascinating issues for future historians of the Empire to grapple with.

Maureen Healy's suggestion about a sequential volume dealing with Austria from the 1980s to the present is fascinating and a legitimate thought experiment. Such a volume would be strikingly different in that it would chart the slow disintegration of the voter blocks that made up the Great Coalition and the rise since the 1980s of new "third way" and deeply populist forces in Austrian politics. Ironically, the state of Austrian politics today reminds one much more of the late Empire, with voluminous factional fragmentation replacing grand coalitional discipline. The question might also be raised about more recent traditions of national leadership. Renner, Figl, Raab, and Kreisky, regardless of their many flaws, were skilled leaders who had a commanding presence among large sections of the electorate. Is such a style of leadership even possible today?

Gary Cohen's observation about the lack of deeply detailed social and economic history in the book is fair and accurate, and this was deliberate. So too was my decision, noted by Günter Bischof, not to engage in cultural or intellectual history in a systematic way. Because the book was conceived as a political/constitutional/regime history with some attention to administrative style and structure, I deliberately focused on the multiple streams of politics, indeed on the very invention of modern competitive electoral politics. I sought to provide a reasonably fulsome social context for political developments, and in that sense civil society is present. As for intellectual history, I did try to provide a cultural and social context for the intellectual revolution of fin de siècle Vienna in Chapter 5, where I sought to re-engage and re-frame Carl Schorske's book. But Gary is correct that readers interested in economic and social structure history will have to consult the excellent work of scholars such as David Good, Roman Sandgruber, Richard L. Rudolph, Max-Stephan Schulze, Michael Pammer, Tomas Cvrcek, John Komlos, and many others.

Peter Becker raises a fascinating issue in what he calls a more anthropological dimension of political history, namely, the cultural role of subordinate or grassroots associations or groups in creating the larger collective personality of the new mass party movements. I remember thinking about this issue when I worked through the materials relating to the Christian Social *Bürgervereinigung*, whom Lueger once characterized as his "grenadiers of social order" and who met regularly in the Rathaus before 1914, and it is plausible that the short-term political decisions and more general normative viewpoints that such groups embraced depended heavily on the personalities of local leaders. This would be intriguing to explore, especially if one had access to personal papers, diaries, or other reminiscences.[3] The book's coverage of changes in higher education policy and especially the lived culture of the universities also encompasses some of the political anthropological perspective that Peter hopes for.

Peter Becker also raises the issue of Seipel's role in the 1920s. Seipel was a brilliant tactician and, aside from Karl Renner in the years 1918–1919, perhaps the single most crucial political actor in the First Republic. He was a wellspring for the radical anti-clericalism of the Social Democrats, and his resistance against any form of collaboration with the Left and his simultaneous reliance on the small Greater German faction made a continuation of the original Great Coalition of 1918–1920 totally impossible.

Finally, a word about comparisons and contrasts. In an age that esteems transnational history, the multiple regions and realms of the old Empire are natural sites for fascinating cross-border comparisons and parallelisms, but I sought in my book to provide some gentle comparisons with a different territorial object, namely, German history. Partly this inclination is autobiographical, since I began my doctoral studies at the University of Chicago intending to write a dissertation in German history under Leonard Krieger, (Krieger left for Columbia University before I began work on my dissertation, however, and instead I had the good fortune to study with two young assistant professors, Bill McGrath and Emile Karafiol, both of whom had written doctoral dissertations on Austrian topics), and I have always approached the Empire through the double visage of German and Austrian historiography.[4] But it does strike me that Jim Sheehan's arguments many years ago about the interconnectedness of German and Austrian history in his classic essay, "What is German History," have even greater relevance today in light of the severe collapse since the 1990s of the classic *Sonderweg* thesis as a way to define and give meaning to *kleindeutsch* German history.[5] The general field of modern German history is in dire need of new interpretive interventions and new multi-generational analytical frameworks, and the current richness and variety that marks Habsburg/Austrian historiography may confirm Sheehan's hunch that, in spite of 1866, the "Germans" have much to learn from the "Austrians."

Let me again thank my colleagues for their stimulating commentaries on my book.

Endnotes

1. In regard to the issue of antisemitism, I remember my colleague and friend Peggy Anderson asking me after my first book on *Political Radicalism* appeared if I was prepared for the storm of criticism that she thought might be just over the horizon because my book could be seen as trying to explain Karl Lueger's antisemitism rather than outrightly condemn it. (For whatever reason, such attacks never emerged.) If one fast forwards to the present, and the ongoing debate about the future fate of the Karl Lueger statue on the Ringstraße facing the Third District, the issues seem uncannily similar.

2. "Regierungserklärung," April 27, 1945, in Karl Renner, *Denkschrift über die Geschichte der Unabhängigkeitserklärung Österreichs*, second edition (Zurich: Europa-Verl., 1946), 78-83.

3. One example of this genre involves Heinrich Hierhammer before 1914. See Herta Hafner, "Heinrich Hierhammer. Vizebürgermeister von Wien, 1905-1918. Ein bürgerlicher Aufsteiger" (Diplomarbeit, University of Vienna, 1988).

4. McGrath was a student of Carl E. Schorske, when he still taught at UC Berkeley, whereas Karafiol was a student of Theodor E. Mommsen and Walter M. Simon at Cornell. In the end the chair of my dissertation committee was William H. McNeill, a global historian whose boldness in assimilating huge historiographical domains to construct high-level interpretive paradigms I found inspiring.

5. "It is perhaps understandable, but certainly unfortunate, that the defeat of Austria in 1866 resulted in her extrusion from German historiography—just as it is regrettable that the political partition of North America resulted in the scholarly separation of Canada from 'American history.' A good deal might be learned if these various histories were brought together again. We know, for example, that ideas, institutions, and individuals from the Habsburg lands continued to have an impact on the political life of the *Kaiserreich*. This was most obviously and disastrously true in the case of rightwing political movements, but the same pattern can be found elsewhere as well. Surely historians should make more of the fact that Social Democracy in Germany and Austria seems to be more alike than either is like any other party in Europe. Similarly, a *grossdeutsch* history of liberalism and of political Catholicism, both of which began before the division might display the evolution of these movements in a new light." James J. Sheehan, "What is German History? Reflections on the Role of the *Nation* in German History and Historiography," *Journal of Modern History* 53 (1981): 2-23, here 18-19.

Review Essay

The Writing of Autobiography

Frank Trommler, *Die hellen Jahre über dem Atlantik: Leben zwischen Deutschland und Amerika* (Vienna: Böhlau, 2022)

Hella Pick, *Unsichtbare Mauern*, trans. Jaqueline Csuss (Vienna: Czernin Verlag, 2022)

Manfried Rauchensteiner, *Betrifft Geschichte: Ein Streifzug durch die Zeiten* (Vienna: Böhlau, 2023)

Günter Bischof

Starting with Stefan Zweig's famous *Die Welt von Gestern*,[1] we are used to literary figures and politicians writing their autobiographies/memoirs[2]—we are less accustomed to academics and journalists looking back on their lives. Hella Pick, the well-known journalist for the liberal British newspaper *The Guardian*, asks the right questions in the final chapter of her autobiography: how candid can I be when I relate my life's story? How far can I go when I reveal my thoughts and experiences? How open should I be about my innermost self? Am I ready to tackle my life story? Will I know myself better in the end? Will it be my catharsis? (425).

There is a rich theoretical discourse about writing auto/biography.[3] In the most basic sense, autobiography "is the story of the life of an individual by him/herself," while biography "is each approximation and effort towards a person (*Annäherung und Bemühung um eine Person*), and his/her accomplishments, and the literary regeneration for third parties." While an autobiography refers back to the subject who is telling their life story, biography is written by a third party.[4] The life stories told are supposed to be exemplary. Modern media also have a voyeuristic interest in human lives and their basic humanity. Artistic-scholarly biographies also question ready-made identity patterns. Autobiographies aim at understanding oneself. The authentic autobiographer hopes to fill lacunae in their memory.[5]

Autobiographers are intent on establishing the facts of their lives, as far as their memories permit; they are far removed from the postmodern skeptical view of the individual that has defined recent biographical writing ever since Pierre Bourdieu's essay in the "biographical illusion," doubting that a life can be told as a coherent life story.[6] Or, as Volker Depkat reminds us, the new biography "oscillates between life itself and the narrative representation of it."[7]

Undoubtedly political memoirs are crucial source material for historians. But what can academics and journalists contribute to the writing of history? Both are extremely well-informed, either observing history unfold—journalists writing "the first drafts of history" themselves—or being close to those "present at the creation." Both are articulate and know what matters in life. These lives of one German-born American academic, an Austrian-born British journalist, and an Austrian academic are characterized by having to come to terms with the Nazi past. The three books deal with encountering the German and Austrian pasts in their travels around the world and coming to terms with issues like the Holocaust personally.

Frank Trommler, the well known *Germanist* who taught most of his career at the University of Pennsylvania has written his memoirs, and a highly absorbing life story it is. For Trommler, the "bright years" of German-American cooperation were the Cold War years. After the fall of the Berlin wall in 1989, but definitely after the September 11, 2001, attacks on the World Trade Center, there was a "darkening" of this bilateral relationship, a certain alienation between the two countries. For Trommler, the closeness between Germany and the US had become his "lifeblood" (*Lebenselixier*) (333). And Trommler starts his book out with the observation that he never was a "fanatical American" (*Amerikabegeisterung*) and that his life's trajectory brought him to America due to many coincidences (13).

Jan Logeman tells us what the American Century means—what Trommler puts at the center of his story:

The decades following World War II are generally regarded as the height of the "American" Century in transatlantic relations. American hard and soft power dominated diplomatic and political as well as economic and cultural relation to a degree that gave rise to the notion of American hegemony. The era saw the project of constructing a "modern" West unfold under the leadership of the U.S. experts and institutions, with European societies often perceiving postwar reconstruction as, in many ways, an "Americanization" of their politics, cultures and economies. The Marshall Plan, productivity missions, as well as American products and popular culture, all added up to a massive flow of transatlantic transfers from the

United States to Western Europe, expanding the reach of America's 'irresistible empire" . . . . As important as the American model became, Europe and Europeans continued to be relevant in science and academia too.[8]

After his arrival in the US in the 1960s, Trommler became one of the most important mediators in the German-American world. Yet Trommler grew up at the end of the Second World War in the Soviet zone of occupation (in Zwönitz, Saxony). This explains why young Trommler was not "Americanized" like his contemporaries in the Western zones. The postwar trauma of his childhood was the internment of his father by the Soviet authorities. His father had built up a successful factory for children's shoes. He was willfully interned by the Soviets as a "capitalist," even though he had been an anti-Nazi. His father returned after three years in Soviet captivity. He was spent and would never be the same again. Trommler comments: "He had used up his life's strength to survive" (37). He was depressed and committed suicide. "His life had weighed him down too heavily" (42). After unification, his hometown Zwönitz honored Trommler's grandfather by naming a street after him and honored his father by including the shoe factory in the city museum (288-290); the legend of the "profit hungry capitalist" father was thoroughly revised in post-Cold War Zwönitz (367).

Even though they managed to hang on to their house, Trommler's family then moved to Offenbach in West Germany. There he attended the humanistic *Gymnasium*, where "America as a source of new youthful self-confidence with film songs, rock'n'roll, jeans fashion and way of speaking remained at a strange distance, even though 'we lived in the heart of the American military presence'" (50). He read about the Nazi years and the Soviet occupiers more than the American occupation (53-54). He prepared for a career in journalism and had an internship with the local paper, the *Offenbach Post.*

Trommler's book then goes into his youthful travels around Europe ("*Hitler's Erben auf Reisen*"). During travels to England, France, Greece, and North Africa, the issue was always whether these young Germans be made responsible for Hitler's war crimes. In a British bar, the barkeeper pronounced "*We forgive you!*" (63). In Greece, Trommler was reminded of the German paratroopers in Crete (66); in Tunisia, Rommels' exploits came up regularly (70). Travel allowed this young man to see the world and grow up and remind him of the legacy "Hitler's Germany" left everywhere.

Trommler also covers his years of university studies in Berlin, Vienna, and Munich. He studied German (*Germanistik*) in Munich and also dabbled in politics. The student opposition was directed against the "fascism of the older generation" (92). Many of his professors in reactionary Bavaria had been cooperating with the Nazi regime. The University of Munich was not interested in bringing back well known émigrés like Alfred Kantorowics, who was determined "to further the cumbersome awakening of the intellectual Left in the stale Federal Republic [*miefige FRG*]" (93). Trommler's personal contacts with Kantorowics awakens in him a lifelong interest in refugee scholars, talented people postwar Germany lost by abandoning their émigrés ("*das andere Deutschland*") (93). Trommler was determined to acquire a doctorate to further his future career in journalism. He wrote his dissertation about the Austrian novelists Joseph Roth, Robert Musil, and Heimito von Doderer and their representation of "the Austrian" (96), picking his topic up while a student in Vienna. He quickly turned the dissertation into a book, and the "young *Piefke*," as Trommler put it, became known as an "Austrian expert," which brought him a coveted invitation from Austria's "culture czar" Wolfgang Kraus to give a talk in his famous *Gesellschaft für Literatur* in Vienna (100-102).[9]

Trommler continued his travels after finishing his studies. He went to England, France, and at last to the United States without ever having developed "enthusiasm for America as a way of life," (*Amerikabegeisterung als Lebensform*), unlike his peers (107). Yet America stayed on his wish list of countries to visit. His colleagues gave him the advice to give lectures on his research on the German-Austrian novel at American universities. He quickly had to learn about American *Germanistik* and where it was practiced. He travelled the country on buses and lectured successfully at Ivy League colleges and from Stanford to Houston. The net result was a lucrative invitation from the German Department at Harvard University to become a visiting lecturer in the fall of 1967. He made enough money to visit Latin America with his girlfriend (later his first wife). Instead of returning to Germany to start a career as a journalist for the *Frankfurter Allgemeine Zeitung*, he became an academic (116-125).

Harvard subsequently hired him back. He now learned to navigate American academia between the "old boys networks" and a younger generation of scholars who wanted to establish a new canon by including twentieth century and contemporary literature to appeal to a growing body of students in the late 1960s. In 1969, the University of Pennsylvania ("Penn") hired him, and before he started he embarked on a journey around the world with his new wife. Again he lectured all over Asia on this tour before he started at Penn in 1970. He sees the 1970s as a transition (*Scharnier*) in his life's story (167). At Penn he began to study German exile literature and the literature of German Democratic Republic, (*DDR-Literatur*), the much-neglected literature in universities of his German *Heimat*. He also began his work as a university administrator and became chairman of the German Department at Penn, turning down a job offer from Princeton University (190).

In his capacity as chair, he got involved in organizing the "Tricentennial Conference," commemorating the first Germans coming to Germantown, Pennsylvania, in 1683. This forced him to take a broader view of the German-American encounter, with its history and immigration trajectory (including ethnic and Jewish studies). German-American relations at the time had reached a Cold War low due to the large rallies in Germany against the stationing of a new generation of American atomic missiles (192). Part of the challenge was to raise the money for this mega-conference, including the publication of the papers. The Thyssen Foundation became the principal sponsor. The German President Karl Carstens gave a keynote address during the concluding dinner. The two-volume publication became a *summa* of German-American relations and Trommler one of its principal impresarios. [10]

In the following years, Trommler got married again, had kids, and dedicated his professional life to the renewal of German Studies in the United States. The generation of émigré scholars had contributed a lot towards the professionalization of *Germanistik* in the US. Now a new generation of younger American *Germanisten* dedicated themselves to making the study of German more attractive to students in the American humanities tradition (209). "German Studies" became more interdisciplinary and opened itself up to women becoming a mainstay in the field (209); the famous GDR writer Christa Wolf's visiting professorships in the US supported this trend. Trommler is an inveterate name dropper, which characterizes all these chapters.

He furthered "reforms" in the German Studies curriculum, which included the adequate teaching of the German language, also as the President of the German Studies Association (GSA) in the early 1990s, right at the time when the Cold War ended. As President of the GSA, he made sure that the community of scholars in German Studies needed to be personally involved in the reforms of the field. He also got support from *Deutscher Akademischer Austauschdienst* (DAAD), investing money in the continued teaching of the German language when it lost its luster with the fall of the Berlin Wall (237, 242-243). With the ending of the Cold War, the GSA meetings in Philadelphia (1988) and Milwaukee (1989) became crucial in an interdisciplinary interpretation of the dramatic events unfolding in Germany and Europe. Here Trommler's contacts with the community of historians since the Tricentennial Conference in 1983 were helpful (239).[11] The new interdisciplinarity of German Studies became a shining beacon in sections like "Germany as the Other: Towards an American Agenda for German Studies" (241). During this time, in 1987, the Kohl Government established the German Historical Institute in Washington, DC, hoping to counteract the dip in the image of the Federal Republic with the opening of the Holocaust Museum (244-245). After unification, which none of the experts (Trommler included) managed to predict, the old Atlantic Bloc was beginning to "drift apart" and Germany (now including the former GDR) had to write its own history (245). Trommler devotes an entire chapter to the "Jewish contribution to German Studies" (252-270). Trommler also welcomed developments of German Studies in the US, such as increasingly concentrating on including "minority cultures" such as Jewish and Turkish Germans and German multiculturalism as well as the Holocaust and the crimes of the Nazi regime in the self-understanding of the new Germany (265).

In the 1990s and beyond, Trommler continued to play a key role as an institutional mediator in interpreting the culture of the reunited new Germany in the United States. He continued to work closely with the DAAD and became the cultural coordinator for the "American Institute of Contemporary German Studies" (AICGS) in Washington, DC. Above all, the culture of the former GDR needed to be included in its programming "to go beyond the well-worn cliches of the Cold War." AICGS acted as a "think tank" that also intended to influence public affairs (292). To correct the mysterious cliches "between the hatred of foreigners in Rostock and the debates about the Holocaust Memorial in Berlin" (297) took an effort in a Washington that was now less interested in Germany. When Chancellor Kohl launched the "excellence initiative," starting three new centers at Harvard, Berkeley, and Georgetown, the German departments around the country were not so pleased—would there be any money left for universities beyond these elite institutions? (312). Soon these centers were complimented by a Midwestern one in Madison, Wisconsin, in cooperation with Minneapolis, and a Canadian one in Montreal cooperating with York University in Toronto.

Saving the German-American Library of the German Society of Pennsylvania was another one of Trommler's grand accomplishments in German-American relations (322-332). This above all meant fundraising from German foundations like Thyssen again. President Joachim Gauck during one of his trips to the US visited the restored Library to add official German appreciation (331). In 1999, he organized another conference in Philadelphia that was assessing German-American relations during their time of "alienation" since unification. The publication following the conference tried to assess American contributions to German history and German contributions to American history.[12] Edward Rendell, the mayor of Philadelphia, gave the concluding keynote (331).

The attacks on the World Trade Center ended "the bright years" of trans-Atlantic relations like a torch. On this day the twenty-first century began, and the close German-American relations was ending (333). The war in Iraq terminated the "common language" between the two countries and cultures, and Trommler's role in AICGS also came to an end. The distance between Germany and the US grew—Americans and Europeans did not communicate well any more ("*redeten aneinander vorbei*") (340). Having spent so much of his time on improving German-American relations, Trommler's disappointment at the end of his book is palpable; he retired and kept writing. Surely there are few people who did more than Trommler to add empathy to his important trans-Atlantic relationship.

Given that Trommler made his name and launched his career with a study of the modern Austrian novel, it is disappointing that he makes the same mistake that many observers of "German émigrés" to the US make, conflating Austrian-born émigré writers and *Germanisten* with "German" ones.[13] In the conference "German Literature, Jewish Critics" at Brandeis University, the Jews born in Vienna Walter Sokel and Egon Schwarz were introduced as German Jews (264). In the case of "German-Jewish authors," he does identify Robert Menasse, Robert Schindel, Ruth Bekermann, and Doron Rabinovici as hailing from Vienna (265-266). The young Austrian *Germanist* Stefan Maurer has pointed out the vital contribution of Viennese Jewish *Germanisten* in the United States by referencing Wolfgang Kraus, the Austrian *Literaturpapst* who got Trommler started. Kraus noted about the postwar period in 1977: "The history of Austria and its great poets and philosophers is written by Americans or the European émigrés," adding "our memory now is located over there, by such a detour we will gain our memory, our self-reflection." In Austria, the appreciation of émigré *Germanisten* came even later than in Germany,[14] maybe because they did not have a strong interlocutor like Trommler.

Hella Pick's is a fascinating life story of one of the second half of the twentieth century's best known international journalists. The subtitle of the book, "The adventurous journey of one of the greatest female political journalists to the summits and abysses of contemporary history" is so much publisher's hype. But hers is a truly absorbing life. As child No. 4672, she was lucky to make it out of Vienna as a young Jew and come on a *Kindertransport* to England after the "Anschluss"; her mother made it to England too three months later; her grandmother lived in Prague and did not make it into exile—she probably perished in Theresienstadt concentration camp. First, Hella lived with a generous host family in London—the Infields—who took her in. England became Hella's new home (31-45). During much of the war, she and her mother lived as "refugees" in the Lake District; they were poor but kept finding kind people who helped them, like paying Hella's tuition fees to go to school (46-69). Toward the end of the war, Hella was accepted as a student at the London School of Economics (LSE), where none other than the famous Socialist intellectual and professor at the LSE, Harold Laski, agreed to pay for her tuition fees behind the scenes (71). During the war, the LSE had been relocated to Cambridge. She studied political science and economics and graduated toward the top of her class (72-83).

Her dream to work for the United Nations in New York did not come true. After a couple of odd jobs, *West Africa*, a weekly publication dealing with decolonization issues in Africa, hired her as a journalist. This was her great luck. She travelled much in the area and was present when many of the British- and French-governed West African countries gained their independence (Ghana, Senegal, Guinea, Nigeria, etc.). She met and became friends with the leaders of these newly independent countries: Kwame Nkrumah Leopold Senghor, Sékou Touré, Alhaji Abubakar Tafawa Balewa (92-138). During her time in West Africa, she began to do freelance work for the BBC and *The Guardian*. Without a job after a couple of years in Africa, *The Guardian* hired her for freelance work and eventually appointed her as the correspondent to the United Nations in New York. So she got her job at the UN after all, but as a journalist, observing and writing on the movers and shakers and the bureaucrats (including Kurt Waldheim). The UN was at the center of the East-West conflict and the "Security Council became the fighting arena for the Cold War" (147). It was an exciting time at the UN. She reported on the Congo Crisis and the Cuban Missile Crisis and other hot spots around the world. The highly admired journalist Alistair Cooke, *The Guardian*'s bureau chief in the United States, became her principal mentor. (149). She met President Kennedy and also began to report on US foreign policy and the civil rights struggle. She covered the march from Selma to Montgomery and met Martin Luther King. In 1964, she also covered the Presidential race between the incumbent Democrat Lyndon Johnson and the reactionary Republican Barry Goldwater. The war in Vietnam became an issue and Johnson won in a landslide (168-170, 190-217).

After all these years in the US, she returned to Europe and became the principal European correspondent for *The Guardian* in Geneva. In 1968, she covered both the student revolt and the beginnings of the US-North

Vietnamese peace talks in Paris. She was supposed to cover the Warsaw Pact invasion of Czechoslovakia but never made it to Prague, covering events from Vienna. She returned to Geneva to cover UN affairs but was dispatched to the US in October 1968 to cover the Presidential race between the Republican Richard Nixon and the Democrat Vice President Hubert Humphrey. She detested Nixon, who won (218-246). She increasingly began to cover Great Britain's application to join the European Economic Community and France's repeated veto. The many technical issues involved were not easy to bring to the attention of *The Guardian*'s readers (266-270). In her final assignment as principal diplomatic correspondent, she covered Eastern Europe and the end of the Cold War and German unification. She spent much time in Poland and all of the Soviet satellite countries and was in a privileged position witnessing the end of the Cold War (304-336, 361-375).

After a thirty-five-year career with *The Guardian*, she retired and began writing books. She was hired to write the life story of fabulously wealthy Aga Khan. After following him around the world and drafting his biography, Aga Khan shared the manuscript with the leadership of the Islamic faith community of the Ismaelites, whose religious leader he was. They did not like it and the book was never published (337-360). Earlier she had been thinking about writing a book on West Africa and decolonization and also a book on the United Nations. Those projects came to naught. Late in her life, she wrote a well-received biography of Simon Wiesenthal, which got her back in touch with her Viennese roots. What impressed her most about Wiesenthal was his lifelong focus on "keeping the memory of the Holocaust and its devastation alive" (403).[15] It was the charismatic Willy Brandt who confronted her with the Holocaust and German World War II memory in an all-night conversation in a London hotel room. It reminded her how, compared to the Germans, the Austrians resisted remembering their Nazi past (254-255). She also wrote a book about postwar Austria's reputation in the world, *Guilty Victim*, which also dealt with Austria's troubled World War II memory (388-414). In the final chapter of her life, she worked for a think tank her friend George Weidenfeld had started to deliberate with top-notch thinkers, politicians, and journalists the future world order. Like Pick, the publisher Weidenfeld was another successful refugee in England from Vienna (415-424).

Pick's book, however, also covers very personal issues—her close but contentious relationship with her mother, who wanted her to get married and have kids (235, 246-247) as well as her love affairs with men. She has a chapter on her love affair with the Indian UN diplomat Narendra Singh while she lived in New York. He was the son of a Maharaja and was supposed to marry a Hindu woman, not a Jewess (173-189). She also dedicates a chapter to her love affair with the German intellectual Ralf Dahrendorf, who became the Director of the LSE, her alma mater. Dahrendorf initially pursued Pick with reckless abandon. He was married with three kids and as it turned out did not want to make a commitment to live together with Pick. She is brutally candid and admits that the sudden end of this affair almost drove her to commit suicide (275-303).

This autobiography makes it clear that Pick has always been proud of her pioneering role as an early and leading female journalist (248) but also very honest about her insecurities in her life in spite of her professional success. As a refugee in England, she was craving security in her life (73). She calls her lifelong insecurity "her invisible cage" (433); earlier she called it "invisible walls" (the title of her book) (19). She usually delved into work to overcome these inner demons (248).

Pick also was on a lifelong search for her identity. During the war, she did not want to speak German. She notices "compared to my obsession to deny my Austrian roots, keeping my Jewish background a secret went even deeper." It would take years "before I could talk about it, let alone embrace it" (51). When she first returned to Vienna in 1949, she just had received her British passport. She was not sure whether she could feel Austrian after she had been uprooted and kicked out of Austria. She wryly comments, "after a while, Austria received an acceptable place in the jungle of my identities" (87). What impressed her about New York, when she began to work there, was that Jews were the majority in the city and also were prominent citizens of the town (137-138). When in Geneva, she had good Jewish friends who went to the synagogue—she did not and continued to struggle with her "unmastered" Jewish identity (234-235). Her research for the Wiesenthal biography brought her back to her "roots" in Vienna. Even though "she was forcefully torn out of her home in 1938," she returned to Austria (often) without holding a grudge (393). She will always remember the crimes committed by Austrian Nazis. Her Jewish identity is "always present in the background," she argues in her final chapter, but her British identity has served as her "anchor' in her life. Her European identity is more a cultural one. In spite of her "bundle of identities," her insecurity is still with her (433). It sounds like she came to terms with her Jewish identity only late in life when she returned to Vienna for an extended period of time—confronting this issue certainly was a kind of catharsis for her. Pick's struggle with that issue is a topic that makes reading this book worthwhile, particularly from the perspective of a student of Austrian history. Amazingly, late in her life, England awarded the refugee Hella Pick the CBE (Commander of the Order of the British Empire) at Buckingham Palace, (Prince Charles substituted for his mother), recognizing her fabulous career by knighting her (431).

About the Warsaw Pact invasion of Czechoslovakia, she notes "Washington protested against the invasion, but did not take any revenge" (239). Washington's response to the invasion of Czechoslovakia, in fact, was indeed very mild. Apart from a protest in the UN, Washington did nothing; "no action" characterized the Johnson administration's response. Secretary of State Dean Rusk feared "if there were military intervention, there would be world war."[16] Pick says she met Foreign Minister Edward Schewardnadse during an opening party of negotiations for the Conference and Security in Helsinki in 1973 (274). During the CSCE conference preparations, Andrej Gromylo was still Soviet Foreign Minister; Schewardnadse represented the Soviet Union in that office in the later 1980s under Michail Gorbachev. She did meet and interview Schewardnadse in Ottawa in February 1990 during "Two Plus Four talks" for German unification (376-379). Like many journalists of her stature, Pick is an inveterate name dropper, having befriended many top world leaders during her long career from Kwame Nkrumah to Willy Brandt and Lech Walesa, the Viennese Cardinal Franz König, and the Austrian Socialists Hannes Androsch and Heinz Fischer (393, 405).

Manfried Rauchensteiner is one of Austria's best-known historians of contemporary history. For a long time, he was *the* military historian in Austria. He lectured in Austrian history at the University of Vienna and served as the Austrian military's chief historian before he became the director of the Museum of Austrian Military History (*Heeresgeschichtliches* Museum) from 1992 to 2005.[17] In his "preface" he sees memoirs as "thinking back" (*Rückbesinnung*) (7). Autobiography "becomes difficult the moment one 'begins to play with one's life's work'" (7). Since he has published a lot, and a number of long books, he decided to publish a selection of shorter pieces (scholarly articles and *Feuilleton* pieces written for newspapers such as the venerable Viennese *Die Presse* and the leading German intellectual weekly *Die Zeit* (7)). These pieces are ordered along the larger themes Rauchensteiner covered in his life. So Rauchenteiner's *Betrifft Geschichte* is an intellectual biography of sorts—we get no interesting personal details of his life like we do in Trommler's and Pick's books.

Each of his book's chapters are made up of four to seven short essays, all of them absorbing and exceedingly well written. Each chapter begins with a collage of items fitting the chapter, usually posters of exhibits he organized at the Military History Museum as its director (and chief curator) and pictures of his weighty books. The first chapter on "Movers and Shakers in History"

(*Gestalter der Geschichte*) covers figures such as Emperor Maximilian and Archduke Carl, who beat Napoleon in the Battle of Aspern in 1809 (11-46) and who had been the subject of Rauchensteiner's post-doctoral *Habilitation* at the University of Vienna. The next chapter covers the First World War. The collage in the beginning features a piece of barbed wire from the mountain front in the South Tyrol, next to Rauchensteiner's magnum opus, *World War I in Austria-Hungary*. The individual essays cover "the murderer" of Sarajevo, Gavrilo Princip; a moving essay on the death of Emperor Francis Joseph in 1916; and a piece on the Villa Giusti, where the armistice was signed between Italy and Austria-Hungary in November 1918 (47-106). Rauchensteiner visits most of the places he writes about, like the Villa Guisti, and gives the reader a good sense of these places. Chapters on the years between the wars follow. He asks the questions: "What was Austria's role within the framework of Hitler's Greater German Reich?" and "What was Austria's part in the rise, firm establishment and the victory of National Socialism?" He does not care to give answers. He mentions that the Americans thought of Austria as "Naziland" (180) but does not further reflect on this view.

The chapter on the Cold War begins with a collage of a poster from an exhibit on the Iron Curtain at the Military History Museum. One would expect Rauchensteiner's book on the early Cold War in Austria *Der Sonderfall* , which was my bible in graduate school,[18] to be in the picture, but instead he features his book on Austrian security policy in the Cold War.[19] The essays in the chapter cover the Soviet invasions of Hungary and the Warsaw Pact "intervention" in Czechoslovakia as well as a chapter on the end of the Warsaw Pact. Rauchensteiner's conservative world view comes through in the critical chapter on Bruno Kreisky ("*König Kreisky und die Briten*"), based on the biting semiannual summary report of the British ambassador in Vienna (225-230). Rauchensteiner, the good archival historian that he is, knows that the Public Record Office in London opens its files exactly thirty years after the event. The British diplomats are usually well educated and well informed and write trenchant observations in such reports. To be at the PRO at the beginning of the year when the new files open is a windfall for astute historians. So he read the Ambassador's document from 1977 in the spring of 2008 and published this piece in *Die Presse* on May 31, 2008.

In the next chapter, Rauchensteiner covers "Biographical" stories from Prince Eugene to Prince Metternich to Carl, the last Habsburg Emperor (*Der himmmlische Carl*) (274-281). This story is on the longstanding efforts to have Carl beatified by the Catholic Church in 2004, which happened under the Polish Pope John Paul II. Sketches of the former defense minister Karl Rösch and the military historian Christoph Allmayer-Beck, a mentor of Ruchensteiner's, complete this chapter. Rauchensteiner does ask the question why Rösch, who became Kreisky's Defense Minister, kept his silence about his Nazi past and World War II involvement—he was member of the SA and the Nazi Party NSDAP, taught in a Nazi Party academy (NAPOLA), and became an officer in the Wehrmacht. Two chapters dealing with museums and exhibits (*Sammeln und Ausstellen*) and diverse matters (*Nicht ganz Alltägliches*) complete the volume. In his chapter on historical exhibitions, he does write about the Military History Museum that he headed (307-313). He writes about its genesis but does not reflect on the critiques of the museum by a younger generation of historians. He also writes about the longstanding efforts "to build an Austrian National Museum/'House of History'" ("*Haus der Geschichte*") (314-329). He is upset by the fact that, in international public opinion, Austria mutated from "everybody's darling" to an "ugly little Alpine fortress suffering from amnesia, full of incorrigible, xenophobic neo-Nazis" (329).

Like the American military historian Stephen E. Ambrose, Rauchensteiner is a very gifted writer. He remarks in his essay on the Congress of Vienna that the kings of small states like Saxony and Naples and "exotic" people like Napoleon's second wife Marie Luise of Austria "were the hangers-on and the ladies of the demi-monde, [*Adabeis und Kokotten*], who made the Congress more colorful, but did not add to the success of the negotiations" (37). In his essay on Prince Eugene defeating the Ottomans in the battle of Zenta, he finds Zenta "a city not worth visiting" ("*die Stadt, die keine Reise wert ist*") (20). Sometimes he adds an off-the-cuff remark like "*C'est la vie*" (154). Sometimes he invents words like Hitler suffering from a "mouth diarrhea" ("*Munddiarrhöe*") of speaking incessantly. He is a learned commentator and uses a lot of citations from German literary treasures like the poet Georg Trakl's observation in his poem *Grodek*: "All streets end in black putrefaction" ("*alle Straßen münden in schwarze Verwesung*") (52-63). This citation (also the title of the essay) comes in a moving piece on refugees within the Austrian-Hungarian Monarchy during the First World War. The numerous essays—some twenty-five of them—published in the weekend *Feuilleton Spektrum* of *Die Presse* are clearly written with a broad readership in mind. Together with the frequent references to exhibitions he curated at the Military History Museum, it makes Rauchensteiner Austria's "public historian." This makes the republishing of these short pieces indeed a sort of intellectual legacy of Rauchensteiner's. He wants to be remembered by his writings, not his life's story.

But all three memoirists battle with the legacies of Nazism in Germany and Austria. That might be a common thread in these books. What comes through explicitly in Pick's memoirs and implicitly in Rauchensteiner's essays is that Austria, after all, has a long postwar history of denying its involvement with National Socialism; Otto Rösch is not the only one.

Endnotes

1. Stefan Zweig, *Die Welt von Gestern: Erinnerungen eines Europäers* (Stockholm: Bermann-Fischer Verlag, 1942; repr. Cologne: Anaconda Verlag, 2013); English version: *The World of Yesterday* (New York: Viking Press, 1943; repr. Lincoln: University of Nebraska Press, 1964).

2. Bruno Kreisky, *Erinnerungen: Das Vermächtnis des* Jahrhundertpolitikers, ed. Oliver Rathkolb (Graz: Styria Premium). This is a one-volume summary of Kreisky's three-volume memoirs; see *Zwischen den Zeiten: Erinnerungen aus fünf Jahrzehnten* (Vienna: Kremayr & Scheriau, 1986); *Im Strom der Politik: Der Memoren zweiter Teil* (1988); *Der Mensch im Mittelpunkt: Der Memoiren dritter Teil*, ed. Oliver Rathkolb, Johannes Kunz und Margit Schmidt (1996); English version: *The Struggle for Austria: Bruno Kreisky on Peace and Social Justice*, ed. Matthew Paul Berg, trans. Helen Atkins/Matthew Paul Berg (New York: Berghahn Books, 2000); Franz Vranitzky, *Politische Erinnerungen* (Vienna: Paul Zsolnay, 2004); Heinz Fischer, *Reflexionen* (Vienna: Kremayr & Scheriau, 1998).

3. Christian Klein, ed., *Handbuch Bigraphie: Methoden, Traditionen, Theorien* (Stuttgart: J.B. Metzler, 2009); Bernhard Fetz, ed., *Die Biographie--Zur Grundlegung ihrer Theorie* (Berlin: De Gruyter, 2009).

4. Michaela Holdenried, "Biography vs. Autobiography," in *Handbuch Biographie*, ed. Klein, 37-43 (here 37).

5. Ibid., 38-43.

6. Christian Klein and Falko Schnicke, "20. Jahrhundert," in Ibid., 251-264 (here 261).

7. Volker Depkat, "The Challenges of Biography and Migration History," in *Quiet Invasers Revisited: Biographies of Twentieth Century Immigrants to the United States*, ed. Günter Bischof (Innsbruck: StudienVerlag, 2017), 299-309 (here 302).

8. Jan Logemann, "More Atlantic Crossings? European Voices and the Postwar Atlantic Community," *Bulletin of the German Historical Institute Supplement* 10 (2014): 7.

9. On Kraus and the *Gesellschaft für Literatur* and its progressive role in catholic, reactionary Vienna, see Stefan Maurer, "Wolfgang Kraus: Impresario of Austrian Literature and Cold Warrior," *Austrian Lives*, ed. Günter Bischof, Fritz Plasser, and Eva Maltschnigg (Contemporary Austrian Studies (CAS) 21) (New Orleans: UNO Press; Innsbruck: Innsbruck University Press, 2012), 25-76.

10 Frank Trommler. Joseph McVeigh, *America and the Germans: An Assessment of a Three-Hundred Year History – Immigration, Language, Ethnicity* 2 vols (Philadelphia: University of Pennsylvania Press, 1985).

11. I can attest to this as I attended both these GSA meetings.

12. Frank Trommler and Elliott Shore, *The German-American Encounter: Conflict and Cooperation between the Two Cultures 1800-2000* (New York: Berghahn Books, 2001).

13. Typical of this would be the British journalist Peter Watson, *The German*

Genius: Europe's Third Renaissance, the Second Scientific Revolution, and the Twentieth Century (New York: Harper Perennial, 2010), 714-742; and Anthony Heilbut, *Exiled on Paradise: German Refugee Artists and Intellectuals in America, from the 1930s to the Present* (Berkeley: University of California Press, 1983).

14. Stefan Maurer, 'Living with Austrian Literature': The 'Austrian Literary Association' and the Émigré Germanists in the United States," in *Quiet Invaders Revisited: Biographies of Twentieth Century Immigrants to the United State,* ed. Günter Bischof (TRANSATLANTICA 11) (Innsbruck: StudienVerlag, 2017), 147-162 (here 147).

15. On Wiesenthal as a Holocaust scholar, see Gerald Steinacher, "The Nazi Hunger: Simon Wiesenthal and the Täterforschung," in *The Second Austrian Republic*, ed. Marc Landry and Eva Pfanzelter (CAS 31) (New Orleans: UNO Press; Innsbruck: Innsbruck University Press, 2022), 191-208.

16. For more detail on the response of the Johnson administration and the CIA, see the essays by Günter Bischof and Donald P. Steury in *The Prague Spring and the Warsaw Pact Invasion of Czechoslovakia in 1968*, ed. Günter Bischof, Stefan Karner, and Peter Ruggenthaler (Lanham, MD: Lexington Books, 2010), 215-248 (here 220).

17. "Manfried Rauchensteiner," *wikipedia.org*, accessed May 14, 2024, https://de.wikipedia.org/wiki/Manfried_Rauchensteiner.

18. Manfried Rauchensteiner, *Der Sonderfall: Die Besatzungszeit in Österreich 1945 bis 1955* (Graz: Styria, 1979).

19. Manfried Rauchensteiner, ed., *Zwischen den Blöcken: NATO, Warschauer Pakt und Ősterreich* (Vienna: Böhlau, 2010).

Book Reviews

Bruce Caldwell and Hansjoerg Klausinger, *Hayek: A Life, 1899–1950* (University of Chicago Press, 2022)

Janek Wasserman

Bruce Caldwell and Hansjoerg Klausinger state their aspirations in the opening pages of *Hayek*: "to provide what we hoped will be considered, for this generation anyway, the definitive full biography of F.A. Hayek" (3). They have achieved this massive accomplishment beyond any doubt, delivering a landmark work of biographical and intellectual reconstruction. The volume, the first of a proposed two, covers the Austrian-British economist's life from his Viennese birth in 1899 through his tempestuous divorce and move from England to the United States in 1950. The book deftly weaves together family and personal biography, intellectual history, and history of economic thought, situating the account within the contexts of *fin-de-siècle* Central Europe, interwar Vienna and London, the ages of Depression and fascism, and world war.

In laying out their methodological position, the authors stress that completeness and accuracy (3) are their lodestars, thereby privileging factual information over critical commentary or engagement with the vast scholarship on Hayek. While this produced some drawbacks—more on these later—this was a well-reasoned choice given their unprecedented access to archival materials. As general editor of Hayek's *Collected Works*, Caldwell had interviews with Hayek, Hayek's family, and friends that others had never seen. He also possessed diaries, datebooks, and other Hayek family archivalia to supplement the existing picture of the economist. Finally, he conducted oral interviews with Hayek's relatives and peers that further enriched the study. Klausinger, the editor of two volumes of the *Collected Works* and the world's foremost scholar on Hayek's German-language work, was the natural collaborator for this project, providing rich contextual knowledge on Austrian history and its institutions, not to mention his meticulous reading of challenging German-language sources. Ironically, the two historians of economic thought do their finest scholarship here on the biographical and personal dimensions of Hayek's life. It is precisely where the authors bring new egodocuments and extensive historical knowledge together that the book offers the newest and freshest insights.

Hayek is divided into six sections and moves chronologically. Parts I and II cover Hayek's youth, Great War experiences, and university days in

Vienna. Parts III and IV span his ascension as a world-renowned economist and move from First Republic Austria to London, not to mention early romantic connections, marriage, and fatherhood. Parts V and VI treat his World War II endeavors and postwar reconstruction work, including the bestselling book *Road to Serfdom* and the establishment of the famed Mont Pèlerin Society. The book concludes (*sans* a true concluding section) with the painful details of Hayek's drawn-out estrangement from his first wife Hella and their acrimonious divorce.

As an encyclopedic reference work, *Hayek* will offer different gems to different readers, rewarding everyone from those unfamiliar with Hayek's world to the most expert. To the initiated, the greatest innovation is the access to Hayek as a son, brother, lover, father, and friend. The opening section on Hayek's genealogy and early years is an imaginative and comprehensive reconstruction of his well-to-do background. (NB: The book lost even more of those details going from manuscript to book, so the online appendix is well worth visiting.) Caldwell and Klausinger animate the cultural context into which the young Fritz entered, offering a glimpse into a Zweigian *Welt von Gestern*. Channeling Hayek's essay "Two Types of Minds," they present him as a "puzzler," ("someone who would keep coming back and rethinking a set of claims"), rather than a "master," ("someone who knew every detail of a literature"), and they show how his naturalist father and scientific relatives inculcated this disposition.[1] Similarly, the authors depict his wartime experience with clarity, supplementing a relative paucity of sources with valuable scholarship on the Habsburg war effort.

While *Hayek* rightly shifts its attentions more to the subject's intellectual and professional development after Part I, less of this material is new or noteworthy, especially because these authors have published extensively on these areas. It remains in the realm of the personal that the book shines. One gets a vivid picture of his friendships with Walter Magg, Herbert Fürth, Fritz Machlup, and later Lionel Robbins. Hayek the intrepid hiker and skier, the dancer, and lover comes into focus. The burgeoning relationship with Helene (Lenerl) Bitterlich, the love of his life and second wife, is told with sensitivity and scrupulous attention to detail. Hayek's sojourn in the United States in 1923–1924 receives its first full treatment, and it reveals his ambivalence about "the unknown civilization that is growing in America."[2] Equally valuable is the reconstruction of early interactions with Ludwig von Mises in the *Abrechnungsamt für Kriegsschulden*, where we learn of some of Hayek's earliest policy work. We gain greater insight, too, into his courtship of and betrothal to his first wife and his gendered attitudes toward marriage and women. In the latter half of the book, the authors depict his personal and professional life in London with intimacy and care. They do not shy away from engaging with his relatives' antisemitism, and the Hayeks' evolving attitudes toward the Nazi state is powerfully told.

The biggest contribution is the examination of the deterioration of Hayek's first marriage, his reconnection with his young love Lenerl, and the protracted separation and divorce proceedings. This saga spanned more than a decade and two continents and resulted in the following outcome: "this perpetual stranger [began] a life in the New World, at a new job and with a new wife, with a slate that had, rather painfully, been wiped very clean indeed" (730). The authors are at their critical and analytic best in sorting through materials from all participants in this sad affair—Fritz and Lenerl, their daughter Christine, Hayek's mother, Lionel Robbins, the lawyers, later recollections from secretaries and friends—and present a balanced assessment.

Of course, *Hayek* recounts some of the most famous episodes in Hayek's life and career, often puncturing or revising old stories. The authors reconsider the relationship between Hayek and John Maynard Keynes—not as one of pure antagonism and enmity but of differences of emphasis in their respective defenses of liberalism. The excavation of the famous story of Keynes and Hayek on air raid duty is delightful. Discussions of relationships with Ludwig Wittgenstein (and his poker) and Karl Popper also gain sophistication. Moreover, as one would expect from these two scholars, all of Hayek's writings receive summary treatments, with some—especially from the late 1930s and 1940s—getting extended coverage. None of these readings are new, but it is valuable because *Hayek* synthesizes the lifetime work of Caldwell and Klausinger.

The criticisms that one can make of such a seminal work pale in comparison to the immense benefits it provides. One issue—as it is for all authorized biographers—is the authors' closeness to their subject. In one footnote (700), they cite Hayek's daughter Christine from an interview with Caldwell: "Poor old Pa. I hope you won't be too harsh on him." *Hayek* puts to rest any fear that the authors will challenge Hayek the scholar or intellectual critically. In doing their best to reproduce Hayek's thought process and intellectual output, they rarely highlight shortcomings—with the lone exception being *The Pure Theory of Capital*, which Hayek himself criticized. Similarly, the authors largely reproduce Hayek's reductive readings of British "men of science," Hans Kelsen, Harold Laski, Karl Mannheim, Otto Neurath, and others. The book downplays shortcomings in the *Road to Serfdom*'s central argument and does not consider reasoned reviews that rejected Hayek's Whiggish intellectual history of individualism and the abuse of reason, especially the notion that French rationalist ideas led to socialism and then to Nazism.[3] Finally, the authors fail to take up the origins of some of Hayek's blind spots on gender, culture, and class. While the authors do admirable work throughout in confronting Hayek's close contact with German nationalism, antisemitism, and even Nazism, his conventional attitudes on women and his almost complete unawareness of poverty or working-class experience undoubtedly informed his project as "one of the last political economists" (11) and as a student of civilization (to use Erwin Dekker's term). The authors addressed some of these shortcomings in their introduction (8-10), yet the lack of engagement with these issues (or with more critical Hayek scholarship) merits some reconsideration.

None of the above comments detract meaningfully from the masterpiece Caldwell and Klausinger have wrought. They have achieved their aim of crafting the defining Hayek biography for our generation. The book will stand alongside Malachi Hacohen's *Karl Popper* (for Central European intellectual biographies) and Robert Skidelsky's *Keynes*, Susan Howson's *Lionel Robbins*, and Jennifer Burns's *Milton Friedman* (for biographies of twentieth century economists) as a paradigmatic work.[4] The book will be the go-to reference work for initiates and experts on Hayek and will merit return visits that will bear fresh fruit. One can only wait with bated breath for the concluding volume, which will further enrich our growing knowledge of this brilliant yet flawed man.

Endnotes

1. One could argue that Hayek borrowed this idea from Isaiah Berlin's "Hedgehog and the Fox."

2. Friedrich Hayek, *The Constitution of Liberty: The Definitive Edition* (Chicago: University of Chicago Press, 2011), 38.

3. For a great example, see Bert F. Hoselitz, "Professor Hayek on German Socialism," *American Economic Review* 35, no. 5 (December 1945): 929-934.

4. Malachi Hacohen, *Karl Popper – The Formative Years, 1902-1945: Politics and Philosophy in Interwar Vienna* (Cambridge: Cambridge University Press, 2000); Robert Skidelsky, *Keynes*, 3 vols. (London: Harcourt/Penguin, 1983-2001); Susan Howson, *Lionel Robbins* (Cambridge: Cambridge University Press, 2011); Jennifer Burns, *Milton Friedman: The Last Conservative* (New York: Farrar, Straus and Giroux, 2023).

Ke-Chin Hsia, *Victims' State: War and Welfare in Austria, 1868–1925* (Oxford University Press, 2022)

Peter Baldwin

Let's not mince words. A book on the development of disabled Austrian soldiers' pensions during the turn of the penultimate century is never going to set pulses racing. And yet, Joseph Schumpeter once claimed to be able to hear the thunder of world history in accounts of public finance. Academics are experts at making interesting subjects boring. More seldom do they make less-than-scintillating topics fascinating. Hsia's book is one such exception.

Students of Austrian history will find much of interest here. The social policy reforms of the post-WWI years—though revised during the Nazi era—laid the foundation of the modern Austrian welfare state after 1945. The interwar years are thus not just the doom-and-gloom scenario so often portrayed. Strong institutional continuities are seen to bridge over the WWI era's revolutionary events once one delves below the waves of events to examine the bedrock of bureaucratic infrastructure. Telling details offer *apercus* into the social history of the period: the extreme shortages of clothing in the period after WWI, for example. So acute were they that, grudgingly, the army sent off demobilized soldiers in their uniforms for simple lack of anything better to dress them in—though not before stripping them of all identifying markings so as to discourage the men from begging in full military regalia.

Sticking to the narrower field of social policy, the inherited classification of the Austrian welfare state (based on Esping-Andersen's classic tripartite schemata) as an example of a corporatist approach is belied here by an account that yet again (see Matthieu Leimgruber's work on Switzerland, *Solidarity Without the State*) uses the history of Europe's smaller nations to shed new light on larger developments. In Hsia's hands, Austrian social policy goes beyond just a way to provide civil servants with gold-plated benefits while ignoring any broader redistribution of burdens to become a forerunner of the social citizenship model in which all members of society are potentially in need of the state's attention, thus supplicants.

But the book's real value stems from the more general light it sheds on the development of social policy writ large. Hsia is not the first to investigate the role of war and military provision for its personnel in social policy's evolution. Theda Skocpol famously argued for the role of Civil War pensions in founding the US welfare state (*Protecting Soldiers and Mothers*). And, of course, the effect of war and the state's need to up the quality of its fighting men as a factor in the welfare state's development has been a leitmotiv since Richard Titmuss.

But Hsia goes further. Part of his argument concerns the state's growing presence in the lives of war wounded—retraining them and directing them to occupations not necessarily of their choice as part of their physical rehabilitation. Nationalist concerns, which would be repeated after the Nazi Anschluss, foresaw agricultural colonies manned by war victims in the eastern provinces. But he also argues for the military disability pensions introduced with postwar reforms starting in 1919 as a cornerstone of universal entitlement.

The book's first half treats the nineteenth century and the old regime of military pensions as the grudging bequest *von oben* of a paternalist state to those of its primarily career soldiers who had fallen in harm's way and could not manage on their own. Benefits were meager and stringently parsed, intended as supplements to other sources of support and extended as charity. Often, they were delivered *in natura* as housing in institutions for invalids. Various reforms in the late nineteenth century of the military benefits system failed to take account of the radical democratization that universal military service had introduced in 1868.

That changed with WWI, mass mobilization and warfare, the Russian revolution, and eventually the threat of similar political radicalization at home. From this emerged the insight that keeping citizens onboard in wartime, and preventing them from becoming restive in the peacetime of defeat, required a pact by which the state agreed to be responsible for their welfare if they were damaged in service to the nation, whether on the front or elsewhere in the war effort.

However, treating war victims as a pressure or interest group cuts in two directions. Universal conscription made military service an appurtenance of citizenship, at least for every male. All were asked to put their lives on the line for the nation, and in return it owed them the duty of support for the sacrifices exacted. Mass warfare, with its widespread casualties, stamped a massive potential pressure group out of the ground—half a million out of a population of six. Add in their dependents, and the political risks of ignoring the victims of war swelled.

Conversely, maimed soldiers were not an interest group in the conventional sense. For brief moments, they might be united by their common plight. But they quickly dissolved back into their more primary political, social, class, or other divisions and identities and, in any case, did not long outlast the end of war as a demographic group or cohesive political force. This ebb and flow explains both the sudden and unexpected victory of generous provision in 1919 and the equally rapid disintegration of the political support for reform during the interwar years.

This is a fine work of social history, based on massive archival research, lucidly written, and with lessons both for Austrian history and the more general development of the welfare state across the industrial world.

One complaint: it should be forbidden to publish books with endnotes where the page number of the text to which the notes belong, or at least the chapter, is not indicated in the header. The cost to the author and publisher of including this is vanishingly small, and the advantage to the reader is immense.

That is followed by a pat on the head: this book is published open-access. Thanks to the Mellon Foundation's funding, the author's recognition that being read is more important than a few dollars of royalties, OUP's willingness to settle for a lump sum upfront rather than unpredictable but likely modest sales, and the insight of the Indiana history department's P&T committee that open-access books are as rigorously peer-reviewed as their paper-and-binding equivalents and intellectually much more effectful, if this review piques your interest, to read the book, all you have to do is follow this link: https://fdslive.oup.com/www.oup.com/academic/pdf/openaccess/9780197582374.pdf (which unfortunately is not the DOI included in the book itself—a dead link. Not all the gremlins have been banished yet.)

Hans Haider, *Ernst Jandl 1925–2000: Eine konkrete Biographie* (J.B. Metzlder, 2023)

Jeroen Dewulf

Hans Haider, an Austrian literary critic, recently published a biography of Ernst Jandl (1925–2000), undisputedly one of the leading poets of his generation, whose work is profoundly Austrian yet simultaneously deeply international in nature. Haider's study is a good example of the kind of work an author biography should be—a well-written book with a clear structure and research materials from both national and international archives that adds new insights to the author's life, places them in the cultural and political contexts of their time, and contributes to the understanding of their work, while providing an objective assessment of their importance.

While the book's subtitle—"*eine konkrete Biographie*"—may suggest otherwise, this biography is not experimental in nature. It provides a traditionally structured, chronological overview of Jandl's life, from his birth in 1925 until his passing seventy-five years later. It does so in 592 pages, divided into 11 chapters, starting with a portrait of Jandl's family in interbellum Austria; his Catholic upbringing; his fathering of a child as a teenager; his first poems in imitation of his mother's religious poetry; his time as a soldier and as a POW; his growing interest in jazz; his study at the University of Vienna; his work as a teacher in Austria and the United Kingdom; his failed marriage; his intellectual development; his lifelong friendship with Friederike Mayröcker; his early poetic work and the eye-opening discovery of concrete poetry; his difficulties in combining his duties as a high school teacher with the desire to become a professional author; his perseverance in achieving this goal in spite of a lack of recognition; his relationship to national and international authors; his problems with publishers at the Walter Verlag and, later, Luchterhand; his revolt against the Austrian PEN-Club; his mental health problems; his growing popularity and, eventually, his celebration as one of Austria's greatest authors of the twentieth century.

Not without reason, Haider started his biography with a description of Mayröcker and Jandl walking through the streets of Vienna. The poetic couple that performed jointly in countless literary events and were buried together in an honorary grave at Vienna's *Zentralfriedhof* would undoubtedly deserve a joint biography. Yet, as Haider pointed out, this will have to be a work of the future, since Mayröcker's archives at the National Library have only recently been made accessible to researchers.

What remains as one's strongest impression after reading this voluminous biography is admiration for Jandl's tenacity in becoming a poet, his "*widerliche[s] lebenszweck*," as he phrased it in the poem "*kommentar*," and to do so in spite of all the adversities he faced at the beginning of his literary career. The latter did not, as one might expect, only come from the conservative establishment that failed to see the importance of his work and belittled it as an infantile repetition of what Expressionists and Dadaists had already accomplished decades ago. The opposition also came from leftist critics, who looked down upon his concrete poetry that, in their narrow view, lacked revolutionary potential. Haider contrasted such opponents by those who did believe in the quality of Jandl's work: Mayröcker, of course, but also other Austrian poets, such as Andreas Okopenko and Erich Fried, the Scottish poet and artist Ian Hamilton Finlay, the Swiss publisher Otto F. Walter, the Dutch curator Martin Mooij, and the German studies scholars Jörg Drews and Wendelin Schmidt-Dengler.

A fascinating discovery is that Jandl already enjoyed international recognition and popularity with his concrete poetry at a time when not a single German-language publisher had cared to publish an anthology. As late as in 1958, the Suhrkamp Verlag even rejected it with the claim that his writings could not be considered poetry. Only a few years later, however, Jandl elated the large audience that had gathered in June 1965 at London's Royal Albert Hall for an "International Poetry Incarnation" and aroused more enthusiasm with his anarchic humor than Allen Ginsberg, Michael Horovitz, Adrian Mitchell, and other famous Beat poets. It was not until the fall of 1966 that the small Swiss Walter Verlag published the soon-to-become legendary *Laut und Luise*, with classic poems such as "*schtzngrmm*," "*wien: heldenplatz*," "*falamaleikum*," and "*lichtung*." A revealing reflection of the skepticism Jandl had to overcome is that this publication came with an epilogue, where Helmut Heißenbüttel felt the necessity to stress that these were actual poems. Soon after, Jandl followed Otto F. Walter to the Luchterhand Verlag, which allowed him to reach a much broader audience with subsequent publications, including the anthologies *sprechblasen* (1968), *der künstliche baum* (1970), *dingfest* (1973), and *der gelbe hund* (1980), often published both in book form and as a vinyl record.

While Jandl is often perceived as a typically Austrian author, whose work is read in connection to Luwig Wittgenstein, Fritz Mauthner, Hugo von Hofmannsthal and the nation's philosophical and literary concern with

Sprachkrise/Sprachkritik/Sprachskepsis; to Austria's tradition of using dialect in literature; and to H. C. Artmann, Gerhard Rühm, Gerald Bisinger and other representatives of the Wiener Gruppe, Haider convincingly demonstrated the international dimension of Jandl's intellectual development. Of importance here are the Bolivian-Swiss poet Eugen Gomringer; the French poets Pierre Garnier and Jacques Prévert; and, in particular, English and American authors such as Ernest Hemingway, Gertrude Stein, E. E. Cummings, and Gerard Manley Hopkins. Haider also paid attention to Jandl's connections to the United States, where in 1971–72, he was a writer in residence at the University of Texas and the University of Wisconsin. This was followed by a lecture tour at twelve additional American universities and, later, an invitation by Ivar Ivask to be a member of the jury for the 1974 Neustadt International Prize for Literature at the University of Oklahoma.

Surprising for an author whom one tends to associate with Austria's leftist intellectual milieu and whose parody of biblical phrases famously caused a scandal at the conservative Walter Verlag is the discovery that Jandl maintained all his life a (critical) connection to the Catholic faith of his youth and looked for ways to unite his Social Democratic ideals with Christian morality. More importantly, Haider showed how this concern impacted his writing and declamation style by highlighting the profound influence of the rosary prayers he had grown up with. Not by accident, thus, Jandl requested to be buried according to Catholic tradition with a rosary wrapped around his hands.

Haider also pointed out, however, that these conservative elements coexisted with political activism, including Jandl's participation in the public protests against Kurt Waldheim's presidential candidacy, his opposition against the German spelling reform, his appeal to the Vienna archbishop to condemn the military intervention in Iraq and, surprising perhaps, his defense of Arnold Schwarzenegger after the Hollywood star had been coitized in the *Kleine Zeitung*. Equally important is that his commitment to intellectual avant-gardism allows connections to contemporary debates. Significantly, Jandl was among the first German-speaking authors to incorporate into his work the linguistic creativity of non-native speakers of German. In his 1970 poem "*da ist ein Garten*," with its line "*im jungen, da ist ein mädchen*," we find an early reflection on the topic of transgender identity, whereas his 1968 radio play *Der Gigant*, an allusion to Cassius Clay/Mohammed Ali, dealt with the history of slavery and its toxic legacy in systemic racism. The latter was just one of several radio plays Jandl developed, often in partnership with Mayröcker, where his impressive rhetorical talent undoubtedly contributed to the success of productions such as the *Fünf Mann Menschen* (1968) and *das röcheln der mona lisa* (1970). Haider also highlighted a broad variety of other projects Jandl was involved in, from literary translations (including Gertrude Stein, Robert Creeley, John Cage, Christopher Middleton, and W. H. Auden), film projects, and jazz performances to the production of children's literature. Although he also worked together with the internet pioneer Franz Krahberger, the digital era unfortunately arrived too late for Jandl to take full advantage of the poetic potential of the new media.

The one regrettable aspect of the book is that Haider placed so much emphasis on Jandl's depressions that particularly the second half of the biography acquired a rather gloomy character. As a result, he failed to convey a good balance between the darker and more cheerful/playful aspects of Jandl's work. Haider also paid surprisingly little attention to the use of Jandl's work in schools and the popularity of his legendary poem *ottos mops* that inspired countless children to experiment with writing their own sound poetry or to "*jandl*" as this practice has come to be known. Precisely this unfortunate omission makes the biography's final sentence—"Ernst Jandl: *Die Show geht weiter*"—feel like an abrupt and somewhat forced optimistic ending.

Overall, however, Haider deserves great praise for his book. This first extensive biography of Jandl is a must-have for all universities in this country with a German studies program.

Martin Senn/Franz Eder/Markus Kornprobst, eds., *Handbuch der Außenpolitik Österreichs* (Springer VS, 2022)

Paul Luif

This handbook is a first in tackling Austria's foreign policy in a comprehensive way; it encompasses more than 800 pages. The volume includes an introduction and a conclusion, nine articles on the processes of Austrian foreign policy, eleven contributions on the different policy areas, ten articles on Austria's relations with (groups of) foreign countries, and five items on Austria's activities in and vis-à-vis international organizations (including the European Union). Most of the articles were written before Russia's invasion of Ukraine. With its large number of contributions, it is not possible for a reviewer to pay tribute to all articles. The main purpose of this review is to expose possible bias and some lacunae in the text and point to literature that has been overlooked.

In the introduction, the editors provide several reasons for publishing the book. First, Austria as a "neutral small state" pursued since the "beginning of the Second Republic [1945] an active and engaged foreign policy" (2/3, numbers refer to the reviewed book). This is obviously not exactly true, since any kind of active foreign policy was only possible after the withdrawal of the occupying powers in 1955. The authors then give a few examples for Austria's activities *directly* influencing international affairs, its neighborhood policy and its policy in the United Nations (UN). The only recent example for influence in world politics concerns Austria's leading role in bringing about the Treaty on the Prohibition of Nuclear Weapons (see below). The establishing of international organizations in Vienna shows Austria's *indirect* influence on global politics. A second reason the authors give for publishing the book has been the changing context of Austria's foreign policy, be it the end of the Cold War, joining the European Union (EU) in 1995, or the increasing complexity of world politics (3/4). Thirdly, in particular after EU membership, the proactive neutrality policy was abandoned and Austria assumed the role of a "pragmatic observer" (5, quoting Müller and Maurer). In public debates, Austria's foreign policy rarely has become visible, except in discussions on neutrality. To fill this void is the fourth purpose of the book. Finally, this book is the first comprehensive analysis insofar as previous publications have been testimonies by diplomats, analyses by specialists of international law, historical accounts,[1] and the study of specific topics by political scientists (6).

Somewhat surprisingly, especially considering by the abandonment of neutrality by Finland and Sweden and their recent applications for membership in the North Atlantic Treaty Organization (NATO), the chapter on neutrality by Senn is the first and obviously one of the book's central chapters dealing with the substance of Austria's foreign policy. After a standard definition of neutrality, the description of "four phases" of Austria's neutrality follows: the "establishment" of an Austrian type of permanent neutrality (diverging from the Swiss role model) and then the globalization of neutrality after 1968 (first Kurt Waldheim and then particularly from 1976 under Bruno Kreisky, 34).[2] A reorientation came after the end of Kreisky's chancellorship in the mid-1980s. Neutrality was reduced to its narrow core, especially after Austria joined the EU. The final, fourth phase is called by Senn the phase of "stagnation" (37). All political parties (except the NEOS) now support neutrality; the "differential" neutrality has become also "de-politicized" (37). According to Senn, these changes have been mostly caused by external factors; Austrian domestic politics are almost never accounted for by him. Thus, his analysis of Austrian neutrality resembles more an international law perspective than a political science assessment.[3] As studies show, domestic influences on the interpretation of neutrality and with it the prospects for Austrian foreign policy played an important role on several occasions. In the early 1960s, the ÖVP tried to reduce the reach of neutrality law to enable a close relationship with the then-European Communities (EC).[4] In the mid-1980s, after the de facto bankruptcy of the nationalized industry, the SPÖ had to accept that, in contrast to its former interpretations, neutrality would be compatible with EU membership.[5] Towards external partners, e.g. in the General Agreement on Tariffs and Trade, it was easier to argue with the obligations of "neutrality" than to justify the protection of agriculture (ÖVP) or "defending" the nationalized industries (SPÖ) against foreign competitors, including the criticism of unjustified large subsidies.

Instead of analyzing the domestic effects on the interpretation of neutrality, Senn stresses the role of neutrality in building an Austrian identity after the Second World War (44). He refers to a book edited by Kovács and Wodak but does not mention the relevant article here. In their sociological analysis, Reinprecht and Latcheva admit that neutrality contributed "to a positive sense of nationhood" in Austria. But they also point out that the "state doctrine of perpetual neutrality made it easier 'to steal out of history' and fail to acknowledge historical responsibility."[6]

What Senn and most other authors have avoided in their discussions about neutrality are its "opportunity costs." One of these costs has been the difficulty for Austria to find close cooperation partners after the end of the Cold War, when the group of neutral and nonaligned countries (the N+N Group) disappeared from European politics and Austria's neighbors in Central Europe all joined NATO (see below).

In their article, Heinisch and Konrad first present a "*Matrixmodell*" (57) of four "arenas" for Austria's foreign policy. In analyzing the government declarations since 1983, they observe an increase of political goals with reference to international affairs as well as a broadening of topics in this area (61/62). Then they discuss the role of the federal government and the parliament. The National Council (*Nationalrat*) and the Federal Council (*Bundesrat*) use their codecision powers only sparingly (64). Heinisch and Konrad discuss the role of the federal president quite extensively, but not so much the role of the federal chancellor. In contrast to Germany, the head of the Austrian government does not have a guideline competency (*Richtlinienkompetenz*). But as the head of the ruling party or the largest party in a coalition government, the chancellor's influence has been significant. It has even been increased by the coordination competency in EU affairs and through the participation in the European Council (meeting of the head of state or government in the EU). This should have called for a more detailed analysis. The foreign ministers are dealt with in the chapter on the political parties (88/89).

Quantitative statistics about the amount of space used in the party manifestos for general foreign policy, defense policy, and European integration are used by Ennser-Jedenastik to show the differences among the political parties (79-83). Less space is used for the analysis of domestic conflicts on foreign policy; these should have been more the focus of a political science study (83/84).

The same holds true for the analysis of the administration's levels in foreign policy by Kneucker. The author presents mainly the legal aspects of the topic. Writing about activists dealing with foreign policy issues, these groups "seem to understand themselves as a counterweight to the economic interests of political parties and lobbies"; he admits that for these "newer phenomenon empirical studies are currently missing" (113/114). Bußjäger deals with federalism and the "foreign policy" of Austria's provinces (*Länder*). He sees bilateral and regional activities of the provinces with (parts of) foreign countries. The cooperation of the federal government with the provinces in the context of the EU is deemed as "basically positive" (136). As already mentioned, Sonnleitner writes that the foreign ministry lost most of its influence in a pertinent area when from 2017 the federal chancellery was charged with EU coordination (149). In addition, the increasing need for legitimization has changed the job description of the diplomats in the foreign ministry. Sonnleitner's assumption that digitalization could change Austria's diplomacy more than EU membership seems to be a bit farfetched (156).

The problem with Austria's media and foreign policy is that the media, except the state-owned ORF, have almost no foreign correspondents. According to Moser, reports from abroad often deal with Germany; populist politicians (like Trump and Orbán) get much (negative) attention (194). Interesting is the reference to a report of US diplomats from 2010 about the isolationist positions of the largest daily *Kronen Zeitung*, which according to the diplomats has also influenced the public's view of neutrality (document published in Wikileaks, 201). This confirms the analysis by Luif on the important and successful opposition by the *Kronen Zeitung* against any abandonment of neutrality during the Schüssel government in the early 2000s.[7]

Brix rightly maintains in his contribution that research and teaching on foreign policy in Austria have no direct influence on foreign policy decision making, except for consultations about international law (218). In my opinion, this has had to do with the need to interpret the scope of neutrality law for foreign policy activities. Compared to other European countries, only a few think tanks dealing with international affairs exist in Austria (219). Vienna University provides most teaching in this area.[8]

After this more detailed review of the contributions dealing with the main structures and institutions of Austrian foreign policy, only a few areas of the second (subject matters) and third (relations with states and international organizations) part will be assessed.

A lengthy contribution by Fattinger and Dialer deals with the Austrian foreign health policy. They start with "Global Health" and then describe Austria as an actor in this area. The authors note that Austria coordinates its policies partly with the German-speaking countries and cooperates also with its Central European neighbors. Austria's health policy has rather successfully influenced EU decision-making (377). But they do not mention that, in March 2021, the delays of the EU authorities in ordering, approving, and distributing vaccines against COVID-19 led Chancellor Kurz to form a partnership with Denmark and Israel to set up a joint research and development fund and possibly production facilities for COVID-19 vaccines. The Austrians got criticized for going it alone (*Die Presse*, 5.3.2021). The quarrels ended after the Commission succeeded in obtaining enough vaccines for the EU member states.[9]

Several articles explain Austria's security policies. But only a few pages are devoted to the external pressures on Austria's *internal* security. Eder mentions the "Salzburg Forum," initiated by Austria in 2000, which is a cooperation of the Central European ministries of the interior (299). But there is no reference to the fact that at the end of February 2016 the Salzburg Forum contacts had probably helped then-Foreign Minister Kurz to successfully close the "Balkan route" during the migrant crisis (2015/16). Days later, German Chancellor Merkel reached an agreement with Turkey about helping the EU with refugees, losing the "race" to Kurz.[10] Frank notes that Austria's military has become more an instrument for internal security (securing the border against illegal migration) than external security and defense (168).

For Roithner, neutrality has been for a long time Austria's most central symbol in its foreign and peace policy (309). He stresses the country's humanitarian disarmament policy. A detailed analysis follows by Kmentt. Austria's foreign ministry was already active with like-minded countries (and together with NGOs) in the "International Campaign to Ban Landmines," which led to the Ottawa Treaty in 1997 (330-332). Another rather effective cooperation between Austria and other "progressive states" as well as NGOs led to the "Convention on Cluster Munitions" in 2008 (333). Austria was even more active in helping to achieve the passing of the Treaty on the Prohibition of Nuclear Weapons (TPNW). Kmentt even gives the names of the Austrian diplomats who, besides himself, were instrumental for achieving this goal (336); so quite a share of the small personnel resources of the ministry were used for it. A conference, organized by the UN, adopted the Treaty by a vote of 122 States in favor, with 1 vote against and 1 abstention on July 7, 2017. It entered into force on January 22, 2021; as of February 2024, ninety-three countries had signed the TPNW, but mostly from the Global South.[11] Besides Austria, only four other European countries ratified the TPNW: the Holy See, Ireland, Malta, and San Marino; among them only three EU states and no NATO members. Kmentt does not mention this rather insignificant ratification by European states (337). In addition, it seems that the activities of Austria were executed outside the Common Foreign and Security Policy (CFSP)/ Common Security and Defence Policy (CSDP) of the EU.

This brings me to one of the notable conundrums of Austria's foreign policy: are those four European countries just mentioned Austria's only close cooperation partners in Europe, in the EU? Austria, in the center of Europe with eight neighboring states (only Germany has more neighbors), does not have major allies in international affairs and in the EU. The TPNW showed that Austria has partners in the Global South, but is this sufficient for influencing decision-making in the EU? In the contribution on Austria's relations with Central Europe, Wineroither presents a chart that clearly shows that in 2020 the Austrian government was not among those that other EU states "generally contact most on European policy matters" (506).[12] According to the chart, the governments of the four Visegrád countries do contact each other closely.

In my opinion, Wineroither neglects in his contribution two important "critical junctures" of Austria's relations with Central Europe. In July 1989, Austria applied for membership in the EC (later EU), and in November 1989 the Berlin Wall fell. Foreign Minister Alois Mock (ÖVP) attempted a dual track policy: working for EC/EU membership and at the same time strengthening the relations with the newly liberated neighbors in the East. Because of limited resources, Austria had to concentrate on joining the EU and "overlooked" the creation of the Visegrád group in 1991.[13] Austria's left was always somewhat suspicious of close relations with the Central Europeans, except for regular meetings with the (Communist) rulers. It resisted Habsburg "nostalgia" and was apprehensive about the early contacts of the ÖVP with dissidents in Central Europe, many of them with religious and conservative backgrounds. The second critical juncture for Austrian foreign policy regarding its eastern neighbors emerged in 1997/98. In July 1997, NATO invited the Czech Republic, Hungary, and Poland to start accession talks with the Alliance. The resignation of Prime Minister Vladimír Mečiar in Slovakia in October 1998 led to a revival of the Visegrád cooperation with its three neighbors. At the same time in Austria, the ÖVP and FPÖ (!) pushed for NATO membership. Their initiative failed since the SPÖ strongly opposed such a move and thus the necessary two-thirds majority in the National Council to renounce neutrality could not be achieved. If Austria had joined its eastern neighbors in their path to NATO membership, it probably could have joined the revitalized Visegrád Group as well. Later attempts by Austria to improve cooperation in Central Europe were only marginally successful. One can clearly notice here the opportunity cost of Austrian neutrality.

Authors like Wineroither forget that the advantage of the Visegrád cooperation does not rest primarily in the official meetings of ministers, which can be loaded with political overtones when the Visegrád Four attempt to reach common positions. A greater value lies in the regular meetings of the officials/civil servants of the different ministries to exchange information about their countries' policies as well as other information on the EU. "Package deals" are regularly concocted for decision-making in the EU Council of Ministers. And cooperation among smaller EU states is successful primarily when it has a long-term perspective; "ad hoc coalitions" are much less effective.

This brings me to the chapter by Maurer on Austrian policies concerning Europe. The article explains EU developments as well as Austria's EU policy. Maurer looks back at Austria's integration policy but does not mention the four power occupation of Austria hampering Austria's relations with the European Coal and Steel Community. There is no mention of the debate in Austria on its neutrality obligations and the Austrian "*Alleingang*," the attempt of the ÖVP to align closely with the EEC in the 1960s.[14]

Maurer is surprised about the speed with which the EU accession negotiations with Austria (as well as Finland and Sweden) could be concluded, forgetting that these countries had already participated in the EU internal market as members of the European Economic Area.[15] Finally, there is no reference to the fact that neutral Austria had to sign, before joining the EU in 1995, a Joint Declaration in which it pledged to be "ready and able to participate fully and actively in the Common Foreign and Security Policy" and to ensure that "the legal framework of the acceding countries will be compatible with the 'acquis.'"[16]

Maurer does not examine the measures (the "sanctions") of fourteen EU countries against the ÖVP-FPÖ government in 2000. The FPÖ was regarded as a dangerous, right-wing populist party. But the evaluation of the Austrian government by a group of three "wise men" in September 2000 resulted in a "clean bill of health on human rights."[17] This episode is again a pertinent example of Austria's lack of close cooperation partners in the EU. The attempt by the government to rectify this situation by creating a "Regional Partnership" in Central Europe failed.

A number of pages are used by Maurer to discuss the Convention on the Future of Europe in 2002/2003 where the smaller EU states (the "seven dwarfs" as Maurer calls them) wanted to affect the outcome, the (later failed) Constitutional Treaty. Austria successfully organized these "dwarfs," but their influence was rather marginal.[18]

Another ad hoc coalition with Austrian participation were the "Frugal Four" (Austria, Denmark, Netherlands, and Sweden). This group of EU countries first opposed any increase of the EU budget. With the outbreak of the COVID-19 pandemic, Germany and France proposed in May 2020 a recovery fund in the form of grants. According to the Frugal Four, the most affected countries should be helped only with loans. Finally, they had to accept that for financing the fund the European Commission could borrow on the capital markets (thus starting EU "deficit spending"). The Frugal Four succeeded in that only €390 billion would be grants; the remaining

€360 billion would be loans (at 2018 prices). They influenced the EU decision making on the budget, but only on the margins.[19]

Even so, Maurer maintains that Austria was reasonably successful in securing its interests in the EU. These successes were not obtained by going it alone, "but by creating 'informal alliances' with other, mostly smaller states" in the EU (724). Austria could have been more influential if it had closer permanent cooperation partners. Austria has clearly lacked them, as the chart presented by Wineroither (506), mentioned above, has shown.

A measure for the (positive) influence of the EU on Austria could be the growth of its economy as an EU member, which Maurer does not use. One can compare the growth of Austria's GDP per capita with, for example, Switzerland, a neighboring country that is not a member of the EU. In fact, after joining the EU, the gap between Austria's lower and Switzerland's higher GDP per capita became smaller. But with the onset of the financial crisis in 2008, the distance increased again significantly.[20]

What is missing in this bulky publication? Migration pops up in many articles, but could have been dealt with in an extra contribution. The EU is mentioned in most articles, but a closer look at Austria's (reluctant) participation in the EU's CFSP/CSDP would have merited closer inspection in view of the Russian invasion of Ukraine. This points again at the problematic of Austria's neutrality policy. Reiter in his article on Austria's relations toward Asian countries maintains that "neutrality plays only a very reduced role" in this context (671). It would be the task of the media, but in particular of the research community, to give a realistic representation of Austria's position in Europe and in the world. With the membership of Finland and Sweden in NATO, neutrality has lost most of its status in the EU. It was the scholars in Finland and Sweden who for decades had examined and debated NATO policies whereas researchers in Austria, as this book testifies, still base their analyses on "neutrality."

Endnotes

1. However, see the comprehensive historical accounts by Michael Gehler, *Österreichs Außenpolitik der Zweiten Republik. Von der alliierten Besatzung bis zum Europa des 21. Jahrhunderts* (Innsbruck: StudienVerlag, 2005), two volumes; Michael Gehler, *From Saint-Germain to Lisbon. Austria's Long Road from Disintegrated to United Europe 1919-2009* (Vienna: Austrian Academy of Sciences Press, 2020).

2. First pointed out in 1982 on basis of Table 1 by Paul Luif, "Österreich zwischen den Blöcken. Bemerkungen zur Außenpolitik des neutralen Österreich," *Österreichische Zeitschrift für Politikwissenschaft* 11, no. 2 (1982): 209–220 (here 215, 216).

3. But see the "international law" article, which actually uses a political science approach by Peter Hilpold, "Das Neutralitätsrecht Österreichs und der Schweiz im „weiten Feld" des internationalen Rechts. Aktuelle Entwicklungen im Vergleich," *Archiv des Völkerrechts*. 60, no. 3 (2022): 268–287 (here 272).

4. Paul Luif, *Neutrale in die EG? Die westeuropäische Integration und die neutralen Staaten* (Vienna: Braumüller, 1988), 102, 113; and in particular Paul Luif, *Der Wandel der österreichischen Neutralität. Ist Österreich ein sicherheitspolitischer „Trittbrettfahrer"?*, 2., ergänzte Version (Laxenburg: Österreichisches Institut für Internationale Politik, April 1998), 23-24.

5. Paul Luif, *On the Road to Brussels: The Political Dimension of Austria's, Finland's and Sweden's Accession to the European Union* (Vienna–West Lafayette, IN: Braumüller–Purdue University Press, 1995), 192–194.

6. Christoph Reinprecht and Rossalina Latcheva, "Neutrality and Austrian Identity: Discourse on NATO and Neutrality as Reflected in Public Opinion," in *NATO, Neutrality and National Identity: the case of Austria and Hungary*, ed. András Kovács and Ruth Wodak (Vienna: Böhlau, 2003), 439–460 (here 456).

7. Paul Luif, "Die alten Schablonen ... ob das Mozartkugeln, Lipizzaner oder die Neutralität sind — greifen in der komplexen Wirklichkeit des beginnenden 21. Jahrhunderts nicht mehr."Die Diskussion über die Neutralität," in *Die umstrittene Wende. Österreich 2000-2006*, ed. Robert Kriechbaumer and Franz Schausberger (Vienna: Böhlau, 2013), 551–584 (here 567-568).

8. Oddly, in the list of courses offered in its Political Science Department provided by Brix, the seminar on EU's internal and external security policies [SE: BAK11: *Die Politik der inneren und äußeren Sicherheit der EU*, SS2020] by Paul Luif is missing (210).

9. Paul Luif, *Austria and the European Union*. Published online: Feb. 24, 2022 (Oxford Research Encyclopedias, Politics), 19, https://doi.org/10.1093/acrefore/9780190228637.013.185.

10. Short remarks on migration can be found in the article by Wineroither on Central Europe (509) and on the Middle East by Harrer (597). On the "contest," see the Austrian side in Christian Ultsch, Thomas Prior, and Rainer Nowak, *Flucht. Wie der Staat die Kontrolle verlor* (Vienna: Molden, 2017),

178/179; the German position in Robin Alexander, *Die Getriebenen. Merkel und die Flüchtlingspolitik: Report aus dem Innern der Macht*, 5th ed. (Munich: Siedler, 2017), 270-271.

11. See, "Treaty on the Prohibition of Nuclear Weapons," United Nations Office for Disarmament Affairs, accessed Feb. 15, 2024, https://disarmament.unoda.org/wmd/nuclear/tpnw/; On the Treaty's participants, see, https://treaties.unoda.org/t/tpnw/participants, accessed Feb. 15, 2024.

12. Analyzing the cooperation space of EU25 in 2006, Naurin found that only three EU states lacked close cooperation partners: Austria, Ireland, and Slovenia. See Daniel Naurin, *Network Capital and Cooperation Patterns in the Working Groups of the Council of the EU,* (European University Institute: Florence, 2007) (= Robert Schuman Centre for Advanced Studies, EUI Working Paper 2007/14), 16.

13. Also see Paul Luif, "Österreich ohne enge Zusammenarbeitspartner in der EU. Neutralität als Hindernis?," in *Österreichisches Jahrbuch für Politik 2022*, ed. Andreas Khol et al. (Vienna: Böhlau, 2023), 341–352.

14. Besides the books by Gehler, an early, comprehensive analysis can be found in Paul Luif, *Neutrale in die EG? Die westeuropäische Integration und die neutralen Staaten* (Vienna: Braumüller, 1988). Contrary to Maurer, Ireland was never a member of EFTA (704).

15. See the extensive discussion in Paul Luif, *On the Road to Brussels*, 148–168.

16. Ibid., 310.

17. Quote from the Financial Times, Sep. 12, 2000; see, Paul Luif, *Austria and the European Union*, 13.

18. Maurer uses two articles from German newspapers as sources. More information by actual participants can be found in Hannes Farnleitner (ed.), *Unser Europa – gemeinsam stärker. Die Kooperation der Klein- und Mittelstaaten im EU-Konvent* (Vienna: MMC Media Med Consulting, 2004).

19. Paul Luif, *Austria and the European Union*, 19/20.

20. Ibid., 21.

List of Authors

Marcel Amoser served as a University Assistant at the University of Innsbruck from 2018 to 2023, where he completed his PhD, focusing on the 1968 movement in Innsbruck, as part of the Doctoral College "Dynamics of Inequality and Difference in the Age of Globalization."

Peter Baldwin was a Distinguished Research Professor at the University of California, Los Angeles.

Duncan Bare is a PhD candidate in history at the University of Graz. He has taught history at the University of Graz and political science at the University of Regensburg.

Markus Barnay studied political science and worked as a TV journalist until his retirement in 2022. Barnay was project manager of the exhibition "vorarlberg: a making-of" and is organizer and moderator of dialogue series on regional history in the Vorarlberg Museum.

Peter Becker is Professor of Austrian History at the University of Vienna. His research focuses on governance in the late Habsburg monarchy, the history of public administration, and the relationship between the successor states and the League of Nations.

Siegfried Beer is a retired professor of late modern and contemporary history at the University of Graz; founder of the Austrian Center for Intelligence, Propaganda and Security Studies (ACIPSS); and also serves as director of the Botstiber Institute for Austrian-American Studies (BIAAS).

Günter Bischof is a Professor Emeritus of the University of New Orleans' History Department and a former Director of Center Austria at UNO.

Ingrid Böhler is the Chair of the Institute of Contemporary History at the University of Innsbruck.

John W. Boyer is the Martin A. Ryerson Distinguished Service Professor of History at the University of Chicago.

Gary B. Cohen is Professor Emeritus of History at the University of Minnesota, Twin Cities, where he served for ten years as director of the Center for Austrian Studies.

Jeroen Dewulf is Professor in the Department of German at the University of California, Berkeley. He is also co-director, with John Connelly, of the Austrian Studies Program at UC Berkeley's Institute of European Studies.

D. Ryan Gray is the Richard Wallin Boebel Professor of Anthropology and Associate Director of the Midlo Center for New Orleans Studies at the University of New Orleans.

Beat Gugger is a freelance exhibition curator with cultural-historical projects. He was co-curator of the exhibition "vorarlberg: a making-of" and member of the expert panel of the Vorarlberg Museum.

Emily Hanish is an Independent Scholar working in the community events industry in San Francisco, California. She holds an MA in History from the University of New Orleans

Maureen Healy is an Associate Professor of History at Lewis & Clark College in Portland, OR. She is the author of *Vienna and the Fall of the Habsburg Empire: Total War and Everyday Life in World War I.* She is co-editor of the *Austrian History Yearbook.*

Pieter M. Judson is a professor for nineteenth and twentieth century history at the European University Institute (Florence). His most recent book, *The Habsburg Empire: A New History* (Belknap-Harvard, 2016) has been translated into twelve European and Asian languages. He is currently co-editing the *Cambridge History of the Habsburg Monarchy.*

Martin Kofler is the Director of the Tyrolean Archive of Photographic Documentation and Art (TAP) in Lienz, East Tyrol and Bruneck-Brunico, South Tyrol.

Martin Knoll is Professor of European Regional History and the Dean of the Faculty of Social Sciences at the University of Salzburg.

Paul Luif was Assistant Professor for international relations at the

University of Salzburg, 1974–1980, and member of the scientific staff of the Austrian Institute for International Affairs from 1980 to 2013.

Hester Margreiter is a research and teaching assistant in Austrian Cultural History at the University of Innsbruck.

Eva Pfanzelter is an associate professor and Deputy Chair of the Department of Contemporary History, Chair of the Digital Humanities Research Center, and Chair of the Faculty Council of the Faculty of Philosophy and History—all at the University of Innsbruck.

H. Glenn Penny is Professor and Henry J. Bruman Chair in German History at the University of California, Los Angeles.

Harald Stadler is Professor and head of the Department of Archaeology of the Middle Ages and the Modern Period at the University of Innsbruck. His books and articles address archaeological topics from the middle stone age to modern times.

Elisabeth Waldhart is a PhD candidate in contemporary archeology at the University of Innsbruck.

Janek Wasserman is Professor of Modern Central European and German History at the University of Alabama. He is the author of *Black Vienna: The Radical Right in the Red City, 1918-1938* and *The Marginal Revolutionaries: How Austrian Economists Fought the War of Ideas*.

Contemporary Austrian Studies

Günter Bischof /Marc Landry, Anton Pelinka/Fritz Plasser/Ferdinand Karlhofer, Editors

Volume 1 (1992)
Austria in the New Europe

Volume 2 (1993)
The Kreisky Era in Austria
Oliver Rathkolb, Guest Editor

Volume 3 (1994)
Austria in the Nineteen Fifties
Rolf Steininger, Guest Editor

Volume 4 (1995)
Austro-Corporatism: Past—Present—Future

Volume 5 (1996)
Austrian Historical Memory & National Identity

Volume 6 (1997)
Women in Austria
Erika Thurner, Guest Editor

Volume 7 (1998)
The Vranitzky Era in Austria
Ferdinand Karlhofer, Guest Editor

Volume 8 (1999)
The Marshall Plan in Austria
Dieter Stiefel, Guest Editor

Volume 9 (2000)
Neutrality in Austria
Ruth Wodak, Guest Editor

Volume 10 (2001)
Austria and the EU
Michael Gehler, Guest Editor

Volume 11 (2002)
The Dollfuss/Schuschnigg Era in Austria: A Reassessment
Alexander Lassner, Guest Editor

Volume 12 (2003)
The Americanization/Westernization of Austria

Volume 13 (2004)
Religion in Austria
Hermann Denz, Guest Editor

Volume 14 (2005)
Austrian Foreign Policy in Historical Perspective
Michael Gehler, Guest Editor

Volume 15 (2006)
Sexuality in Austria
Dagmar Herzog, Guest Editor

Volume 16 (2007)
The Changing Austrian Voter

Volume 17 (2008)
New Perspectives on Austrians and World War II
Barbara Stelzl-Marx, Guest Editor

Volume 18 (2009)
The Schüssel Era in Austria

Volume 19 (2010)
From Empire to Republic: Post-World War I Austria

Volume 20 (2011)
Global Austria: Austria's Place in Europe and the World
Alexander Smith, Guest Editor

Volume 21 (2012)
Austrian Lives
Eva Maltschnig, Guest Editor

Volume 22 (2013)
Austria's International Position after the End of the Cold War

Volume 23 (2014)
1914: Austria-Hungary, the Origins, and the First Year of World War 1
Samuel R. Williamson, Jr., Guest Editor

Volume 24 (2015)
Austrian Federalism in Comparative Perspective

Volume 25 (2016)
Austrian Studies Today

Volume 26 (2017)
Migration in Austria
Dirk Rupnow, Guest Editor

Volume 27 (2018)
Austrian Environmental History
Patrick Kupper, Guest Editor

Volume 28 (2019)
Democracy in Austria
David M. Wineroither, Guest Editor

Volume 29 (2020)
Myths in Austrian History
Christian Karner, Guest Editor

Volume 30 (2021)
Visual Histories of Austria
Martin Kofler, Hans Petschar, Guest Editors

Volume 31 (2022)
The Second Austrian Republic
Marc Landry and Eva Pfanzelter, eds., Christian Stenico, Associate Editor

Volume 32 (2023)
Covid-19 and Pandemics in Austrian History
Marc Landry and Dirk Rupnow, Editors